Civilizing Missions in Colonial and Postcolonial South Asia

Civilizing Missions in Colonial and Postcolonial South Asia

From Improvement to Development

Edited by
Carey A. Watt and Michael Mann

ANTHEM PRESS
LONDON · NEW YORK · DELHI

Anthem Press
An imprint of Wimbledon Publishing Company
www.anthempress.com

This edition first published in UK and USA 2011
by ANTHEM PRESS
75-76 Blackfriars Road, London SE1 8HA, UK
or PO Box 9779, London SW19 7ZG, UK
and
244 Madison Ave. #116, New York, NY 10016, USA

Cover image: A full-page advertisement for 'Pears' soap,
taken from the 1929 edition of *The Times of India Annual*.
The illustration depicts an Indian woman, seated inside
an open lotus flower holding a baby and a sceptre. India, 1929.
© Images of Empire, British Empire & Commonwealth Museum, UK

British Library Cataloguing in Publication Data
A catalogue record for this book is available from the British Library.

Library of Congress Cataloging in Publication Data
Civilizing missions in colonial and postcolonial South Asia :
from improvement to development / edited by Carey A. Watt and Michael Mann.
p. cm.
Includes bibliographical references and index.
ISBN-13: 978-1-84331-864-4 (hardcover : alk. paper)
ISBN-10: 1-84331-864-4 (hardback)
1. India–History–British occupation, 1765-1947. 2. Great Britain–Colonies–Asia–Social
policy. 3. India–Civilization–British influences. 4. India–Colonial influence. I. Watt, Carey
Anthony. II. Mann, Michael, 1959-
DS463.C553 2011
954.03–dc22
2011003908

ISBN-13: 978 1 84331 864 4 (Hbk)
ISBN-10: 1 84331 864 4 (Hbk)

This title is also available as an eBook.

TABLE OF CONTENTS

Introduction

THE RELEVANCE AND COMPLEXITY OF CIVILIZING MISSIONS c. 1800–2010[1]

Carey A. Watt

Hearing the phrase 'civilizing mission' usually conjures up the idea of European colonialism, so it seems to be a rather dated nineteenth-century expression. In the nineteenth- and twentieth-century era of imperialism the civilizing mission was an ever-shifting set of ideas and practices that was used to justify and legitimize the establishment and continuation of overseas colonies, both to subject peoples and to citizens or subjects in the homeland. For the British Raj in India the civilizing mission meant many things, including bringing the benefits of British culture to the subcontinent in the form of free trade and capitalism as well as law, order and good government. British rule was supposed to bring an end to a supposed condition of chronic warfare, violence, disorder and despotic rule in India, and it would institute peace and order in the form of Pax Britannica. At its core, the civilizing mission was about morally and materially 'uplifting', 'improving' and later 'developing' the supposedly 'backward' or 'rude' people of India to make them more civilized and more modern. A fundamental *difference* between colonial subjects in India and their British overlords was posited, with Indians and other subject peoples placed at lower or 'inferior' positions in new 'scales of civilization', and the British (and Europeans generally) at the top.[2] Indians were thereby condemned to continually try to catch up to their British rulers and 'European civilization', which claimed to be – and was widely accepted as – the universal or 'silent referent'.[3]

Civilizing Missions Today?

Since 2003, however, the civilizing mission phrase has gained traction once again. The Anglo-American invasion and occupation of Iraq has encouraged a renewed, twenty-first-century consideration of civilizing missions. Though there has been much speculation that British and American motives were primarily about ensuring access to oil, and thus related to strategic and economic interests, justifications of the March 2003 attack rested on depictions of Iraqi leader Saddam Hussein as an Oriental despot. He was allegedly a cruel, barbaric, inhumane and fanatical or irrational dictator who was preparing to use 'weapons of mass destruction' (WMD) against civilized members of 'the international community'. Attempts were also made to link the Iraqi leader to the nefarious Osama bin Laden and Al Qaeda, and thereby to the 'fanatical' and 'barbaric' forces of Islamic terrorism that became the focus of the American 'War on Terror' after 9/11 (the terrorist attacks on the United States of 11 September 2001).[4]

Self-proclaimed civilized peoples in states such as Britain and America declared that they needed to be protected while the people of Iraq and neighbouring states needed to be liberated from a dictatorial and dangerously uncivilized regime. Americans and Britons were to be welcomed with open arms as liberators, according to former US Defence Secretary Donald Rumsfeld, and America and Britain (and the 'Coalition of the Willing') would bring peace, good government, democracy and capitalist modernity to Iraqis. The invasion and occupation was also supposed to 'remake the Middle East' by spreading democracy and modernity to other allegedly backward Arab or Muslim states and peoples in the region.[5] Former British Prime Minister Tony Blair (1997–2007) initially justified the Iraq war on the basis of the imminent threat of Saddam Hussein using his hidden arsenal of WMD, but by 2006 he reframed his justification for war with new assertions that the invasion was part of a struggle between 'democracy and violence', and a battle about 'modernity' and 'civilization'.[6] The irony is that the benefits of enlightened Western civilization and liberal democracy were 'given' to Iraq and Iraqis through violence and coercion, by means of a 'shock and awe' military campaign. As Michael Adas has noted, however, technological superiority in military affairs has also been deployed as a prominent marker of civilizational supremacy and a justification for colonial civilizing initiatives.[7]

Similar civilizing mission arguments have been used to justify and legitimize the war in Afghanistan. Afghanistan became the epicentre of the global 'War on Terror' immediately after 9/11, because it was ruled by the Taliban – a group of 'fundamentalist Muslims' that was hosting Osama bin Laden and Al Qaeda. Over forty countries currently have troops in Afghanistan and operations have been sanctioned by the United Nations (UN), but the International Security Assistance Force – Afghanistan (ISAF) is led and dominated by the North Atlantic Treaty Organization (NATO) in conjunction with the United States and its efforts to fight terrorism through Operation Enduring Freedom.

Americans have the largest number of troops in the country and the British hold the number two spot.

The fundamental goals of ISAF are threefold: increasing *security* (creating 'a secure and stable environment'), supporting *reconstruction and development* with government, international and nongovernmental (NGO) partners, and 'building capacity' for *governance* among Afghans ('strengthen the institutions required to fully establish good governance and rule of law and to promote human rights').[8] These objectives may sound familiar to anyone knowledgeable about European colonial civilizing missions in the nineteenth century, with NGOs as twenty-first-century missionaries – bringing modern attitudes, institutions and practices to the world's underdeveloped peoples – despite the existence of tensions between NGOs and military or government officials.[9] Though there is more emphasis on newer terms or concepts such as 'security', 'human rights', 'governance' and 'building capacity', an apparent need to develop and civilize a chaotic and 'backward' Afghanistan is clear. Afghanistan's difference, in the sense of its inferiority, is implicit too. Moreover, one might also note the self-imposed responsibility of a more advanced or 'civilized' power to pacify Afghanistan, and to morally and materially improve, uplift and modernize an unstable or 'failed' state. According to ISAF and the United States, Afghanistan must be uplifted to a universal standard of civilization that is based on European or Western standards (the 'silent referent').

ISAF and American military forces quickly deposed the Taliban government and dispersed Al Qaeda operatives in late 2001, but a so-called counterinsurgency is still being waged against the Taliban nearly a decade later. In fact, Taliban 'insurgents' have gained strength in recent years and ISAF and American success in Afghanistan is far from certain, however 'success' is defined. The nature of the Afghan threat has shifted too. The original goal of the war was to oust the Taliban and deny Al Qaeda a base from which it could support anti-Western terrorism and directly threaten the security and 'way of life' of American or other Western citizens. More recently the objective has morphed into preventing Pakistan and the rest of South Asia from sliding into a state of anarchy that would be dangerous for the West. Pakistan has been destabilized by American pressure to support the 'War on Terror', especially in the nebulous border areas of the 'northwestern frontier' that were such a concern to the Raj in the nineteenth century. US and ISAF operations in southern and southeastern Afghanistan – and in Pakistan itself – have only aggravated Pakistan's problems by pushing Taliban fighters across the porous border and enraging the local populace, which has long resisted modern state-building projects. Many Western leaders fear that if Pakistan collapses its nuclear weapons could fall into the hands of Islamic extremists or 'Islamists' who might threaten India, Pakistan's rival and former foe, and this would have dire consequences for the entire subcontinent.

Evidently, it is considered imperative to establish a Pax ISAF or Pax Americana in Afghanistan, which would allow it to grow into a 'civilized' liberal democracy and member of the 'international community'. As one of the twenty-six member countries of NATO Canada is part of ISAF and has had troops in Afghanistan since 2001 though the scope of its mission increased dramatically in 2006. In 2007, as the war dragged on and 'security' in Afghanistan began to deteriorate, public support began to wane and the Canadian government sponsored a study that was published in early 2008 as the *Independent Panel on Canada's Future Role in Afghanistan.*[10] This document repeatedly makes the point that Afghanistan is different, yet once again in the sense of being inferior. It does not explicitly say that it is 'uncivilized', but it states that Afghanistan is a 'divided tribal society' and 'developing country' that is 'shockingly poor and dangerous'. Moreover, Afghanistan is characterized by 'corruption', 'criminality' and a lack of 'discipline' in its police and military forces, as well as by 'insecurity' and 'violence' – all in a 'region of violent instability'.[11] Such images of 'backwardness' have received further support from media descriptions of Afghans 'living in the Stone Ages' or, more generously, living in 'medieval conditions'. Afghan society is therefore apparently timeless and static. The solution is 'improvement', 'development' or 'capacity building'. In fact, the report of Canada's independent panel mentions 'building capacity', which is the newest addition to the lexicon of development, twenty-eight times. Old habits die hard, however, and 'improvement' is discussed on more than thirty occasions while the need for 'development' is stressed 142 times – an average of 1.6 times per page, in spite of the fact that between 2002 and 2006 over 90 per cent of the international funds committed to Afghanistan were spent on military affairs rather than development.[12] Development encompasses both 'moral and material' dimensions, with comments regarding the need to improve the capacity of Afghans for 'accountable, honest and effective governance' and the obligation 'to enhance roads, bridges and electrification so that ordinary Afghans can see progress'.[13]

The Canadian panel describes the Taliban as a monolithic group that ruled as 'a radical Islamist regime of exceptional violence' and 'coercive repression'. The Taliban-led 'insurgency', meanwhile, is characterized by its 'proven brutality'.[14] Conversely, the American and ISAF counterinsurgency is led by progressive forces, 'including most of the great democracies', that seek to support Afghans in their quest for 'the democratic rule of law and the full exercise of human rights'.[15]

One important marker used to highlight Taliban depravity and backwardness is its treatment of women. This is significant because the social condition of women was commonly used by European colonial regimes in the nineteenth century as a marker of 'civilization' or 'backwardness'. In the case of the British Raj, the works of James Mill, Thomas Babington Macaulay and James Tod all cited examples of the poor condition of Indian women to demonstrate India's 'rudeness' or 'barbarity' and thereby justify British rule. The *Independent Panel on Canada's Future Role in Afghanistan* highlights the prevalence of gender discrimination in Afghanistan and the fact that illiteracy rates for women are about 87 per cent, while asserting that the Taliban's 'mistreatment of women is particularly notorious'.[16] Images of Afghan women 'imprisoned' in head-to-toe *burkhas* have provided a potent symbol of the Taliban's turpitude, and thus a justification for the Afghan war – notwithstanding the fact that many ISAF warlord allies are equally abhorrent in terms of their attitudes toward women.[17]

While the objectives and justifications of the Afghan war are reminiscent of nineteenth-century European colonial civilizing missions in many important respects, significant differences must be acknowledged. The ISAF campaign is not intended to be a long-term multigenerational or permanent project of colonial occupation and many NATO members hope to withdraw their forces as soon as possible. Canada's parliament, for example, has passed a motion that requires the withdrawal of combat troops in 2011. As imperial historian Anthony Hopkins has recently reminded us, however, the 'brief occupations [of the colonial era] had the habit of becoming long-term commitments'.[18]

The ISAF project is not an attempt to create an empire on the part of one European state either. Over forty countries are involved in the ISAF effort, which would make for a very messy colonial state, even if we admit that the British tolerated French, Dutch and Portuguese colonial enclaves in India right up till 1947. Moreover, international organizations such as the UN are closely involved, as are a great many NGOs. Thus, for most members of the ISAF mission the Afghan war is complex and expensive, and they are reluctant participants. Lastly, there is a sovereign Afghan government that has made democratic gestures by holding – many observers would say 'fixing' – elections, and it has repeatedly 'invited' American and ISAF forces to help in its security and development initiatives.

Nonetheless, an international military intervention in Afghanistan that is dominated by Western nations and NATO, and which seeks to 'improve' and 'develop' Afghans morally and materially, has many of the hallmarks of a colonial civilizing mission. Even the involvement of the UN cannot shield ISAF from this taint. Mark Mazower's intellectual history of the UN shows that its ideological origins were deeply influenced by an 'imperial internationalism' that was itself informed by Britain's civilizing mission, and elements of UN Eurocentrism persist today.[19] More important, perhaps, is the fact that the populations of the United States and other NATO members are overwhelmingly Christian and that 99 per cent of Afghans are Muslim. This makes the 'War on Terror' seem like a 'War Against Islam', and it evokes memories of European colonialism, notably the civilizing efforts of Christian missionary societies in the nineteenth century. Prior to the 1857 Rebellion in India, for example, Hindus and Muslims already believed that the British, as Christians, were trying to subvert their 'rude' and 'inferior' religions in order to 'Anglicize' or 'civilize' them. Thus, when rumours circulated in early 1857 that the recently introduced Enfield rifle would henceforth require Indian sepoys to bite the end off cartridges greased with pig or cow fat – offensive and polluting to Muslims and Hindus respectively – this provided a catalyst for a mutiny that quickly escalated into a full-scale rebellion. A recent case related to Iraq and Afghanistan involving the US arms manufacturer Trijicon has some troubling parallels with the Raj's Enfield rifle misstep. Trijicon was founded by a devout Christian and it has been supplying British and American troops with weapons that feature coded references to the Bible on their gunsights, while the firm's website claims that America's greatness is based on its adherence to Biblical standards.[20] British and American military authorities have expressed concern about how the existence of Christian references on ISAF weapons might be perceived by Afghans, including the possibility that Taliban propagandists could point to them as proof of a Western 'crusade' against Islam. Many Canadians, meanwhile, have taken to displaying Christianized 'Support our Troops' decals on their cars, which feature the silhouette of a Christian cross in the upper hollow of the bow. Such examples recall aspects of nineteenth-century European colonial civilizing missions that denigrated local religions and cultures as inferior while asserting the superiority of Western Christianity as rational and progressive.

The names given to military missions can be problematic as well. Operation Enduring Freedom speaks to American rhetoric about the United States as the 'land of the free' or home of freedom and liberty, and perhaps to 'superior' Western liberal traditions that date from the Enlightenment. Canada's penchant for Greek and Roman names such as Apollo, Athena, Argus and Medusa for its ISAF missions is even more interesting.[21] This is because British officials and writers in the colonial era, including Mill, Macaulay and R. S. S. Baden-Powell (founder of the Boy Scouts), consistently invoked the Greco-Roman classical world as the model for the British Empire. The British and their empire supposedly represented the apogee of human civilization and the culmination of a line of civilizational progress that stretched back directly to Greece and Rome. Such a blatant appropriation of the legacy of

Greece and Rome was an enormous distortion and simplification of history, but it was used effectively to convey the impression that the British had a legitimate moral duty to 'share' its superior civilization with the world.[22] While Canada's affinity for mission names that come from the Western classical world might remind Afghans of British imperialism, it could also prompt memories of a much older empire: that of 'Alexander the Great' c. 330 BCE and the Seleucid dynasty that succeeded him. After all, the Canadian mission is based in Kandahar, which is probably the descendant of 'Alexandria in Arachosia' – one of the many cities in Asia founded by Alexander. The name Kandahar is likely a variant of Iskander, which is how Alexander was known locally. To most people in Central, South or West Asia, however, Alexander is not referred to as 'the Great'. That honorific is a Western convention. In Asia, for example, Jawaharlal Nehru was quite generous when he stated that Alexander was 'a famous conqueror but a conceited young man',[23] and that his accomplishments were greatly exaggerated, because he is more widely known as 'the accursed' or a two-horned devil.[24]

There is also an implicit 'scale of civilization' or 'development' that puts the Western liberal democracies of NATO at the top and 'backward' states such as Afghanistan at or near the bottom – obligated to catch up with the help of Western tutelage. In the twenty-first century, however, the difference is that we have moved from older ideals of 'uplift', 'improvement' and 'development' to an emphasis on 'building capacity'. International organizations and NGOs had a role in colonial-era civilizing efforts, too, and the ISAF objective of returning 'Afghanistan to Afghans' smacks of colonial paternalism. For well over 100 years, from the early nineteenth century till the 1940s, the British Raj was famous for saying that India would have self-government – an 'India for Indians' – when Indians were 'ready' for it.

Many Afghans see the American and ISAF presence as yet another unwelcome foreign occupation. Taliban leader Mullah Mohammed Omar refers to it as an 'occupation' with 'colonialist objectives', and he specifically describes the United States as an 'arrogant enemy' and the government of Afghan President Hamid Karzai as 'the stooge Kabul administration'.[25] Mullah Omar's comments show how ISAF efforts to prop up a weak and venal Afghan administration in Kabul reek of British colonial-era 'indirect rule' policies. It is easy to ignore or discount such assertions when they come from the Taliban, but that is not the case when similar remarks come from a group like RAWA (Revolutionary Association of the Women of Afghanistan). RAWA represents Afghan women and it originally supported the US and ISAF war in Afghanistan, but has since turned against it and now asks that all American troops leave the country. During the course of a public lecture tour in major American cities, a RAWA activist named Zoya said that 'the United

States has attempted to use the establishment of democracy, the liberation of women and the war on terror to legitimize its "occupation" of Afghanistan'.[26] Thus, we have an interesting case of Afghan women – ostensibly beneficiaries of the Afghan war and a key focus group for ISAF 'development' – identifying and condemning the discourse of an American civilizing mission being used to legitimize an occupation.

Of course, the United States has been the key actor in both Iraq and Afghanistan, and since the end of the Cold War in the early 1990s America has been hailed as the world's first 'hyperpower'. The US has unmatched military muscle and, until the recent global financial meltdown of 2008–09, unmatched economic might. Some commentators have been encouraging the United States to assume a more active and direct imperial role, including British historian Niall Ferguson. Ferguson acted as an advisor to Republican presidential candidate John McCain in the 2008 American election, and he has encouraged America to don the imperial mantle formerly worn by the British in order to create a global Pax Americana.[27] Not surprisingly, he is also an apologist for the British civilizing mission or 'civilizing process' of the nineteenth and twentieth centuries.[28] Ferguson regrets the violence and 'blemishes' of imperial rule, but he justifies imperialism and colonialism by arguing that the British Empire helped modernize and improve the world. After all, he says, one cannot have a great empire and globalization without gunboats and a little violence or coercion. The empire made 'the world we know today' by promoting capitalist globalization on the British model ('Anglobalization' to Ferguson) as well as the global dissemination of nine distinctive British values: the English language, English forms of land tenure, Scottish and English banking, common law, Protestantism, team sports, the limited 'nightwatchman' state, representative assemblies and 'the idea of liberty'.[29]

To Ferguson, British imperial administrators, soldiers and missionaries were vital to the success of the empire in the nineteenth and twentieth centuries: they imposed British and European values on colonial peoples around the globe, and they made our modern world. The problem identified by Ferguson is that America is 'an empire in denial' and will not properly assume its noble burden despite being Britain's natural heir. It has the wealth, military power and technology, but it 'lacks the drive to export its capital, its people and its culture to those backward regions which need them most urgently and which, if they are neglected, will breed the greatest threats to its security'.[30]

Deepak Lal, an economist born in late colonial India, but long since principally resident in the United States and Britain, is another proponent of American imperialism. Lal's book *In Praise of Empires* derives from a speech entitled 'In Defense of Empires' given at the American Enterprise Institute in 2002, and it was expanded into a monograph in 2004.[31] Like Ferguson, Lal bemoans the fact that the United States has been reluctant to take up its imperial responsibilities. He dates the beginning of British imperial decline as the end of World War I, and chastises US president Woodrow Wilson for preventing America from taking over British imperial duties. In fact, Wilson is blamed for destroying the 'Age of Empire' at the Versailles peace conference in 1919 and ushering in a destructive 'Age of Nations', which supposedly created global disorder and economic disintegration for 100 years. The growth of American power as 'the world hegemon' since the 1990s has presented a new opportunity for the emergence of a global empire and a return to the natural order of things, and Lal claims that 'not since the fall of the Roman Empire has there been a potential imperial power like the US today'.[32] Once again, it is interesting that the classical world is 'western' and only looks westward: Rome → London → Washington.

Lal and Ferguson both assert that empires provide peace, order, security and greater global prosperity. Lal wants a return to the liberal international economic order (LIEO) created by the British Empire and Pax Britannica in the nineteenth century, which 'was wholly benign and allowed many of the current developing countries to begin modernization'.[33] Now, of course, it must be a Pax Americana, but concepts of 'development' and 'modernization' are still based on a Western model that claims to be universal. Furthermore, there is an implicit hierarchy with Western-style 'developed' and 'modern' states towering above 'developing countries' and Ferguson's 'backward regions'. This is reminiscent of the 'scales of civilization' constructed in the colonial era. To make matters worse, Lal singles out Muslims for particular disparagement. Firstly, he argues simplistically that Arab Muslims destroyed the (Western) classical world in the seventh century CE and threatened 'the West' until the end of the Ottoman siege of Vienna in 1683. The implication is that the classical world was solely a 'Western' achievement, and that it was neatly and cleanly separated from Asia and Africa. It ignores the enormous contributions of Arab Muslims – from places such as the Bayt al-Hikmah (House of Wisdom) in Baghdad – to 'Western' science and culture, and it wrongly implies that Muslims have been the bogeymen of 'Western' progress and modernity for 1300 years. Secondly, Lal avers that Muslims are naturally aggressive, militaristic, despotic and full of rage. Thirdly, the Muslim world has allegedly resisted the transition to modernity, especially in the Middle East. American imperialism is needed 'to create a new order in the Middle East' and help Muslims come to terms with (Western) modernity, but it should be indirect American rule 'backed up by the threat or actual use of force'.[34] Clearly, Lal has not given much thought to the work of Edward Said, and *In Praise of Empires* is rife with pernicious Orientalist stereotypes. Unfortunately, this is not surprising as it helps support 'the War on Terror' and Western-led wars in Iraq and Afghanistan, which are both Muslim-majority states.

Sadly, Deepak Lal and Niall Ferguson read like nineteenth-century British imperialists and their arguments are often very similar, particularly the presumption that empires promote 'benign' globalization.[35] However, they differ on one very key point. Lal does not advocate spreading or imposing Western cultural values, and he argues that America should only promote the West's material and economic beliefs to create a 'liberal international economic order'. He warns against trying to spread Western cultural or 'cosmological beliefs' because this could cause resistance and a violent backlash, but he is not clear on how to separate 'material values' from cultural or cosmological values.[36] Is it possible to separate the values of liberal capitalism from liberalism in general? On this point Niall Ferguson is much more credible. Ferguson makes it clear that liberal economics comes packaged with cultural values, whether they are associated with religion, team sports or simply the idea of liberty. Using the example of the missionary-explorer David Livingstone in nineteenth-century Africa, he points out that the objective of opening up the African interior to British trade was to create an 'artery of civilization' and uplift backward Africans with the gift of British culture. Ferguson acknowledges that similar assumptions were at play in India prior to 1857.[37] In other words, the dissemination or imposition of Western economic values and institutions cannot be separated from the spread of Western culture.

One might expect that support for imperial adventures and civilizing missions would have waned in recent years given the continuing 'development' problems and violence in Iraq and Afghanistan, but an Intelligence Squared debate held in London on 19 October 2007 showed that this is not necessarily the case. A motion stating that 'We should not be reluctant to assert the superiority of Western values' was passed by a vote of 465 to 264, and arguments in support of the motion referred to 'Western civilization's' support for rational and critical methods, its emphasis on 'improvement' and its respect for women's and minority rights.[38] James Mill and Thomas Babington Macaulay would have been proud.

More sophisticated perspectives on twenty-first century imperialism and civilizing missions can be found in the work of scholars such as Anthony Hopkins, Kenneth Pomeranz, Edward Said and William Dalrymple.[39] Shortly after the invasion of Iraq and only a couple of months before his death in 2003, Said prepared a new introduction to *Orientalism* and, among other things, he addressed the issue of how Orientalist intellectuals who should know better have helped empires construct ideas of difference that condone violence, war and occupation.[40] He wrote of 'an aggressive attack on contemporary Arab and Muslim societies for their backwardness, lack of democracy and abrogation of women's rights' while 'jejune publicists' peddle simplistic notions of 'Western' modernity, enlightenment and democracy. The centrality of a 'colonial difference' perspective and adherence to a superior 'us' versus an inferior 'them' attitude is clear. Moreover, Said reminded us that 'every single empire in its official discourse has said that it is not like all the others, that its circumstances are special, and that it has a mission to civilize, bring order and democracy, and that it uses force only as a last resort. And, sadder still, there always is a chorus of willing intellectuals to say calming words about benign or altruistic empires'.[41] For his part, Dalrymple also refers to the Iraq invasion and he bemoans 'Western' arrogance about the supposed superiority of a construct called 'the West', and resulting civilizing missions that have repeatedly used violence to uplift 'savages' or even exterminate 'inferior races'.[42]

Anthony Hopkins' commentary in *The New York Times*, 'Lessons of "Civilizing Missions" are Mostly Unlearned', discusses the 'reconstruction' of Afghanistan and the beginnings of the American debacle in Iraq, and it was published on 23 March 2003, just a few days after the invasion. Hopkins uses his considerable knowledge about British imperial history to great effect and offers plenty of insight into the difficulties inherent in attempting to carry out a 'civilizing mission'. He points out that the British launched 'the world's first comprehensive development plan', believing that liberal notions of free trade and constitutional government, supported by the more generic force of Victorian values, including Christianity, would transform the world. The vanguard of the British Empire was convinced that it would only have to 'show the light' and peoples in foreign lands would follow, but 'the gratitude they expected for bringing the benefits of the West to the Rest was either not forthcoming or was short-lived. . . . When disillusion set in, the recipients were blamed, but never the plan'. While Hopkins acknowledges that 'the time and circumstance' of America's imperial civilizing mission is different, he also observed that reconstruction efforts in Afghanistan were running into 'familiar difficulties' in 2003 while foreseeing the problems of the Iraq occupation: 'Whatever the initial reception, it is inevitable that foreign rule will be resented, especially in a postcolonial world . . . people cannot be forced into freedom – they have to grow into it'.[43]

Kenneth Pomeranz's 'Empire & "civilizing missions", past & present' is wide-ranging both in temporal and geographic terms, and it considers American imperialism and civilizing campaigns from the 1970s into the twenty-first century. Pomeranz's approach is refreshing because he explores the efforts of non-Western empires such as the Ottomans, Japan and Qing China to 'civilize' their subject populations, even if they concentrated on general issues such as discipline rather than European notions of enlightenment and progress. Moreover, he outlines a general shift from civilizing missions being used to justify imperial rule over 'uncivilized' peoples who lacked the reason or self-control required for self-government in the nineteenth century, to a growing emphasis on more measurable ideals of 'development' in fields such as education, finance, infrastructure and public health after 1900. Pomeranz calls this 'developmentalism', and while it had the benefit of implying a need for continuing imperial guidance, it was also problematic in the sense that it raised expectations, costs and risks. Imperial administrations frequently failed to meet expectations and this highlighted the stinginess of their civilizing missions and undermined claims to superiority, leaving them open to criticism from nationalists and other groups.

Ironically, Pomeranz argues that until about 1970 modern Western and Asian imperialisms had much in common. Recent American civilizing efforts, however, have broken with earlier Asian-Atlantic models. While the United States has focused on 'development' and 'nation-building' with a more extensive global vision than the British, it has been reluctant to make real commitments to development and has retreated from hands-on nation-building. As Pomeranz puts it, America broke the link 'between hegemony and the promise of development that was prominent in most other modern empires'.[44]

Our broad discussion of twenty-first-century civilizing missions related to Iraq and Afghanistan underlines the fact that historians, scholars and public intellectuals have continued to discuss imperialism and civilizing missions right up to the present day, and thus the topic of the 'civilizing mission' remains extremely interesting, relevant, and even controversial. We have also seen that ideas and practices related to civilizing missions are historical in the sense that they change over time, and that they can be complex and contradictory, which leads us to the essays included in this book.

The Present Book

This collection of essays on civilizing missions in colonial and postcolonial South Asia builds on an earlier volume published by Anthem Press, *Colonialism as Civilizing Mission: Cultural Ideology in British India*, edited by Michael Mann and Harald Fischer-Tiné in 2004. While some of the chapters in the new book revisit aspects of the British colonial state's civilizing agenda in the nineteenth and twentieth centuries, the present collection devotes much more attention to the tensions, ambiguities and paradoxes of civilizing missions carried out (a) by the Raj, (b) by various missionary and nongovernmental organizations (NGOs), and (c) by Indians themselves – during the colonial era and in the decades after independence was achieved in 1947. More attention is given, for example, to how Indians 'reassembled' and 'internalized' elements of the colonial civilizing mission to carry out what we call 'self-civilizing' initiatives.[45] This widens the discussion of 'the British civilizing mission' in India to the point where we must address the issue of 'civilizing missions' in the plural.

The book also highlights some of the unintended consequences of civilizing missions. For example, British civilizing efforts often stressed discipline, violence and martial qualities rather than enlightenment and liberty, and colonial initiatives were frequently redirected or co-opted by 'men on the spot', missionaries and other nongovernmental organizations – and Indians. But Indian self-civilizing missions had much in common with British efforts in that they were largely élite male bourgeois projects that tried to turn the low castes, lower classes, peasants and women into pliant citizens through various forms of education or tutelage. The focus on élites, however, does not represent a return to an older political history of colonial or nationalist élites that was excoriated by the Subaltern Studies movement in the early 1980s. The nine essays included here may often analyze the ideas and actions of élites, but they do so using a variety of creative historiographical approaches. Social, cultural and postcolonial history is used to explore the complexities and ambiguities of civilizing missions in India, while some contributors bring perspectives from other disciplines. In addition, several papers borrow from recent world history innovations to move beyond national or regional frames and put South Asian events in broader global context.

The chapters in this volume are arranged in rough chronological order and cover a 200-year period from the beginnings of the East India Company's state in the late eighteenth century until the early twenty-first century and thus well into the postcolonial era. Of course, ideas and practices related to colonial and 'self-civilizing' missions changed over time. Generally speaking, notions of civilizational difference and the civilizing mission were rather more fluid and inchoate *circa* 1800 than they were in the late-nineteenth-century imperial heyday.[46] Concepts of European 'difference' and 'superiority' hardened upon the building of a Company state with an 'Anglicizing' impulse in the 1820s and 1830s, and even more so after the 1857 Rebellion and the articulation of schemas of 'scientific' racism following the publication of Charles Darwin's *Origin of Species* in 1859. However, imperial and civilizational confidence began to wane shortly after the appearance of Rudyard Kipling's 'White Man's Burden' in 1899.[47] Moreover, the sensational and shocking Japanese victories over 'European' Russia in 1904–05 dented Western claims to superiority and gave impetus to a growing sense of Asian pride and a surge in Indian nationalism. These shifts in European – Asian relations were followed by 'enlightened' Europe's internecine savagery during the First World War and the exposure of the Raj's uncivilized brutality in the Jallianwalabagh massacre of 1919. As the 'moral improvement' aspects of the British colonial civilizing mission were undermined in the early twentieth century more emphasis was gradually placed on economic development because it could be quantified and measured. But Indian moral and material self-civilizing efforts gathered pace in this same period of declining British confidence, and they continued into the post-1947 period.

The first part of the book, 'The Raj's Reforms & Improvements: Aspects of the British Civilizing Mission', features two chapters that explore the Raj's civilizing efforts. In 'Conjecturing Rudeness: James Mill's Utilitarian Philosophy of History and the British Civilizing Mission' Adam Knowles analyzes James Mill's seminal *History of British India*, which was published in 1817, just at the moment when the East India Company became the 'paramount' or supreme power in the subcontinent after the final defeat of the Marathas. Mill's *History* was an immediate success and was tremendously influential throughout the nineteenth century in shaping British attitudes toward India as a 'rude' and 'backward' society. It thereby provided a foundation for the Raj's civilizing mission while helping to establish the legitimacy of British rule. It also helped define India as 'different' in the sense of being inferior and at the bottom end of 'the scale of civilizations', and thus in need of a firm British hand to 'improve' and 'progress' upward to a higher stage of civilization. However, Knowles shows that Mill's argument regarding India's supposed 'rudeness' was based on conjecture and was in fact a problematic application of conjectural historiography. Moreover, Mill came from 'rude' Scotland and was sceptical of Britain's own claims to civilization during the 1800s and 1810s. This highlights the paradox and tenuousness of British claims to civilizational superiority. Arguably, one of the cornerstones of the colonial civilizing mission was suspect, and this might help explain recurrent British anxiety and insecurity about their cultural eminence as well as self-conscious efforts to display confidence. As Margaret MacMillan stated in the introduction to her *Women of the Raj*, officials and non-officials believed that they were 'part of the great civilizing mission', but the British in India could not tolerate uncertainties or ambiguities. They had to be confident and act the part of the superior ruler.[48]

Michael Mann's essay, 'Art, Artefacts and Architecture: Lord Curzon, the Delhi Arts Exhibition of 1902–03 and the Improvement of India's Aesthetics', also appears in the first section of the book. Mann shows how a number of British commentators on art and aesthetics from the 1840s onward, such as E. A. Freeman, William Morris, George Birdwood, John L. Kipling, George Watt, Percy Brown and Viceroy Curzon, underlined the 'difference' of Indian arts. Despite occasional praise for Indian artisans and craftsmanship vis-à-vis laments about the decline of the artisan in industrializing Britain, Indian art, architecture and aesthetics were commonly disparaged as monstrous, fanciful, superstitious, irrational, undisciplined and barbarous. In short, Indian arts – like Indian people and institutions – needed to be 'improved' and 'civilized' through a benevolent British paternalism. Such efforts reached a pinnacle of sorts in the Delhi Arts Exhibition of 1902–03, which was part of Lord Curzon's grand Delhi Darbar celebrations in honour of the accession of Edward VII.[49] However, Mann demonstrates that there were clear limits to British improvement initiatives. Materially, for example, the Raj was reluctant to fund the kind of arts education recommended by individuals such as J. L. Kipling, and financial parsimony was a recurrent problem for the British civilizing mission. There were ideological constraints too. Architecture was protected as a domain for Britons only (though there were tensions between military engineers and civilian architects), while Indian arts would only be improved to 'traditional' standards of a romanticized Indian past. In other words, Indian art and aesthetics might become more rational, practical and disciplined, but they could not become truly 'modern' or fully civilized. In making this point, Mann highlights one of the central paradoxes of colonial civilizing missions: the civilizing project could not succeed because 'difference' between the rulers and the ruled had to be maintained, and success of the civilizing mission would mean the end of colonial rule. Without such notions of difference colonialism could not be justified.[50] Thus, the Delhi Arts Exhibition used 'modern' and 'scientific' taxonomic schemes to present a different 'traditional' India consistent with the princely India that was so conspicuous at Curzon's lavish *darbar*.

The second part of the book, 'Colonialism, Indians and Nongovernmental Associations: The Ambiguity and Complexity of "Improvement"', features three chapters that cover the period from the early 1800s until the late colonial era of the 1930s, and it delves further into the complexities and ambiguities of civilizing missions in colonial India. Jana Tschurenev's essay, 'Incorporation and Differentiation: Popular Education and the Imperial Civilizing Mission in Early Nineteenth Century India', explores the important issue of education under Company rule in the early nineteenth century and she highlights several areas of complexity. Tschurenev shows how British educational initiatives in India were part of a wider 'universal' effort to 'improve' the minds of 'the rising generation' throughout the world – including in Britain itself. Indian minds infected with vice, corruption, immorality, laxity and timidity had to be conquered with British virtues of diligence, honesty, industry and rationality. Indian youth were to be 'enlightened, educated and made happy'. The promise of universal improvement ran into trouble, however, when it met with a 'grammar of difference' in early colonial India. Educational goals were compromised to fit local colonial needs and ethnic, class, caste or gender issues in India. It quickly became apparent that Indian students should not be taught the same things as European or Eurasian children, and the question of 'how much civilizing was appropriate or safe for Indians?' was soon being raised. If the same pedagogical materials and approaches were used to teach young Indians and Britons, what would that say about British claims of civilizational superiority? As in the case of artistic or aesthetic education in later nineteenth century examined by Michael Mann, there were very real limits to the promise of 'civilizing' Indians, and these problems were further compounded by the familiar issue of a lack of financial commitment from the colonial state.

Tschurenev also shows that new and more centralized 'universal education' depended on a wide array of intermediaries for its delivery to students. In Britain as well as India, missionary societies and voluntary associations were key to the new education, and this added another layer of complexity between the civilizing projects of the state and the society it attempted to improve and govern. In India the situation of an emergent colonial state was rendered more complex by the addition of several layers of intermediaries between nongovernmental missionary or voluntary organizations and Indians, including British women, Eurasians and Indians. Each group had its own agenda and set of priorities in administering the colonial civilizing mission, which made it extremely difficult for the colonial state to inculcate the 'superior' values of European culture cleanly and directly. Indian 'self-civilizers', for example, chose to emphasize practical skills and knowledge that would lead to employment opportunities and material advances rather than the 'moral uplift' that was so prominent in the rhetoric of the civilizing mission.

In Britain, India and other parts of the empire in the early nineteenth century the new popular education was delivered through monitorial schools, with Chaplain Andrew Bell's institution in Madras playing a key role in the development of the new model. In such schools more advanced students would 'monitor' the progress of their juniors and the core curriculum featured short lessons in reading, writing, and arithmetic that could be memorized easily, but there was also an emphasis on moral uplift and the eradication of crime and delinquency. While monitorial schools promised a cheap and effective means of improving the 'rising generation' and thereby helping a society move up in the 'scale of civilizations', there were problems too. Learning often descended into rote memorization and, as the term 'monitor' indicates, there was much emphasis on monitoring and surveying the students. Tschurenev notes that the new monitorial system of education employed many modern disciplinary technologies, with students disciplining fellow students and the master with supreme powers of surveillance. Moreover, there was a consistent stress on 'system, method and order' with the objective of making students diligent, industrious and disciplined.

In fact, 'discipline' is oddly one of the most important words in the lexicon of the civilizing mission. As the work of Michel Foucault and sociologists such as Christopher Dandeker has shown, discipline and 'disciplinary regimes' or 'disciplinary technologies' have been an integral part of 'modernity' for the last two hundred years.[51] This highlights yet another paradox of the civilizing mission: the liberal promise of moral and material uplift and improvement to higher stages of civilization – and education to enlighten and promote happiness – was frequently redirected toward much darker ends. The bombast of civilizing initiatives highlighted the freedoms, liberties and moral and material progress promised by modern European civilization, but colonial subjects and the lower social orders and other marginal groups in Europe and North America were more likely to receive instruction about industry, obedience and discipline and suffer increasing regulations and limitations on personal or collective autonomy. Uday Mehta has ruminated on this paradox of liberalism, including the fact that liberal ideas matured during the very period in which so many European states established overseas empires, and that liberals such as John Stuart Mill – who was employed by the East India Company for twenty-five years – would accept the exclusion of slaves, aboriginal peoples, colonial subjects and other groups from promises of liberal universalism (which emphasised inclusion!).[52] Mehta maintains that there was an ambiguity at the heart of liberalism that allowed for notions of difference and exclusion that went hand-in-hand with colonialism in India and elsewhere.

David Washbrook's article 'India, 1818–1860: The Two Faces of Colonialism', from *The Oxford History of the British Empire* series, highlights similar tensions between the Raj's rhetoric about modernizing, reforming and Anglicizing India and its actual performance as a state.[53] Washbrook argues that while the Company state created after the achievement of 'paramountcy' in 1818 claimed that it was reforming Indian society according to Western liberal and utilitarian principles it was actually making India more 'Oriental' and 'different' in the pejorative sense of being 'backward' and 'despotic'. The Company state was in fact 'a very military state' that was more interested in securing revenues to maintain its army than in reforming or civilizing India.

Washbrook also draws attention to the dominance of the military in colonial India. The East India Company pointed to the eradication of 'evils' such as *sati*, *thuggee* and infanticide as evidence of its reformist initiatives, along with the general pacification of India after 1820. This was trumpeted as the creation of Pax Britannica. While such claims were exaggerated they also ignored the fact that the Raj's armies grew at a rapid pace while Indian society was demilitarized. The role of military forces in leading civilizing missions has remained paradoxical to the present day, as the recent American-led campaigns in Iraq and Afghanistan have shown. Despite Anthony Hopkins' dictum that 'people cannot be forced into freedom',[54] violence or the threat of violence has remained an integral part of civilizing missions – and of civilization itself.[55] Even in areas of informal empire, such as China, the imperatives of Western tutelage demanded that violent lessons be given in order to reinforce the importance of 'civilized norms' of behaviour.[56]

Superiority in the realm of science and technological progress was used as a marker of higher European civilization, including science as applied to the manufacture of increasingly more powerful, destructive and violent weapons of war. As Ronald Wright notes, French and British civilizing missions in the late nineteenth century, at the height of European imperial power, were supported by the invention of automatic weapons such as the Maxim gun.[57] However, the violence inherent in colonial rule and Western civilization was blatantly exposed during World War I. The human carnage and environmental destruction wrought by four years of trench warfare in the heart of Europe, all facilitated by the most scientifically advanced weapons of war, undermined European colonial claims to superiority. Though there were already some doubts about claims to civilizational progress and supremacy before 1914, including some within Europe itself, the war encouraged a wider 'Afro-Asian assault on the civilizing mission ideology'.[58]

In India, this process was given a considerable fillip by the 13 April 1919 Jallianwalabagh massacre in the city of Amritsar. Army troops under the command of General Dyer opened fire on an unarmed crowd of Indian demonstrators who were protesting the Rowlatt Acts, which continued wartime restrictions on civil liberties, in a walled 'garden' enclosure. Nearly four hundred Indians were killed and over one thousand were wounded. General Dyer was forced to resign but he did not express regret for his actions, which he saw as a necessary form of colonial tutelage to impart an important moral lesson to disobedient Indians.[59] Despite official condemnation in Delhi and London, Dyer's actions were supported by many Britons and he was given a hero's welcome upon his return to England. For a great many Indians, meanwhile, the Jallianwalabagh massacre was a watershed event that unmasked the fundamental brutality and violence of British colonial rule. It also revealed the hollowness of the Raj's civilizing mission proclamations and helped support the rise of Mohandas Gandhi's non-violent *satyagraha* campaigns in the 1920s and 1930s.[60]

Harald Fischer-Tiné's paper 'Reclaiming Savages in "Darkest England" and "Darkest India": the Salvation Army as Transnational Agent of the Civilizing Mission' ties together the disciplinary and martial aspects of the British civilizing mission in nineteenth- and twentieth-century India. As with the essays of Jana Tschurenev and Prashant Kidambi in this book, however,

Fischer-Tiné looks beyond India to explore how civilizing missions in the subcontinent were complicated by links to activities, processes and networks in the British metropole as well as wider global flows of ideas and practices. The Salvation Army was founded in London by William Booth in 1878 and by 1910 it was active in more than thirty countries and had an international staff. It first established itself in India in 1882 under the leadership of Frederick De Lautour Tucker, a former Indian Civil Service officer who changed his name to Frederick Booth-Tucker in 1888. The Army was an evangelical Christian institution though, as Fischer-Tiné points out, it had a distinctly military flavour in Britain and overseas. It used military-style ranks, uniforms, music and language, and it viewed its mission of spreading Christianity and uplifting the 'savage', 'unruly' and 'submerged' elements of society in warlike terms. When the Army landed in India in 1882, for example, Booth-Tucker referred to it as an 'invading force' while aggressive 'boom marches' were used in the 1890s to intimidate Indians, and they sometimes led to the destruction of 'pagan temples'. Moreover, India was seen as a 'bridgehead' from which the rest of the Asian continent could be conquered.[61]

In keeping with its military orientation, Salvationists focused on making Indians more industrious, disciplined and obedient. There was also much importance placed on turning itinerant loafers, vagrants and 'criminals' into settled or sedentary subjects of the empire, especially in the Army's 'settlements' and 'industrial homes'. The stress on industry, subjection, discipline, obedience and limiting individuals' freedom of movement was compounded by the Salvation Army's autocratic and anti-democratic inclinations. These qualities conflicted with the promises of 'uplift', 'improvement' and 'progress' made by proponents of the civilizing mission in India. Instead, Indians were confronted with an authoritarian and illiberal military civilization of the type noted by David Washbrook – the 'other face' of colonialism. Of course, colonial officials could argue that Indians would not be ready for self-government on the Westminster model until they had achieved a sufficient level of maturity, discipline and 'civilization'. This in turn highlights another inconsistency of civilizing missions: promises of uplift, improvement and development were always delayed to an unspecified future date. As Louis Lindsay noted in his essay 'The Myth of a Civilizing Mission', colonial subjects were made to wait for 'distant and incalculable benefits', but the gifts of the civilizing mission never arrived.[62]

Notwithstanding an apparent alignment of interests and goals between colonial authorities and nongovernmental Salvationists, the Army's Indian outpost was often viewed with suspicion and it did not become a 'partner of empire' until 1910. Many British officials and non-officials feared that the Army's brash tactics might foment unrest in India, but there were also concerns about Salvationists 'going native' – adopting local dress, names and behaviour – for greater success with the 'lowest Indians'. Such practices erased the 'difference' between 'superior' Europeans and 'backward' Indians, and undermined the legitimacy of the civilizing mission and colonial rule itself.

The global scope of the Salvation Army's work also blurred the boundaries between the British and their colonial subjects, and it created ambiguity at the heart of the Raj's civilizing mission ideology. Though the Army was founded in Britain and initially focused on reclaiming the 'sunken millions' of the British urban poor, it was enmeshed in a global flow of ideas and personnel that included Africa and Asia within its orbit. The Salvation Army borrowed from British experiences in 'Darkest Africa' to address the dangers of British degenerates in the 'urban jungle' of 'Darkest England', and Booth-Tucker applied this knowledge in 'Darkest India'. But the Army also used new information and experiences from India for its work in the United States, Canada, Scandinavia and Japan. In India the Salvationists provided educational and medical services while also providing relief during emergencies, but cooperation with the Raj after 1910 occurred in two main areas: reclaiming India's so-called Criminal Tribes and reforming itinerant European 'loafers'. The latter harmed the prestige of the British in India and they were an embarrassment to their fellow Europeans because their laziness and indigence undermined claims of civilizational superiority. Such vagrants were another manifestation of the British 'savage within' that obscured the differences between 'backward' Indians and 'civilized' Britons. Apart from illustrating the interesting history of the Salvation Army in India and as a global nongovernmental organization in the nineteenth and twentieth centuries, Fischer-Tiné demonstrates the problematic ambiguities and paradoxes of the civilizing mission for the British. If civilizing missions were required to uplift white 'savages' in the 'urban jungles' of Britain and to reclaim and civilize degenerate 'white loafers' in India, how could the British sustain their assertions of colonial difference and superiority? Was 'Darkest England' really different from 'Darkest Africa' or 'Darkest India'?

Andrea Major's paper on the Sarda Act, 'Mediating Modernity: Colonial State, Indian Nationalism and the Renegotiation of the "Civilizing Mission" in the Indian Child Marriage Debate of 1927–1932' is the last chapter in section two and it reveals another level of complexity related to the civilizing mission in the late colonial era. By the 1920s the Raj was beyond its peak and had lost the confidence of the late nineteenth century that had culminated in Curzon's viceroyalty. As noted above, there was growing Asian confidence in the years following the epochal Japanese victory over Russia in the Russo-Japanese War, and this was compounded by the global divulgation of European savagery and barbarity during the First World War. As Major points out, the debate on the Sarda Act showed that colonial officials in the 1920s were often reluctant to pursue an agenda of reform, especially when it touched on delicate 'domestic' issues such as religion and the status of Indian women. This led to accusations – from many quarters – that the British had abandoned their commitment to the civilizing mission. After all, since the Company enacted legislation regarding *sati* and widow remarriage in 1829 and 1856, the British had, by the time the Sarda Act was passed in 1929, used the position of women as a marker of civilizational progress for one hundred years.

In the end, colonial officials reluctantly supported Sarda's initiative in modified form, but it seemed by that point that Indian social reformers had wrested the control and direction of the civilizing mission away from the British. The situation was more complex than that, however, because colonial officials had to deal with pressures from various British and Indian groups in an era of increasing nationalism and Indianization of the bureaucracy. On the Indian side there were real or potential divisions between men and women, Hindus and Muslims, and orthodox conservatives versus reformers. On the British side, there were differences of opinion between London, Delhi and the provinces, while British women tended to get caught between the interests of Indian women and the colonial state. There was also growing international scrutiny of the Raj's affairs. The Government in India tried to balance its commitment to India's 'moral and material progress' with the practicalities of governance, and this led to foot-dragging, obfuscation and ambiguity.

The discussion of Sarda's efforts to modernize Indian marriage practices leads us into part three of *Civilizing Missions in Colonial and Postcolonial South Asia*, entitled 'Indian "Self-Civilizing" Efforts c. 1900–1930'. Andrea Major points out that social reformers such as Har Bilas Sarda were in part attempting to 'modernize' and 'civilize' Indian marriage practices to align them with more advanced domestic conventions associated with Western modernity, and in this sense they were 'self-civilizers'. Michael Mann and Harald Fischer-Tiné addressed how Indians 'internalized' aspects of the colonial civilizing mission in the introduction and three chapters of *Colonialism as Civilizing Mission* (2004), but in this volume we delve deeper into this topic by exploring several examples of 'self-civilizing' projects. In section three of the book the topic is analyzed in essays by Shobna Nijhawan and Prashant Kidambi, but the theme appears in several other chapters too. As we have noted above, the subject is discussed by Jana Tschurenev and Andrea Major, but it is also featured in essays by Shahid Perwez and Carey Watt in the final part of the book.

Over the course of the nineteenth century millions of Indian minds were 'colonized' as European discourses of progress and Western civilizational superiority were diffused through a 'colonial culture' that included educational institutions, print culture and the English language itself. Indians gradually accepted new civilizational hierarchies constructed by Britons such as Mill, Macaulay and Herbert Spencer that ranked Europeans as superior and Indians (along with other colonial subjects) as 'backward' or inferior.[63] Indeed, Indians also came to view the European paradigm of civilizational progress as the only one to follow. As Dipesh Chakrabarty has put it, European narratives of progress, modernity and civilization became the 'silent referent' in the nineteenth century. In a form of 'asymmetric ignorance', colonial subjects were compelled to know 'Europe' while Europeans were free to ignore Africa, Asia and other parts of the non-Western world.[64] Furthermore, in order to become 'modern' and 'civilized' and thus be entitled to the possibility of eventual freedom and self-rule, non-Western peoples were obliged to copy European economic, political and cultural institutions or practices. These included nationalism, liberal democracy, industrial capitalism (or socialism) and use of the English language. The internalization of these tenets of the civilizing mission and related notions of inferiority meant that Indians were plagued by a sense of 'lagging behind' and were condemned to continually 'catch up' to peoples or races of higher rank in the 'scale of civilizations' – notably their British colonial overlords.

Gandhi famously bemoaned the enslavement of India's nationalist politicians by the English language and British or European ideals in *Hind Swaraj*, written in 1909 before he returned to India. He remarked that even if the leaders of the Indian National Congress were to achieve independence and the British left India, the country would effectively still be ruled by the British because the minds of so many urban middle-class politicians had been penetrated by British values.[65] Though we should not fetishize Gandhi's text, as Dipesh Chakrabarty warns in his influential article 'Postcoloniality and the Artifice of History', we can acknowledge that Gandhi was able to step outside the powerful frame of the civilizing mission ideology, albeit with the help of British critics of 'Western civilization' such as John Ruskin and Edward Carpenter.[66] Of course, many Indians had sufficient agency to select, translate and reassemble Western influences with their own values, and some reformers and revivalists echoed or anticipated Gandhi by insisting on the superiority of Indian 'traditions'. Nonetheless, in many areas of cultural, economic and political life European paradigms and narratives were dominant. The challenge for Indian nationalists was to construct an 'Indian modern' without accepting all of the Western colonial 'civilizing discourse', and yet still be modern in the sense of promising 'improvement' and remaining capable of participating in a competitive and hierarchical world system.[67]

Shobna Nijhawan provides an interesting commentary on Indian self-civilizing efforts in her essay '"Civilizing Sisters": Writings on How to Save Women, Men, Society and the Nation in Late Colonial India'. She shows that middle-class Hindu women carried out a 'women's civilizing mission' against Indian men during the 1910s and 1920s in order to 'save the Indian nation'. In a sense, this was a civilizing mission twice-removed because Indian women used Hindi journals as a space for redeploying nineteenth-century civilizational arguments made by James Mill, James Tod, and Herbert Spencer against Indian men who had themselves become besotted by the 'superior' Western paradigm. Mill, Tod and Spencer had stipulated that the poor or degraded status of women in India indicated that it was a backward society in need of British paternal guidance, and Indian women argued that their own liberation would release female energies that would free 'enslaved' and 'colonized' Indian males. Women challenged male attempts to domesticate or regulate them, and they promised to create a modern woman who could accommodate the best elements of Indian tradition in order to provide national service to 'uplift' and ultimately free India. This kind of creative appropriation of civilizing mission ideals for self-empowerment has also been used recently by Dalit activists such as Chandrabhan Prasad. He has organized celebrations of Lord Macaulay's October 25th birthday since 2004, because Macaulay's deprecation of Hindu civilization along with his promotion of the English language and rational, scientific education would liberate Dalits from centuries of caste oppression.[68] As with Indian women in the 1920s, Dalits like Prasad have found parts of the Raj's civilizing mission rather helpful to their cause.

The second chapter in part three is Prashant Kidambi's 'From "Social Reform" to "Social Service": Indian Civic Activism and the Civilizing Mission in Colonial Bombay, c. 1900–20', and it examines an 'internal civilizing mission' undertaken by middle-class Indian liberals and directed at the urban poor. Kidambi puts Indian initiatives related to 'the discovery of poverty' in global perspective, but he also shows how reformers internalized much of the colonial ethic of 'improvement' and 'discipline' – though British Victorian ideals were melded with Brahminical or Muslim *ashraf* expectations of piety and decorum.[69] Indian liberals frequently borrowed from the lexicon of the colonial civilizing mission to justify their 'uplift' and 'redemption' campaigns. For example, men and women of the urban poor were depicted as 'backward', 'irrational', 'intemperate', 'degenerate', 'rascally', 'dangerous', 'filthy' and 'unhygienic'. Predictably, the goal of voluntary associations under the direction of Bombay's middle-class intelligentsia, such as the Social Service League and Seva Sadan, was to 'enlighten' and 'improve' and ensure 'discipline' and 'obedience' while also inculcating greater 'thrift' and 'cleanly habits' through various educational initiatives. New phrases such as 'social work', 'social welfare' and 'national efficiency' entered the lexicon in the early twentieth century, however, and this reflected the influence of 'modern' and 'scientific' global innovations in attempts to 'reclaim' and 'civilize' the urban poor.

Kidambi's paper also highlights the class or bourgeois aspect of civilizing missions. His study of colonial Bombay in the early twentieth century shows how well-to-do middle-class liberals sought to 'civilize' the poor in their image, with a seemingly illiberal emphasis on discipline and obedience. The bourgeois aspect of civilizing initiatives is also apparent in Harald Fischer-Tiné's essay on the Salvation Army. Most of the Army's officers came from the middle classes, albeit the lower end, and they espoused middle-class values. Salvationists in Britain started out by focusing on reclaiming the urban poor and working classes. Moreover, some members of the Servants of India Society and the Prarthana Samaj saw themselves as missionaries, rather like the Salvation Army, while both the Army and the Seva Sadan established 'industrial homes'. Indian associations and Salvationists also received financial support from Indian capitalists, including the Tata family, who supported reform of the 'Depressed Classes'. The Depressed Classes designation underlines the entanglement of class and caste in India, since it combined the lower or working classes with the lower castes, including untouchables. Notably, much of the Salvation Army's work among the Criminal Tribes in the early twentieth century was directed at untouchable communities.

In the end, Kidambi argues that the initiatives of Indian liberal reformers in Bombay were relatively ineffective in 'civilizing' the urban poor. They were more successful in garnering legitimacy for Indian leaders. As in the case of the British civilizing mission, merely proclaiming high-minded intentions regarding the 'uplift', 'improvement' and 'civilizing' of so-called degenerate and backward peoples contributed to the rulers' moral authority and political legitimacy.

The final part of the book is 'Transcending 1947: Colonial and Postcolonial Continuities', which features two chapters that explore how aspects of the colonial and 'internal' Indian civilizing missions persisted into the postcolonial era. In effect, civilizing missions had to continue because the colonial civilizing mission was neither complete nor successful in 1947, particularly in its objectives of 'moral improvement'. Shahid Perwez's essay 'Female Infanticide and the Civilizing Mission in Postcolonial India: A Case Study from Tamil Nadu c. 1980–2006' examines state efforts to curtail female infanticide through programmes such as the Cradle Baby Scheme (CBS) and Girl Child Protection Scheme (GCPS). Perwez shows that these initiatives were part of the Tamil Nadu government's development and welfare policies, which focused on 'developing' the rural population, and especially rural women, to a higher and more modern scientific standard. The practice of female infanticide in rural areas was construed as 'backward' and 'criminal' with poor and low-caste rural women basing their actions on 'superstitious' *jathagam* astrology. The modern state saw its role as one of 'intervention' to survey and monitor the actions – and bodies – of rural women in order to promote the social welfare and overall development of Tamil Nadu. Moreover, the state was supported and assisted by many NGOs, and this is reminiscent of the 'civilizing' role that nongovernmental voluntary or missionary societies played in the colonial period.

Another important colonial – postcolonial continuity is that the state of Tamil Nadu's CBS and GCPS projects were effectively urban-based campaigns to 'civilize' rural India. Sunil Khilnani's observation in *The Idea of India* that 'the British Raj lived in the city' indicates that colonialism and the colonial civilizing mission also lived in the city: they were fundamentally urban.[70] To be sure, civilizing missions could focus on 'backward' urban groups, as Prashant Kidambi's paper shows, but they also spread outward from cities to the villages of the rural hinterland. In fact, Gandhi's campaigns focused on India's peasants because the peasants had not been colonized. The political authority of the Raj had difficulty extending itself to rural areas, but more importantly to Gandhi, the minds of the peasants, unlike India's urban, middle-class and English-speaking elites, had not been contaminated or 'colonized' by 'Western civilization'.[71]

The last chapter in part four is 'Philanthropy and Civilizing Missions in India c. 1820–1960: States, NGOs and Development', in which I analyze the relationship between philanthropy and civilizing missions over a 140-year period by looking at three different case studies. The first looks at East India Company incursions into the field of charity after 1820, the second at Indian social service and philanthropic initiatives with links to the Indian nationalism between the 1890s and the 1940s (including Gandhi's 'Constructive Programme'), while the third considers the efforts of the post-1947 'Nehruvian' state to establish itself as the principle source of philanthropy in the form of social welfare and social justice. The essay shows surprising continuities across these different moments. Each new effort, whether British or Indian, claimed to be rational, modern and scientific while denouncing existing or 'traditional' Indian forms of charity as 'wasteful' or 'superstitious'. Moreover, there was a consistent emphasis on the need to inculcate discipline and austerity in the recipients of charity, despite slight changes in terminology over the decades: from 'utility' and 'industry' in the 1830s to 'efficiency' after 1900, and then to 'development' and 'scientific planning' in the 1940s and 1950s. Those directing the philanthropic endeavours – whether British or Indian, governmental or nongovernmental – were by definition 'different' and 'superior' in the sense of being more 'rational' and 'modern', and hence more 'civilized'. Therefore, greater political legitimacy was conferred on the individuals, organizations or states that provided the charity. The latter point regarding legitimacy is highlighted in Prashant Kidambi's essay on civic activism in colonial Bombay, but the 'Philanthropy and Civilizing Missions' chapter also underlines the complexity and ambiguity of civilizing missions in colonial and postcolonial India in other ways. It underscores the overlap between British and Indian attitudes toward social groups deemed 'backward' or 'inferior' on the basis of class, caste, race or gender; it draws attention to the ambiguous role of nongovernmental or 'civil society' organizations; it highlights the shift from 'improvement' to 'development'; and it accentuates the coercive, disciplinary and illiberal elements of civilizing missions. As such, it recapitulates many of the insightful arguments made by the book's other contributors.

Postcolonial Britain: An Area for Further Research?

Ideally, this book would not only go beyond the colonial period and the temporal boundary of 1947, but also beyond the geographic space of South Asia. One promising area for future research on civilizing missions related to British colonialism and the peoples of South Asia would be the issue of 'New Commonwealth' immigration to Great Britain from the 1950s onward. This research would explore the continuation of the colonial civilizing mission in postcolonial Britain and efforts to 'civilize' immigrants from former British colonies, especially India, Pakistan and Bangladesh, whether arriving directly from South Asia or from Africa (Uganda and Kenya).

In the case of France and the French empire, for example, historians such as Joan Wallach Scott have written of an internal French civilizing mission directed at individuals of Algerian or wider North African ancestry within France.[72] Scott argues that the French campaign to ban headscarves or veils worn by women in France is a continuation of a failed *mission civilisatrice* in Algeria. With rising levels of immigration to France from Algeria and other former North African colonies from the late 1950s onward, and especially after Algeria became independent in 1962, the civilizing mission shifted its attention to 'immigrants' within France. Many of these so-called 'immigrants' were actually born in France, but, nonetheless, many 'regular' white French citizens saw them as unwelcome 'guests' from North Africa and expected or encouraged them to go 'home'. By the end of the 1970s it became apparent that 'North Africans in France', whether born in France or Maghreb, either could not or would not 'go home'. A French republican state based on ideas of universal equality could not accept the 'difference' of its North African residents or citizens and was determined to 'civilize' and assimilate them. However, since the early 1980s at least two generations of French youth of North African ancestry have resisted France's postcolonial civilizing mission.[73]

Britain has also faced problems related to immigration from its former colonies.[74] As Roy Porter states in his history of London, 'Britain's imperial chickens came home to roost with flaring racial tensions from the 1950s, associated with New Commonwealth immigration'.[75] British authorities instituted measures to try to control Asian, African and Caribbean immigration in the 1960s and 1970s, but in 1961 the number of Indian and Pakistani immigrants managed to increase to 48,000. By 1981 more than 15 per cent of London's population of 6.6 million was born outside the United Kingdom with 296,000 born in Asia.[76] Cultural differences encouraged racial intolerance and hatred, and Enoch Powell's infamous April 1968 'Rivers of Blood' speech indicated the depth of white British fears about immigration.

Many Britons of the majority white culture viewed 'black immigrants', a category which included Africans, Caribbeans and Indians or Pakistanis, as too 'different' to fit into British society. Historians such as Thomas Metcalf and Judith Brown acknowledge that imperial ideas of Indian 'difference' and 'inferiority' made their way to Britain and were well established by the 1960s, further contradicting longstanding promises of liberal inclusion.[77] Furthermore, Indian fiction about London in the 1960s and 1970s, such as Kamala Markandaya's *The Nowhere Man* (1972), features characters trying to settle in London who stated that the colonial attitudes of the Raj had reached across the ocean and followed them to Britain.[78]

Tensions related to 'New Commonwealth' immigration periodically erupted into violence, and for older Britons mass immigration was difficult to comprehend or accept. Any violence carried out by 'black immigrants' seemed to prove their true 'primitive' essence – despite the role of white Britons and the police in such tragic incidents.[79] Hence there was a need to educate and 'civilize' the new 'immigrants' – to erase their difference and make them more British and thus more 'civilized'. The civilizing mission had not succeeded in India and other colonies so it had to be continued in Britain, in the metropole itself.

In an essay from 1982 entitled 'The New Empire Within Britain' Salman Rushdie argues that the 'new empire' was a Britain that had not yet been 'cleansed of the filth of imperialism'.[80] 'Problem' black or Asian 'immigrants' were the new 'colonized', even though 40 per cent or more of the 'black immigrants' in Britain were British citizens by birth, with the police as the 'colonizing army' and 'regiments of occupation and control'. Moreover, black and Asian colonial subjects of 'the empire within Britain' had to be treated like the 'wild', 'half-devil and half-child' peoples of Kipling's 'White Man's Burden'. Though Rushdie does not explicitly refer to a 'civilizing mission' in his essay, it is certainly implied by his reference to Kipling. Like the youth of North African ancestry living in France during the 1980s, Rushdie's essay was an impassioned attack on condescending imperial attitudes and institutional racism, and it was an act of resistance against Britain's postcolonial civilizing mission.

Though postcolonial Britain's problems related to 'difference', accommodation and racism date as far back as the 1950s, an article published in *The Indian Express* by C. P. Bhambhri in August 2009 bemoaned the British government's post-9/11 and 7/7 (the London suicide bombings of 7 July 2005) attitude toward Muslims and other minorities in the United Kingdom. 'The growing intolerance of cultural diversities in Western countries is either a product of a "fear complex" or a desire to completely "homogenise" their societies on the basis of their self-belief that their cultural values are "superior" to all other cultures, especially Islamic culture'. [81] Bhambhri was writing in the context of the American-led 'War on Terror', but, like Rushdie in 1982, he invoked Kipling's 'White Man's Burden' and deemed British attitudes a return to the 'White Man's civilizing mission'.

There has been a growing body of scholarship regarding 'South Asians in Britain', including recent works such as Michael H. Fisher, Shompa Lahiri and Shinder S. Thandi's *A South-Asian History of Britain* (which features two chapters on the post-1947 period),[82] Judith Brown's *Global South Asians*,[83] and the collaborative project *Making Britain: South Asian Visions of Home and Abroad, 1870–1950*,[84] led by the Open University in conjunction with the University of Oxford and King's College London. While such works address the issue of discrimination and racism directed at South Asian immigrants or British citizens of South Asian ancestry, it appears that little has been written about this as a continuation of the colonial 'civilizing mission', now focused on people of South Asian ancestry within Britain. This situation may well change in the near future.

Notes

1 My thanks to Michael Mann, Prashant Kidambi and Samira Farhoud for their helpful comments on earlier versions of this introduction.

2 See Michael Mann's discussion and definition of 'civilizing mission' in '"Torchbearers Upon the Path of Progress": Britain's Ideology of "Moral and Material Progress" in India. An Introductory Essay' in Harald Fischer-Tiné and Michael Mann (eds.), *Colonialism as Civilizing Mission: Cultural Ideology in British India* (London & New York: Anthem Press, 2004), 1–26. See also Thomas R. Metcalf on the 'civilizing mission' and the importance of 'difference' in *Ideologies of the Raj* (Cambridge: Cambridge University Press, 1996), 1–6, 39, 66–68 and *passim*, and, regarding France's *mission civilisatrice*, see Alice Conklin's pioneering study, *A Mission to Civilize: the Republican Idea of Empire in France and West Africa, 1895–1930* (Stanford: Stanford University Press, 1997).

3 Dipesh Chakrabarty, 'Postcoloniality and Artifice of History: Who Speaks for "Indian" Pasts', *Representations* 37 (Winter 1992), 1–26. In this influential article Chakrabarty argues that Europe claimed to be the universal model of progress in the nineteenth century and thus became the 'silent referent' in all narratives of development and the 'transition' to 'modernity' and modern civilization in the form of European liberalism

and capitalism. Chakrabarty called for new and radically heterogeneous histories that would help to 'provincialize Europe'. See also Dipesh Chakrabarty, *Provincializing Europe: Postcolonial thought and historical difference* (Princeton: Princeton University Press, 2000).

4 Saddam Hussein took on a superficial similarity to Tipu Sultan, the Muslim leader of the South Indian state of Mysore in the 1780s and 1790s, who reputedly had links to French agents provacateurs during the Napoleonic Wars, and was finally killed by the British in 1799 after his power had already been eroded considerably. William Dalrymple also noted this similarity in 'An essay in imperial villain-making', *The Guardian*, 24 May 2005, <http://www.guradian.co.uk>.

5 John J. Mearsheimer and Stephen M. Walt have argued that the Israel lobby in the United States played a critical role in encouraging the American attack on Iraq, because it and many Israeli politicians believed that remaking the Middle East by ousting despots and promoting democracy would serve Israel's 'security interests'. See John J. Mearsheimer and Stephen M. Walt, chapter 8, 'Iraq and Dreams of Transforming the Middle East', in *The Israel Lobby and U.S. Foreign Policy* (Toronto: Penguin Canada, 2007), 229–62. This is especially interesting because Theodor Herzl, the European founder of modern Zionism who penned the famous text *The Jewish State* in 1896, justified the creation of a state for Jews in the Middle East on the grounds that it would form a bulwark of civilization in the region. In this sense, late-nineteenth and early-twentieth-century attempts – during the era of colonialism – to create the state that became Israel in 1948 were seemingly part of a civilizing mission in the Middle East.

6 Blair's comments were made on 21 March 2006, the third anniversary of the war. See 'Blair "takes on" Iraq war critics', BBC News http://news.bbc.co.uk/2/hi/uk_news/politics/4827680.stm, accessed 14 December 2009.

7 Michael Adas, 'Contested Hegemony: The Great War and the Afro-Asian Assault of the Civilizing Mission Ideology', *Journal of World History* 15, 1 (2004), 31–63. In an essay published in 1982, Salman Rushdie also noted: 'One of the key concepts of imperialism was that military superiority implied cultural superiority, and this enabled the British to condescend to and repress cultures far older than their own; and it still does'. Salman Rushdie, 'The New Empire Within Britain', in *Imaginary Homelands: essays and criticism 1981–1991* (London: Granta Books, in association with Viking Penguin, 1991), 129–38.

8 'About ISAF Afghanistan: Mission', http://www.isaf.nato.int/en/our-mission/, accessed 14 December 2009.

9 For an examination of the Salvation Army as an international NGO that conflicted and cooperated with the British Raj in the late nineteenth and twentieth centuries, see Harald Fischer-Tiné's 'Reclaiming Savages in "Darkest England" and "Darkest India": the Salvation Army as Transnational Agent of the Civilizing Mission' in part two (chapter four) of this book. His essay is also discussed below, in the second section of the introduction ('The Present Book').

10 *Independent Panel on Canada's Future Role in Afghanistan*, http://dsp-psd.pwgsc.gc.ca/collection_2008/dfait-maeci/FR5-20-1-2008E.pdf (accessed 1 December 2009). Though the report provides a long list of experts who were consulted by the panel it is interesting that no historians of South or Central Asia are listed. Some readers may find it difficult to imagine Canadian involvement in any kind of 'civilizing mission', but we must remember that Canada was a 'White Dominion' within the British Empire, and that it undertook its own mission to civilize Canadian aboriginal peoples (First Nations, Métis and Inuit). For example, in the late nineteenth and twentieth centuries

the Canadian government worked with various Christian churches to remove over 150,000 aboriginal children from their families and villages to place them in 'Indian residential schools' so that they could be 'civilized' to European standards.

11 *Independent Panel on Canada's Future Role in Afghanistan*, 3–7, 18, 20.

12 Janice Gross Stein and Eugene Lang, *The Unexpected War: Canada in Kandahar* (Toronto: Viking Canada, 2007), 266.

13 *Independent Panel on Canada's Future Role in Afghanistan*, 4, 17.

14 *Independent Panel on Canada's Future Role in Afghanistan*, 7, 10.

15 *Independent Panel on Canada's Future Role in Afghanistan*, 7.

16 *Independent Panel on Canada's Future Role in Afghanistan*, 12.

17 On the issue of brutal and misogynistic warlords in the Afghan government supported by ISAF and the US see, for example, Kathy Gannon, *I is for Infidel: From Holy War to Holy Terror – 18 Years Inside Afghanistan* (New York: Public Affairs, 2005), and Malalai Joya *A Woman Among Warlords: the extraordinary story of an Afghan who dared to raise her voice* (Scribner 2009).

18 A. G. Hopkins, 'Lessons of "Civilizing Missions" are Mostly Unlearned', *New York Times* (23 March 2003). Some commentators have actually admitted that it would take decades for ISAF and the Americans to achieve their development objectives in Afghanistan. See, for example, Canada's *Independent Panel on Canada's Future Role in Afghanistan*.

19 Mark Mazower, *No Enchanted Palace: The End of Empire and the Ideological Origins of the United Nations* (Princeton and Oxford: Princeton University Press, 2009), 14–21 and *passim*. It is quite startling that Mazower's book on the ideological origins of the United Nations contains frequent references to the British imperial civilizing mission. The topic is discussed on approximately twenty of the book's first one hundred pages.

20 See 'Gunsights' biblical references concern US and UK forces', BBC News, <http://news.bbc.co.uk/2/hi/americas/8468981.stm>, 20 January 2010.

21 *Independent Panel on Canada's Future Role in Afghanistan*, 79.

22 On this point, see Louis Lindsay, 'The Myth of a Civilizing Mission: British Colonialism and the Politics of Symbolic Manipulation' (University of the West Indies, Jamaica: Institute of Social and Economic Research, 1981), 8–9, 29–30. See also Edward Said, *Culture and Imperialism* (New York: Vintage Books, 1994), 15–16.

23 Jawaharlal Nehru in *Glimpses of World History* (New Delhi: Penguin Books India, 2004 [first published 1934]), 54–57.

24 See Michael Wood, *In the Footsteps of Alexander the Great: A Journey from Greece to Asia* (Berkeley & Los Angeles: University of California Press, 1997), 13, 130–36 .

25 Mullah Omar's is quoted in Ahmed Rashid, 'Omar vs. Obama', *The Globe and Mail* (Toronto), 30 November 2009.

26 See Ashley Blum, 'RAWA Activist discusses Afghanistan war', <http://www.rawa.org/rawa/2009/10/14/rawa-activist-discusses-afghanistan-war.html>, accessed 14 December 2009. Zoya uses an assumed name for reasons of personal security. See also 'Afghan Women Resist Occupation and Fundamentalism – RAWA Tour USA 2009' at <http://www.rawa.org>. Malalai Joya makes similar points in her book *A Woman Among Warlords*.

27 Niall Ferguson, *Empire: the rise and demise of the British world order and the lessons for global power* (New York: Basic Books, 2004 [first published 2002]), ix–xxvi.

28 A substantial discussion of British efforts to 'civilize' and 'Anglicize' its colonial subjects, especially in Africa and India, occurs in chapter three 'The Mission' in Ferguson, *Empire*, 93–136.

29 Ferguson, *Empire*, xxii–xxiii.

30 Ferguson, *Empire*, 317.

31 Deepak Lal, *In Praise of Empires: Globalization and Order* (New York & Houndmills: Palgrave Macmillan, 2004).

32 Lal, *In Praise of Empires*, xix–xxiv.

33 Lal, *In Praise of Empires*, xxv.

34 Lal, *In Praise of Empires*, xvii, 99, 85–104, 187–90.

35 Ferguson and Lal also seem to be 'imperial internationalists' in the mould of South African Jan Smuts and Briton Alfred Zimmern. In the first half of the twentieth century Smuts and Zimmern were hopeful that the League of Nations and its successor the United Nations could be instruments of a global civilizing mission informed by British imperial values. Moreover, like Ferguson and Lal, Zimmern expected that Americans would succeed the British after 1940 to become 'leaders of freedom' in the world. See Mazower, *No Enchanted Palace*, 18–23, and chapters one and two, 28–103, regarding Smuts and Zimmern, respectively.

36 Lal, *In Praise of Empires*, xxv–xxvi.

37 See chapter three, 'The Mission', in Ferguson, *Empire*, 93–136, 101–10 & 128–36 focus on Livingstone. India is discussed on 110–28.

38 'We should not be reluctant to assert the superiority of Western values', Intelligence Squared, <http://www.intelligencesquared.com/iq2-video/2007/we-should-not-be-reluctant-to-assert-the-superiority-of-western-values> (accessed 21 December 2009).

39 A. G. Hopkins, 'Lessons of "Civilizing Missions" are Mostly Unlearned', *New York Times* (23 March 2003); Kenneth Pomeranz 'Empire & "Civilizing Missions", Past & Present', *Daedalus* 134, 2 (Spring 2005), 34–45; Edward Said, 'A window on the world', *The Guardian* <http://www.guardian.co.uk> 2 August 2003; William Dalrymple, 'A lesson in humility for the smug West', *The Sunday Times*, <http://entertainment.timesonline.co.uk/tol/arts_and_entertainment/books/article2651452.ece> 14 October 2007. Dalrymple's article summarizes his argument against the 'We should not be reluctant to assert the superiority of Western values' motion in the Intelligence Squared debate that occurred in London a few days later, on 19 October 2007.

40 Said speaks of Bernard Lewis and Fouad Ajami but we can just as easily insert the names of Deepak Lal and Niall Ferguson.

41 Said, 'A window on the world'.

42 Dalrymple, 'A lesson in humility for the smug West'.

43 Hopkins, 'Lessons of "Civilizing Missions" are Mostly Unlearned'.

44 Pomeranz, 'Empire & "Civilizing Missions"'.

45 The notion of 'reassembling bits of the "civilizing mission" into something else' is discussed in Frederick Cooper and Ann Laura Stoler, 'Between Metropole and Colony: Rethinking a Research Agenda', from Frederick Cooper and Ann Laura Stoler (eds.), *Tensions of Empire: Colonial Cultures in a Bourgeois World* (Berkeley & Los Angeles: University of California Press, 1997), 1–56, especially 31–32. The last section of *Colonialism as Civilizing Mission* was entitled 'The Civilizing Mission Internalized' and it contained three of the book's thirteen chapters.

46 Robert Travers, *Ideology and Empire in Eighteenth-Century India: The British in Bengal* (Cambridge: Cambridge University Press, 2007), 6–9.

47 Rudyard Kipling's poem was penned at the apogee of the British empire in 1899 and it invited the United States, which had recently become an overseas colonial power during

the Spanish-American War of 1898, to share in the imperial burden of civilizing the backward peoples of the world.

48 Margaret Macmillan, *Women of the Raj* (New York: Thames and Hudson, 1988), 10–11. The term 'officials' refers to Britons serving the Raj in its civil or military branches, while 'non-officials' were professionals, planters, businessmen, scholars and some missionaries who were not 'officially' part of the Raj.

49 A *darbar* (or *durbar*) was a court or aristocratic court ceremony that was used by various Indian dynasties as well as the British in India.

50 The paradoxical need to maintain 'difference' has been the subject of interesting commentary by several scholars including: Michael Mann, '"Torchbearers Upon the Path of Progress": Britain's Ideology of "Moral and Material Progress" in India. An Introductory Essay' in Fischer-Tiné and Mann (eds.), *Colonialism as Civilizing Mission*, 1–26, the editors' introduction to the section entitled 'The Imperial Mission' in Alice L. Conklin and Ian Christopher Fletcher (eds.), *European Imperialism, 1830–1930: Climax and Contradiction* (Problems in European Civilization Series) (Boston & New York: Houghton Mifflin Company, 1999), 55–57, and Cooper and Stoler, 'Between Metropole and Colony: Rethinking a Research Agenda', in Cooper and Stoler (eds.), *Tensions of Empire*, 1–56, and Pomeranz, 'Empire & "Civilizing Missions"'.

51 Michel Foucault, *Discipline and Punish: The Birth of the Prison*, trans. by Alan Sheridan (New York: Vintage Books, 1995), Christopher Dandeker, *Surveillance, Power and Modernity: Bureaucracy and Discipline from 1700 to the Present Day* (Cambridge: Polity Press, 1990). Dipesh Chakrabarty also discusses the post-1850 Victorian fetish of discipline, order and routine in 'The Difference – Deferral of Colonial Modernity: Public Debates on Domesticity in British Bengal', in Cooper and Stoler (eds.), *Tensions of Empire*, 376–77.

52 Uday Mehta, 'Liberal Strategies of Exclusion', in Cooper and Stoler (eds.), *Tensions of Empire*, 59–86.

53 D. A. Washbrook, 'India, 1818–1860: The Two Faces of Colonialism', *The Oxford History of the British Empire*, vol. III, ed. Andrew Porter (Oxford: Oxford University Press, 1999), chapter 18, 395–421.

54 Hopkins, 'Lessons of "Civilizing Missions" are Mostly Unlearned'.

55 Elizabeth Kolsky, *Colonial Justice in British India: White Violence and the Rule of Law* (Cambridge: Cambridge University Press, 2010), has taken some of David Washbrook's points about Company violence, militarism and despotism a step further, especially regarding British-Indian law. On page 30, for example, Kolsky writes: 'Not only was physical violence a persistent and integral feature of British rule in India, law was its most reliable and consistent accomplice'.

56 Pomeranz, 'Empire & "Civilizing Missions"', 40–41.

57 Ronald Wright, *A Short History of Progress* (Toronto: House of Anansi Press Inc., 2004), 33–34. See Lindsay, 'The Myth of a Civilizing Mission', 9–10, and Cooper and Stoler, 'Between Metropole and Colony: Rethinking a Research Agenda', in Cooper and Stoler (eds.), *Tensions of Empire*, 16–17 & 31–32, on this point too.

58 Adas, 'Contested Hegemony', 40–63.

59 See 'General Dyer's Report on the Massacre' and 'General Dyer's Statements Before the Hunter Committee' which are included in 'Accounts of the Amritsar (Jallianwala Bagh) Massacre, 1919', in Tracey J. Kinney (ed.), *Conflict and Cooperation: Documents on Modern Global History* (Toronto: Oxford University Press, 2006), 106–107.

60 *Satyagraha* is the term that Gandhi coined to convey the importance of non-violent 'firmness in the pursuit of truth' (*satya*), in which 'truth' could have various meanings

including mastery of self or, indeed, national independence for India. Gandhi, of course, had been expressing trenchant criticism of 'European civilization' since the publication of his text *Hind Swaraj* (usually translated as 'Indian Home Rule') in 1909.

61 On the transmutation of military values into civilian life during the nineteenth and early twentieth centuries, see also Carey Watt, '"No showy muscles": the Boy Scouts and the global dimensions of physical culture and bodily health in Britain and colonial India', in Nelson R. Block and Tammy M. Proctor (eds.), *Scouting Frontiers: Youth in the Scout Movement's First Century* (Newcastle: Cambridge Scholars Publishing, 2009), 121–42, especially 130–32.

62 Lindsay, 'The Myth of a Civilizing Mission', 12, 18 and *passim*.

63 The deleterious psychological effects of European colonialism, in terms of encouraging a sense of inferiority among colonial subjects, have been noted by many authors including Frantz Fanon, *Black Skin, White Masks*, translated by Charles Lam Markmann (Pluto, 1986 [first published 1952]), Edward Said, *Orientalism* (New York: Vintage Books, 1978) and *Culture and Imperialism* (New York: Vintage Books, 1994), and Louis Lindsay, 'The Myth of a Civilizing Mission', 17–20, 32.

64 Chakrabarty, 'Postcoloniality and the Artifice of History', 2.

65 Mohandas K. Gandhi, *Hind Swaraj*, in Rudrangshu Mukherjee (ed.), *The Penguin Gandhi Reader* (Penguin Books USA, 1996), 12–20.

66 David Arnold, *Gandhi* (Harlow & London: Longman, 2001), 64–70. See also David Hardiman, *Gandhi in his Time and Ours: the global legacy of his ideas* (New York: Columbia University Press, 2003), 66–93. Chakrabarty's comment about not fetishizing *Hind Swaraj* is in 'Postcoloniality and the Artifice of History', 8. We should note that Gandhi has also been accused of pursuing his own civilizing mission in his efforts to 'uplift' and 'educate' India's untouchables. See Arnold, *Gandhi*, 169–73, Hardiman, *Gandhi in his Time and Ours*, 123–55, and B. R. Ambedkar, *Gandhi and Gandhism* (Jullunder: Bheem Patrika Publications, c. 1970). See also Watt's chapter 9, 287–92, below.

67 See Chakrabarty 'The Difference – Deferral of Colonial Modernity'. Chakrabarty focuses primarily on Bengali nationalists and the issue of domesticity in colonial Bengal, yet his insights have wider relevance. On the topic of contesting and negotiating Western modernity and civilization see also Adas, 'Contested Hegemony', and Andrea Major's chapter in part two of this book.

68 See 'Macaulay's Children', *The Economist*, vol. 373, issue 8399 (30 October 2004), 48, and Chandrabhan Prasad's website, <http://chandrabhanprasad.com/index.aspx>. Dalit means 'the oppressed', and it is the term used and preferred by former 'untouchables' since c. 1970.

69 *Ashraf* refers to well-to-do or 'respectable' Muslims.

70 Sunil Khilnani, *The Idea of India* (New York: Farrar, Straus and Giroux, 1999), 116. Of course, cities and urban life have been coterminous with 'civilization' since the first complex societies or 'civilizations' based on agriculture emerged 5,000 years ago in Mesopotamia, the Indus valley (Harappa and Mohenjo-Daro) and several other locations.

71 Arnold, *Gandhi*, 76.

72 Joan Wallach Scott, *The Politics of the Veil* (Princeton: Princeton University Press, 2007).

73 Scott, *Politics of the Veil*, 46–47, 66, 81, 162. See also Paul A. Silverstein, *Algeria in France: Transpolitics, Race, and Nation* (Bloomington: Indiana University Press, 2004).

74 Ironically, the very empire that attempted to render its colonial subjects fixed and sedentary in the nineteenth century also encouraged migrancy and movement in the

twentieth. On this point see John C. Ball, *Imagining London: Postcolonial Fiction and the Transnational Metropolis* (Toronto: University of Toronto Press, 2004).

75 Roy Porter, *London: A Social History* (London: Penguin Books, 1994), 354.

76 Porter, *London*, 354.

77 Metcalf, *Ideologies of the Raj*, 234, Judith M. Brown, *Global South Asians: introducing the modern diaspora* (Cambridge: Cambridge University Press, 2006), 119–21.

78 John C. Ball, *Imagining London: Postcolonial Fiction and the Transnational Metropolis* (Toronto: University of Toronto Press, 2004), 187–90.

79 See chapter four, 'London Cosmopolis' in A. N. Wilson's *London: A Short History* (London: Phoenix/Orion Books), especially 133–34.

80 Rushdie, 'The New Empire Within Britain', first published in 1982.

81 C. P. Bhambhri, 'A Civilizing Mission Unveiled', *The Indian Express*, 19 January 2007 <indianexpress.com>, accessed 7 August 2009. 7/7 refers to the terrorist attacks in London that occurred on 7 July (hence 7/7) 2005, which killed 52 people and were carried out by four suicide bombers of Muslim background. As noted at the beginning of the introduction, 9/11 refers to the terrorist attacks on the United States that occurred on 11 September 2001, which were carried out by men affiliated with Al Qaeda and radical Islam.

82 Michael H. Fisher, Shompa Lahiri and Shinder S. Thandi, *A South-Asian history of Britain: four centuries of peoples from the Indian sub-continent* (Oxford/Westport, CT: Greenwood World Publishing, 2007).

83 Brown, *Global South Asians* (2006).

84 *Making Britain: South Asian Visions of Home and Abroad, 1870–1950*, see <http://www.open. ac.uk/Arts/south-asians-making-britain/>, accessed 7 March 2010.

Part One

THE RAJ'S REFORMS AND IMPROVEMENTS: ASPECTS OF THE BRITISH CIVILIZING MISSION

Chapter One

CONJECTURING RUDENESS: JAMES MILL'S UTILITARIAN PHILOSOPHY OF HISTORY AND THE BRITISH CIVILIZING MISSION

Adam Knowles

Introduction: *The History of British India* as an Exercise in Futility

A deep ambivalence characterizes James Mill's *The History of British India*. Mill, the historian of India who never went to India, wrote ostensibly in the style of Scottish conjectural history, grafting this short-lived mode of historiography and onto a particularly rigid strand of utilitarian thinking.[1] The result of this philosophical amalgam was a ponderous narrative now infamous for its disparaging comments about the 'rude nations' of the world, and a work of purportedly 'standard', 'canonical' or 'hegemonic' status, often being assigned the position as the single most important work in the historiography of South Asia.[2] The ambivalence running through the *History* is a result of its 'rude' subject matter combined with the difficulty of aligning this rudeness with Mill's aim of providing the world with utilitarian knowledge, for it seems that Mill himself considered the work, along with its subject matter, regrettably inutile.[3] The *History* was a book that need not have been written and a work of limited utility, for it could, in the eyes of its own author, only teach about the rude people of India. Mill offered the *History* as a 'service' to spare the utility of future generations, encompassing everything one could need to know about India 'once and for all'.[4] In carrying out this service, Mill established many of the ideological and textual underpinnings for the British civilizing mission, which was still inchoate when the *History* was first published in 1817. Mill's work became a cornerstone for establishing discourses of colonial difference that supported the colonial civilizing mission.

Despite his seeming concern for reforming India, Mill perceived colonialism as an endeavour counter to utilitarian ends. 'The love of domination', Mill reminded the reader, 'has always the greatest sway in the most ignorant state of the human mind'.[5] The irony was intentional and was rooted in the allegorical nature of the *History*, through which Mill intended to awaken British readers into recognizing their own rudeness. The *History* was supposed to serve as a mirror which British readers held up to themselves to feel embarrassed about their own rudeness and love of domination. The ambivalence of Mill's work was thus twofold: the *History* only retained its utility as a justification for colonial rule, yet colonial rule as a whole is anti-utilitarian. As a result, the book was intended to lay the groundwork for its own elimination. Nonetheless, despite Mill's qualms with colonialism, he could still enjoy a profitable job at the East India House and actively participate in strengthening Britain's hold on India. As long as the colony existed, it should at least be governed as well as possible.

With the peculiar confluence of philosophical strands woven into the *History*, Mill worked within an idiosyncratic strain of thinking seemingly running counter to many of the basic notions of the European Enlightenment. The *History* conforms neither to Mary Poovey's characterization of the Enlightenment as relying on 'neutral' facts gathered through calculation, nor to what Martin Jay has characterized as the 'ocularcentrism' of the Enlightenment, since Mill trusted his principles over his eyes.[6] This mistrust of needing to see his subject in order to form an impression of it was deepened by Mill's tacit assumption that a carnivalesque atmosphere of chaos was rampant in India, a veritable miasma of impressions which would permanently taint the eyes, and thereby the reason of anyone who experienced it, including those who lived within the carnival. Whereas the festival or carnival formed the ideal of transparency for Rousseau,[7] it was the bearer of a contagious opacity for Mill, thus exemplifying Stephen Greenblatt's claim regarding colonial knowledge production that 'the explanatory power of writing repeatedly tames the opacity of the eye's objects by rendering them transparent signs'.[8] In the face of this dense opacity, Mill's rationality revealed itself to be fragile and constantly susceptible to jagged partial impressions. This rationality was at once the robust infallible reason of the Enlightenment, but it was also violable, open to incursions and pollution wherever inutility reared its ugly head, including in the mother country. For its part, Mill's India was woefully wrapped up within partial impressions of itself, unable even to grasp itself, unable to know what it was without being gathered together in the fold of a Western rationality that risked polluting itself by gathering together such a raw mass of rude material into a cohesive whole. Working under the sign of what Edward Said referred to as 'radical realism', the assertive and creative power of the copula in Orientalist texts,[9] Mill first had to think what India was, write it, then allow others to see it through the gaze of the reformer. In this manner, Mill served as the tabulator of a grid of faults and sketched a topography of rudeness, establishing a blueprint for those preparing the 'sweeping away' that would allow a civilizing mission to supplant what came before it.

Under Mill's peculiar concept of utilitarianism, the *History* rendered itself superfluous, but only on the condition that it first state its own superfluity in a scope of words coextensive with itself. Mill thus wrote in the mode of an apology – a curious tone for a work stretching to over two thousand pages. The scope of the task Mill set for himself was recognizably ambitious: to develop a *final* philosophy of man, to write a *final* work on the history of India, to *finally* rank all the civilizations of the world, to lay out precise and *final* plans for governing these civilizations, all while laying the groundwork for civilizing them through proper governance. Despite this ambitious scope, Mill was convinced of his ability to provide a work of such finality since he considered himself to be in possession of the philosophical principles of an absolute science of human nature. This science, in the words of Elie Halévy's classic text on the philosophical milieu in which Mill wrote, 'allows human nature to be overcome in the interest of mankind'.[10] Overcoming human nature was achieved through a process of understanding that very nature completely and the 'general laws of human nature' by which it is governed.[11] Through a familiarity with these universal laws, the axiomatic framework underpinning the certainty of Mill's conjectural history, one could conjecture on a subject for which evidence is missing (or, in Mill's case, has been ignored) and even supplant empirical evidence with this superior Western reasoning derived from a knowledge of universal laws. Similarly, the British civilizing mission carried out in the name of the universal laws would also overcome human nature 'in the interest of mankind'. Rudeness in Mill's thinking was thus doubly conjectured: firstly by Mill's refusal to visit India and, secondly, in his writing India's history through great conjectural leaps. As will be shown, this form of conjecture occupies a unique position in the development of the Western rationality in whose name European colonial civilizing missions were carried out.

In her striking intellectual history of this rationality, Mary Poovey has described this form of conjecture as constituting a 'dissenting opinion' against the epistemology of what she calls the 'modern fact', an epistemology that was developing into its mature form by the middle of the 19th century.[12] In Poovey's depiction, the modern fact is characteristically positivistic, empirically verifiable, often numerical, and was constructed as a 'neutral' unit of knowledge. Mill rejected this very type of fact and considered his failure visit India as an asset attesting to his authority as a historian of India, for seeing India would provide him with nothing more than 'partial impressions' which would conform to the expectations the observer already possessed.[13] In a later essay expanding her research into 'the modern fact', Poovey comments directly on Mill's *History*, stating: 'According to this position, no eyewitness account, no matter how intimate the conditions under which it was produced, could overcome the inherent limitations of the human senses or the 'constitution of the human mind'.[14] While Poovey deftly traces the background and pedigree of Mill's Scottish Enlightenment thinking and his deference to 'general principles', this paper intends to build on her account by taking the additional step of linking Mill's anti-empirical history of philosophy to his utilitarianism, and the place of his utilitarianism in the British colonial civilizing mission.

Mill's utilitarianism did not merely stand beside his conjectural philosophy of history, but was an integral component of it. A rude nation like India functioned according to rude principles, and its operation would be simple to understand according to these universal principles. Utilitarianism allowed Mill to streamline his conjecture, for a process that would produce only rude knowledge did not need to be carried out with much precision. Furthermore, once the rude nation had been assigned an inferior position in the scale of civilizations, knowledge collection could cease, for a rude civilization could offer nothing of worth to an advanced civilization. Indeed, it would even be a necessary consequence of this argument to say that what the 'rude' peoples themselves possessed or knew was not even tantamount to knowledge. As Mill gathered and assembled this knowledge, the *History* constantly worked to efface itself. Its main intention was merely to convince his readership that they, too, should feel no obligation to understand India, except to understand that it need not be understood.

Approaching *The History of British India*: Mill's Science of Human Nature

It is an irony of history that James Mill, the self-ordained prophet of philosophical progress, descended from Scotland, a place which David Hume referred to as 'the rudest, perhaps of all European nations'.[15] After an ill-fated attempt to become a preacher, Mill moved to London, where he embarked upon a career as a freelance writer and began composing occasional pieces about India. In these early writings, Mill presented himself as a staunch opponent of colonialism and repeatedly called for the abolition of the East India Company. In the *Edinburgh Review* he wrote that 'the English public must be in a position to make decisions about this change based on reliable information'.[16] In a later article, Mill dampened his demand for reform, stressing that regardless of what form of government the colony of India should have, it should be based on 'as accurate a knowledge as possible'.[17] Composed over a twelve-year period and first published in 1817, Mill intended *The History of British India* to provide this knowledge. As Mill became increasingly enmeshed in India and his reputation as an 'expert' rose, he began to temper his criticism of the EIC, the most important employer in London for such experts. Mill's critical stance disappeared altogether when the EIC offered him a position as an Examiner.[18] In 1812, Mill had written that the EIC's monopoly was a 'relict of a semi-barbarous' age.[19] By 1832, he would be among an elite group of officials chosen to defend the monopoly before a Select Committee of Parliament after a long career at East India House in London.[20]

From 1805 to 1817, the years during which Mill composed his *History*, the East India Company's position in India changed drastically as it began to solidify an ever-growing and valuable empire in India. With the definitive defeat of the Marathas in 1818, the Company's trade revenues soared to over £22 million as the colonial state grew in both size and importance.[21] Seldom has a work appeared at such an opportune moment, for Britain was eager to coronate a 'standard' work in the growing field of knowledge about India when Mill appeared with his book in 1817, thus filling a lacuna in the literature of early nineteenth century Great Britain with a work that the author himself described as 'a motley kind of production'.[22] This motley nature is at least partially attributable to Mill's idiosyncratic mix of conjectural history and utilitarianism, which is, in Jennifer Pitts' words, an 'ill-advised synthesis' of the two.[23]

In Mill's brand of utilitarianism, the possibility of moral goodness and pleasure is based on one's external situation. Accordingly, the possibility of improving one's personal or moral well-being is contingent on reforming one's own society.[24] Since this society consists of institutions and establishments, any personal improvement can only take place when these external institutions are governed by just laws which promote the pleasure of the greatest number. Mill intended his philosophy to be the exposition of these very laws, laws to be based on what Elie Halévy has called a 'calculus of morals'.[25] Mill himself referred to his thinking as a 'science of human nature', a science aimed at determining universal laws for promoting this greatest good.[26] This science, in turn, rested on the fundamental assumption that human nature was completely transparent and knowable through universally valid rational thought, and Mill claimed that given sufficient time he could 'make the human mind as plain as the road from Charing Cross to St. Paul's'.[27] While perhaps Mill's least explicitly theoretical work, the *History* was in part conceived as a practical tabulation of calculations in support of Mill's science. Although much has been made of Mill's use of a purportedly Benthamite science in the *History*,[28] Mill created a work which Bentham himself found 'melancholy' and 'disagreeable'.[29]

In the *History*, Mill employed utilitarian philosophy in a twofold manner: as a guide for reform and as a benchmark for measuring rudeness. Eric Stokes, who showed Mill's unwavering dedication to utilitarian reform, masterfully documented Mill's use in the first sense.[30] It remains nonetheless a neglected aspect of Mill's thought that he faltered in the second sense, applying utility only weakly as a measure of rudeness and its obverse – civilization. Mill did not structure his criticism of India around a consistently expressed philosophy of utilitarianism, and never attempted to precisely define utility. Donald Winch has claimed that Mill intended for utility to become 'a universal principle for judging all societies at all times'.[31] Winch's assertion requires a certain amount of reading backwards based on a broader knowledge of Mill's writings, for the *History* itself provided only weak, platitudinous examples of the application of the utility principle. Within the *History* itself, Mill's strongest statement of utility as a standard for judging cultures is buried in an Appendix to Vol. II, a critique of 'Hindu' astronomy and algebra. Mill stated:

Exactly in proportion as *Utility* [Mill's italics] is the object of every pursuit, may we regard a nation as civilized. Exactly in proportion as its ingenuity is wasted on contemptible and mischievous objects, though it may be, in itself, an ingenuity of no ordinary kind, the nation may be safely denominated barbarous.[32]

In this manner, Mill wielded a double-edged argumentative sword. On the one hand, he recognized that astronomy and algebra in India had reached levels which rivaled, if not bested, those in Europe. On the other hand, he rebuked India for using this great knowledge to futile ends, namely, superstitious astrology: 'the most irrational of all pursuits; one of those which most infallibly denote a nation barbarous'.[33] Command of knowledge or advanced sciences as such was not sufficient to make a nation civilized, for knowledge itself was not an end, but a means. If any means, even a highly sophisticated one, was not properly employed towards a sound end, then a civilization would be all the more rude for possessing a sophisticated means and applying it towards a barbarous end. In such a case, when a potentially utilitarian means was employed for superstitious ends, then a nation's barbarity was reinforced. In other words, a nation would be considered more barbaric for having sophisticated means but not making use of it. Such a mode of argument is watertight, if one happens to reside in Mill's hermetic world of utility.

By requiring both the possession and proper employment of utilitarian ends, Mill transformed utility into both a material-developmental concept and a cognitive-developmental concept, providing ample ideological ammunition for the British civilizing mission. Barbarity, therefore, is not merely recognizable on rugged means, but on the cognitive recognition of the potential use of such rugged means for utilitarian ends. Progress, development and rudeness moved out of the realm of the purely material for Mill and this cognitive aspect hints at philosophical and pseudo-scientific theories of race then only in the making.[34] Since the Hindus were a rude nation, Mill speculated that they received their complicated knowledge of astronomy from 'nations more advanced in civilization than themselves'.[35] Ultimately, though, the details of the question were 'not worth resolving', since determining exact information about rude nations never served utilitarian ends.[36] Mill's ends-means system of judgment was singularly rigid, and not only hopelessly Eurocentric, but hopelessly interlocked within the idiosyncratic *Weltanschauung* of one man – a man, in Pitts' words, of 'limited imagination'.[37] By introducing a specific system of ends into his scale of civilizations, he distorted what had been a relatively open material-developmental term into a closed cognitive-developmental term.[38] For Adam Smith and his successors, such a stark cognitive aspect had not yet been calculated into the system of development, and the potential for malicious use of such a theory was ominous, although Mill did believe that these cognitive defects could be improved upon, or educated out of the rude peoples of the world if their external situation was changed.

While Mill wrote the *History* partially because of growing interest in London regarding the Company's expansion in India, he could have, according to his own portrayal of his philosophical idealism, used the same explanatory tools to write a history of any arbitrarily chosen geographical or historical space. This conviction resulted in a history in which India played merely a supporting role based on an intentionally selective process of writing and source selection. Its slant always erred on the side of what could be known about India as a European colony, not as a space that had ever been anything but a colony. This neglect of India's past was rooted in a qualitative judgment on the utility of knowledge about India, not a mere delineation of Mill's chosen subject matter. Getting lost in the mythology and observation of a rude nation as Sir William Jones had done was an ill-advised, retrograde step into an irrational past which Europe had left behind, and a past which Mill felt India could be brought out of through the salutary application of European thought over time. As Dipesh Chakrabarty has written of this phenomenon: 'Historicism—and even the modern, European idea of history—one might say came to non-European peoples in the nineteenth century as somebody's way of saying 'not yet' to somebody else'.[39] Mill was a key author of this 'not yet', and the colonial civilizing mission that drew its ideological resources from Mill's *History* purported to close the gap between this backward Indian 'not yet' and the modern, progressive 'now' represented by Europeans.

Mill was confident in Britain's ability to grant India good government, and to bring India out of the 'dark ages' and 'rudeness' into civilized modernity. As a result, he perceived the *History* to be fulfilling an invaluable service towards determining the manner in which the colonial government should be shaped. Rendering this service meant that the *History* would not only be a *descriptive* work narrating past events, but also a *prescriptive* work for determining the course of future events. The latter consideration constituted Mill's true core of interest in India, for: '[a]ll speculation, and all experience, is an attempt from the view of the order of past events to anticipate the order of future ones'.[40] Mill, therefore, would *pre*scribe the future, in the most literal sense of the term.

The Scale of Civilizations

Mill's descriptive philosophy of history had one central axiom at its core: that Britain stood at the pinnacle of the scale of civilizations, while India was at an undetermined location somewhere near the bottom.[41] This cleft was due to a fundamental dichotomy separating rude and civilized nations and it is the same fundamental dichotomy upon which civilizing missions were premised throughout the colonies.[42] Mill's primary task was not to prove the validity of the dichotomy, but merely to flesh it out with detail, for the dichotomy itself was based on *a priori* truths and was itself not in need of proof—it was in fact prior to any sort of proof. Mill attempted to defend himself against the charge of *a priori* judgment in an article on Hinduism published after the *History*: 'These conclusions, incontestable as they appear, do not rest solely on reasonings a priori: they are confirmed by an appeal to history, in every age and quarter of the globe'.[43] Despite this defense, Mill's 'appeal to history' was nothing more than a confirmation of the very *a priori* notions of rudeness he possessed from the outset of the work.

Ostensibly, Mill took up the task of proving the superiority of European thought, but since he did this entirely within a linguistic and conceptual framework rooted in pre-existing assumptions of European superiority, the results of Mill's conclusions were already necessarily contained within the questions themselves. While the superiority of British thinking did not, according to Mill, give Britain justification to rule the world, it did mean that Britain was at least obligated to administer its existing colonies well.[44] Proper knowledge of India would be critical for proper administration. As Mill wrote:

To ascertain the true state of the Hindus in the scale of civilization, is not only an object of curiosity in the history of human nature; but to the people of Great Britain, charged as they are with the government of that great portion of the human species, it is an object of the highest practical importance.[15]

But Great Britain was not yet ready to fulfill this charge, for there was a significant caveat: something was rotten in this 'greatest civilization', and Mill sought to embarrass his countrymen into change by comparing his civilized Britain to his constructed figure of lowly India. This would shame the British public into recognizing that it could not feign to bestow good government upon India or any other colony unless Britain's own (domestic) affairs could first be brought into order. As Javed Majeed points out, this created a tension in the *History* due to Mill's ambivalence about the utility of possessing colonies, especially when the affairs of the home country were in such a supposed state of disarray.[16]

In order to form this unique social critique, Mill combined a dogmatic philosophy of rude nations with exhaustive diatribes about the state of his own society, often argued through the screen of Indian affairs in order to camouflage a radicalism that could have been interpreted as subversion if applied directly to Britain.[17] Indeed, it could even be asked if Mill was actually attempting to civilize Britain itself. Constructed in this manner, the *History* served as a type of grand allegory through which the rude nations were merely placed in the narrative to provide a contrast to the civilized ones, functioning as rhetorical devices or tropes decontextualized from their own existence. Approached as an argumentative allegory filtered through the screen of a decontextualized imagination of India, Mill's criticism of the Brahmins, for example, should be read as intended for the priests of the Catholic Church, his derisive treatment of Indian princes should be read as aimed at the British monarchy, and his attacks on the zamindars should be read as directed towards the British landed gentry.[18] The effectiveness of these attacks as components of a cohesive argument both in and for itself hinges on one critical point: finding narrative fodder with which he can describe India as one of the lowest civilizations in the world, while the exalted British nation was simply the highest *a priori*, despite its need for reform.[19] For the latter point, no argument was needed and asking the question would itself be a form of rudeness. Recognizing Britain's superiority was definitional; it was, in the hermetical world of Western rational thought, inextricably bound to thinking rationally. Whoever did not think so was not thinking rationally, for there was, according to Mill, 'European good sense and intelligence', but 'there really seems to be no other'.[50]

In his grandiose rhetorical experiment in Orientalism, Mill's concepts of rude and civilized were merely axiomatic and as such required no empirical evidence to support their validity. For this reason, Mill refused to visit India and made little effort to seek out information from those who had been in India. Mill trumpeted this perceived lack of experience as a singular qualification – if not *condition* – for writing a history of India. Mill presented this argument in the 'Preface', where he attempted to argue his way up a tricky philosophical slope, turning common sense on its head by claiming he could – indeed *should* – write a history of India 'without ocular knowledge of the country, or acquaintance with its languages'.[51] Being detached from India meant that one could avoid the pernicious influence of 'partial impressions' and step back to view the whole. The need to avoid being distracted by partial impressions in order to view the whole motivated Mill to make the extraordinary and oft-quoted statement:

> Whatever is worth seeing or hearing in India, can be expressed in writing. As soon as every thing [*sic*] of importance is expressed in writing, a man who is duly qualified may obtain more knowledge of India in one year in his closet in England, than he could obtain during the course of the longest life, by the use of his eyes and ears in India.[52]

The fact that Mill not only never went to India, but also regarded direct experience of India as detrimental to writing a proper history has earned him scorn and ridicule.[53] Just as Mill rejected ocular knowledge of India, he was equally suspicious of any Indian historiography. He was little troubled by what he perceived as the absence of an indigenous tradition of historical writing, for the 'wildness and inconsistency of the Hindu statements evidently place them beyond the sober limits of truth and history'.[54] This 'wildness' was something 'Eastern' or inherently 'Oriental' which Mill also traced in his brief writings about China. Even though Mill admitted that there was something akin to a Chinese historiography, it is 'worthy of no regard', for 'the people of Europe can hardly form any conception of the extent to which the principle of exaggeration carries almost all the Eastern nations'.[55] Thus, Mill did not merely rely on European sources because they were the only sources he believed were available: he intentionally rejected any 'Oriental' sources in favor of 'Orientalist' sources. Although the Orientalists created works which were infused with a 'love of the marvellous [*sic*]'[56] and carried opinions which Mill was 'constrained to convert',[57] the Orientalists were at least trained in European 'good sense and intelligence', and were therefore better representatives of 'Oriental' culture than the 'Orientals' themselves.

Mill's anti-Orientalist project was based on both the notions of Indian stagnation and changeability – concepts which were not mutually exclusive. Led by Sir William Jones, the Orientalists were responsible for the translation of a number of purportedly classical Indian texts which Mill was willing to take into account in describing modern India because India for him had changed very little since the classical ages.[58] Perhaps, Mill speculated, as the result of a process of cultural osmosis spreading out from the epicenter of the European classical age, India had advanced rapidly to the initial stages of civilization, but then fallen into a stagnation of 'extraordinary durability'.[59] Due to this stagnation, one could use any randomly selected ancient texts to illustrate the current state of India. Hence, the Orientalists had not merely carried out work useful for historians describing how India was in ancient times, but also work that could be equally useful for the researcher describing contemporary India. Because of their skills as translators, Mill could not completely avoid the Orientalists, yet he attempted to seek out alternative sources such as the reports of missionaries, travelers and administrators in order to break out of the Orientalist mould.[60] Mill's task was to filter through this mass of partial impressions to create a picture of the whole.

Although Mill vigorously attacked Jones, he felt that Jones' work could be used without irony or contradiction because he regarded Jones solely as a translator. For Mill, translation was a value-neutral, one-to-one process of correspondence.[61] This process of correspondence was even simpler in the case of a translation from an 'inexact' language of 'barbarians' into the 'precise' language of a civilized nation.[62] Bernard Cohn fittingly tags this approach to Indian knowledge as 'establishing correspondences',[63] and Mill never faltered in his confidence that the purportedly superior cultural and linguistic apparatus of the English language could offer an appropriate correspondence for everything which could be expressed in a rude Indian language. It is precisely this manner of translation which results in the production of difference, the very difference through which Europe justified its need to civilize the world of difference.[64] As a mediator of difference, Jones served simultaneously as Mill's intellectual nemesis and as an indispensable source for the *History*. Mill regarded Jones as the protector of a body of knowledge that India had lost, resulting in a long stretch of cultural hibernation. This stagnation did not prove that India was immutable, for it was the very potential for mutability and curing rudeness which was a precondition for the validity of Mill's prescriptive philosophy of history. Mill stated clearly: 'The peculiarities of the Hindus are not so very unalterable as they have been represented'.[65] Cultural stagnation could be overcome, and it was India's potential for progress which opened up the possibilities of India's improvement through a British civilizing mission.

Mill demonstrated this potential for change most clearly in his 1813 article on the Sikhs, a 'race' of Indians he neglected in the *History*.[66] Mill attempted to prove that the Sikhs were 'merely Hindus', but Hindus who had thrown off the injustices of the caste system, thereby improving their external situation. The Sikhs proved that rude people were not only capable of being educated, but could even educate themselves for the better under the proper circumstances. Pitts thus errs on this point by claiming that Mill saw cognitive defects as incurable or innate, for the potential for improvement is an underlying tenet of his philosophy of good government.[67] The utility of a good government must first be assessed based on a culture's ranking, for each level of development demands a unique style of government. A culture's ranking can be determined based not on the utility of the ends of their culture, but on their ability to recognize and promote such ends. Thus we have Mill's circle of utility: self-contingent utility folded back on itself to both determine and regulate its own use.

Mill's process of gathering sources for the *History* extended well beyond the mere assessment of the sources' utility, for all sources, whether from Orientalists, travelogues or missionaries, were themselves only another form of impressions, all necessarily partial. It was the proper task of the historian to 'judge' these sources, 'extracting perfectly the light of evidence from a chaos of rude materials'.[68] It is important to note here that European sources on India were not exempted from the label of 'rude' in Mill's nomenclature. At best, any source could merely provide the raw material to be processed by a discriminating historian. This historian must fulfill two charges: passing a moral judgment on the source with utility as the measure and passing a judgment on the truth or falsity of the statements the source makes.[69] Truth for Mill was based on 'real' causes. It was the task of the historian to 'discriminate between real causes and false causes; real effects and false effects, between good ends and evil ends; means that are conducive, and means that are not conducive to the ends which are applied'.[70] What Mill as a historian knew was known through this science, and the historian acquired scientific thinking through a mastery of the relevant qualifications. The list of qualifications was daunting:

> In short, the whole field of human nature, the whole field of legislation, the whole field of judicature, the whole field of administration, down to war, commerce, and diplomacy, ought to be familiar to [the historian's] mind.[71]

For the historian in possession of these qualifications, this universal knowledge would only need to be augmented by minimal local knowledge in order to write the history of a rude nation. After performing this process on India, Mill maintained little humility about the effectiveness of his universal science of human nature. 'And I believe', he pronounced, 'there is no point of great importance, involved in the History of India, which the evidence I have adduced is not sufficient to determine'.[72] The quote is not only relevant for proving Mill's self-assuredness, but also for giving insight into how his epistemology was rooted in his science of human nature.

In Mill's epistemology, truth was found in the whole which the philosopher-historian pieces together according to a blueprint of true principles or laws of human nature which function like a type of social Newtonian physics of absolute action-reaction movement. In this science, individual facts cannot alone amount to truth, for truth only emerges from general principles,[73] general principles at all times based on European ideals held to be universal. One could not 'know' anything about India without Mill's book, for all other books on India are merely collections of impressions not yet filtered and judged by the historian. Majeed thus errs in claiming that 'Mill's world is the world of measurable concrete objects',[74] for Mill's world was first developed by constructing a scale for the measurements of objects (in this case the scale of civilizations), thereby producing knowledge through the interpretation of the objects as manifestations of universal principles – a project of scientific analysis which supersedes, indeed supplants, the objects themselves. Mill demonstrated his conception of the effectiveness of his own arguments after his exposition of the rudeness of the Hindus: 'everything we *know* of the ancient state of Hindustan conspires to prove it was rude'.[75] 'Know' was not simply a word that Mill utilized carelessly, and the italics in this passage are significant. Mill saw himself as presenting an irrefutable argumentative explication of something he felt the rational thinker should have found patently obvious in the first place. After reading Mill, one would *know* something about India because evidence had been presented according to irrefutable principles, and the reader who did not think that way clearly suffered from a cognitive deficiency.

The Orientalists harbored this deficiency in its most pernicious form, and with the *History* Mill began a concerted campaign to temper their influence on British attitudes toward India. Mill, in fact, seemed to be irked that the dreamy imaginations of the Orientalists had forced him into doing such a thing in the first place: that is, stating the obvious, and showing that a rude nation was rude. In the process of this exposition, Mill hoped to eliminate the temptation for otherwise reasonable thinkers to linger uselessly in the fantastic past of a rude people. 'For Mill', as Pitts has stated, 'once a society was deemed backward, there was little more about it that one needed to know'.[76] In this reductive system, Mill elevated himself to the position of a mediator through whom knowledge of India was created, finalized, and then placed in the category of 'rude ideas'. Only if the British colony of India were to expand, and remain a field of British civilizing efforts, would one ever be obliged to consult anything beyond Mill's *History* to learn about India. That history would then become a story of improvement, enlightenment, and civilizational progress.

The anti-empirical rationality underpinning Mill's philosophy of history was deeply rooted in the intellectual tradition of the Scottish Enlightenment.[77] Throughout the footnotes of the *History*, Mill acknowledges the influence of such Scottish Enlightenment historians as David Millar, David Hume, William Robertson, and Dugald Stewart. This 'school' of historical thought, referred to most commonly under the terms 'philosophical' or 'conjectural' history, traces its origins to Adam Smith's four-stage theory of economic-historic development.[78] Smith's stages – the ages of hunters, shepherds, agriculture, and commerce – provided the framework not only for a teleology of economic development, but also for a 'teleology of civility'.[79] The scale of this teleology was based on the axiomatic idea of a necessary tendency for economic or material progress to increase over time. Given this scale, any 'nation' could be assigned a ranking along a scale of development or non-development, which was, theoretically, not a corollary to a state of inferiority or superiority, but an assessment based on a purportedly value-neutral scale of difference. Within this teleology, a historian could 'conjecture', according to Stewart's term, what happened when sources were missing for particular events. To do this, one would surmise what must have happened in a particular instance based on the teleology of events typical for a (European) society at the particular stage of the society under question. Stewart, whose lectures Mill attended as a student in Edinburgh,[80] described this form of judgment as follows:

> In this want of direct evidence, we are under a necessity of supplying the place of fact by conjecture; and when we are unable to ascertain how men have actually conducted themselves upon particular occasions, of considering in what manner they are likely to have proceeded, from the principles of their nature, and the circumstances of their external situation.[81]

Any nation, whether rude or civilized, was only a type, a manifestation of a general category of 'external situation'. Mill's rude nations represented a stage of development whose history consisted of cycles of warfare and superstition, and inexact pronouncements to which civilized nations need not heed. Information about these events, nothing more than various species of rudeness replacing themselves, had no value, even in respect to Europe's rude past.

Like Stewart before him, Mill proposed a break with the past, between modern society and its own history.[82] Attempting, for example, to determine the dynastical lineage of 'barbarian' rulers, whether Anglo-Saxon, South American or Babylonian, had no value for Mill because it provided no pedagogical lessons which could help humanity progress. If one chose to squander time on such futile endeavors, the process would be simple enough: barbarian kings come in cycles; occasionally a great man arises and sets into motion a new cycle; if he were truly great, he could even provide the impetus for carrying an entire civilization to the next level of development.[83] In this manner, conjecture became history, for the teleology of a rude nation was so straightforward that everything could simply be conjectured. And whenever answers could not be found, or were lacking, one could always fall back on Mill's handy historical trope of the rude: 'rude times give no reasons'.[84] Yet for Mill's unique blend of conjectural history and utilitarianism, there was an ironic twist in writing the history of a time without reason: precisely because the time was so rude, and conjecturing about it so simple, writing its history was a task entirely without utility.

Mill's imaginative history of India has provoked negative reactions from its very inception.[85] Successive waves of revision have criticized Mill not only for providing a justification for colonialism, but also for purely philosophical and historiographical inconsistencies. The *History*, in this sense, was a flawed example of both historical and philosophical thinking. As a philosophy of history, it failed to define its most basic terms.[86] Although 'rude' and 'civilized' turned out to be fundamental concepts in the book, Mill neglected to properly define these concepts except through the hermetic circle of rationalism – which held the basic tenet that anyone who did not already know what 'rude' and 'civilized' meant thereby proved his or her rudeness. In the final section of this paper, three methods of argumentation Mill employed to carry out his conjectures on rudeness will be discussed. Firstly, Mill relied on utilitarian ideas, although the book never provides a proper explication of utilitarianism. A nation in this scheme was rude precisely in proportion to its ignorance of both the ends and means of utility. Secondly, Mill's concept of rudeness was often defined retrospectively as specific traits of rudeness were revealed through his descriptions of India. Thirdly, Mill relied on a bastardized concept of conjecture in which he filled in details about the state of India based on what he 'knew' about other rude cultures. For this type of argumentation, Mill often employed literature about South America, Africa and other parts Asia, but also the rude nations of Western Europe's past to provide material for conjecture in his purported 'appeal to history, in every age and quarter of the globe'.[87] Taken as a whole, these methods of argumentation will be outlined in order to question not only Mill's affinity with the concepts of conjectural history, but to counter the notion that he did indeed apply a consistent philosophy of history. As a result, questions will be raised about Majeed's description of the *History* as a 'carefully articulated body of ideas'.[88]

Conjecturing Rudeness: Mill's Historiographical Method

Given the scope of the *History*, it does indeed seem to be a carefully crafted text. Mill followed an ambitious plan for examining seven of the most important aspects of 'Hindu' culture: its form of government, laws, taxes, religion, manners, art, and literature, followed by a detailed summary entitled 'General Reflections'.[89] In each individual section, Mill followed the pattern of the *History* as a whole but on a smaller scale: enough evidence was given for the rudeness of the subject matter in order to then give Mill reason to drop the line of pursuit. This is the first method of argumentation to be discussed. In this way, Mill dealt with a broad variety of aspects of Indian society, especially those he considered to be most pernicious. Here Mill tried his hand as a critic of topics ranging from weaving to warfare and from pottery to poetry, and, in the process, he revealed a striking eristic simplicity.

In this broad process of critique, Mill seemed only minimally concerned with accuracy. Determining, for example, the exact number of gods in the Hindu pantheon was for him an immaterial question of minutiae, and attempting to answer it precisely had no utility since Hinduism 'remains a vestige of a lower stage of civilization'.[90] If it could simply be shown that Hinduism recognized many gods, and, as any good utilitarian would know, the worship of those gods was time consuming, then sufficient evidence of the inutility of polytheism was provided. Hence, if polytheism were inutile, knowledge *about* polytheism would be equally inutile – especially detailed knowledge. Mill ceased his line of inquiry in an equally abrupt manner in his treatment of Hindu cosmology, for 'rude nations derive a peculiar gratification from pretensions to antiquity'. Any estimates about the age of the world would be nothing more than the delusions of 'a boastful and turgid vanity'. Continuing down this path, he stated that, since Hinduism 'never contemplated the universe as a connected and perfect system, governed by general laws, and directed to benevolent ideas', it was only 'mean superstition'.[91] In this rejection of Hinduism, Mill used utilitarianism not only as a standard for pointing out criticisms, but also as a shorthand form for avoiding tedious historical explanations. The historian who proceeded in this way could work efficiently and always rely on the trope of the rude, for whatever is rude could be brushed off with minimal explanation. By articulating such criticisms of Hinduism, Mill followed the trusted path of utilitarian critique, but his work becomes of most interest for the intellectual historian where he embarked on his own imaginative type of critique. These portions of his text were at once the most colorfully ridiculous and the most pernicious.

In his second mode of argumentation, Mill employed a particularly dogmatic tone. As shown in the example of astronomy above, he took any point on which India could possibly garner praise for being civilized according to his own criteria and found an argumentative means of twisting it into yet another instance of baseness, for India's culture was nothing but the 'playsome whimsies of monkeys in human shape'.[92] Further examples abound, some of which parallel his criticisms of China, offering a semblance of systematic methodology in his thinking.

Mill pursued a detailed analysis of the arts and crafts of India, ranking them on a relative technological scale by using China as a foil. The Indian plow, for example, 'consists of a few pieces of wood, put together with less adaptation to the end in view, than has been elsewhere found among some of the rudest nations',[93] while the Chinese plow was 'the most rude and inefficient instrument that can well be imagined'.[94] One wonders, then, which was ruder. Both nations also shared ineptitude in respect to the use of glass. Indians had (though seemingly lost) the knowledge to produce a 'rude species of glass, which was manufactured into trinkets and ornaments for the women', but it had never occurred to them to put it into the windows of houses or to use it as an optical aid like the Europeans. Just as in the case of astronomy, India possessed a useful means, but never could use it for the proper ends to which it is so 'admirably adapted'.[95] The Chinese fared even worse on this point. After praising the quality of Chinese porcelain, Mill reminded the reader that this art was 'a very simple one, and was in fact invented by some of the rudest people'. Furthermore, he was surprised that they should have been in possession of this craft, 'which is so analogous to that of making glass', yet the Chinese never took the next step in the scale of progress 'to invent that beautiful and useful manufacture'. The Hindus nonetheless languished in a circle of rudeness even below that of the Chinese, at least in regards to their arts, for '[i]n almost every manufacture, and certainly as a manufacturing people in general, the Hindus are inferior to the Chinese'.[96]

Moving away from plows and pottery, Mill then made surprisingly laudatory remarks about Indian jewelry, which he admitted was perhaps the finest in the world. After this initial conciliatory gesture, he stepped back, for Indian jewelry was produced with 'imperfect tools', and 'dexterity in the use of imperfect tools is a common attribute of a rude society'.[97] He employed the same rhetorical maneuver when he praised India for inventing chess. Chess was no doubt an 'ingenious' game, but such games were typical of the 'rude condition', for they relieved the 'pain of idleness' which dominated life 'prior to the birth of industry'.[98] Not surprisingly then, a 'love of repose reigns in India', for 'the savage is listless under every clime'.[99] This general love of gaming and idleness among the savages seemed to explain why a 'taste for buffoonery is very generally part of the character of a rude people'.[100] And if one visited the home of rude people, one would see 'hospitality, generously and cordially displayed'. While such hospitality was not bad per se, it 'helps to cast into the shade the odious passions which adhere to man in his uncultivated state'.[101] Rudeness, thus, was adept at disguising itself, and the philosopher-historian had to avoid falling victim to the pernicious influence of the shadow cast by such odious passions. For here lurked the dreaded partial impressions, impressions which would have blurred Mill's search for what he already knew – and thus taint his rationality.

Mill's powers of conjuring up an imagined India from afar were often astounding. In perhaps his most audacious conjecture, he expanded the aforementioned notion of physical dexterity to describe the source of the Hindus' sense for fine tactile skills: 'The delicacy of their texture is accompanied with great acuteness and sensibility in all their organs of sense... [T]he Hindu is a type of sensitive plant'.[102] It is little wonder, then, that Alexander Walker, an early reviewer of the *History*, felt the need to reprimand Mill on this point in an unpublished correspondence with Mill. Commenting on this section of the *History*, Walker wrote: 'Let us always remember that they are human beings, living and acting under the influence of our common nature'.[103] But the sensitivity of this race of plant-men only ran so deep, for we then learned of a deplorable practice in India: 'The British government', Mill informed us, 'has interfered to prevent the sacrifice of children by throwing them to the sharks in the Ganges'.[104] With such a wise British intervention, India could begin its inexorable march along the path of historical progress to leave what Majeed, in a surprising repetition of Mill, has referred to as the 'childhood the British found it in'.[105] As Tejaswini Niranjana has noted, the links between Mill's declaration of India's 'childhood' and the civilizing mission is clear-cut: 'The maturity-immaturity, adulthood-childhood opposition feeds right into the discourse of improvement and education perpetuated by the colonial context'.[106]

Having acutely reinforced the danger of partial impressions through the above examples, Mill reiterated his own importance as a historian capable of passing judgment. From his detached perch upon the bench of utilitarian knowledge, he followed a simple argumentative style: once he discovered such rude traits in the Indians as a love for buffoonery, repose, gaming, hospitality, a certain vegetable quality of corporeal texture, or attention to the nutrition of the local river shark population, he then declared such traits to be general characteristics of rude nations. As Walker remarked with masked condescension: 'It is impossible not to admire the ingenuity that is employed to prove the Hindus savages. Every art in which they have obtained any excellence is that which is peculiar to a rude age'.[107] India was therefore *a priori* rude to Mill, and rudeness first gained a definition as it is illustrated through the very traits Mill discovered in India. Rude, for Mill, was an *a priori* concept retroflexively defined, or a type of *a priori a posteriori* concept. If that was a contradiction in terms, then it was a contradiction Mill seemed capable of accepting. It is perhaps best understood as an example of what Gayatri Chakravorty Spivak refers to as a 'successful cognitive failure'.[108]

Mill's process of conjecture worked in many directions, as is evident in his third style of argumentation: filling in details about India based on what he knew of other rude nations. As Mill told Ricardo, he saw his book 'as no bad introduction to the study of civil society in general', demonstrating his intention to draw conclusions which would be valid not only for the study of India, itself a rather trivial subject for him, but for the study of all nations, be they rude or civilized.[109] For this, Mill relied on a style of symbiotic textual conjecture. Where sources were missing for illustrating particular aspects of India's rudeness, he conjectured based on the conclusions of histories which described other supposedly rude nations, including, most prominently, Robertson's *History of America* (1777). Mill's use of the work was shrewd. Comparing India to Native Americans provided Mill a particularly effective rhetorical device, and he attempted to make such comparisons regularly throughout the work, placing India below Native Americans in the scale of civilizations. Such an analogy with American indigenous peoples thus served as a form of shorthand slander against Indians, for it incorporated a bundle of readymade, negative stereotypes which many informed readers would have already possessed. In this manner, the Orientalist trope was reinforced by the trope of 'the American savage' in order to augment the general trope of the rude that Mill, ensconced in his London 'closet', was in the process of formulating.

Mill's treatment of Indian architecture provided another telling example of the stereotypes he worked both with and against. Since India had been praised for grand and beautiful works of architecture, he needed to prove that these works were either not grand, or that such grand works can be erected at a very rude stage of civilization. His argumentation focused mostly on the latter technique, drawing in a broad range of sources which attested to the existence of architectural feats displaying mere gaudy pomposity, but not sophistication (and certainly not utility), which could be constructed based on simple architectural principles within the grasp of rude nations. Comparisons were, according to Mill, the 'only means of precise judgment of the indications of civilization'.[110] For this reason, he reproduced verbatim two pages of testimony from translated Spanish sources on the grandiose simplicity of temples among the Aztecs and Incas, two rude societies in the parlance of the time. Mill then continued in a spirit of egalitarianism to trace a similar rudeness in the Gothic cathedrals of Europe, which were constructed while European civilization was at a 'comparatively low' state.[111] Modern Europe, Asia and Mexico were brought into a societal and civilizational comparison, while further ancient examples were also included to give the comparison a temporal dimension. While Herodotus described Egyptian temple construction, Polybius held court on Persia. Sicily, Ceylon, Babylon, Constantinople and China appear dispersed throughout the footnotes. In this surfeit of historical evidence, Mill even managed to find a utilitarian thread: as a certain Dr. Ferguson informed us in a quote from his *History of the Roman Republic*, 'Rude nations...sometimes execute works of great magnificence for the purposes of superstition or war; but seldom works of mere convenience or cleanliness'.[112] India's architectural feats were perhaps imposing sights to behold, but they did not encourage positive notions in the beholder. Instead, they were lasting monuments to rudeness.

By citing a wide range of eras and peoples to reinforce his argument about the rudeness of Indian architecture, Mill covered all the bases of his self-proclaimed 'appeal to history'. Temporally and geographically examined, architecture was acquired at an early stage of civilization. Even where it could be admitted that great works were built, they did not serve the utilitarian purposes of 'convenience and cleanliness'. Rude nations might have built with skill and magnitude, but, unfortunately, 'the unsophisticated decision of a sound understanding...[has] magnified [it] into the proofs of the highest civilization'.[113] The 'unsophisticated decisions' of the Orientalists were the most pernicious, for they failed to notice that the temples of Mexico were grander than those of the Hindus, and that modern Persian houses possessed a sophisticated vaulted roof absent in India, and that the Hindus constructed all of their architectural grandeur without the aid of the arch – a windfall of civilization first introduced by the 'Muslim conquerors'.[114] Therefore, one could hardly follow in the footsteps of the Orientalists to declare that the Hindus were civilized, for doing so would have required admitting too many other rude nations into the elite club of 'civilization'.

Mill's process of selective reasoning was no less dogmatic for being broad, and it relied on an essentially circular logic. Instead of revealing a willingness to question his *a priori* designation of India as rude, Mill twisted any indication of Indian achievements into further proof of Indians' rudeness, employing, according to Walker, 'a tone of indiscriminate censure'.[115] Mill delivered his most precise determination on the low ranking of Indian culture in a sweeping *tour de force* of Orientalist[116] hauteur:

There can be no doubt that they are in a state of civilization very nearly the same with that of the Chinese, the Persians, and the Arabians; who, together, compose the great branches of the Asiatic population; and of which the subordinate nations, the Japanese, Cochin-chinese, Siamese, Burmans, and even Malays and Tibetians are a number of corresponding and resembling offsets.[117]

Mill thus turned the scale of development from the Scottish conjectural tradition into a refined tool for lumping together indiscriminately, and in this scheme India was relegated to the lower levels of the civilizational hierarchy. Among these cultural castaways, little precision was required in ranking the rude civilizations amongst themselves, for doing so had no utility. Once a nation had been assigned a place on the wrong side of the rudeness versus civilization dichotomy, one only needed to know enough about it in order to show that it needed improvement. But since all rude nations had to develop through the same rational teleological process, the amount of prerequisite information necessary for making these improvements would be nominal. For this reason, Mill apologized duly after his exposition on Hindu rudeness. Writing about the non-British aspects of Indian history had robbed him of too much of his own time, and he attempted, through the logic of his dichotomy, to make the reader aware of his regret for languishing so long in the inutile world of the rude in order to perform his great 'service' for the nation and humanity.

Conclusion: Mill and the Civilizing Mission

Through his dichotomous logic, Mill argued his way around the globe, encompassing rudeness in its entire breadth, both past and present. In following this course, one comes to understand that Mill's India was rude because it resembled ancient Babylon, which in turn was rude because it resembled the Aztecs around 1500, who themselves were rude because they erected temples similar to those of the rude Chinese, who, like all the others, were rude simply because they were rude. All of these cultures were rude merely because they were different from modern Europe, which also continued to be unacceptably rude. Europe's rudeness consisted of having the means for utilitarian change and yet too often failing to employ them. One cannot be faulted for declaring Mill hopelessly Eurocentric, but this description can be considered too imprecise. More accurately stated, Mill was hopelessly *ego*centric.

Imagining a future civilizational *tabula rasa* before him, a space open to a complete reworking through a civilizing mission, Mill could gather all the knowledge about India once and for all, for India would have to be thoroughly civilized as part of a global developmental progression that would gradually supersede the need for not only a history of *India*, but the need for *history itself*. Mill's 'once and for all' functioned not because the quality of Mill's historical scholarship was intended to be timeless, but because the work claimed to offer a manual for civilizing away the very interest in such rude histories. The prescriptive intentions of the *History* would thereby destroy the relevancy of the descriptive portions of the work, and once the prescriptive portions of the work had been carried out, the entire work could be jettisoned in the name of the very utility which it served. This 'once and for all' thus became a function of the 'not yet' of colonial difference. As a successful 'canonical text', Mill's *History* established a bulwark of colonial difference which supported the British colonial civilizing mission.

Notes

1 James Mill's *History*, originally published in 1817, has appeared in various editions. The most accessible and commonly available edition today is a 1968 reprint of Horace Hyman Wilson's annotated version from 1858: James Mill, *The History of British India* (New York: Chelsea House, 1968 [reprint London, James Madden /Piper, Stephenson and Spence, 1858]).

2 For a few examples: Ronald Inden refers to the *History* as 'the oldest hegemonic account of India within the Anglo-French imperial formation'. Inden, *Imagining India*, 2nd ed., London, Hurst, 2000, p. 45; 'The standard history was that of James Mill...' Romila Thapar, *The Penguin History of Early India: From the Origins to A.D. 1300*, New Delhi, Penguin, 2002, p. 7; 'Mill's text, unsurpassed as a general British history—and as a canonic text for training of East India Company servants—for the rest of the century...' Nicholas Dirks, *Castes of Mind: Colonialism and the Making of Modern India*, Delhi, Permanent Black, 2001, 32.

3 For the sake of brevity, the quotation marks will be left off of 'rude' without implying a tacit approval of Mill's value judgments.

4 Mill, *History of British India*, I:16.

5 Mill, *History of British India*, V: 347.

6 Martin Jay, *Downcast Eyes: The Denigration of Vision in Twentieth-Century French Thought* (Berkeley: University of California Press, 1993), 83–148.

7 Jay, *Downcast Eyes*, 92–4.

8 Stephen Greenblatt, *Marvelous Possessions: The Wonder of the New World* (Chicago: University of Chicago Press, 1992), 88.

9 Edward W. Said, *Orientalism* (New York: Vintage Books, 1994 [reprint, 1979]), 72–3.

10 Elie Halévy, *The Growth of Philosophic Radicalism* (Boston: The Beacon Press, 1966), 27.

11 Mill, *History of British India*, I: 27.

12 Mary Poovey, *A History of the Modern Fact: Problems of Knowledge in the Sciences of Wealth and Society* (Chicago: University of Chicago Press, 1998), 218.

13 Mill, *History of British India*, I: 23.

14 Poovey, 'The Limits of the Universal Knowledge Project: British India and the East Indiamen', *Critical Inquiry* 31, no. 1, (Fall 2004): 187.

15 Quoted in: David Hume & John Hill Burton, *Life and Correspondence of David Hume* (Edinburgh: W. Tait, 1846), 472.

16 James Mill, 'East Indian Monopoly', *Edinburgh Review*, vol. 19, no. 37, Nov. 1811, 230.

17 James Mill, 'Malcolm's *Sketch of the Sikhs*', *Edinburgh Review* 21, no. 42 (July 1813): 433.

18 The publication of the *History* would make Mill into such an expert. Mill wrote to Dumont: 'What will more surprise you is, that said book has been the principle cause of placing me in the service of the East India Company'. Mill to Dumont, 13 Dec. 1819, published in David Ricardo, Piero Saffra and M. H. Dobb (eds.), *The Works and Correspondence of David Ricardo*, Vol. VIII, (Cambridge: CUP, 1951), 40; In a revealing letter to Zachary Macaulay, Mill describes his selection for a post as Examiner based partially on the reputation which the *History* garnered him: Mill to Z. Macaulay, 13 Apr. 1819, published in Macaulay & Viscountess Knutsford, *Life and Letters of Zachary Macaulay* (London: E. Arnold, 1900), 347–8.

19 James Mill, 'East Indian Monopoly', *Edinburgh Review* 20, no. 40 (Nov. 1812): 489.

20 James Mill, 'Testimony before the Select Committee', 16 Feb. 1832, in *British Parliamentary Papers: Minutes of Evidence Before the Select Committee*, vol. 11 (Shannon: Irish University Press, 1970).

21 Sugata Bose and Ayesha Jalal, *Modern South Asia: History, Culture, Political Economy*, 2nd ed. (Oxford: OUP, 2004), 56.

22 Mill to David Ricardo, 6. Oct. 1816 in Ricardo, *Works*, Vol. VII, Piero Saffra and M. H. Dobb (eds.) (Cambridge: CUP, 1951), 75.

23 Jennifer Pitts, *A Turn to Empire: The Rise of Imperial Liberalism in Britain and France* (Princeton: University Press, 2005), 121.

24 Colin Heydt, 'Mill, Bentham and 'Internal Culture', *British Journal for the History of Philosophy* 14, No. 2 (2006), 275–301, 280.

25 Halévy, *The Growth of Philosophical Radicalism*, 31–33.

26 Mill, *History of British India* I: 22; *History of British India* III: 291; 'science of government' is a common phrase in the work which is replete with various combinations of 'scientific' phrases. See *History of British India* I: 99; *History of British India* II: 140 & 349; *History of British India* VI: 42.

27 Mill to Francis Place, 6 Dec. 1817, quoted in: Graham Wallas, *The Life of Francis Place, 1771–1854* (London: Longmans, Green & Co., 1898), 91.

28 Javeed Majeed repeatedly employs the formulation 'Mill and Bentham', portraying the two as one mind. See Majeed, *Ungoverned Imaginings: James Mill's the History of British India and Orientalism* (Oxford: Clarendon Press, 1992), 123–150.

29 Jeremy Bentham, John Bowring (ed.), *The Works of Jeremy Bentham*, Vol. X (Edinburgh: W. Tait, Simkin, Marshall, & Co., 1843), 450.

30 See Eric Stokes, *The English Utilitarians and India* (Oxford: Clarendon Press, 1959), 52 ff.

31 Alexander Winch (ed.), *James Mill: Selected Economic Writings* (Edinburgh: Oliver & Boyd, 1966), 390.

32 Mill, *History of Birtish India* II: 105.

33 Mill, *History of British India* II: 106.

34 Thomas R. Metcalf traces the role of Mill and the Orientalists in the gradual process of introducing racist ideologies to India. See Metcalf, *Ideologies of the Raj* (New Delhi: Foundation Books, 1998), 80–92.

35 Mill, *History of British India* II: 75.

36 Mill, *History of British India* II: 79.

37 Pitts, *A Turn to Empire*, 133.

38 Pitts, *A Turn to Empire*, 131–133.
39 Dipesh Chakrabarty, *Provincializing Europe: Postcolonial Thought and Historical Difference* (Princeton: Princeton University Press, 2008), 8.
40 Mill, 'Affairs of India', *Edinburgh* 16, no. 31 (1810): 127–57, 136.
41 Indeed, Mill does not claim to have a philosophy of history of his own, although he does claim to be writing 'philosophical' history. For perhaps the best example of Mill's own description of his approach to history, see: Mill, review of *History of the Reign of James II* by Charles Fox, *Annual Review* 7 (1808): 99–114.
42 For a more detailed account on the colonial rule of difference see, Ranajit Guha, 'The Small Voice of History', in Shahid Amin and Dipesh Chakrabarty (eds.), *Subaltern Studies* IX (Oxford: OUP, 1996): 1–12; for a re-working of colonial difference in the larger framework of postcolonial studies, see the chapter 'Border Thinking and Colonial Difference' in: Walter Mignolo, *Local Histories/Global Designs: Coloniality, Subaltern Knowledges, and Border Thinking* (Princeton: Princeton University Press, 2000), 49–90.
43 Mill, 'Religion and Character of the Hindus', *Edinburgh Review* 29, no. 58 (Feb. 1818): 377–403, 382.
44 See Mill, *History of British India* VI, 286; Mill did not ascribe to any manifest notion of the burden of a civilizing mission. In the article 'Colony', which he published after the completing the *History*, he systematically followed the canon of Adam Smith's anti-colony arguments to speak out against *all* colonies, including India. Mill, 'The Article Colony', in *Essays from the Supplement to the Encyclopædia Britannica* (London: Routledge/Thoemmes, 1992), 3–33; Eric Stokes asserts otherwise, claiming Mill 'shared the aggressive Evangelical conception of the British civilizing mission while disowning the religious objective'. Stokes, 302.
45 Mill, *History of British India* II: 107.
46 Majeed, *Ungoverned Imaginings*, 190–4.
47 On the eve of the *History's* publication, Ricardo wrote: 'it is calculated to excite a great deal of attention'. D. Ricardo to Richard Malthus, 16 Dec. 1817, Piero Saffra and M. H. Dobb (eds.), *The Works and Correspondence of David Ricardo* VII (Cambridge: CUP, 1951), 223; for a detailed description of the political situation at the time, see: Uday Singh Mehta, *Liberalism and Empire: India in British Liberal Thought* (Oxford: OUP, 1999).
48 Majeed makes this claim. Although he makes pretensions to originality, such ideas were already presented in earlier sources. See D. Forbes, 33; William Thomas, *The Philosophic Radicals: Nine Studies in Theory and Practice, 1817–1841* (Oxford: Clarendon Press, 1979), 108.
49 In the *History*, Mill does not describe his scale in detail, except to rank and compare nations already assumed as rude against each other. He mentions the scale in passing in an article published after the *History*, assigning England, Holland, Switzerland and Germany (in reference to the Protestant areas of the latter two) first-tier status, above the second-tier nations Portugal, Spain and Russia, with France as a stronghold of Catholicism falling somewhere in between. Mill, 'Hindus', 382–3.
50 Mill, Review of: 'De Guignes, *Voyage à Pekin*', *Edinburgh Review* 15, no. 28 (July 1809): 407–29, 429.
51 Mill, *History of British India* I: 21.
52 Mill, *History of British India* I: 23.

53 Of these various reactions, Ranajit Guha's is perhaps the most aggressive: Ranajit Guha, *Dominance Without Hegemony: History and Power in Colonial India* (Cambridge: Harvard University Press, 1997), 1–99.

54 Mill, *History of British India* I: 115.

55 Mill, '*Pekin*', 417–8.

56 Mill, *History of British India* I: 113.

57 Mill, *History of British India* I: 292.

58 For Mill's conjectures about the earliest stages of Indian civilization see: Mill, *History of British India* I: 118 ff.

59 Mill, *History of British India* I: 122–3.

60 Mill's tone and vocabulary of rude nations bears similarities to the missionary Charles Grant's denouncement of the Bengalis, which Mill repeatedly cited. Charles Grant, B. R. Garg (ed.), *Observations on the State and Society Among the Subjects of the Great Britain*, (Delhi: Associated Publishers, 2003).

61 For a critical analysis of this process of translation, see: Tejaswini Niranjana, *Siting Translation: History, Post-Structuralism, and the Colonial Context* (Berkeley: University of California Press, 1992).

62 Language was an indicator of a civilization's advancement for Mill. For a discussion of Mill's philosophy of language, see Peter König, 'Carl Gustav Jochmanns Rezeption der Philosophic Radicals', in Michael Schwidtal and Armands Gütmanis (eds.), *Das Baltikum im Spiegel der deutschen Literatur* (Heidelberg: Universitätsverlag, 2001), 165–180.

63 Bernard Cohn, 'The Command of Language and the Language of Command', in *Colonialism and its Forms of Knowledge* (Princeton: University Press, 1996), 16–56, 53.

64 Such acts of translation and the desire to render terms transparent in the universal language of reason is present today in academic writings within area studies which come fortified with a glossary of foreign terms. Dipesh Chakrabarty points to this problem inherent in the project of translation, which seeks to render concepts in the language of the universal when he says: 'What translation produces out of seeming "incommensurabilites" is neither an absence of relationship between dominant and dominating forms of knowledge nor equivalents that successfully mediate between differences, but precisely the partly opaque relationship we call "difference"'. Chakrabarty, *Provincializing Europe*, 17.

65 Mill, 'Hindus', 381.

66 Mill, 'Malcolm's *Sketch of the Sikhs*', *Edinburgh Review* 21, no. 42 (July 1813): 432–44. Mill did not expand this case study in the *History*.

67 Pitts, *A Turn to Empire*, 133–140.

68 Mill, *History of British India* I: 26.

69 'The course of history should be so directed as to present in clear and instructive light the natural rewards of virtue and the punishments of vice'. Mill, 'Review of *History of the Reign of James II* by Charles Fox', *Annual Review* 7 (1808): 99–114, 101.

70 Mill, *History of British India* I: 18–19.

71 Mill, *History of British India* I: 26.

72 Mill, *History of British India* I: 31.

73 Poovey, *Modern Fact*, 256–7.

74 Majeed, *Ungoverned Imaginings*, 164.

75 Mill, *History of British India* II: 115 (Mill's italics).

76 Pitts, *A Turn to Empire*, 140.

77 Poovey, *Modern Fact*, 214–263.
78 Pitts, *A Turn to Empire*, 25–59.
79 Murray G. H. Pittock, 'Historiography', Alexander Broadie (ed.), *The Cambridge Companion to the Scottish Enlightenment* (Cambridge: CUP, 2003), 258–79, 262.
80 Jane Rendall, 'Scottish Orientalism: From Robertson to James Mill', *Historical Journal* 25, no. 1 (1982): 43–69, 45.
81 Dugald Stewart, 'Conjectural History', Alexander Broadie (ed.), *The Scottish Enlightenment: An Anthology* (Edinburgh: Canongate, 1997), 670–1.
82 Knud Haakonssen, *Natural Law and Moral Philosophy: From Grotius to the Scottish Enlightenment* (Cambridge: CUP, 1996), p. 301.
83 See Haakonssen for a discussion of Mill's emasculation of history: Haakonssen, 298.
84 Mill, *History of British India* I: 207.
85 See Major Vans Kennedy, 'Remarks on the Sixth and Seventh Chapters of Mill's *History of British India*', *Transactions of the Literary Society of Bombay* 3 (1823): 117–171; cf. Anonymous, review of *The History of British India* by James Mill, *Edinburgh Review* 31, no. 61 (Dec. 1818): 1–44.
86 For a similar criticism of Mill's historical writing, see Haakonssen's comments on Mill's inconsistent historical approach. Haakonssen, 297–9.
87 Mill, 'Hindus', 382.
88 Majeed, *Ungoverned Imaginings*, 140.
89 These are the individual chapters of the infamous Book II 'Of the Hindus'.
90 Mill, *History of British India* I: 231.
91 Mill, *History of British India* I: 107.
92 Mill, *History of British India* I: 242.
93 Mill, *History of British India* II: 16–7.
94 Mill, *'Pekin'*, 422.
95 Mill, *History of British India* II: 32.
96 Mill, *History of British India* II: 33.
97 Mill, *History of British India* II: 22.
98 Mill, *History of British India* II: 31.
99 Mill, *History of British India* I: 333.
100 Mill, *History of British India* I: 335.
101 Mill, *History of British India* I: 327.
102 Mill, *History of British India* I: 332.
103 Alexander Walker, 'Remarks on James Mill's *History of British India*', 1819, unpublished manuscript in the National Library of Scotland, Edinburgh, Walker of Bowland Papers, MS 13737, folio 93.
104 Mill, *History of British India* I: 288.
105 Majeed, *Ungoverned Imaginings*, 145.
106 Niranjana, *Siting Translation*, 22.
107 Walker, 'Remarks', MS 13737, folio 153.
108 Gayatri Chakravorty Spivak, 'Subaltern Studies: Deconstructing Historiography', in Ranajit Guha (ed.), *Subaltern Studies* IV (Oxford: OUP, 1985), 330–363, 334.
109 Mill to Ricardo, 19 Oct. 1817 in Ricardo, *Works* XII, 194.
110 Mill, *History of British India* II: 7.
111 Mill, *History of British India* II: 7.
112 Quoted in Mill, *History of British India* II: 9.
113 Mill, *History of British India* II: 9.

114 Mill, *History of British India* II: 10.
115 Walker, 'Remarks', MS 13737, folio 161.
116 'Orientalist' is used here in the broader Saidian sense. David Ludden identifies three categories of Orientalism which Said tends to conflate: Orientalist scholars such as William Jones, Orientalism as imagery and perspective and, finally, 'a venerable set of factualised statements about the Orient, which was established with authorized data and research techniques and which had become so widely accepted as true, so saturated by excess plausibility, that it determines the content of assumptions on which theory and inference can be built'. Ludden demonstrates Mill's pivotal role in producing and solidifying the third category. See: Ludden, 'Orientalist Empiricism', Caroline A. Breckenridge and Peter van der Veer (eds.), *Orientalism and the Postcolonial Predicament* (Philadelphia: University of Pennsylvania Press), 250–278, 251 ff.
117 Mill, *History of British India* II: 150–1.

Chapter Two

ART, ARTEFACTS AND ARCHITECTURE: LORD CURZON, THE DELHI ARTS EXHIBITION OF 1902–03 AND THE IMPROVEMENT OF INDIA'S AESTHETICS

Michael Mann

Prologue: On the Political Implications of Art and Architecture

In the long decade after the victorious Boer and Boxer Wars in Africa and China and before the outbreak of the First World War, the short period marking the heyday of British (as well as other European states') imperialism, it was the British Empire in India which became the focus of Great Britain's imperial grandeur and splendour. To commemorate the announcement of Edward VII as Emperor of India, the then Governor General and Viceroy of India, Lord Curzon (1898–1905), declared in 1901 his intention to organize a Coronation Darbar to be held at Delhi. The Delhi Darbar of 1902–03 was a massive demonstration of Britain's global military power, almost 40,000 soldiers including Indian regiments having just returned from the African and Asian theatres of war paraded in front of the Viceroy and the assembled dignitaries of Britain, Germany and India. The Delhi Darbar was also a lucid demonstration of colonial cultural patronage, collecting and displaying the best samples of contemporary Indian artefacts at the Delhi Arts Exhibition, which was part of the huge official programme accompanying this rather pompous imperial function.[1]

The Delhi Arts Exhibition was part of a rather young tradition of industrial and art exhibitions, which began in 1851 with the 'Great Exhibition of the Works of Industry of all Nations' in London, to be followed by the Paris International Exhibition of 1855. The global industrial showcase took place again in London in 1862, in Paris in 1867 and 1878 and, more significantly, at the 'Indian and Colonial Exhibition' in London in 1886. At all exhibitions, imported Indian artefacts had a considerable presence. For many visitors and critical observers it seemed that Indian industrial art represented aesthetic 'order' in contrast to Britain's 'disorder'.[2] This confusion of stereotypes intensified an already ongoing discussion on the aesthetic improvement of British industrial products. One of the major questions was whether – and to what extent – Indian patterns and methods could or should be transferred to develop English craftsmanship whose quality of design, as it was maintained, had deteriorated with industrial mass production. For a short moment it seemed that Indian artefacts – if not the Indian artisan himself – might be superior to their English counterparts.[3]

The debates regarding official art education policy taking place in England were exported to the Indian colony.[4] The political question about whether Indian art and the Indian artisan needed stately patronage briefly took priority on the colonial agenda of education during the second half of the nineteenth century. Taking the London School of Design founded in 1837 as a model, a first school for the teaching of crafts was established in Madras in 1850, followed by the Schools of Art and Industry in Calcutta and Bombay in 1854 and 1857 respectively. The famous Mayo School of Industrial Arts at Lahore set up in 1875 clearly documented the colonial state's ambitions to develop the skills and tastes of the Indian artisan as well as the quality of his handicraft with respect to beauty and utility.[5] This was also true for the ornamental arts of the construction and decoration of buildings.[6] The Indian exhibits in the various London exhibitions were later featured in the South Kensington Museum, and they came to represent the most comprehensive showcase of Indian artefacts in Britain. They were not regarded as a collection of curiosities but as a reservoir that should be utilized for the development of India's resources.[7] To ensure improvement, the Indian artisan would need education for the development of his profession, which was to be undertaken by superior British governmental guidance.

Architecture as the highest form or expression of art, however, remained the sole domain of the British. Within Europe and British India 'experts' more or less agreed with each other that India's architecture had either declined and needed improvement or, more radically, that it was not worth any development because of Indians' lack of aesthetic principles. Apparently, India's handicraft sector was worth using as an example for Britain's industrial manufacturing whilst India's fine art and architecture were not even taken into consideration for educational purposes. This contradiction is perhaps best expressed by John Ruskin, the famous leader of the British Arts and Crafts Movement. Applauding Indian decorative design he simultaneously dismissed art and architecture. Shocked by the 'mutiny' of the Indian 'sipahis' in North India, he ascribed the barbarous massacres against innocent English women in Kanpur to the Indian people at large instead of Indian soldiers. Ruskin believed that at some earlier stage Indians had abandoned nature as a guiding principle, which was clearly visible in arts and architecture with its monstrous figures and grotesque decorations.[8]

With respect to architecture the development of aesthetics was not considered possible if not desired. From the very beginning, therefore, Indians were excluded from the highly political debate on the question of a representative imperial style in terms of architecture which was also to epitomise a kind of 'colonial national style', a question which became important particularly in the second half of the nineteenth century. Basically two main schools of thought appeared reflecting the two above-mentioned positions. On the one hand we have the 'aesthetic imperialists' who argued in favour of European architecture representing the colonial state. They opted either for a Christian, mediaeval Gothic architecture or for a neo-classical style in the tradition of Andrea Palladio (1508–80) and Christopher Wren (1632–1723). The latter was actually preferred as it stood for the essence of modern English values. On the other hand the 'native revivalists' proposed an uninterrupted tradition of Indian arts and architecture to be utilised by the colonial state as means of representation.[9]

These two opposing positions reflected the basic mistrust between the military architects and engineers who ran the Public Works Department, established in 1854 as a kind of elite club, and who did not want any interference from a few civilian architects 'going native'.[10] The argument continued until the beginning of the twentieth century. When Lord Curzon planned the Delhi Darbar, he clearly opted for the 'native style', or the so called 'Indo-Saracenic', as the most adequate architecture to represent the British Raj in India because the urban historical environment of Delhi rendered no other style possible. However, when the same Lord Curzon proposed the building of Victoria Memorial Hall in 1902, he very clearly decided in favour of the Palladio-Classicism as the only representative architecture of the British Empire. The significance of this decision is evident in the fact that Calcutta was the seat of the British Empire in India, and thus stood for the foreign colonial regime.[11] Perhaps no public building other than Victoria Memorial Hall better represents the climax of British imperialism, planned by certainly the most imperialistic viceroy ever in charge of India.

As architecture remained the exclusive domain of British imperialism in India, the 'Palladio-Classic' style was simply executed by military engineers whilst any developmental efforts in the realm of architecture were restricted to the 'Indo-Saracenic' style. However, no Indian architect ever enjoyed training and education in an English institution, and even the famous Bhai Ram Singh of Lahore, who went on to become the Raj's best known Indian architect and designed prestigious 'Indo-Saracenic' buildings, started as a carpenter and later enrolled at the city's Mayo School of Industrial Art.[12] 'Indo-Saracenic' architecture, too, remained the exclusive domain of the British in India, the exception proving the rule. On the other hand, the Delhi Arts Exhibition marked the end of official attempts by the British to improve and develop Indian arts and artefacts or, more generally speaking, the development of India's aesthetics. The international exhibitions on arts and industry, the preservation and display of the Indian exhibits at museums, as well as the Delhi Arts Exhibition – none generated any significant development in the sense the British envisioned.

The Delhi Arts Exhibition did certainly aim at the development of Indian craftsmanship, though only to satiate British and European upper class demands for rare 'Oriental' commodities and luxuries. To guarantee the standard of Indian craftsmanship, British policy wanted to develop the quality of Indian handicrafts with respect to the tastes of a limited foreign market and not to create additional competition to English industrial wares. For this reason, developing India's aesthetics did not mean 'improvement' according to western standards but rather preserving the 'traditional' manufacturing industries of India. The Delhi Arts Exhibition of 1903 thus resembled an imagined, romanticized, and therefore 'traditionalized' India which is more about British aristocratic ideas of a lost paradise in England due to the industrial revolution than about the state of the art, architecture and aesthetics in India.

Art and Architecture as a Marker of Progress

The question of progress in the arts came into focus in Europe during the eighteenth century. Arts were supposed latecomers in the enlightened discourse of progress in civilizations, the terrain being occupied by religious, political and historical issues. Like their predecessors, arts were now placed in the universal context of human, cultural and civilizational development. From a very general perspective, this discourse of development was based on the hypothesis that all civilizations originated from a common ancient people or nation – a 'historic centre' – from where knowledge ultimately diffused. To mark the beginning of civilization and also to mark the different branches of human development, 'modern' sciences such as linguistics, botany, biology and history, which now also included the history of arts, operated with the notion of *Ursprung*, *Urheimat* and *Urtext*. In fact, the metaphor of a tree with its roots, trunk and branches was used for describing the 'linear system' of sciences thus generated and established.[13]

The history of science that aimed at explaining the development of such a 'linear system' and attempted to come up with a hierarchy within this process of development became the very core of sciences and humanities. At the turn of the eighteenth century, the newly established academic discipline of Indology reckoned the civilization of the Indian subcontinent amongst the oldest of the world. Arts and architecture of India were seen as an ancient part of the global cultural heritage initially influencing the cultural development of mankind. However, the 'classical age' of what was defined as 'Hindu' architecture as well as the Gandhara architecture lasted from the second century BC to the third century AD. The end of the then European influenced culture, i.e. the Greek-Bactrian, also brought the 'classical age' of India's art and architecture to a close. From then onwards, it was agreed upon by European indologists and historians, now joined by art historians, that the continuous decline not only the arts of politics but also of arts generally, and particularly south Indian architecture, signified the decadent end of an erstwhile great tradition.[14]

This discourse was by no means homogeneous. Different opinions existed about the quality and aesthetic of India's early art and architecture. Either it was classified as primitive *ab origine* or as of high quality which was on a path of steady deterioration. Two eminent German art critics, B. Rode and A. Riem, opined that primitive art preceded the rise of taste and that India was in fact the best example to demonstrate this observation. As Indian architecture, for example, lacked Palladian principles of architecture, it could only be considered as an essay in the infancy of art, the product of unregulated fancy and arbitrary rules. This was indicated by Indian artists' puerile taste in decoration and their preference for gigantic monsters instead of natural men. The primitivism, it was maintained, resulted from the tropical climate which supposedly caused the tiring of the spirit and impeded all desire to improve the arts.[15] Hegel confirmed this assertion and pushed the argument further by maintaining that the predetermined national spirit of the Indians prevented them from developing arts and architecture.[16]

It was not only the 'tropical climate' – a part of the 'Oriental discourse' dominant in the second half of the eighteenth century – that was used to explain India's people's physical weakness, effeminate character, spiritless arts and lack of political principles, and other characteristics part of the well known catalogue of stereotypes, which was established as 'knowledge' at the beginning of the nineteenth century. In addition, the 'national spirit' was also meant to explain the unformed and primitive arts of the Indians, which remained unchanged since time immemorial, in contrast to Europe's development based on dynamism. The idea of dynamic development combined with the idea of a 'national spirit' helped, on the other hand, to establish the notion of a static India (as *pars pro toto* of the Orient), with its immemorial immutability, its unchanging irrationality and its poetic and artistic fantasy.[17] Hence, art and architecture were just another medium to mark the difference between Europe and the Orient and to define (dynamic) Europe by *othering* the (static) Orient.

During the first half of the nineteenth century the inferiority of the civilization of the Orient was taken for granted by European scientists as well as by British politicians. However, the people at large, particularly in Britain, remained rather unaffected by this perception. It was to a large extent shattered by the Great Exhibition of 1851, when exhibits from India demonstrated the high quality of her artisan design and the aesthetics of her artefacts. For the first time since the East India Company had established as paramount ruler of the Indian subcontinent, doubts about European superiority became part of a public discussion in England as well as in British India. How was one to deal with the fact that Indian handicraft was possibly, at least in some fields, superior to contemporary English craftsmanship? The Arts and Crafts Movement led by William Morris and John Ruskin had already lamented about its decline and had demanded its development.[18] Now it seemed that Indian aesthetics could be used for the improvement not only of England's industrial but also of her craftsman's products.

To make matters worse: In the immediate decades after the 'Company State' had been abolished and British India was declared crown colony in 1858, the public debate on the state of the Indian arts also took place in Calcutta and in Lahore. The reversal of a widely internalised perception, however, would ultimately have caused a serious crisis in the self-understanding of the colonial regime in India whose legitimacy was mainly founded on the self-imposed civilizing mission. To educate, order and discipline its Indian subjects was without doubt the essential part of the colonial state's political mandate. What was also worrying for some time was the fact that debates were at no time and at no place unanimous, as opinions differed considerably upon the Indian artisan, Indian arts and even Indian architecture.[19] Yet, what in the first place seemed to be only confusing was actually inconsistent and sometimes also contradictory, in any case arbitrary but, at the same time, constituting the British colonial regime.

Between 1840 and 1910, E. A. Freeman, James Fergusson, John Ruskin, John Lockwood Kipling, George Birdwood and Edwin Lutyens dominated the debate on India's art and architecture. In his *History of Architecture*, published in London 1849, Freeman (1823–92) observed some similarity between the Islamic and the Gothic architecture, both romantic styles if described in terms of north European aesthetic categories of the nineteenth century. However, whilst Islamic architecture was characterised as fantastic and fairytale-like, it was Gothic, the style of the European genius, which proved western dynamism over eastern stasis. The cultural bias turned into a racial difference when Freeman extended the question of aesthetics to the character of a people stating that Semites were basically uncreative. Attesting at least some historical relevance to Islamic architecture, for example the Alhambra of the Moors in Spain, Freeman maintained that its overall lack of invention and therefore inability of autonomous development could only be overcome by external inspiration and influence.[20] Asserted cultural superiority thus helped to justify political dominance and colonial rule as a civilizing mission.

Contrasting Freeman's rather negative notion of Islamic architecture James Fergusson (1808–86) who resided in India from 1835 to 1842 simply saw some lack of discipline hindering the otherwise inventive Muslim. In his popular book *Illustrated Handbook of Architecture* (1855) he argued that wanting discipline was also an indication of deficiency in the higher qualities of art. He missed order and particularly rationality which Fergusson exclusively claimed for European architecture. Ordering Indian art and architecture, and therefore actually all Islamic architecture, became part of a general mandate to discipline and develop Islamic nations and Muslim people. Like Freeman, Fergusson asserted racial superiority. His interest in Indian architecture was based on his conviction that there must have been some kind of pure, rational principles in Aryan architecture which could be utilised for European constructions. If India and her architecture could be useful at all, it was thanks to her Aryan descent. For the same reason he believed that the East could temporarily provide the West with some rational models, but the West would have to select and to apply them fruitfully.

To develop his model or 'systems' of architecture, Fergusson did not argue culturally or historically. Instead he used geological metaphors to describe cultural refinement within the sequence of civilizations. This model was not orientated towards the popular theory of the time, Darwin's evolutionist model, but created a model of slow and ceaseless motion putting layer upon layer only interrupted by catastrophic events as it had been developed in Charles Lyall's influential *Principles of Geology* (1830–33).[21] The principles, theories and, above all, rationality of the emerging (natural) sciences were applied to cultural sciences to provide them with a likewise rational substructure. However, this application supported the emergence of races (and racism) as a decisive marker of cultural difference and civilizational inferiority. In a lecture titled 'On the Study of Indian Architecture' delivered at the London Society of Arts in 1866 Fergusson did not talk about principles and forms of Indian architecture but about its utility for a better understanding of the ethnology, history and religions of the subcontinent. Since India and the South were fundamentally different from Europe and the North, it was the Europeans who were able to look at India's architecture from an external and fresh perspective. Only European experts could adequately judge the quality of India's aesthetics and decide where to begin with their development.[22]

Fergusson's opinion about the right who was to judge Indian affairs became clearly visible during the heated controversy on the Ilbert Bill which occupied the British and Indian public in British India in 1883–4. The argument centred around the question of whether an Indian judge should be empowered to sentence Europeans as proposed in the said bill. In his monumental *History of Indian and Eastern Architecture*, which was published in London in 1876 and for which he is widely renowned, Fergusson supported like others before him the 'diffusion theory' according to which Indian art and architecture were shaped by foreign, particularly Greek influence. When Rajendralal Mitra, the first Indian archaeologist in service of the British, rejected this theory some years later, it was Fergusson who vehemently opposed any Indian interference in European sciences.[23] He accused Mitra for his inability to work scientifically showing the Indian's deficiency in power of judgement. Because of his racial inferiority Mitra, like all Indians, could not think and judge rationally.[24] Therefore it was exclusively left to the European to judge from a distant and rational position.

With respect to Indian, Islamic and Oriental arts and architecture the step from a rather cultural to a resolutely racist interpretation of civilizations was taken by John Ruskin (1819–1900). While Fergusson preferred the geological metaphor, Ruskin operated with a climatic model. To classify the different regions of cultural development he divided the globe into five climatic zones. India became the example for the tropics and Arabia the example for the desert while the grape and wheat clime was applied to Europe. Furthermore, Ruskin indiscriminately called the Arabian, Persian and Indian architecture roughly 'Byzantine' and subsumed it together with all the other hot and humid countries under the rubric 'south-savage' whilst the 'north-savage' was represented by the 'Norman'. Apparently, Ruskin preferred a North-South division instead of the more common East-West to signify the differences in global cultural development.

India was supposedly savage because moisture and heat were not conducive to the growth of mind or for art, which is why Indians could only develop some subtlety of intellect and not become learned and produce noble art. Therefore, Indians and Arabs ignored natural forms only to produce grotesque ornaments and horrifying monsters.[25] The Orientalist stereotype of climes responsible for the development of different cultures was, however, shortly to be applied to racial conceptions. For a brief moment, Ruskin gave special attention to India when the 'Mutiny'[26] of the British Indian regiments in 1857 let loose his satanic racism which enabled Ruskin to mark the fundamental and insurmountable differences between the civilized British and the barbarous Indians. The following quote from Ruskin highlights his vitriolic tone:

> All ornamentation of that lower kind is pre-eminently the gift of cruel persons, of Indians, Saracens, Byzantines, and is the delight of the worst and cruellest nations, Moorish, Indian, Chinese, South Sea Islanders, and so on. I say it is their peculiar gift; not, observe, that they are not capable of doing this, while other nations are capable of doing more; but that they are capable of doing this in a way which civilized nations cannot equal. The fancy and delicacy of eye in interweaving lines and arranging colours – mere line and colour, observe, without natural form – seems to be somehow an inheritance of ignorance and cruelty, belonging to men as spots to the tiger or hues to the snakes. [...] Get yourself to be gentle and civilized, having respect for human life and a desire for good.[27]

At a lecture delivered at the Museum of Oriental Art in 1859 Ruskin directly referred to the events of the 'Mutiny'. Praising India's art as delicate, refined and inimitable, Ruskin's 'racial turn' becomes visible in his characterization of India assuming that 'the love of subtle design seems universal in the race; and is developed in every implement that they shape, and every building that they raise; it attaches itself with the same intensity, and with the same success, to the service of superstition, of pleasure, of cruelty'.[28] Again the complete catalogue of Orientalist stereotypes is arbitrarily applied to India's people. However, the prejudicial notion of the emotional 'Oriental' is enriched by the term 'cruel'. In his infamous introduction to *The History of British India* (3 vols, London 1817) James Mill opened with the two words 'Rude nations', which are only to be applied within a paragraph to Egyptians, Chinese and Indians. Now John Ruskin characterized Africans and Asians not only as uncivilized but as barbarous nations whose arts and artefacts may be appreciated, whose people however were categorically dismissed as an object of development.

Echoing Ruskin some twenty years later, George Birdwood, author of the much praised two volume catalogue on *The Industrial Arts of India* for the South Kensington Museum, also dismissed Indian sculpture and architecture as monstrous, and blamed the evil influence of the Brahman *purāna*s for ultimately preventing Indian art and architecture from any development in spite of, as he believed, the good mystic influence of the Aryans. At the same time Birdwood declared that western industrial design was certainly having a bad influence on the Indian artisan and his craftsmanship, in particular on the village artisan, who was actually the true bearer of Indian (Aryan) art. Once again the Indian village became the essence of India and, as another facet of 'Orientalism', village art the essence of India's arts. Moreover, imagined as a romanticized community, the Indian village resembled the idea of a self-sustaining medieval (pre-modern) European agrarian society, which was now lost. It was only this idealized vivid presence of India's Middle Ages which was to give an idea of improvement for the deteriorating European craftsmanship and decaying artisan design.[29]

In India it was Rudyard Kipling's father, John Lockwood Kipling – professor for architectural sculpture at the Bombay School of Arts until 1875 and principal of the newly founded Lahore Mayo School after that – who actively promoted the development of Indian arts and crafts. To support the formative phase of the colleges, he founded the *Journal of Indian Art* which later came to be known as the *Journal of Indian Art and Industry*. The periodical was sponsored by the British Indian government from 1883 to 1917 to promote trade as well as taste. Much of his career as a teacher in arts Kipling donated to the development of Indian arts and artefacts and above all the artisanal works. Frustrated, he lamented that no trained Indian architect ever left government schools of arts, somewhat missing the point i.e. architecture was supposed to remain the exclusive domain of the British. At the same time he demanded that the Indian *mistri*, the native constructor of buildings and designer of decorations, would need some training to develop a more systematic and rational approach to his profession. As an essential part of this educational programme, the *mistri* master builder was to be prevented from simple or imitative copying and mass production. To be sure, Kipling was definitely in line with the British Arts and Crafts Movement and the romanticization of 'traditional' craftsmanship.[30]

This de-contextualization of art and architecture was part of the civilizing mission in British India. Samuel Swinton Jacob (1841–1917), one of the most prominent British architects for buildings in the 'Indo-Saracenic' style in India, published his monumental six volume *Jeypore Portfolio of Architectural Details* in 1890. Here he presented, as samples for British Indian buildings, 375 plates of architectural drawings depicting basic elements from historic buildings throughout north India. This was a rather random selection of north Indian architecture that was shown as the essence of Indian architecture to assist British architects to freely choose 'historic elements' for their constructions provided by this non-historical presentation. Likewise and at the same time, the British meticulously identified India's major historical sites, which also included Mughal architecture, and protected them through the Archaeological Survey of India. Preservation, protection and presentation, however, occurred outside the historical context in which these buildings and constructions were created.

Randomly and arbitrarily, British architects selected familiar elements like cupolas and domes with 'oriental' elements like *jāli* (carved wooden or stone screens), *chattra* (small domed pavilion-like constructions on top of a building) and *lajja* (roof-like overhangings of a building to protect the walls from sun-radiation) to put them together *ad gusto* for any purpose at any place and at any time. 'For the colonial builder, that is, the elements of Indian architecture represented not an aesthetic tradition within which he worked, but an external "Oriental" aesthetic, whose elements, at the deepest level, were rather similar and interchangeable'.[31] A timeless and static India was created by British architects and it was presented by an architecture which became known as 'Indo-Saracenic'. The hybrid and eclectic 'composite architecture' – one can hardly speak of 'fusion' – became reason for much criticism from the purist representatives of colonialism who pleaded for a simple but nevertheless impressive 'Palladio-Classic'. It was regarded as the colonial 'national style' which can be found, in fact, in all former British colonies.

The Indo-European Debate on Indo-Saracenic vs Palladio-Classic Architecture

The debate on the 'proper' architectural style for British India reached its climax in the middle of the 1870s. Basically it centred on the question of whether an exclusively European style or an improved Indian style would best represent the British Raj. The supporters of the European Palladio-Classic architecture were mostly government employees in the Public Works Department (PWD). A decade later, consulting architects were appointed to the provinces of British India and the central government started a massive programme for developing the infrastructure of the subcontinent ranging from irrigation canals to railway networks, security establishments like barracks and prisons to representative buildings like general post offices, court houses and big railway stations. As most of the architects of the PWD had been military engineers, the representative government buildings were executed in a rather vulgar neo-Palladian style whereas the ordinary buildings expressed the spiritless taste of military planners.[32]

John Ruskin had argued in a similar way, though from a completely different angle, in his appraisal of the classical architecture, simply and sadly executed by slaves, in contrast to Gothic architecture, executed by free and individual craftsmanship.[33] However, in 1877 the Public Works Member of the Viceroy's Council stated that the European architecture certainly was the most appropriate for the Raj's European representative constructions such as residences, churches, railway stations and offices, while for buildings representing the Indian populace like schools, hospitals, mosques and markets some sort of native style should be applied.[34] This distribution of buildings and styles is highly interesting. There is an Indian and a British sphere, a separate space for more 'traditional' public buildings like schools, markets and mosques and one for 'modern' governmental buildings like post offices and railway stations. On the one hand, the 'traditional sphere' was to be represented by the likewise 'traditional' 'Indo-Saracenic' whilst, on the other hand, the sphere of modern technology and efficiency was to be represented by the 'Palladio-Classic' architecture.

Ultimately the debate on the 'proper' architecture to represent British colonial rule in India culminated in the Mayo College at Ajmer, the college for educating the young princes of the British Raj. Named after the then viceroy, Lord Mayo (1869–72), the argument between 'modernists' and 'traditionalists' as well as among the 'traditionalists' lasted for five years demanding several plans and reports on the appropriate architecture. To cause some kind of enthusiasm and identification with the Raj it was decided to apply the 'Indo-Saracenic' style as composite architecture uniting 'Musli'' as well as 'Hindu' elements. Following James Fergusson's substantial work, Indian architecture was simply distinguished, like the society of the subcontinent at large, according to the major religious communities – that is 'Hindus' and 'Muslims'. Moreover, only sacral buildings seemed representative for the architecture, profane buildings like *dharmsalas*, *haweli*s and *sarai*s were not taken into consideration. Although Fergusson admitted the variety of India's architecture, he nevertheless insisted on reducing its characteristics to either 'Hindu' or 'Saracenic'.[35]

The British indiscriminately called all architecture of 'Muslim' countries, from Moorish Spain where Europeans first encountered an Islamic society to Mughal India, 'Saracenic'. During the debate on an Indian style, 'Arabian', 'Islamic' and even 'Byzantine' elements were moulded in a hybrid historistic architecture that, despite including some 'Hindu' elements from Rajputana, firmly subordinated them. Mayo College at Ajmer became the first building in British India to be executed in this new and yet eclectic style.[36] Until the beginning of the twentieth century most public buildings including prestigious government buildings were constructed in the 'Indo-Saracenic' manner, many of them in Madras, such as the Madras Law Courts and the Board of Revenue Offices. The latter, for example, mingled local Indian and British 'Indo-Saracenic' elements whereas the former resembled an arbitrary arrangement of various styles and elements. A 'fine' example of 'Indo-Saracenic' architecture is certainly the Madras University Senate House designed and planned by the most outstanding 'Indo-Saracenic' architect, Robert F. Chisholm (1840–1915).[37]

Though British architects designing in the 'Indo-Saracenic' style claimed to be reviving Indian architecture by original contributions, none of them used a term like 'Neo-Indo-Islamic' or 'Anglo-Indian' to classify his own work, and not one example of the 'movement' can be called   an authentic exercise in Indian architecture. All buildings were based on western models and Indian architectural themes were reduced to mere entablature. The late critic of 'Indo-Saracenic' architecture, E. B. Havell, accused British architects at the beginning of the twentieth century of constantly misinterpreting and misrepresenting Indian aesthetics and complained that the British architect used the Indian tradition as a set of historical representation to be added to the established repertoire of Classic and Gothic. For him, their work was far from being an authentic contribution to Indian architecture.[38] From this perspective, 'Indo-Saracenic' architecture resembles the then British-Victorian romantic-picturesque imagination of an Indian past encapsulated within the Britishers' own buildings.

However, to judge and select, to merge and fuse particular Arabic, Saracenic, Mughal, and Rajput components, crowned by a few Gothic elements into a modern and representative 'national' architecture demonstrated the colonial regime's ability to contribute to India's aesthetic improvement. According to British self-understanding, architecture became a field for experiments – a development from rudeness to refinement. In this way the architecture of 'rude and cruel nations' like the Saracens and Arabs as well as Rajput-Muslim Indians, which stood for the despotic character of their political rulers, was civilized through aesthetic refinement into a 'benevolent paternalism', as colonial rule was commonly characterized by the British. The continuity of British rule on Indian soil can hardly be characterized as political and only partly as historical with respect to the succession to the Mughals, but rather as an aesthetic continuity that portrayed the colonial regime in legitimate succession to Indian regimes. For this reason, architecture became another stage on which the colonial regime tried to perform its historical mission.

For more than three decades the 'Indo-Saracenic' style dominated representative architecture in British India though, as has been stated above, plenty of public buildings were still executed in a vulgar 'Palladio-Classic' style. Yet, during Lord Curzon's time as viceroy, Palladio and Wren returned to the imperial architectural stage. To commemorate Queen Victoria in British India, the viceroy decided to have the Victoria Memorial Hall planned in the familiar European style, which had also given the British settlement in Bengal the title 'City of Palaces'. Curzon declared that even if the memorial was erected in Delhi (which was among other reasons out of the question because it was the seat of the former Timurid dynasty) the 'Indo-Saracenic' style would not be able to capture the unique and inimitable architecture of the Mughal.[39] At the same time, the viceroy only regarded the 'Indo-Saracenic' architecture appropriate for the Delhi Darbar, for its intention was to raise enthusiasm and loyalty among the Indian population and, in the long run, to preserve the political continuity of imperial rule.[40]

It was in this ideological setting that the Delhi Arts Exhibition took place. Lord Curzon personally initiated it as part of the official programme of the Delhi Darbar. At first sight the Delhi Arts Exhibition did not very much differ from the preceding, above mentioned industrial exhibitions in Europe and India. Handicrafts and artefacts from various regions of the subcontinent were on display and offered for sale. However, a closer inspection of the selection of handicrafts, their arrangement and the manner of display, as well as the intention of the whole venture, make clear that it was more than just a pompous show of Indian craftsmanship. It actually represented another attempt to 'traditionalize' India and to set it in contrast to 'modern' British colonial rule. Superficially, the Delhi Arts Exhibition must be interpreted as an attempt to prevent the decay of Indian craftsmanship and to develop its products. From a more critical perspective, though, it should be interpreted as another example of the colonial state's attempt to count, select, organize, arrange and display not only men and nature but also art and artefacts according to its own needs and ends. Art and artefacts became more directly implicated in the Raj's 'civilizing mission'.

On the Development of Arts and Artefacts: The Delhi Arts Exhibition of 1902–03

The Delhi Darbar lasted from 29 December 1902 to 10 January 1903. The Delhi Arts Exhibition was declared open on 30 December 1902 and lasted for more than six weeks until the end of February 1903.[11] More than 48,000 visitors saw the display of Indian handicrafts, dubbing it *ajaib ghar* or 'House of Marvels'. The temporarily 'with the canons of the Indo-Saracenic architecture' erected building was a spacious hall measuring 220 by 80 feet and four rooms were designated to the four government Schools of Art in Madras, Lahore, Bombay and Rangun. Additionally, two galleries presented the loan artefacts and jewellery, whilst '[i]n an outer verandah, representative craftsmen from all parts of India practised their various arts'.[42] In his opening speech Lord Curzon repeated, though with his very characteristic personal emphasis, the well known 'radical' British position towards Indian industrial art and artefacts:

> Ever since I have been in India I have made a careful study of the art industries and handicrafts of this country, once so famous and beautiful, and I have lamented, as many others have done, their progressive deterioration and decline. When it was settled that we were to hold this great gathering an Delhi, at which there would be assembled of every Province and State of India, Indian princes and chiefs and nobles, high officials, native gentlemen, and visitors from all over parts of the globe, it struck me that here at last was the long thought opportunity of doing

something to resuscitate these threatened handicrafts, to show to the world of what India is still capable, and, if possible, to arrest the progress of decay.[43]

Only under the personal guidance of British rule and in particular the rule of the present viceroy Curzon, India's much adored but dramatically decaying handicraft could be rescued from further decay. To demonstrate the potential of Curzon and the colonial state, the viceroy took the opportunity of the Delhi Darbar to show Indian handicrafts to India and the world. Implicitly he maintained that Indian monarchs and princes have lost sight of their own cultural heritage and that it was once more the British who were capable of detecting, appreciating and protecting the traditional values of India. In his speech, delivered at the Bengal Asiatic Society in February 1902, Curzon stated frankly that 'a race like our own, who are themselves foreigners, [are] better fitted to guard; since '[t]he British Government are free from [...] either religious fanaticism, or restless vanity, or of dynastic or personal pride. [T]heir responsibility [is] the greater for inaugurating a new era and for displaying that tolerant and enlightened respect to the treasures of all, which is one of the main lessons that the returning West has been to teach the East'.[44]

The British mandate in India was not only to guard and protect and to teach the lesson of modern civilization's values, but also to determine and judge the quality and standards of handicrafts and industrial products of India. During his inaugural speech, Curzon also pointed out that it would have been very easy and satisfying but also very ugly to have presented a show illustrating the industrial and economic development of India.[45] Apparently Curzon was referring to industrial products from machine work thus echoing the old but still ongoing British critique of the spiritless and ugly industrial designs, whether in Britain or in India. However, one wonders what kind of industrial show Curzon may have organized for the global spectator, considering that there was hardly any industry in India at that time besides jute in Calcutta, cotton in Bombay and the harness and saddlery factories in Kanpur, all of them meeting British commercial and security ends rather than Indian economic needs.[46]

Curzon pursued three aims with the exhibition: first of all, it had to be an arts exhibition and not an industrial show; secondly it had to be exclusively and genuinely Indian excluding anything European; and thirdly, the aim was that the exhibition would exhibit only the best artisan work. The exhibition was to display 'all that is rare, characteristic, or beautiful in Indian art'.[47] In a letter addressed to the local governments and administration in March 1902, the central government had already formulated the same issue, yet more crisply, for '[T]he main test to be applied in each case will be that of artistic merit, the handicrafts selected being those that have already attained a certain pitch of proficiency and are capable of further development'.[48] Conceptually more important, however, was the simultaneous exhibition of present-day products along with samples of the past. The loan exhibition as part of the Delhi Arts Exhibition featured a collection of borrowed items from various museums in British India, as well as from private persons, mainly Indian rulers. The message of the two-tiered exhibition was quite clear: the arts of the past, pure and of high quality, ought to give an example for the development of the spoilt and decayed art of the present.

The same point was made by George Watt, organizer of the artefacts for the exhibition and author of the official catalogue. In the second paragraph of the 'Introduction' he explained:

> There are two distinguishing features of the present Exhibition which deserve particular attention. Of these the *first* is that the exhibits have been collected as the result of personal choice and selection – special efforts having been directed to the exclusion of all traces of the modern foreign influences which have tended to debase the ancient indigenous arts of India. And in the *second* place an important divergence has been made from the methods of classification usually followed at exhibitions, in that the exhibits are arranged according to their kind and not their places of origin. It is thus made possible convenient for visitors to compare, almost at a glance, productions of one kind from all parts of India both near and remote.[49]

If Lord Curzon was responsible for the general setting of high standards, it was George Watt who personally supervised the quality of the exhibits whilst Percy Brown, then principal of the Mayo School of Arts in Lahore and assistant director of the Delhi Arts Exhibition, travelled around the country selecting and collecting the items for the exhibition. In short: three Europeans decided what the most representative pieces of beautiful Indian art and artefact were. Yet, Watt went a step further. In distinction to previous exhibitions, the artefacts of the Delhi Arts Exhibition were taken out of their local and historical context. Officially for the convenience of visitors, exhibits were arranged in a manner which made comparisons easy. Guideline for this arrangement must have been European principles of aesthetics, an operation which could be undertaken easily because, as it was generally agreed upon, Indian arts did not possess aesthetic principles.[50] Actually, however, the deconstruction of time and space, as we have discussed above, was one of the main cultural tools of the foreign regime in constructing its colonized society.

As Narayani Gupta rightly pointed out in the preface of the reprinted edition of the catalogue, it had the quality of a gazetteer and an ethnographical dictionary.[51] Indeed, the artefacts were listed, named and ordered according to the established and familiar arrangement of the District, Provincial and Imperial Gazetteers of India. At the same time the arrangement reminds of H. H. Risley's contemporary *Tribes and Castes of Bengal-Ethnographical Glossary* with its rigid and de-contextualizing alphabetical 'order of things'.[52] Apart from the strict ordering into rubrics like 'Metal Wares', 'Stone Wares', 'Glass and Earthen Wares', 'Wood Work', 'Ivory, Horn and Leather, etc.' and 'Lac, Lacquer, etc.' as well as 'Textiles', 'Embroidery', 'Carpets' and ultimately 'Fine Arts' (all of them subdivided into several 'Divisions'), the comments on Indian art within these rubrics is far more interesting than the description of the artefacts – at least for the historian.

For the convenience of the reader, the artefacts of 'Division 7 – Stone-Carving' were set in a chronological and systematic order distinguishing the three stages: '(a) corresponding with the excavation of cave temples and the construction of topes, (b) the building of Hindu, Chalukyan, and Jain temples, and (c) of Pathan and Mughal mosques, tombs and palaces. In other words, stone-work first assumed importance in India with the Buddhist topes and cave temples'.[53] In analogy to the chronology of India's pre-British past, art history was also divided according to religious categories, i.e. Buddhist, Hindu and Muslim eras. It is also interesting to note that Mughal architecture and art, in particular the stone-decoration as it was developed during the reign of Mughal Shah Jahan (r. 1727–58), was labelled 'Indo-Saracenic'[54] – not 'Mughal' or 'Indo-Persian' – which placed British historistic 'Indo-Saracenic' architecture in the line of the art-historical inheritance and cultural tradition of the Indian subcontinent. Within this context, the British regarded the revival or reform of 'Indo-Saracenic' architecture as a modernizing development.

Much is lamented about the decay of the artisan. Muslim 'Indo-Saracenic' craftsmanship dwindled over centuries, with former Muslim artisan-employers becoming the employees of Hindu-masters. More generally speaking, '[t]he artisans are profligate, apathetic, indigent and of intemperate habits. If their work be not desired they are ready to starve; but to change their social position, their modes of life or their craft customs, they will not. The number of good artists is extremely limited'.[55] Percy Brown, author of the catalogue's chapter on 'Fine Arts', joins in the negative characterization of the Indian artisan and his artefacts, stating that:

[a] study of the numerous examples in the Exhibition reveals, in some of them, a certain amount of aptitude on the part of the modeller in seizing

a likeness which is encouraging, but the greater portion of these products are in other particulars somewhat ordinary. The principal faults are the lack of feeling, which it is feared will take some time to overcome, and an ignorance of the construction of the figure of face which only a long and constant study of life and antique can remedy. The latter is probably the root of the whole matter, for although the training given is of the best, the length of time devoted by the average art student to conscientious study is generally somewhat limited.[56]

It is agreed upon that the abilities of Indians are limited. Even if best education is provided, the character of Indians makes it a rather frustrating and almost impossible task to develop art and artefacts. Of course, there is still hope as Lady Curzon's extensive orders for robes and gowns by the embroiderers of Banaras demonstrate. Subsequently, they produced a purified and refined style of embroidered textiles that is likely to expand in the future.[57] Only British initiative can, if at all, rescue and reform Indian handicrafts.

To start with, the Delhi Art Exhibition did not simply put artefacts on display but set up a committee to examine, classify and judge the exhibits. The 'Judging Committee' consisted of eight members out of which two were Indians, one of them the above-mentioned Ram Bhai Singh from the School of Arts at Lahore. The renowned 'Indo-Saracenic' architect Samuel Swinton Jacob, who also designed the Delhi Darbar, became president of the jury. Among the exhibits of each section and division the jury selected the best and awarded prices, certificates and medals to individual artisans and organizations like the Schools of Arts.[58] Stephen Wheeler, the unofficial reporter of the Delhi Darbar in 1903, remarked that the hundreds of awards will have taught workers that there is an improved standard of artistic merit and that there is advantage following it.[59]

Public decoration and ornamentation seemed to be the British government's only role for promoting Indian arts and artisans. The Schools of Arts ware part and parcel of the official 'development-programme'. At an earlier stage Curzon himself had pointed out that, for example, 'Fresco-painting is an art which the Indian craftsman once excelled [...] This art is not extinct in India, and is being fostered and revivified in Institutes and Schools of Art'.[60] To strengthen the position of the Schools of Art and Industry in Bombay, Madras, Lahore and Calcutta, Lord Curzon gave special attention to a paragraph to be included in the University Act of 1904. It stated that the said institutes should give training on subjects like designing, painting, illumination, modelling, photography and engraving, depending on what the pupil intended to pursue after leaving school. To enable easy access to the schools it was suggested that free admission and scholarships should be granted and only gradually replaced by the payment of fees.[61]

Whether the suggestion of Percy Brown, the assistant director of the Delhi Arts Exhibition, to finance a limited number of teachers, instructors, students and pupils of the Schools of Art and Industry materialized or whether it came to naught is not known.[62] In any case the colonial government saw its responsibility for the development of arts and artefacts merely in terms of idealistic support. If any major initiative including financial aid was to be taken, it was the responsibility of the 'Princes of India'. The two-tiered arrangement of the Delhi Arts Exhibition already indicated the duality of Curzon's idea. In his opening speech Curzon had already pointed out, that '[if] the Indian art [...] is to continue to flourish or is to be revived, it can only be done if the Indian Chiefs and aristocracy, and people of culture and high degree, undertake to patronize it [...] I should like to see a movement spring up among the Indian Chiefs and nobility for the expurgation, or, at any rate, the purification, of modern tastes, and for a reversion to the old-fashioned but exquisite styles and patterns of their own country'.[63]

According to the vernacular press it was not very likely that such a movement would emerge. Very clearly writers pointed out the deficiencies of the Delhi Exhibition. The most impressive analysis appeared in the *Hitavadi*, a Calcutta journal.

> Patronage extending to a few artisans by a handful of rich men will not improve the condition of the country at large. [...] The Delhi Exhibition would have gratified the writer if it had given encouragement to the requirement of the masses. A display of rich jewellery and rich cloth may increase the beauty of an Exhibition, but it will serve no useful purpose in the way of bettering the economic condition of the country. Those who can afford to indulge the luxury may view with pleasure the encouragement which has been given in the Delhi Exhibition to the finer indigenous arts; but the masses are not at all interested in the progress of such arts.[64]

The Tribune from Lahore criticized the Delhi Darbar including the Arts Exhibition since 'the poor had no place or part in the celebrations at Delhi'.[65] However, the poor were never thought of being part of the show as Lord Curzon and the British protectors of Indian art simply did not intend to address them. The target audience was first and foremost Indian rulers and princes and secondly Indian art teachers and qualified artisan. The most ironic critique was also published in *The Tribune*, heralding the achievements of British art patronage as part of a larger civilizing programme:

> Of the many spectacles, ceremonials and events which made the great Darbar memorable, the opening of the Art Exhibition was not only the first function of the fortnight, but the foremost among those which answer to the Oriental ideal of a Coronation celebration – viz., the affording of a tangible token of the Rulers' solicitude for the well-being of the masses. [...]
>
> The little energy and enterprise that has been hitherto devoted by our countrymen to the revival of indigenous industries has been confined to a few of those articles alone which supply our everyday needs and requirements. But we have absolutely neglected those higher and characteristically Indian branches of our industries which once lost can never be replaced, and which satisfy needs no less crying (as far as the upper sections of the community, at any rate, are concerned) than those relating to the body. No doubt the want of food, clothing, home utensils, ordinary furniture and so forth, is of primary importance, and demands our first attention. But rightly considered, the want of things which satisfy the impressible craving for the bright, beautiful and the elegant – to remind mortals that the world is not all hurry, dust and struggle – is an equally supreme want after the merely animal stage is past.[66]

This lengthy quotation indicates how uncomfortable the writer and possibly many other Indians felt with the Darbar and the Art Exhibition at Delhi. If there was anything like an 'Oriental ideal of a coronation ceremony', the display of artefacts was certainly a *novum* and definitely out of place. Moreover, the show of high quality handicrafts and in particular expensive jewellery was also a misfit as it most cynically ignored the needs and wants of those who struggled in the dust of everyday life.[67] If India was to become a civilized nation it certainly did not need public or princely patronage for the improvement of her handicrafts but support for the basics of livelihood. The Bombay plague as well as drought and severe famine in many parts of the Indian subcontinent in the closing years of the nineteenth century had once again demonstrated the colonial regime's inability to provide for the elementary necessities of its population. It seemed that the politics of development had missed its target, at least from the Indian point of view.

Epilogue: Of Patronage and Politics

Developing arts, artefacts and architecture in British India actually remained restricted to the development of traditional, or what the British regarded as traditional, craftsmanship. Much of it was part of a massive invention of tradition by British administrators and art teachers as well as Indian artisans. Selected items of this traditionalized artisan India were thought fit for the aesthetic improvement of European and in particular British industrial decoration and design. To keep Indian design clear and pure (according to a British understanding) India had to be protected from the evil influences of European industrial development and, for that reason, to be prevented from getting industrialized at all. Placed in the contemporary context, Britain was, besides financial and commercial profits, to gain aesthetic profit from her colonial relationship. However, this was not the main intention of Lord Curzon's patronage. Within a broader framework of politics he polarized between the 'Orient' and the 'West' locating and demarcating differences as probably none had done before him.

Certainly Lord Curzon supported the achievements of modern Europe and in particular Britain, including the industrial age. However, in keeping with many of his contemporaries in Britain, he disagreed with the development of industrial design and was worried about the decline of traditional craftsmanship. However, whereas in England the Arts and Crafts Movement of William Morris and John Ruskin suggested to improve the individual artisan and to introduce non-ornamental design as part of a comprehensive reform of the industrial society, in India Curzon separated the 'colonial sphere' into two distinct entities: On the one hand British India, represented by modern technology and plain Palladio-Classic architecture and, on the other hand, Indian India, represented by the 'Princes', traditional ornamentalized artefacts as well as the 'Indo-Saracenic' style.[68] Curzon's Delhi Art Exhibition marks the zenith of a process which had been ongoing for a century or so, attempting to traditionalize India's cultural achievements and contributing to marking the boundaries between what was regarded as traditional and modern.[69]

Curzon never thought of a comprehensive reform of the Indian society. On the contrary, he envisaged a traditional India, idealistically and to some extent logistically patronized by British officials and financially supported by Indian princely patrons. Generally speaking, the Delhi Arts Exhibition was the colonial state's last attempt to attract public support, princely patronage and private enterprise for the development of India's traditional art and craft. However, with this kind of policy Curzon represented English aristocratic attitudes of a 'lost paradise' in Britain projected on the contemporary Indian society rather than an Indian modernity envisaged and represented by appropriate institutions. If there was any hope for an Indian modernity, whatever one may have thought it to be at that time, it was drowned in the colonial sea of an imagined traditional Indian pomp on display during the Delhi Darbar and the Delhi Arts Exhibition.

With respect to architecture, the debate on the 'proper' representation never silenced. The critique on the historistic 'Indo-Saracenic' style did not vanish. At the beginning of the twentieth century Herbert Baker, who was to become famous for his neo-classic architecture of the Secretariat Buildings in New Delhi, plainly postulated that 'Palladio is the game'.[70] Any Indian style, Baker argued on another occasion, does not have the 'constructive and geometrical qualities necessary to embody the idea of law and order'. Only classical architecture and particularly that of Wren, therefore, represented European rationalism and eminent qualities of good government.[71] In the same vein, Edwin Lutyens argued stating that he did not believe that there was any real Indian architecture or any real tradition.[72] Not only for aesthetic reasons but mainly on political grounds was Palladio-Classic architecture on the agenda.[73] New Delhi therefore became the architectural embodiment of neo-Palladio-Classic style[74] – certainly as vulgar (and political) as its contemporary European counterparts in the Soviet Union, Italy, Germany, Great Britain and the US of the 20s, 30s and 40s.

Notes

1 For the Coronation Darbar at Delhi *vide* Michael Mann, 'Pomp and Circumstance in Delhi, 1877–1937 oder: Die hohle Krone des British Raj', in Peter Brandt, Arthur Schlegelmilch and Reinhard Wendt (eds), *Symbolische Macht und inszenierte Staatlichkeit. 'Verfassungskultur' als Element der Verfassungsgeschichte* (Bonn: Dietz Verlag, 2005), pp. 101–35, cf. 112–24.

2 Thomas R. Metcalf, *An Imperial Vision. Indian Architecture and Britain's Raj* (Delhi: Oxford University Press, 2002), 142.

3 N. Pevsner, *Pioneers of Modern Design: From William Morris to Walter Gropius* (The Museum of Modern Art: New York, 1949).

4 Partha Mitter, *Art and Nationalism in Colonial India, 1850–1922: Occidental Orientations* (Cambridge: Cambridge University Press, 1994), 29–62.

5 Peter H. Hoffenberg, *An Empire on Display. Indian, English and Australian Exhibitions from the Crystal Palace to the Great War* (Berkeley etc.: University of California Press, 2001).

6 Pervaiz Vandal and Sajida Vandal, *The Raj, Lahore and Bhai Ram Singh* (Lahore: National College of Arts, 2006), 114–5.

7 T. R. Metcalf, *An Imperial Vision*, 144–5.

8 Cf. *ibid.*, 141–2.

9 Philip Davies, *Splendours of the Raj. British Architecture in India, 1660–1947* (London: John Murray, 1985), 192.

10 *Ibid.*

11 T. R. Metcalf, *An Imperial Vision*, 202–3.

12 P. Vandal and S. Vandal, *The Raj, Lahore and Bhai Ram Singh*, 123–243.

13 Partha Mitter, *Much Maligned Monsters. History of European reactions to Indian arts* (Oxford: Clarendon Press, 1977), 189–92.

14 Deborah Swallow, 'Colonial architecture, international exhibitions and official patronage of the Indian artisan: The case of the gateway from Gwalior in the Victoria and Albert Museum', in Tim Barringer and Tom Flynn (eds), *Colonialism and the Object.*

Empire, Material Culture and the mMuseum (London and New York: Routledge, 1998), pp. 52–67, *vide* 54.

15 B. Rode and A. Riem, 'De la peinture chez les anciens', in Johann Joachim Winckelmann (ed.), *Histoire de l'Art chez les Anciens*, 3 vols., (Paris, 1803), vol. II, pt. 2, 57–84, part. 64–6.

16 Georg W. F. Hegel, Vorlesungen über die Ästhetik (1835–1838). II. I. C. Die eigentliche Symbolik; II. II. *II*.1. a. Das Ideal als aus freiem künstlerischem Schaffen entsprungen; II. III. *III*. 3. c. Das Ende der römischen Kunstform in http://www.textlog.de

17 Cf. P. Mitter, *Much Maligned Monsters*, 217–8.

18 Elizabeth Cumming and Wendy Caplan, *The Arts and Crafts Movement* (London: Thames and Hudson, 1991). Rosalind P. Blakesley, *The Arts and Crafts Movement* (London: Phaidon, 2006).

19 Mark Crinson, *Empire Building. Orientalism and Victorian Architecture* (London and New York: Routledge, 1996), 37–61.

20 *Ibid.*, 40–2.

21 *Ibid.*, 43–5.

22 Cf. Bernard S. Cohn, 'The transformation of objects into artefacts, antiquities, and art in nineteenth-century India', in *idem, Colonialism and its Forms of Knowledge* (Delhi etc.: Oxford University Press, 1997), 76–105, particularly 91–3.

23 Fergusson's two volumes were revised and enlarged by J. Burgess's *Indian Architecture* and R. Spier's, *Eastern Architecture* (London, 1910) which are still regarded as an early standard work on Indian architecture. Rajendralal Mitra published *Antiquities of Orissa*. 2 vols, Calcutta 1875–80, and *Buddha Gayā. The great Buddhist Temple*, Calcutta, 1878.

24 Martin Brandtner, 'Koloniale Archäologie: Monopolisierte Vergangenheitsdeutung und Herrschaftslegitimation in Britisch-Indien', in Stephan Conermann (ed.), *Mythen, Geschichte(n), Identitäten: Der Kampf um die Vergangenheit* (Hamburg: E. B. -Verlag, 1999), 303–66.

25 Cf. P. Mitter, *Much Maligned Monsters*, 240, 246–7.

26 To stay within the argumentative and historical context I use the phrase 'Mutiny'. In the meantime the event is called 'Great Rebellion', 'War of Independence' or, what I rather prefer, 'War of Liberation'. All these denominations are 'labels' which represent different historical perspectives.

27 Quote from M. Crinson, *Empire Building*, 60 and P. Mitter, *Much Maligned Monsters*, 247.

28 As quoted in P. Mitter, *Much Maligned Monsters*, 247–8.

29 George Birdwood, *The Industrial Arts of India*, 2 vols. (London 1878). Cf. P. Mitter, *Much Maligned Mosnters*, 236–7 and T. R. Metcalf, *An Imperial Vision*, 152–3.

30 T. R. Metcalf, *An Imperial Vision*, 156–8, 162–4.

31 Thomas R. Metcalf, 'Past and Present: Towards an Aesthetics of Colonialism', in: *idem, Forging the Raj. Essays on British India in the Heyday of Empire* (Delhi etc.: Oxford University Press, 2005), 169–83, quote 175.

32 P. Davies, *Splendours of the Raj*, pp. 193–4; T. R. Metcalf, *An Imperial Vision*, 164–6.

33 Cf. T. R. Metcalf, *An Imperial Vision*, 150.

34 *Idem*, 'Architecture and Representation of Empire: India, 1860–1910', in *Forging the Raj. Essays on British India in the Heyday of Empire* (Delhi etc.: Oxford University Press, 2005), 105–139, esp. 105–6, 109, 128.

35 P. Vandal and S. Vandal, *The Raj, Lahore and Bhai Ram Singh*, 27–8.

36 The story of Mayo College at Ajmer has been told by T. R. Metcalf, 'Architecture and the Representation of Empire', 116–22.

37 P. Davies, *Splendours of the Raj*, 195–9.
38 G. H. R. Tillotson, 'Indian Architecture and the English Vision', in *South Asian Studies* 7 (1991): 59–74, esp. 60–1, 67–8. P. Mitter, *Much Maligned Monsters*, 270–7.
39 Public Meeting, Calcutta, February 6, 1901, in Thomas Raleigh (ed.), *Lord Curzon in India. Being a Selection from his Speeches as Viceroy & Governor General of India, 1898–1905*, 2 vols. (London: Macmillan and Co, 1906), vol. 1, 252–261, esp. 258–9.
40 Address of Lord Lytton, in J. Talboys Wheeler, *The History of the Imperial Assemblage at Delhi* (London 1877), 84.
41 George Watt, *Indian Art at Delhi 1903. Being the Official Catalogue of the Delhi Exhibition 1902–1903*, (first publ. 1903, repr. with an Introduction by Narayani Gupta Delhi etc.: Motilal Banarsidas, 1987), xiv.
42 Lord Curzon, 'Extract from Budget Speech' (March 25, 1903), in T. Raleigh (ed.), *Lord Curzon in India*, vol. 2, 228. Stephen Wheeler, *History of the Delhi Coronation Darbar* (first publ. London 1904, repr. Delhi and Chandigarh 1991), 88–9.
43 Speech of Lord Curzon (December 30, 1902), 'Indian Art Exhibition at Delhi', in T. Raleigh (ed.), *Lord Curzon in India*, vol. 2, 223–4.
44 Speech of Lord Curzon at the annual meeting of the Bengal Asiatic Society of Bengal (February 7, 1900), in *ibid.*, vol. 2, 199–213, esp. 202–3, 205.
45 *Ibid.*, 224.
46 For the expanding leather industry at Kanpur to supply the growing miltary demand within British India but also other parts of the British Empire, namely South Africa and China, cf. Henry G. Walton, *A Monograph on Tanning and Working in Leather in the United Provinces of Agra and Oudh* (Allahabad, 1903), p. 28. All industries met the ends of the imperial regime and certainly not those of the 'national' interests of India.
47 Speech of Lord Curzon (December 30, 1902), 'Indian Art Exhibition at Delhi', in T. Raleigh (ed.), *Lord Curzon in India*, vol. 2, 224–5.
48 As quoted in J. T. Wheeler, *History of the Imperial Assemblage at Delhi*, 88.
49 G. Watt, *Indian Art at Delhi*, 1–2.
50 This was again highlighted by Curzon in his speech at the Bengal Asiatic Society where he claimed that India's great artistic achievements were all exotics imported into the country in the train of conquerors, who had learnt their architectural lessons in Central Asia, Arabia and in Afghanistan, cf. T. Raleigh (ed.), *Lord Curzon in India*, vol. 2, 202.
51 Narayani Gupta, Preface, in *idem.*, xi.
52 Herbert H. Risley, *Tribes and Castes of Bengal. Ethnographical Glossary*, 2 vols. (Calcutta, 1892).
53 G. Watt, *Indian Art at Delhi*, 64.
54 *Ibid.*, 65.
55 *Ibid.*, 149.
56 *Ibid.*, 452.
57 *Ibid.*, 380.
58 *Ibid.*, Introduction, xvii and *passim*.
59 S. Wheeler, *History of the Delhi Coronation Darbar*, 96–8. Stephen Wheeler was the son of the above mentioned J. Talbot Wheeler, official reporter of the Imperial Assemblage in 1877.
60 Speech of Lord Curzon at the annual meeting of the Bengal Asiatic Society of Bengal (February 7, 1900), in T. Raleigh (ed.), *Lord Curzon in India*, vol. 2, 273–4.
61 Suresh Chandra Ghosh, *The History of Education in Modern India, 1757–1986* (Hyderabad: Orient Longman, 1995), 126.

62 From Percy Brown, Assistant Director, Exhibition of Indian Art Manufacturers, Delhi, To The Director General of Education. Exhibition of Indian Art Manufacturers at the Coronation Assemblage at Delhi, No. 351 – A, dated the 6th September 1902, Home Department, Education 1902 (part A). Proceedings October. F.N. 87–88, National Archives of India, New Delhi.

63 Speech of Lord Curzon (December 30, 1902), 'Indian Art Exhibition at Delhi', in T. Raleigh (ed.), *Lord Curzon in India*, vol. 2, 227.

64 *Report on the Native Papers in Bengal*, No. 3 of 1903 (*Hitavadi*, Calcutta 9 January 1903): 31.

65 *Selections from the Native Newspapers published in the Punjab* XVI, No. 4: 24–6, quote: 26, The *Tribune*, Lahore.

66 *Ibid.*, No. 5, 29, The *Tribune*, Lahore, dated 22 and 23 January 1903.

67 Much of the critique pointed out the enormous expenditure for the Delhi Darbar against the background of famine and starvation, *ibid.*, vol. XIV, No. 33, S. 445, *Sat Dharm Parcharik*, dated 8th August 1902. Mortimer Menpes, *The Durbar*, London 1903, 203.

68 P. Mitter, *Much Maligned Monsters*, 222.

69 Generally speaking, this is true for all dichonomic constructions like the urban-rural contrast, high and low classes or Europe and the Orient. It is not even an exclusively European phenomenon.

70 T. R. Metcalf, 'Architecture and the Representation of Empire', 133–4.

71 Thomas R. Metcalf, 'Architecture and Empire: Sir Herbert Baker and the Building of New Delhi', in: *idem, Forging the Raj. Essays on British India in the Heyday of Empire* (Delhi etc.: Oxford University Press, 2005), 140–152, quote 146.

72 Cf. Christopher Hussey, *Sir Edwin Lutyens* (London 1963), 277–9.

73 For the discussion in the Indian press, particularly the Calcutta *Dawn Magazine*, in the wake of the debates on the architecture of New Delhi in 1901–13 *vide* Haridas Mukherjee and Uma Mukherjee, T*he Origins of the National Education Movement (1905–1910)* (Calcutta: National Council of Education, Bengal, 1957), 2nd edn 2000, 241–5 and App. C-F, 321–7.

74 For New Delhi see Andreas Volwahsen, *Imperial Delhi. The British Capital of the British Empire* (Munich etc.: Prestel, 2002).

Part Two

COLONIALISM, INDIANS AND NONGOVERNMENTAL ASSOCIATIONS: THE AMBIGUITY AND COMPLEXITY OF 'IMPROVEMENT'

Chapter Three

INCORPORATION AND DIFFERENTIATION: POPULAR EDUCATION AND THE IMPERIAL CIVILIZING MISSION IN EARLY NINETEENTH CENTURY INDIA

Jana Tschurenev

Introduction

In the first three decades of the nineteenth century, public education began to assume a special place within the colonial civilizing mission in India. On the one hand, an important shift occurred in the East India Company's approach towards education and learning, a shift which culminated in the 'great education debate'.[1] Leaving behind the patronage of 'the learned natives of India', the Committee for Public Instruction, which had been installed in 1823, formulated a consciously interventionist educational policy in the frame of a civilizing mission.[2] Instruction in Western sciences in the English language was assigned a special role in winning the consent and cooperation of the Indian middle classes for the colonial project. Thereby, however, the Bengal Committee of Public Instruction – in accordance with the Court of Directors of the Company in London – almost exclusively concentrated its resources on higher education, hoping that knowledge would diffuse 'downwards' from there and thus transform Indian society as a whole.[3]

At the same time, crucial developments also happened in the field of elementary, or popular, education, even if this field was frequently neglected and sometimes even discouraged by the Company. The efforts of privately operating educationalists (British as well as Indian), missionaries and voluntary educational associations found entrance in the colonial statistics and are also well known to historians.[4] However, they attracted much less scholarly attention than the ideological (and financial) battles over higher education. It is difficult to judge if the early nineteenth century non-state activities led to an *expansion* of popular education, since even British sources point to a decline of the pre-existing indigenous educational institutions.[5] However, what did happen was an important *transformation* of elementary schooling: new schools were founded, and existing facilities were replaced or incorporated into new systems of superintendence. Thus, missionaries and educational associations triggered a process by which the nature of Indian education was radically altered. They imported the idea of a school building 'as the norm of the age', which was a radical break with a 'learning and popular culture [that] has been oriented to the outside'. They introduced a politics of centralized control 'over definitions of truth and meaning', new teachings methods, routines and rituals, which changed the 'relationships between student, teacher, text and the world'.[6] This chapter is concerned with the transformation of *popular education* in the context of a *non-governmental civilizing mission*.

I want to look at the shift from elementary education as an informal private activity towards standardised public institutions from the perspective of imperial entanglements, because there are striking similarities between Britain, India and other British-controlled territories, for instance in Western Africa. For Britain, Margaret Archer has identified a cycle in the history of educational change that started with 'private enterprise' and the 'mono-integration' of schooling with religious institutions in the early modern period and finally led to the creation of a state education system. As an intermediary step in this process schooling was put on a public, although not yet governmental, basis.[7] This meant that parents and Church lost the immediate control over the activities of teachers, who became accountable to the new sponsors and providers of schooling: voluntary associations, or, as they would be called now, non-governmental organizations (NGOs). The formation of such organizations that were engaged in the expansion and improvement of popular schooling was not confined to England. On the one hand, committed individuals in Bengal, Madras and Bombay gathered in local organizations of a similar nature. On the other hand, local initiatives in different parts became connected by a network of missionary and school societies that covered the entire empire and cooperated in what was commonly called the 'spread of universal instruction'. The general aim of the organizations was, as the *Bombay Native Education Society* put it, 'to introduce a regular system of useful and liberal instruction'.[8] This 'regular system' was a combination of classroom arrangements and technologies that became known as the monitorial system of education. While Foucault referred to monitorial schools as the pedagogical example par excellence for the emergence of new techniques of discipline and subject formation,[9] the system – having itself imperial origins – has recently been analysed as one of the first global currents in the field of elementary schooling.[10] In this way, the transformation of schooling in India took place in an imperial, and even global, frame.

This paper starts with a short introduction of the missionary and school societies, who – operating from England and in India – engaged with the spread of a new kind of popular education in India, and whose 'civilizing' agendas will be analysed in detail. These agendas were shaped by two conflicting tendencies that can be termed, following Cooper and Stoler, *incorporation* and *differentiation*. According to Cooper and Stoler, civilizing missions implied a tension between universal and particularistic elements. While the colonial reform projects were, on the one hand, highly inclusive – all colonial subjects were to be civilized – they raised, on the other hand, questions of 'how much civilizing' was useful and when 'too much civilizing' became politically dangerous. The 'uplift' had to be limited according to a complex and flexible colonial 'grammar of difference', in whose production and maintenance, as I want to show, educationalists also participated.[11] The first section of this paper focuses on the tendency of incorporation, which in this context meant the universalistic zeal of the educationalists. School societies aimed at the inclusion of children living all over the 'habitable globe'[12] into cheap and effective elementary schools, operating according to the new standardised disciplinary techniques. The second section then explores the aspect of differentiation, from a research perspective that can be labelled as 'intersectionality'.[13] The imperial educationalists suggested different curricula for different target groups that were defined by interplay of the categories of race or culture, class and gender. Education was to be limited so as not to remove people from their social position or their 'respective sphere', as the educationalists termed it. As I will argue in the third section, the two tendencies of incorporation and differentiation, which characterised the educational agendas, also operated on the level of the voluntary associations. Membership was not confined to male British middle class subjects. On the contrary, the associations aimed at securing wide support and participation, even within a hierarchical framework. I will look at the position of British women and Indian middle class reformers within the voluntary associations; at processes of selective appropriation; conflicting interests; and struggles to change the setting of asymmetrical power relations among the agents of the civilizing mission. The paper will close with some remarks on how the ambitious plans and the strategies of the civilizing missionaries had to be constantly refined in the course of the interaction with the local teachers as well as the students. This interaction, together with certain tensions between the educational agendas and the means adopted to achieve them, led to consequences that were neither intended nor anticipated by the missionaries and middle class school activists.

1. Incorporation: Universal Education for Civilization

Probably the most active group among the suppliers of a new kind of public elementary education in the British Empire of the early nineteenth century were Protestant missionaries.[14] In Bengal, the Baptist missionaries of Serampore – Joshua Marshman, William Carey, and William Ward – 'conducted' more than a hundred 'native schools' in the surrounding villages in 1818.[15] Robert May and J. D. Pearson, who were sent out by the London Missionary Society, set up a local system of more than thirty schools around Chinsura, starting in 1814.[16] The Church Missionary Society's schools around Burdwan were often cited as successful models,[17] while the Tranquebar Mission was highly active around Madras, Tanjavur and Tiruchirapally in the South.[18] The missionaries' educational activities were not isolated efforts of individuals. They were highly organized, and connected to an imperial educational movement. On the one hand, missionary pamphlets on education, such as the Serampore trio's *Hints Relative to Native Schools* or *On Indian Civilization*, written by Christian Samuel John of Tranquebar circulated among British Indian, British and even European audiences.[19] On the other hand, the missionary educationalists stationed in India received strong ideological and material support in the form of teaching materials, manuals and trained teachers from two influential organizations that operated from England. Most important was the British and Foreign School Society (BFSS), founded in 1814. The BFSS combined the promotion of non-denominational elementary education in England with a strong missionary zeal. It was primarily based in evangelical and dissenting circles but also supported by liberals and utilitarians. The other organization, the National Society for the Education of the Poor in the Principles of the Established Church (National Education Society, NES), represented the more conservative Anglican faction. While competing with each other in Britain, both societies cooperated in other parts of the empire and jointly supported the activities of missionary and bible societies abroad. In contrast to the missionary societies, the BFSS and NES were not 'transnational' or 'international' organizations with metropolitan headquarters and colonial affiliations, although they did have imperial or global connections and goals.

In South Asia, agents of the Baptist, London and Church Missionary Societies (henceforth BMS, LMS, CMS) as well as their wives formed themselves into local societies specifically dedicated to promoting education, such as the Society for Native Schools (SNS), which was founded in 1816 as the educational arm of the Serampore Trio, or the interdenominational Ladies' Society for Native Female Education (LSNFE) in Calcutta. However, what made the missionaries' educational efforts really influential was their involvement in the novel 'Europeo-Native institutions', i. e. associations run jointly by British and Indian middle class reformers. Such institutions were established in all three Presidencies. The first of them, the Calcutta School Book Society (CSBS), was founded in 1817. It was supplemented by the Calcutta School Society (CSS) one year later. The Madras School Book Society and the Bombay Native Education Society (BNES) followed in 1820 and 1822 respectively.[20] All these associations not only shared certain organizational features, they also established close ties with one another by means of regular correspondence, personal visits and overlapping memberships. They exchanged relevant information and circulated what would be now called 'best practises' in the field of education. Moreover, they undertook joint fundraising efforts and legitimated each other by exchanging and cross-referencing their reports. Their strategies comprised the 'improvement' of existing schools by means of supervision, establishment of model schools and teacher training institutions (BFSS, NES, LSNFE, CSS, BNES) and the supply of materials (BFSS, NES, SNS, CSBS, BNES) as well as the direct installation of local school systems. What most strongly connected the missionary and school societies was their common cause: they perceived one another as cooperating in the improvement of society through the universal spread of an 'improved' mode of education and therefore forwarding the 'great work of uplifting mankind'.[21]

Let us now turn to this universal agenda. Here, I will concentrate on the British side of the discourse, or in other words, the support of colonial educational ventures from the home base of Great Britain. Since 1813, the BFSS was presenting itself as fighting the 'cause of universal instruction', or, as its committee member James Mill claimed in a widely circulating pamphlet, 'schools for all'.[22] The mission of the BFSS included not only children of any denomination or religion in England, but also all the new 'fellow-subjects' living in the British Empire, who had come into the reach of philanthropic school activists. Not 'a single child' in the world was to be left 'without instruction', boy or girl.[23] This highly inclusionary impulse was shared by all the associations concerned: the educational projects in Bengal always searched for means to reach as many people as possible. Their ultimate goal was the 'general instruction and illumination of the population' and thereby the transformation of Indian society as a whole.[24]

How can one account for this strong impetus for educational expansion? One important factor was that British public opinion became increasingly convinced about the 'evils of popular ignorance'[25] and about the powers of education as the means to cure those evils. Karen Jones and Kevin Williamson have shown how changes in the character of political knowledge occurring in late eighteenth century Britain conditioned the construction of an urgent need to instruct the entire population. Social reformers in the administration as well as a concerned public began to interpret social tensions as being 'problems with the principles and habits of the population' that, in turn, resulted from their ignorance. Because of its ability to form 'sound principles' and 'good habits',[26] – and thus remove the source of all evil – popular schooling appeared as a 'multi-valent tactic'[27] or a highly flexible tool for social reform.

However, it was not just any kind of instruction or schooling that appeared to possess these immense powers. The educational reformers perceived the existing schools as highly insufficient with regard to pedagogical techniques, curriculum and disciplinary methods. In England, Joseph Lancaster could not see that the 'wretched' schools catering for 'the industrious classes' led to any 'improvement' and criticized that corporal punishment was the only instrument to ensure due attention of students.[28] The latter point was also stressed by William Adam and Alexander Duff in Bengal who complained that in the vernacular village schools (*patshalas*), students could not at all acquire 'self-acting' and 'self-judging' capacities.[29] Thus, against the background of new educational goals, modern reformers rejected prevalent forms of schooling, both in the colony and in Britain. 'True' education, as these reformers thought, had to 'improve' and even 'conquer' the 'minds of the rising generation'.[30] In short, education had to instil the 'right' principles and habits. School societies therefore aimed not only at the expansion of education but sought also to 'improve' the quality of education. This meant, in the end, a displacement of the prevailing pedagogical culture. Moreover, the strong inclusionary impulse demanded a form of pedagogy and school organization that allowed for an effective and efficient instruction of large numbers of pupils.

The pedagogical method that promised to answer the new educational goals – targeting the minds, rationality and efficient operation – was the monitorial (also labelled as 'British', 'National', or simply 'new') system of education. Formulated in the early years of the nineteenth century it was based on two reform 'experiments' that were both connected with educating a particular social group. In Madras, the Scottish science lecturer and chaplain Andrew Bell who was superintendent of a school catering to orphaned children of the European military from 1789 to 1797, was searching for an effective means to produce 'good scholars, good men, and good Christians'. Therefore, he combined teaching practises from local village schools with 'system, method and order' and re-modelled his school accordingly.[31] Some years later, the Quaker Joseph Lancaster, a young schoolmaster in London, initiated a campaign for the education of the poor, suggesting several of the 'improvements' that he had introduced into his school as the basis for large-scale elementary education.[32] The 'discoveries' of Bell and Lancaster closely resembled each other and were gradually combined into a standard model.[33] Based on the 'distinguishing characteristic'[34] of students mutually instructing each other, i. e. more advanced students ('monitors') teaching their less advanced peers, the monitorial system included a number of innovations. Teaching was based on a sequence of short, standardised successive lessons. Students were grouped in classes according to their progress in the curriculum and constantly re-ranked within the classes according to their performance. Monitorial schools introduced a strict disciplinary regime, which, ideally, replaced corporal punishment with 'emulation' on part of the students and panoptic surveillance on part of the master.[35]

To nineteenth century educationalists, the model appeared as a cheap, rational and effective 'machine' for the diffusion of useful knowledge. Detailed records of the numbers of students in attendance, the numbers of sums written and lessons spelled or committed to memory allowed subscribers to supervise the students' progress. Such accountability standards recommended the monitorial system for the educational projects of voluntary associations, who were dependent on subscriptions and donations and had to prove to the public that their money had not been spent in vain. The spread of monitorial schools was thus connected to the 'largest philanthropic movement' in the history of education.[36]

The core curriculum of monitorial schools included lessons in reading, writing, and arithmetic. The teaching of basic literacy, however, was always directed to a higher end. In England, the BFSS and NES promoted the monitorial system as a means of combating poverty, crime and the erosion of traditional authority. They hoped to achieve this by orderly arrangements to help develop good habits, and by religious instruction that was supposed to instil moral principles in the students.[37] For the empire at large, the missionary and school societies employed the monitorial system – of course 'improved and adapted to the circumstances of the country'[38] – as an instrument to morally uplift students and thereby enhance society's scale of civilization.

For the civilizing missions pursued by the protestant missionary societies as well as the BFSS, two reference points seem to be important. First, drawing from the evangelical discourse, they assigned a special mission to 'the sons of Britain' in the empire and the world. Perceiving signs of 'providence' in various historical developments – especially the 'commitment' of India to Britain's 'guardian care'[39] – they called on those who had already received the 'blessings' of protestant Christianity to extend those blessings to others. Since the British public knew about 'the awful state of the Heathen, and of myriads even of our own fellow subjects', who were 'perishing for lack of knowledge', they had the duty to spread the Gospel.[40] In this twin project to reclaim poor Britons for Christianity and convert the 'heathen' abroad, missionary, bible and education societies 'form[ed] a whole, and, like the different parts of a machine, all work[ed] together'.[41]

Secondly, the educational mission appropriated elements of the new concept of history as a sequence of progressive stages. French and Scottish Enlightenment philosophers had introduced the idea that each society must pass through the same stages of development. In this way, it was possible to rank countries according to their present state of civilization – a state that was, however, changeable. It became the task of the philosopher of history to identify the laws that governed social change.[42] While James Mill, applying John Millar's philosophy of history to India, emphasized the crucial importance of good government and found that 'something far beyond the power of mere schooling' was required to uplift Indian society, the missionary discourse saw the healing principle in the spread of popular education.[43] Again, ignorance appeared as the source of 'mental corruption' and, in turn, of social evils. The Serampore missionaries believed that it was the 'lack of knowledge', that '[sank the Hindus] far below the most savage nations in vice and immorality'.[44] For the educationalists concerned, the 'knowledge' or 'ignorance' of a population decided about the placement of a country on the scale of civilization.[45] Moreover, education not only appeared capable to elevate the relative position of a particular country, but was also believed to have the power to uplift humanity as a whole. In this way, the BFSS perceived the supporters of 'Indian instruction' in the CSS also as the 'friends of mankind'.[46] In short, when pleading the 'cause of universal instruction' in Britain, the educationalists combined elements from two oppositional currents of thought. The reference to 'providence' legitimated the imperial mission, while the liberal notion of a malleable 'scale of civilization' opened a new field to employ the multi-valent tactic of popular instruction.

The assumption that the scale of civilization could by upgraded by means of education rested on the notion of a general equality of human potential: 'Let us no longer be told', stated the BFSS, 'that the African race is an order of inferior beings while we can point to Hayti [sic] as a proof, that when their intellect has a fair chance for cultivation, they will naturally rise in the scale of civilization to a point infinitely higher, than can be fairly claimed by many of those who have proudly despised it'. A report from a school 'for the children of Africans' in New York tells: 'In fact, let the enemies of these neglected children of men perform a pilgrimage to New York, and at the Shrine of Education recant their principles, and confess that the poor despised African *is as capable of every intellectual improvement as themselves*'.[47] In like manner, William Ward of Serampore, while on a fundraising tour for 'Native Female Schools' in England, expressed his conviction that properly educated Hindu women would not only equal their men but were, moreover, capable of becoming the 'Hannah Mores and Elizabeth Frys of India'.[48] The notion of a *perfectibilité* of all human beings contrasts, on the one hand, with the biological racism and social Darwinism that gained popularity in the second half of the nineteenth century.[19] On the other hand, the educational discourse of the early nineteenth century found its own means to limit potential claims of equality.

2. Differentiation: Useful Knowledge for Different Social Positions

The inclusionary impetus of the universal educational mission contrasted with the notion that different people had to be educated in different ways according to the social position they were to occupy after they left school. This future position was again related to the social background of students: birth and living conditions defined the social 'sphere' a student belonged to. Thinking of French 'utopias', Andrew Bell was afraid of the 'risk of elevating, by an indiscriminate education, the minds of those doomed to the drudgery of daily labour, above their condition, and thereby rendering them discontented and unhappy in their lot'.[50] The Serampore missionaries expressed the same concern with regard to the population of Bengal: 'instruction […] should be such as to render the inhabitants of a country happy in their own sphere, but never take them out of it'.[51] Christian Samuel John, in his 'proposals for the civilization of the natives by Free schools', hoped that his students would 'become good subjects, submitting to all their superiors whom Divine providence had placed over them, so that each might learn what his duties were'.[52] In this way, the reference to 'providence' not only conditioned Christian universalism; it also legitimated hierarchical schemes of differentiation. In short, the incorporative zeal of 'schools for all' was bound by the danger of coursing objectionable social mobility instead of 'uplift' within a particular 'sphere'. Popular education somehow had to find a balance 'between the Scylla of brutal ignorance and the Charybdis of literary education' that might led to rising expectations.[53]

Again, the monitorial system seemed to offer a solution. It appeared as a tool to impart exactly as much and exactly the kind of knowledge that was seen as necessary for a particular subaltern group to become 'useful' to themselves and society. Concentrating on the educational projects of the Serampore missionaries, the writings of Andrew Bell and the reports of the Ladies' Committee of the BFSS, I want highlight this by exploring cases of 'indigent Christians', 'natives' and, finally, female education.

2.1 'Half-castes' and 'Indigent Christians' as Mediators

The Madras asylum superintended by Andrew Bell (1789–97) was designed to cater for 'the orphan and distressed male children of the European military'. Bell found his 'half-caste' students a 'degraded race'; their fathers having died or disappeared nothing protected them against the 'corrupting' influence of their Indian mothers.[54] Interestingly, he used their 'half-caste' background as the primary category of description, although about one fourth of the students were the children of exclusively 'European' couples.[55] In 1809, the Serampore missionaries opened the first monitorial model school in Calcutta, the Benevolent Institution for the Instruction of Indigent Christians. It catered to a similar social group although one primarily classified by the missionaries in religious terms as 'country-born Christians'.[56] In both cases, the students belonged either to the so-called 'half-castes' or 'Eurasians', who were partially of Portuguese, English or other 'European' descent – a population that was distinguished by a complex interplay of 'race' and class. Or they were 'indigent' or 'poor whites', still privileged in terms of 'race', but subaltern in terms of class.[57] However, no clear boundaries separated both groups; and both occupied a highly problematic position in colonial society. Their public conduct, and even their mere existence, seemed to exhibit the instability of the colonial 'grammar of difference'.[58] Therefore, a variety of disciplinary and social engineering projects were designed for 'half-castes' and 'white subalterns' in South Asia, especially since there were hopes to transform them into useful intermediaries.[59]

These hopes were already entertained by Andrew Bell. He planned to 'rescue' his students from their 'state of depravity and wretchedness' with the help of systematic arrangements, order and discipline. Bell tried to counterbalance the bad effects of early association (that is to say the influence of the mothers) and produce instead 'habits of diligence, industry [...] and honesty' as well as 'principles of religion and morality' in his students. In short, he wanted to 'giv[e] society an annual crop of good and useful subjects' capable of occupying a mediating position between 'European gentlemen' and 'native servants'.[60]

This very position was also projected for the students of the Benevolent Institution. As children 'bearing the Christian name'[61] and thus connected to the British by the bond of religion, they were supposed to learn '[to] comprehend directions given them by English gentlemen, which their superior colloquial acquaintance with the native language and idiom, enables them to convey to native servants with ease and effect'.[62] Therefore, they were taught English and Bengali lessons and, in addition, given non-denominational religious instruction. However, when the Benevolent Institution opened its gates, the street children appeared as completely unfit for their future role as subordinate clerks or supervisors of the so-called native schools. The first teacher of the Benevolent Institution complained that it was 'no uncommon thing to hear boys of five or six years old [speaking] a language which would shock even a wicked man in Europe'.[63] In order to describe the children admitted into the school, the missionaries repeatedly used the phrase 'a sphere still lower': lower than the poor in Britain; lower than the military orphans in whose school in Calcutta they were not even accepted; and, what concerned their 'benefactors' most, still lower than the common Indian population.[64] If they were not given the means to 'procure support by the pen', they were left to 'wander the streets' looking for jobs that not even the poorest Hindu or Muslim would do.[65] The latter fact, in the eyes of the Serampore missionaries, most strongly legitimated the call on the public – in Bengal and in Britain via the BFSS – to financially support the Benevolent Institution. However, as the missionaries also emphasized, the curriculum was limited in order not to 'injure any other class of people'.[66] There would be no danger that the graduates would compete with the offspring of well-to-do British in Calcutta for better posts.

2.2 'Native Schools': Praeparatio Evangelica, Conquering Minds

In their programmatic *Hints Related to Native Schools* (1816), the Serampore missionaries established a plan for building a net of public elementary schools for the population of Bengal under the supervision of a voluntary association. The model curriculum laid down in this booklet, a 'course of moral and scientific instruction', became adopted by the other missionary educators, as well as educational societies (CSS, BNES) in all three Presidencies and beyond.[67] The *Hints* emphasized the urgent necessity to educate the 'natives' by pointing in vivid terms at their 'degraded state'. The core of the problem, in the missionaries' imagination, was that the Hindu 'system' of religion was 'tending to produce and perpetuate ignorance of the worst kind, and this ignorance, on the other hand, tend[ed] to add to the horrors of the system'. As a first step to disrupt this circle they proposed the instruction in an 'improved' and orthographically standardized vernacular. The vocabulary of the students was to be enriched by repeatedly copying and reading a selection of 'their best words', the 'correct meaning' of which was to be learned by heart. All this was supposed to 'facilitat[e] the reception of ideas which may enlarge and bless the mind in a high degree'.[68] Thus, the basic literacy skills were just a preparatory measure, as – it should be remembered – the ultimate end of instruction was to 'improve' the minds of the students. In England, educationalists hoped to achieve this through the channel of religion. In Bengal, the missionaries had to find a substitute, as they depended on the cooperation of local teachers as well as parents' demand.[69] They found this substitute in 'Western' science, which is not surprising considering the fact that amateur research and science education, in other words, a rational knowledge of 'God's creation', played an important role in the evangelical project in general.[70] In the *Hints Relative to Native Schools*, some basic knowledge in astronomy, natural philosophy and geography, together with history and chronology was put against the

Brahmin cosmology which much abhorred William Ward in his 'view' on the 'Hindoos'.[71] However, although the missionaries stressed the powers of scientific knowledge, the 'facts' to be taught were mixed with Christian beliefs. History lessons included a 'biblical' and a 'secular' branch. An emphasis on the common origin of all mankind, as given in the Bible, was hoped to break the 'tyranny' of Brahmins and the inequality of caste. Moreover, the geography and history lessons were centred on Britain, according to 'her pre-eminence among the nations which the God of providence has given her'.[72] In short, what was presented to the Bengali youth as universal rationality was indeed strongly interspersed with ethnocentric and religious elements.

In order to impart these ideas, the Serampore Trio suggested employing the machinery of the monitorial system. What Bell and Lancaster recommended for acquiring basic literacy, was now to be used for memorizing 'facts'. A set of compendia and wall tables containing such 'facts' were distributed in the schools. The sentences were then written by the students under a monitor's dictation, corrected and repeatedly re-read. In this way, the missionaries hoped that sentences such as '[t]he earth moves round the sun in three hundred and sixty five days, which motion forms the year', or '[t]he moon encompasses the earth in twenty-nine days and a half, thus forming the lunar month' were 'committed to memory' and, in this way, the minds of the students would become 'imprinted' with useful ideas.[73]

For the Serampore missionaries, the 'useful ideas' had a double purpose: they aimed at eradicating 'superstition' and mythical cosmology, which was seen as a prerequisite for the adoption of the gospel. Moreover, because 'India must be indebted to the West' for the communication of these ideas, 'generations yet unborn will pour benedictions on the British name' for having received them.[74] In this way, education even had the power to contribute to the stabilization of the British rule in India. But the missionaries also pointed at where they saw the limits of 'native education': it must not alienate the common people from 'manual labour' and their 'paternal calling'. Vernacular education would place the students under better circumstances 'by [their] ideas being enlarged and [their] powers aroused to a greater exertion in [their] own calling'. Only the Indian elites and middle classes who possessed 'wealth and leisure' enough should get a private English education. Otherwise, there would be 'thousands of natives [...] drawn from their proper employments by the golden expectations inspired through their being able to copy an English letter' without 'employment for all' of them. In this way, a 'thickening crowd' would be 'allured to real misery'. But even more important was that English education would put common Bengali people in the position to compete with the 'body of Christian youth' – the 'indigent' Christians who were to act as cultural brokers. Connected to the

missionaries by their religion, language, habit and 'mode of life', they had
stronger claims for employment and social 'uplift'.[75]

It is an interesting point that racial notions of fundamental difference come
into play when the missionaries define and legitimize different educational
agendas for different target groups. The civilizing mission directed at Hindus
was meant to advance, enlighten and educate them, but with important
restrictions that went beyond of the idea of differentiated social spheres and
the assumed demands of the labour market. 'A Hindoo', the Serampore trio
stated, 'must ever remain a Hindoo, inferior to the European by the force of all
those habits which his superior exertions have rendered natural to him'. These
'superior exertions' were traced to the rougher climate of Europe, where, as
the missionaries thought, harvest required more intensive labour.[76] While
the missionaries assumed a 'single origin' of mankind, a belief in the effects
of climate accounted for the difference in 'mental culture' among human
beings.[77] In the framework of a culture-climate-theory[78] the missionaries
legitimized British rule over the 'relaxed and timid Asiatic', who, not 'less
happy because inferior in ability [...] may sit in his [European] neighbor's
peaceful shadow', profiting and learning from his 'more powerful and more
enlightened mind'.[79] Here, the British appeared not only as more advanced
but also more able than the colonized subjects, which is quite a contradiction
to the language of the BFSS as well as to the fundraising campaign for 'native
female education' which William Ward of Serampore himself conducted in
England. In the colony, categories of civilization, religion and culture merged
in the making of a 'cultural differentialism', which can be regarded as the first
'register' of racism.[80]

2.3 Poor Girls, Indian Women: Reconstructing the Domestic Sphere

If basic literacy and religious instruction aimed at the moral and material
'uplift' of the lower classes in England, there was a specific additional
component for Eurasian youth in Madras and Calcutta: a bilingual education
that would allow them to become 'mediators' between the colonizers and the
colonized. In the 'native schools', religion was partially substituted by science
in order to prepare the ground for the adoption of protestant Christianity,
which was regarded by the missionaries as a rational religion. And there was
also a particular agenda for the girls or women within these groups.

The Ladies' Committee of the BFSS felt a 'necessity [...] for imparting to
Females, belonging to the labouring classes [...] such a portion of education
[...] as shall enable them to discharge the duties of their stations which, as
women, they are destined to fill'.[81] In this context, needlework assumed a crucial

role in the curriculum. Working class girls in Britain and Eurasian girls in Bengal were supposed to acquire skills that enabled them to work as servants in respectable households, find suitable marriage partners, or if neither could be arranged, to make a living from needlework instead of turning to prostitution or informal relationships.[82] However, needlework was much more than a 'useful art'. It became a symbol of constant employment within the domestic sphere, which figured as the women's realm in evangelical discourse. Therefore, the social agenda of female education for both working class girls and 'native' women was, basically, the reconstruction of the domestic sphere.

Together with needlework, religious instruction was considered to be crucial to female education 'in every part of the empire'.[83] Only religion was seen as capable to instil in the girls 'holy principles' that would eventually lead to 'virtuous conduct'.[84] Female domestic virtue was seen to be of particular importance because of the woman's role as mother, and thus,the earliest association of children. The BFSS ladies' committee found that 'it cannot be expected [of] mothers, who are destitute of every moral principle, [to] be the means of instructing their offspring in the duties they owe to God, their parents, or to society'.[85] Since 'Asiatic mothers', the imperial feminists thought, had 'little control [...] over their children',[86] they still had to be taught how to gain and practise motherly authority. However, whenever she was well instructed in her duties, 'the universal rational mother'[87] was seen as a potential agent of civilization.

As a particular agenda for the colonies, 'rescue' and 'liberation' came into play. Indian women, by means of instruction in needlework and the Christian religion would, it was believed, 'acquire habits of industry' and adopt 'a holy principle to keep them from evil and direct them to good', which would lead Indian men to 'grant' their wives 'more liberty'.[88] In this way, education was seen as instrumental for rescuing Indian women from 'domestic slavery'. Moreover, female education became connected to a central project in the establishment of the colonial civilizing mission: the abolition of 'suttee'.[89] To British social reformers, the practise of (self-)burning of wives on the funeral pile of their deceased husbands became representative of the status of women in Hindu society. On the initiative of William Ward, who was one of the strongest advocates of a legal ban on 'suttee' in Bengal, the BFSS ladies started a subscription in order to send a qualified headmistress to Calcutta who was supposed to establish a model or central school for spreading Christian female education. Teaching Indian women their motherly duties was of special importance also with regard to suttee, because it was these duties they sadly neglected if they chose to die with their husbands.[90] Thus, by invoking a universal motherhood, public female education targeted the heart of the domestic sphere. From there, it was hoped, society at large would be uplifted. Because the assumed position of women was regarded as a crucial marker for the level of the development of a country – an idea that the missionaries shared with philosophers of history – the improvement of the women's lot would directly enhance the state of Indian civilization. What scholars working on the link between schooling and the (re-)production of social stratification called the 'hidden agenda of education' or the 'hidden curriculum', it appears, was made perfectly explicit by agents of the early nineteenth century civilizing mission.[91] However, there is need for specification. First of all, there was no single and homogeneous social agenda of 'education of the poor' or 'native instruction'. In England, for instance, the supporters of the Anglican Andrew Bell followed a more conservative approach as compared to the dissenters and especially the Utilitarians in the BFSS.[92] With regard to India, the BFSS in England was less restrictive than the Baptist missionaries in Bengal. However, the programs and reports discussed share – to a large extent – the notion that education should enable the individual to become a recognized agent within a particular social position, assigned to him or her according to social and cultural background as well as gender. At the same time, it was meant to restrict social mobility, strengthen authority and produce disciplined subjects. However, the educational projects are not so much about the re-construction of the existing set of power relations but linked to the production of a new – metropolitan-liberal and colonial – social order and the making of a new 'grammar of difference'.

Moreover, as Pavla Miller has emphasized, one cannot assume that this 'rhetorical curriculum' was identical to the 'curriculum-in-use' or even to the 'received curriculum'.[93] Similarly, Sumit Sarkar stresses that the demonstration of the hegemonic intentions of colonial education policies offers no proof that hegemony was actually achieved.[94] In this line, I want to discuss now three important factors that hindered a direct implementation of the educational agendas discussed above. There were conflicting interests and negotiations about the common agenda within the voluntary associations among the civilizing missionaries themselves. Moreover, the individual agency of the local teachers and students came into play. Finally, the means adopted did not always lead to, and sometimes even contradicted the projected ends, so that only some of the educational and social results of the educational programmes had actually been intended by some of the educationalists.

3. Hierarchical Inclusion, Selective Appropriation, Renegotiating Positions

Just as the students were differentiated along the lines of 'race', class and gender, the educational reformers themselves cannot be seen as a homogenous group either; the two conflicting tendencies of incorporation and differentiation also operated within the group of the 'civilizers'. The *Missionary*

Register – from its first edition – called on 'the poor' to 'take their share' in the 'benevolent exertions' of missionary and school societies. The inclusion of working class contributors and members had a double purpose. It could substantially assist the societies financially while, at the same time, the 'care for others' would encourage morality.[95] The *Missionary Register* thus envisaged the wide participation of common people in 'benevolent' organizations as a countermeasure to the emerging political culture of the working class as well as other 'vices'.

Also British women were particularly called on to 'offer themselves to take that share in the work which can be taken by none but females'.[96] Because 'Indian manners [forbade] females to be placed under the tuition of men', the education of girls and women was regarded as a special responsibility of the 'Ladies in Britain'. Two elements from the evangelical-imperialist discourse were combined to present them as the 'natural guardians of these unhappy Widows and Orphans in British India'.[97] On the one hand, their 'Britishness' committed them to participate in the imperial social mission. On the other hand, women's responsibility for the domestic sphere defined the specifically female tasks within this mission. While the evangelical ideology of 'separate spheres' excluded women as independent missionaries and especially from preaching it regarded them as indispensable, but subordinate, 'help-meets'. However, these ideological elements were used by women for claiming a special authority, a 'female colonial authority' based on maternal care for other women and for children.[98] This authority, even though it was partially based on an ideology which confined women to the private, enabled 'respectable' women to enter the public sphere; to found committees within the established societies or even to establish associations run by women independently such as the LSNFE.[99] Moreover, it even helped to overcome the sometimes strong opposition to independent female missionary agency. Engaging with female education enabled single women to go abroad as professional educators and to leave behind the restrictions of the domestic sphere. Midgley has demonstrated these opportunities for self-empowerment within an 'imperial frame' by the example of Mary Ann Cooke, the teacher who was sent to Calcutta by the BFSS in response to William Ward's campaign. Quitting her low-prestige position as a governess, Cooke was the first unmarried woman who went to India in the missionary context and eventually assumed an influential and prominent public position.[100] The highly ambiguous role of British women in the imperialist projects has been widely discussed in feminist and cultural historical literature.[101] Since history 'is replete with ironies in which the dominated become agents of domination',[102] British 'ladies', who were subordinated within the bourgeois order of gender, participated in the subjection of others in terms of 'race' and class. The engagement in the colonial civilizing mission could become a part of personal empowerment strategies as well as gender politics at home.

At this point we can turn to look at the participation of indigenous elites in the so-called 'Europeo-native institutions' from the same perspective of incorporation, differentiation and selective appropriation for renegotiating one's social position. The grand designs of the protestant missionaries, their highly ambitious projects for educating, converting and 'uplifting' the whole of India, strongly contrasted with the lack of missionary staff and financial resources. The educational projects thus depended on the support of the Indian middle classes as well as on the work of Indian teachers. The proceedings of the formation of the CSBS explicitly state that the inclusion of the *bhadralok* was meant to assure their '*active cooperation* as well as *acquiescence* [...], a measure which tends to obtain the labours and gratuitous services of some, the pecuniary contributions of many and the good wishes of all'. In this way, the indigenous middle classes were hoped to be made active agents as well as sponsors of the 'uplift' of Indian civilization – of course within the frame of colonial hierarchies. British leadership was supposed to ensure that Indian charity would be directed 'from absurd into judicious channels'. When compared to Indian troops led by British officers, 'Europeo-native institutions' such as the CSBS seemed 'destined to accomplish its *moral and intellectual*, as troops of this character have, the *military* conquest of this country'.[103]

This claim to leadership found its expression in the structure of the CSBS, which included Bengali 'gentlemen' up to the level of secretaries, while the highest level of the institutional hierarchy was reserved to the British. The CSS and BNES show a similar structure. However, in spite of this hierarchical framework and the explicit hegemonic prominent reformers like Radhakanta Deb, Mrityunjay Vidyalankar or Ramkamal Sen joined the CSBS and CSS, while many more committed individuals acted as superintendents of schools, wrote school books and compiled materials. Moreover, a lot of well-to-do Bengalis subscribed to and sponsored the numerous schools as well as the societies initiated by the British educationalists.[104]

The new Indian middle classes participated in and supported the educational ventures, because they connected them to their own agendas, a process that would not have been possible without the universalistic elements of the civilizing mission. As Brian Hatcher has shown for Vidyasagar, Bengali educationalists adapted and 'vernacularized' the British-bourgeois 'improvement' discourse.[105] In a context of high social mobility, engagement with social reform was a means of strengthening a respectable Hindu identity. On the one hand, public schools, the compilation of school-books and the circulation of new genres of printed literature that appeared were instrumental in the standardization of the vernacular languages and to the invention and formalization of cultural traditions against the British. On the other hand, the new wealthy middle classes represented themselves as 'sentinels of culture' and distinguished themselves as the civilizers of the Indian population.[106]

For this 'vernacularized' civilizing mission, certain elements were selected from the British educationalists' offers, while others were not. On the one hand, the school books on mathematics, written by missionaries May and Harle in Chinsura were unanimously promoted by the CSBS; they were even quite popular with Bengali schoolmasters. The CSBS's best-selling publications were treatises on natural philosophy. The pedagogical techniques of the monitorial system seemed to have been quite attractive as well. While the CSBS printed and distributed *Bell's Instructions* in Hindi and Bengali, the CSS adapted the 'indigenous' or 'copy-book system', as proposed by the SNS.[107] In general, it was scientific, organizational, and technical knowledge, together with language teaching materials, that was encouraged by the Indian members of the educational associations and demanded by the wider audience.

Highly controversial with the *bhadralok*, however, was the establishment of public female schooling. Although J. H. Harington, secretary of the CSS, assured the BFSS ladies that 'the Gentlemen of the Calcutta School Society will, I am sure, give [Mary Ann Cooke] the kindest reception',[108] this was not the case. After her arrival in Calcutta, the CSS refused to pay Cooke's salary stating that its priority, under conditions of limited funds, was the education of boys. Miss Cooke (after her marriage, Mrs Wilson) therefore first connected her work to the CMS and later continued under the auspices of the female-led LSNFE.[109]

Bengali public opinion was not against female education in general. Some members of the CSS compiled a pamphlet in favour of female education, gathering 'evidence' from the Sanskrit 'scriptures' so that it would not contradict Hindu traditions. Contrary to missionary opinion, girls were certainly educated, usually not in schools but according to an apprenticeship model of learning. A number of wealthy Bengali families had their daughters more formally educated by private tutors at home.[110] Cooke's venture, however, had caused opposition among the *bhadralok* within the CSS. The first problem was the religious nature of her educational plans. It must be remembered that the BFSS saw Christianity as the only means to lead women to 'holy principles' of conduct and for the re-modelling of private life. Also in Bengal, the lines between the public and the private sphere were re-drawn and a new domestic culture, in which women played a crucial role, was in the making. For example, modernization was deemed appropriate for activities in the public sphere, where there could be interaction with the British. The zone of women, spirituality and the home, meanwhile, became a refuge of self-assertion.[111] This (female-religious) domestic base of the new Bengali culture must have appeared as threatened by the efforts to impart Christian education to girls. Moreover, the practise of holding public examinations of students, which were meant to assure the public that its subscriptions and donations had not been spent in vain, also implicated that girls would be exposed to the eyes of Indian and British 'gentlemen'.[112] This might account for the fact that Miss Cooke's schools were frequented by lower caste girls. The opposition against female education was, more precisely, an opposition against *public* female education and Christian religious instruction for girls.

The engagement of the new Indian middle classes with the 'Europeo-native' educational institutions can be read as the beginnings of the 'internalization', or 'appropriation', of civilizing missions and the emergence of 'self-civilizing' projects that were later continued by Indian social reformers and nationalists, amongst them a number of women (cf., Shobna Nijhawan, in this volume). This selective appropriation included the content as well as the organizational form of the civilizing mission. As Carey Watt (also in this volume) shows, institutionalized philanthropy was part of the 'civilizing' repertoire of Indian social reformers. Within a framework of hierarchical inclusion, British women as well as 'native gentlemen' followed their own agendas, in some ways adapting to the limits of their position, in some ways going beyond the limitations it implied. It would not suffice, therefore, to point at the exclusionary tendencies of nineteenth-century civil society only as, for instance, critics of Habermas' conception of the bourgeois public sphere have done: the terms under which different groups of actors gained access to or were included or incorporated into associations, and the ways in which they were able to change the conditions of their participation were equally relevant.[113]

4. Demand and Supply, Technologies and Effects: The 'Copy-Book System'

Thus far, this paper has explored why different groups of people became involved in the provision of educational services for others. In this section I investigate the demand side to which the providers of schools constantly reacted.[114] What did parents and pupils appreciate regarding the new 'native' schools? First and foremost, there was a high demand for knowledge of the English language. Students were eager to acquire account-keeping skills in both the old and the new English forms of arithmetic and they wanted to learn and practise an accurate and elegant hand-writing. The demand for schools that offered qualifications for future employment was so strong that parents even sent their sons to schools directly controlled by missionaries – despite the fact that people feared that they could be converted to Christianity and alienated from their families. In contradiction to the agenda of missionary education to foster moral subjectivities, the schools were regarded as potentially demoralising in the Bengali population.[115] This again might help to explain the special concerns about female education.

The motives to attend the new native schools thus considerably differed from the educationalists' aim to further the 'moral and intellectual improvement' of the entire population with the help of vernacular educated mediators. 'The culture of the mother tongue', explained the BNES, 'has proved pleasing and profitable, and the road, in consequence, to intellectual and moral attainments, made plain and easy'. English lessons, on the contrary, were seen as detrimental to the 'improving' agenda of education, and not only in terms of an unintended social mobility. 'The acquisition [...] of English', the report of the BNES continued, 'has hitherto invariably tended to render a native negligent of his own vernacular dialect, and consequently, whatever knowledge he might become acquainted with through the medium of English, there was a risk of being unable to communicate it to his own countrymen and would thus have been of no use in extending mental and moral improvement amongst the natives'. As a consequence, the English school of the society later admitted students who were already proficient in Marathi or Gujarati only.[116] Robert May stopped giving English lessons after discovering that these lessons were the only motivation of his teacher training candidates to attend his central school in Chinsura.[117] Thus, the British educationalists' designs were not only confronted with the wishes of the indigenous elites who participated in the educational associations; they also had to react to parents' and students' demand for certain skills, and their lack of interest for other curricular elements. Conflicts finally resulted from the interaction with local teachers.

An interesting story about how educationalists were searching for efficient strategies and means of control can be found in the sequence of reports of the SNS. According to the 'system' suggested in the *Hints Relative to Native Schools*, the Serampore missionaries designed the curriculum, supplied the wall tables containing useful (moral and scientific) 'facts', organized a regular inspection of the schools and checked the school registers. While the work of teaching had to be done by the monitors, i. e. by the students themselves, Bengali teachers were supposed to supervise their schools and report about them (number of students attending; number of lessons learned), while other 'natives' were employed as superintendents of schools. The hope was thus to spread 'useful knowledge' with the help of agents who were unconscious of the plan they were fulfilling as they just obeyed the rules of the system. Four years later, this reliance on local teachers had appeared as a major obstacle to the effective operation of the monitorial 'machine'. The Serampore missionaries complained about the 'extreme duplicity of those who must be used as instruments of diffusing knowledge' and who undertook 'the work of teaching wholly on mercenary principles'. It is not surprising that teachers who were basically paid according to the number of their students frequently inflated this number by adding names to the lists and, when superintendents visited, gathering children who were otherwise not attending. Although understanding it in the 'differential' racist terms of 'native character', the missionaries knew the basic reason for this problem: 'Schools supported by [public] contribution, are in danger [...] of sinking into the state of small endowed schools in England, in which the Master drawing his support from a source which renders him independent of the parents of the children he instructs'.[118] This means that, based on their British experience, the missionaries were aware of the problem of the new 'rational' means to ensure teachers' accountability: the registers and inspection were not necessarily effective. The transformation of schooling from a private enterprise into a public institution implicated radical changes in the position of the teacher. Before, he was paid by the parents with money and small presents such as food and tobacco. As an agent of a school society, he not only lost control over the curriculum but also status and income. The salary was usually much lower than the support teachers used to receive from the community. This changing position of the teacher, which Krishna Kumar connected to the making of the state education system, can already be observed in the intermediary phase when voluntary associations put schooling on a public base.[119]

The question of how to ensure poorly paid teachers' accountability, combined with the problem that 'the Children [were] to follow their own inclination whether they will attend School or not',[120] made the missionaries turn to a new strategy that they termed the 'indigenous' or 'copy-book system'. This system, which was later adapted by the CSS, re-established the private support of the teachers by the parents, while at the same time providing the teachers with so-called 'scientific copy-books'. These copy-books contained the same kind of 'facts' as the compendia and wall tables suggested in the *Hints*. In contrast to usual books, they left sufficient space for the students to copy the printed sentences several times and even contained a number of empty pages to write them down again from memory. The condition for a school to receive these copy-books was that superintendents were allowed to regularly examine students. Teachers would then be paid a small reward, according to the number of 'facts' their students had committed to memory. The missionaries thus limited their expenditure per school, in order to reach more schools than before. The copy-books were intended to secure the support of the parents who would save the relatively high cost of paper for writing practice and the cooperation of the teacher in the rote learning of 'facts' was ensured by payment for results.

The ultimate end of the 'copy-book system' was the improvement of the mind and conduct of the students. The monitorial system knew two mechanisms that hoped to achieve this: forming favourable 'habits' by means of orderly and systematic arrangements, which is basically the disciplinary mechanism analysed by Foucault – targeting the body in order to reach the soul. In India, however, the users of the monitorial techniques rather relied on a second mechanism, the 'imprinting' of the mind with 'useful ideas'. This was the function assigned to the copying and rote-learning of 'rational' and 'moral' statements. Memorizing 'facts' was imagined to translate into the formation of right principles and, in turn, into a reformed way of conduct.

As examinations proved, students were indeed often successful in repeating the lessons. Memorizing and reciting the written word was not uncommon to them, as it resonated with prevalent modes of learning. However, they 'appear[ed] to feel very little interest in the glorious truths they daily commit to memory'. It is difficult to assess whether and to which extent the missionaries' 'hope [that] the instructions even as such will not be entirely lost, but that in future life, by the power of the holy spirit, they may produce fruit'[121] became true. What can be said, however, is that one unintended consequence of the installation of the copy-book system was the emergence of what Krishna Kumar has called a pedagogical culture, in which 'the text-book is the curriculum' and in which the school became associated with the rote-learning of unconnected statements which, drawn from another cultural context, had no meaning outside the classroom.

Conclusion: Tensions of Empire and the Limits of the Civilizing Mission

In the early nineteenth century, an imperial civil society movement emerged which regarded the promotion of popular schooling as the panacea for rising the scale of civilization of mankind in general as well as for the 'uplift' of particular countries. In this context protestant missionaries, supported by two influential educational associations in England and cooperating with Indian social reformers in 'Europeo-native institutions', promoted a new kind of public elementary education in India. An analysis of these educational projects can help to point out some of the ambiguities, tensions and limits of the British imperial civilizing mission.

In order to establish a new colonial social order, it seemed to be crucial to 'civilize' all colonial subjects, British as well as Indian, rich and poor, men and women; however, not all were to be 'civilized' in the same way. 'Indigent Christians' were meant to act in an intermediary position between colonizers and colonized, and they therefore received a bilingual education.

'Native schools' were supposed to disrupt the circle of 'ignorance' and 'superstition' by introducing Western science. In contrast to the East India Company, which was defining its educational policy in terms of Orientalism vs Anglicism, the non-governmental promoters of mass schooling thereby linked their social reform agenda to *vernacular* literacy.[122] The Christian education of girls, finally, appeared crucial to the re-modelling of family life according to bourgeois-evangelical standards. The universal educational mission was thus differentiated according to a complex grammar of difference, in the making of which several discursive strands interplayed. The idea of stable social 'spheres' to which people belonged according to their birth still resembled the estates of the *ancient regime*. The languages of 'race' and 'culture' as well as femininity and motherhood already pointed at the new essentialist and naturalist mode of differentiation. The role of education in this differentiated civilizing mission was to prepare students to become 'useful' in their respective spheres. Thus, the 'bounded universality' of the civilizing mission points at one of the 'basic tension[s] of Empire': 'otherness' was always unstable, and social boundaries had to be constantly re- redrawn and re-legitimized.[123]

Also the complex interactions and negotiations among the agents of the civilizing mission sometimes led to unexpected deferrals of boundaries. Although male British middle class educationalists followed agendas of colonial control, patriarchal domination and bourgeois hegemony, they could not simply implement them. Because they were dependent on a wide-range of support and cooperation, they had to cope with the agency and the particular agendas of others. To Indian social reformers and British women, the selective appropriation and re-interpretation of the civilizing mission opened spaces for negotiating their social position and 'uplift' beyond the projected scale, even if sometimes again at the cost of others.

Looking at 'tools' of the civilizing mission, it is not surprising that there was a large gap between the nearly unlimited hopes in the *perfectibilité* of subjects and societies and the actual performance of the new schools, the number of which, moreover, was restricted by want of money as well as local resistance. While the want of financial resources led the civil society educationalists to increasingly apply for state money, the confrontation with the agency and interests of teachers, parents and students produced a local variation of the monitorial system of education, in the 'machinery' of which great expectations had been set. However, it is highly questionable whether the assumed link between memorising 'facts', establishing moral principles and changing the actual conduct of the student worked as intended. The 'copy-book system' rather marked the beginning of a pedagogical culture in which rote-learning from text-books became central. Thus, the non-governmental efforts in education prepared the way for the making of a colonial education system – which is a highly relevant consequence – but did not actually change the world-views and subjectivities of the students in the intended way.[124] Such tensions between the grand imperial designs, the actual performance of the tools of social engineering and the limitations posed by severe material constraints are among the factors that led to metropolitan disappointments, the declining credibility of the promises of uplift and civilization and the shift from the ideology of an imperial civilizing mission toward social Darwinism and essentialist constructions of difference in the second half of the nineteenth century.

Acronyms

BFSS	British and Foreign School Society
BNES	Bombay Native Education Society (= Bombay Native School-book and School Society)
BMS	Baptist Missionary Society
CMS	Church Missionary Society
CSBS	Calcutta School Book Society
CSS	Calcutta School Society
LMS	London Missionary Society
LSNFE	Ladies Society for the Promotion of Native Female Education (Calcutta)
NES	National Society for the Education of the Poor in the Principles of the Established Church (= National Education Society)
SNS	Society for Native Schools (= Educational branch of the Baptist Serampore Mission)

Notes

1   L. Zastoupil and M. Moir (eds), *The Great Indian Education Debate: Documents relating to the Orientalist-Anglicist controversy, 1780–1840* (Richmond: Curzon, 1999).

2   Cf. N. Castells, 'Public Instruction and Public Justice: The Twin Faces of the East India Co.'s Civilizing Mission', in this volume; H. Fischer-Tiné, 'Vom Wissen zur Macht. Koloniale und nationale Bildungsmodelle in Britisch-Indien, ca. 1781–1920', in K. Preisedanz and D. Rothermund (eds.), *Südasien in der „Neuzeit* (Wien: Promedia, 2003), 90–112.

3   Cf. the Proceedings and Reports of the Committee for Public Instruction 1829–1832, in the India Office Records: IOR/F/4/1170/30639; IOR/F/4/1289/51641; IOR/F4/1386/55228. In Madras, Thomas Munro did not share this higher education focus, and indeed suggested to build a public school system under the auspices of the Company. After his death, however, the Bengal policy also reached Madras. Cf. R. E. Frykenburg, 'Modern Education in South India, 1784–1854: Its Roots and Its Role as a Vehicle of Integration under Company Raj', *The American Historical Review*, 91 (1986).

4 Cf. 'Fisher's memoir on Native Schools', 1826, in A. N. Basu (ed.), *Indian Education in the Parliamentary Papers, Part I (1832)* (Bombay, Calcutta: Asia Publishing House, 1952); B. T. McCully, *Indian Education and the Origins of Indian Nationalism* (Columbia University Press: 1940); S. Nurullah and J. P. Naik, *A Student's History of Education in India, 1800–1947* (Bombay: Macmillan, 1955); C. Deer, *L'Empire Britannique et l'Instruction en Inde (1780–1854)* (L'Harmattan, 2005); T. Allender, 'How the State Made and Unmade Education in the Raj, 1800–1819', in Tolley, Kim (ed.), *Transformations in Schooling. Historical and Comparative Perspectives* (New York: Palgrave Macmillan, 2007), 67–86.

5 A. D. Campbell, 'On the State of Education of the Natives in Southern India', *Transactions of the Literary Society of Madras*, 1 (1834), 350–360. Cf. Dharampal, *The Beautiful Tree. Indian Indigenous Education in the Eighteenth Century* (New Delhi: Biblia Impex Private Limited, 1983).

6 N. Kumar, *The Politics of Gender, Community, and Modernity. Essays on Education in India* (New Delhi: Oxford University Press, 2007), 29, 31. Kumar concludes this for higher education, but her observations are equally true for the field of elementary instruction. Cf. also K. Shahidullah, *Patshalas Into Schools: The Development of Indigenous Elementary Education in Bengal, 1854–1905* (Calcutta: Firma KLM, 1987).

7 M. Archer, *Social Origins of Educational Systems (University Edition)* (London et al.: Sage, 1984). Cf. also M. J. Maynes, *Schooling in Western Europe: A Social History* (Albany: State University of New York Press).

8 *The Third Report of the Proceedings of the Bombay Native Education Society: 1825–26* (Bombay: 1827), 28.

9 M. Foucault, *Discipline and Punish. The Birth of the Prison* (Vintage Books: 1995), 135–194; D. Hogan, 'The Market Revolution and Disciplinary Power: Joseph Lancaster and the Psychology of the Early Classroom System', in *History of Education Quarterly*, 3 (1989).

10 M. Caruso and E. Roldán Vera (eds), *Pluralizing Meanings: The Monitorial System of Education in Latin America in the Early Nineteenth Century*, *Paedagogica Historica* 41, no.5 (2005); P. Ressler, *Nonprofit-Marketing im Schulbereich. Britische Schulgesellschaften und der Erfolg des Bell-Lancaster-Systems der Unterrichtsorganisation im 19. Jahrhundert* (Frankfurt am Main et al.: Peter Lang, 2010); J. Schriewer and M. Caruso (eds), *Nationalerziehung und Universalmethode – frühe Formen schulorganisatorischer Globalisierung* (Leipzig: Leipziger Universitätsverlag, 2005); J. Tschurenev, *Imperial Experiments in Education. Monitorial Schooling in India, 1789–1835*, PhD thesis (Humboldt University Berlin: Comparative Education Centre, 2008).

11 F. Cooper and A. L. Stoler 'Between Metropole and Colony. Rethinking a Research Agenda', in *idem* (eds), *Tensions of Empire: Colonial Cultures in a Bourgeois World* (Berkeley et al.: University of California Press, 1997); quotes from 10, 7, 3.

12 10th *Annual Report of the British and Foreign School Society* (BFSS), 1815, 14.

13 K. Crenshaw, 'Demarginalizing the Intersection of Race and Sex: A Black Feminist Critique of Antidiscrimination Doctrine, Feminist Theory and Antiracist Politics', *University of Chicago Legal Forum* 1989: 139–167. P. Hill Collins, *Black Feminist Thought: Knowledge, Consciousness, and the Politics of Empowerment* (Boston: Unwin Hyman, 1990), 221–238; Knapp, Gudrun-Axeli, '"Intersectionality" – ein neues Paradigma der Geschlechterforschung?' in R. Casale, and B. Rendtorff (eds), *Was kommt nach der Geschlechterforschung? Zur Zukunft der feministischen Theoriebildung* (Bielefeld: Transcript, 2008), 33–53.

14 S. Seth, 'Secular Enlightenment and Christian Conversion: Missionaries and Education in Colonial India', in *Education and Social Change in South Asia*, ed. K. Kumar and

J. Oesterheld, 22–43 (Hyderabad: Orient Longman, 2007); M. A. Laird, *Missionaries and Education in Bengal, 1793–1837* (Oxford, 1972); B. Holmes (ed.), *Educational Policy and the Mission Schools. Case Studies from the British Empire* (London: Routledge and Keagan Paul, 1967). The *Missionary Register* shows that Western Africa became another focal point of missionary educational activities. Cf. also C. G. Wise, *A History of Education in British West Africa* (London et al.: Longmans, Green and Co, 1956), 1–13.

15 W. Carey, J. Marshman, and W. Ward, *The Second Report of the Institution for the Support and Encouragement of Native Schools in India* (Serampore: Mission Press, 1818), 9.

16 *Reports Connected with the Native Free Schools at Chinsurah Under the Superintendence of Mr. May, 1818*, IOR/F/4/605/15020; *Report relative to the Native Free Schools at Chinsurah. Death of Mr. R. May and appointment of Mr. Pearson to succeed as superintendent of the Schools, 1819*: IOR/F/4/617/15371.

17 *Memoir of the Rev. John James Weitbrecht, Late Missionary of the Church Missionary Society at Burdwan, in Bengal. Comprehending a History of the Burdwan Mission, Compiled from his Journal and Letters by his Widow* (London: James Nisbeth and Co., 1854); Letter from T. Thomason to W. B. Bayly (Bancoora, 5th March, 1819), reporting about his visit of the Burdwan schools, published in *Second Report of the Calcutta School Book Society* (Calcutta, 1819), 80–83.

18 H. Liebau, 'Faith and Knowledge: The Educational System of the Danish-Halle and English-Halle Mission,' in A. Gross, Y. V. Kumaradoss and H. Liebau (eds), *Halle and the Beginning of Protestant Christianity in India* (Halle: Franckesche Stiftungen, 2006), Vol. 3; *Memoir of the Rev. C. T. E. Rhenius: Comprising Extracts from his Journal and Correspondence, with Details of Missionary Proceedings in South India, by his Son* (London and Edinburgh, 1841).

19 W. Carey, J. Marshman, and W. Ward, *Hints Relative to Native Schools together with an Outline of an Institution for their Extension and Management* (Serampore: Mission Press, 1816). Extracts from this pamphlet appeared in a range of missionary publications, such as the *Missionary Register*, or the German reports of the Tranquebar Mission (*Neuere Geschichte der evangelischen Missions-Anstalten zur Bekehrung der Heiden in Ostindien*), as well as in the reports of the *British and Foreign School Society*. C. S. John, 'On Indian Civilization', *Missionary Register* (1813), 369–84. This text was also published and repeatedly referred to in the above-named reports.

20 This paper is primarily based on a reading of reports, programmatic texts and published correspondence of the organizations named above, most important being the BFSS, BMS, SNS, and CSBS as well as the *Missionary Register*. For the 'Europeo-native institutions' cf. also N. L. Basak 'Origin and Role of the Calcutta School Book Society in Promoting the Cause of Education in India, especially Vernacular Education in Bengal (1817–1835)', in *Bengal Past and Present* (1959), 30–69.

21 J. Osterhammel, '"The Great Work of Uplifting Mankind". Zivilisierungsmissionen und Moderne', in B. Barth, and Osterhammel (eds), *Zivilisierungsmissionen* (Konstanz: UVK, 2005), 363–425.

22 Mill, James, *Schools for All, in Preference to School for Churchmen Only: or, the State of the Controversy Between the Advocates for the Lancasterian System of Universal Education, and Those, who Have Set up an Exclusive and Partial System Under the Name of the Church and Dr. Bell,* London, 1812; reprint ed. by J. Stern (Bristol: Thoemmes Press, 1995).

23 There are numerous references to the 'cause of universal instruction / education' in the introductory remarks to the early annual reports of the BFSS; for the gender issue cf. 16th Annual Report of the BFSS, 1821, 34.

24 Letter from W. H. Pearce, one of the Secretaries of the CSS, to G. Forbes, a Member of its Committee (August 29th, 1819), in 2nd Report of the CSBS, 83.

25 J. Foster, *An Essay on the Evils of Popular Ignorance* (London, 1820).

26 J. D. Pearson, *The British System of Education as Adapted to Native Schools in India* (Calcutta: Mission Press, 1830), 51.

27 K. Jones and K. Williamson, 'The Birth of the Schoolroom. A Study of the Transformation in the Discursive Conditions of English Popular Education in the First-half of the Nineteenth Century,' *Ideology and Consciousness*, 19 (1979): 63, 71.

28 Lancaster, Joseph, *Improvements in Education, as It Respects the Industrious Classes of the Community: Containing, a Short Account of Its Present State, Hints Towards Its Improvement, and a Detail of Some Practical Experiments Conducive to That End* (London, 1803).

29 In the *Calcutta Review* II (4), 142: 301–376, Alexander Duff reviewed William Adam's 2nd and 3rd Reports on the State of Education in Bengal and Behar, 1836 and 1838. At p. 321, Duff is affirmatively quoting Adam's critique of the teaching methods adopted by the village teachers.

30 3rd Report of the BNES (1827), 19–20; 'Proceedings prior to the final Establishment of the Society &c.,' Annex XIV to the 2nd Report of the CSBS, 67–74.

31 A. Bell, *An Experiment in Education, Made at the Male Asylum at Madras, Suggesting a System by Which a School or Family May Teach Itself Under the Superintendence of the Master or the Parent* (London, 1797), v, 9.

32 Lancaster, *Improvements in Education*.

33 There has been some discussion on the 'Indian origin' of the monitorial system of education. B. K. Sarkar proudly emphasized 'England's debt to India in Pedagogy'. (The Futurism of Young Asia and other essays on the relations between the East and the West, Berlin, J. Springer, 1922, 146). Nurullah and Naik followed this line of interpretation – the British 'imported' the monitorial system from India – in their *Student's History*. However, as I have argued elsewhere, the knowledge flows connected to the monitorial system were much more complex. Bell's colonial 'experiment,' drawing from Tamil pedagogical practises as well as from Scottish enlightenment ideas and a variety of other sources, was then transformed in the metropole into a standardised pedagogical method, again in combination with other sources. J. Tschurenev, 'Diffusing Useful Knowledge: The Monitorial System of Education in Madras, London and Bengal, 1789 – 1840', *Paedagogica Historica* XLIV (3), 2008; idem. *Imperial Experiments in Education*, 28–53.

34 A. Bell, *Instructions for Conducting a School* (London, 1808), p. 3; Pearson, *British System*, 21.

35 Foucault, *Discipline and Punish*, 135–194; Jones and Williamson, 'Birth', 73–78; P. Miller, 'Worlds of Social Control: Civilizing the Masterless Poor', in her *Transformations of Patriarchy in the West, 1500–1900* (Indianapolis: Bloomington, 1998), 143–182.

36 J. Bowen, *The Modern West Europe and the New World* (A History of Western Education Vol. 3) (London: Methuen, 1981).

37 Cf. Jones and Williamson, 'Birth', 71; Bell, *Experiment*, 32. Religion was at the core of the curriculum in the 'British' as well as the 'National' schools with the difference only in a non-denominational or Anglican orientation. It must be kept in mind that although schooling became disconnected from the Church, education and knowledge were still being understood in religious terms by many of the philanthropic educationalists.

38 Marshman, Carey and Ward, *Hints Relative to Native Schools*, p. 19. The aspect of 'adaptation' to local needs is stressed by several users of the monitorial system in Bengal; cf. Pearson, *British System*, v; 2nd report of the CSBS (1819), 94.

39 Marshman, Carey and Ward, 2nd Report of the SNS (1818), 4.

40 'An Appeal, particularly to Churchmen, on the duty of propagating the Gospel', in *Missionary Register* (1813), 1–11.

41 A. Fuller, 'Extract from a Sermon on behalf of the BFSS,' in 10th Annual Report of the BFSS (1815), 66.

42 Cf. R. L. Meek, *Social Science and the Ignoble Savage* (Cambridge: Cambridge University Press, 1976), 1–4; 160–173; J. Goodman, 'Languages of Female Colonial Authority: the educational network of the Ladies committee of the British and Foreign School Society, 1813–37', in *Compare* 30, 1 (2000): 7–19.

43 Mill, James, *History of British India* (London 1840), 4th edition, Vol. V, 541.

44 Marshman, Carey and Ward, *Hints*, 7–9.

45 This had also a problematic component: Foster, in his *Essay*, feared, that England could also lose its leading position, if the government would not solve the problem of the degraded state of ignorance of the population.

46 14th Annual Report of the BFSS (1819), 27 (emphasis in the original).

47 13th Annual Report of the BFSS (1818), 32; 12th Annual Report of the BFSS (1817), 39.

48 W. Ward, *Farewell Letters to a few Friends in Britain and America, on Returning to Bengal in 1821* (London: Black, Kingsbury, Oarbury & Allen, 1821), 84, quoted in C. Midgley, 'Female Emancipation in an Imperial Frame: English women and the campaign against sati (widow-burning) in India, 1813–30', *Women's History Review* 9, no. 1 (2000), 100.

49 C. Hall has traced the discursive shift from 'educability' to biological racism and linked it to important events in the colonies, such as the 'mutiny'. (*Civilizing Subjects*, Oxford, Polity Press, 2002).

50 A. Bell, Postscript to the 2nd edition of his *Experiment*, 1805.

51 Marshman, Carey and Ward, *Hints*, 11.

52 John, 'On Indian Civilization', 374, 380.

53 C. F. Kaestle, '"Between the Scylla of Brutal Ignorance and the Charybdis of a Literary Education": Elite Attitudes toward Mass Schooling in Early Industrial England and America', in L. Stone (ed.), *Schooling and Society* (Baltimore and London: John Hopkins University Press, 1976), 177–191.

54 Bell, *Experiment*, 7–8.

55 A table giving the parentage of Bell's students in 1794 includes (as the children of privates): 39% illegitimate children of Indian mothers; 38% legitimate children of Indian mothers; 21% legitimate children of European mothers; 2% not given. 'Register of Boys on the Foundation of the Male Asylum for 1794,' quoted in P. McCann, 'The Indian Origins of Bell's Monitorial System,' in P. Cunningham and C. Brock, eds., *International Currents in Education. Proceedings of the 1987 Annual Conference of the History of Education Society of Great Britain held jointly with the British Comparative and International Education Society* (1988), 33.

56 Annual Reports of the Benevolent Institution for the Instruction of Indigent Christians in Calcutta, Serampore, 1810–1830; cf. also G. F. Bartle, 'The Role of the British and Foreign School Society in Elementary Education in India and the East Indies 1813–1875', in *History of Education*, 23 (1994): 17–33.

57 Cf., H. Fischer-Tiné, *'Low and Licentious Europeans': Race, Class and 'White Subalternity'* in *Colonial India* (New Delhi: Orient Longman, 2009); T. Hubel, 'In Search of the British Indian in British India: White Orphans, Kipling's Kim, and Class in Colonial India', in *Modern Asian Studies* 38 (2004): 227–251. The category of 'indigence' became a focal point of the metropolitan regime of governing poverty around 1800; cf.,

P. Colquhoun, *A Treatise on Indigence* (London, 1806); D. Mitchell, *The Constitution of Poverty, Toward a Genealogy of Liberal Governance* (London et al.: Routledge, 1991).

58 Cooper and Stoler, 'Between Metropole and Colony'. Cf. A. L. Stoler, *Race and the Education of Desire* (Durham and London: Duke University Press, 1995).

59 C. J. Hawes, *Poor Relations. The Making of a Eurasian Community in British India 1773–1833* (Curzon, 1996); D. Arnold, 'European Orphans and Vagrants in India in the Nineteenth Century', *The Journal of Imperial and Commonwealth History* VII (1979): 104–128; H. Fischer-Tiné, 'Britain's other Civilizing Mission: Class-prejudice, European "Loaferism" and the Workhouse System in Colonial India' in *Indian Economic and Social History Review* 3 (2005): 295–338.

60 Bell, *Experiment*, 6–7.

61 Report Relative to the Benevolent Institution (1812), 3.

62 Report Relative to the Benevolent Institution (1816), 5–6.

63 Report Relative to the Benevolent Institution (1813), 9–10.

64 Report Relative to the Benevolent Institution (1812), 4; (1813), 5. Most of the children admitted were not living in 'orderly' households; in many cases, their fathers were either unknown, had already died, or left the family. The children were either supported by mothers, most of them working as servants, or by poor relatives. A considerable number of children lived 'on charity' or as beggars on the streets. Many of them were 'Portuguese' Catholics.

65 W. Carey, J. Marshman and W. Ward, *The First Report of the Institution for the Encouragement of Native Schools in India* (Serampore, 1817), 40.

66 Report Relative to the Benevolent Institution (1817), 9.

67 'Abstract of Reports on Native Education in India', *Missionary Register* (1819), 102–121; 2nd Report of the CSBS (1819), 80–83; 5th AR Bombay Education Society (1820).

68 Carey, Marshman and Ward, *Hints*, 7, 11–13.

69 In the field of higher education, Gauri Viswanathan has analysed a similar process of substitution. The classical curriculum of the grammar schools and the old universities of Oxford and Cambridge did not suit the plans of British educationalists in India. Searching for means to gain cultural hegemony, they turned to English literature, long before this was established in the curricula in Britain itself. Cf. *Masks of Conquest. Literary Studies and British Rule in India* (London: Faber and Faber, 1990).

70 S. Sivasundaram, *Nature and the Godly Empire* (Cambridge: Cambridge University Press, 2005). Recent research in the history of the Tranquebar mission has shown the same connection between missionary and scientific activity. Cf. A. Gross, Y. V. Kumaradoss and H. Liebau (eds), *Halle and the Beginning of Protestant Christianity in India* (Halle: Franckesche Stiftungen, 2006).

71 Carey, Marshman and Ward, *Hints*, 13–16. W. Ward, *A View of the History, Literature, and Mythology of the Hindoos: Including a Minute Description of their Manners and Customs, and Translations from their Principal Works*, Vol. I (London: Kingsbury, Parbury and Allen, 1822).

72 Carey, Marshman and Ward, *Hints*, 14.

73 *Ibid.*, 19–24.

74 *Ibid.*, 13.

75 Carey, Marshman and Ward, 1st Report of the SNS, 39–40.

76 *Ibid.*, 41.

77 W. Carey, J. Marshman and W. Ward, *The Third Report of the Institution for the Support and Encouragement of Native Schools in India* (Serampore, 1820), 3.

78 The climate theory employed by the Serampore missionaries established the link between climate, mode of subsistence, and culture in a very general sense. This contrasts with more 'physical' theories, which assume direct effects of climate on 'energy' or bodily strength. This line can be followed from Montesquieu's *De L'esprit des Loix* (Genève, 1748) to the 'science' of 'Ethno-Climatology', which was formulated in the later nineteenth century. Cf. J. Hunt, 'On Ethno-Climatology; or the Acclimatization of Men', in *Transactions of the Ethnological Society of London*, II (1863), 50–83.

79 Carey, Marshman and Ward, 1ˢᵗ Report of the SNS, 41.

80 S. Hall, 'The Multi-Cultural Question', in B. Hesse (ed.), *Un/settled Multiculturalisms. Diasporas. Entanglements. Disruptions* (London: Zed, 2001), 216. Also other scholars have demonstrated how racism was sometimes 'cultural' – as in the case of the Serampore missionaries – before it turned into the biological register and that both variants easily slip into each other. Cf. C. Hall, Introduction to *Civilizing Subjects*; W. D. Hundt, *Negative Vergesellschaftung. Dimensionen der Rassismusanalyse* (Münster: Westfälisches Dampfboot, 2006).

81 10ᵗʰ Annual Report of the BFSS (June 1815), viii (emphasis in the original).

82 Report Relative to the Benevolent Institution (1816), 11–12. This school, from the beginning, had a strong female branch.

83 10ᵗʰ Annual Report of the BFSS (1815), iix.

84 *Ibid.*

85 16ᵗʰ Annual Report of the BFSS (1821), 25–26.

86 Report Relative to the Benevolent Institution (1813), 8.

87 Goodman, 'Languages of Female Colonial Authority', 17.

88 'Call on British Females', in *Missionary Register* (1815), 397–400.

89 Midgley, 'Female Emancipation in an Imperial Frame'. A number of scholars have discussed the connection of the abolition of 'suttee' with the British civilizing mission. Among them, the arguments of G. C. Spivak ('Can the Subaltern Speak?', in C. Nelson and L. Grossberg (eds), *Marxism and the Interpretation of Culture* (Urbana: University of Illinois Press, 1988), pp. 271–313) and L. Mani (*Contentious Traditions. The Debate on Sati in Colonial India* (University of California Press, 1998)) have been most widely received. Cf. J. Tschurenev, 'Between Non-interference in Matters of Religion and Civilizing Mission: The Prohibition of *Suttee* in 1829', in H. Fischer-Tiné and M. Mann (eds), *Colonialism as Civilizing Mission* (London: Anthem Press, 2004).

90 'Appeal on behalf of the Native Females of British India' in *Missionary Register* (1820), 433–435.

91 For the Indian context, the issues of a 'hidden agenda' and the connection between education and the (re-)production of social stratification have been discussed, among others, by the contributors to S. Bhattacharya (ed.) *The Contested Terrain. Perspectives on Education in India* (Orient Longman: 1998); cf. also N. Crook (ed.), *The Transmission of Knowledge in South Asia* (Delhi, 1996).

92 Cf. S. Trimmer, *A Comparative View of Education Promulgated by Mr. Joseph Lancaster, in his Tracts concerning the Instruction of the Children of the Labouring Part of the community; and of the System of Christian Education founded by our pious Forefathers for the Initiation of the Young Members of the Established Church in the Principles of the Reformed Religion* (London: Rivingtons, 1805); J. Fox, *A Scriptural Education the Glory of England: Being a Defense of the Lancastrian Plan of Education, and the Bible Society, in Answer to the Publications of the Rev. C. Daubeny, Archdeacon of Sarum, the Rev. Dr. Wordsworth, the Rev. Mr. Spry &c. &c,*(London: Royal Free School Press, 1810).

93 Miller, *Transformations of Patriarchy in the West*, 224–5.

94 S. Sarkar, 'Orientalism Revisited: Saidian Frameworks in the Writing of Modern Indian History', in *The Oxford Literary Review* 16, 1–2 (1994): 205–224.

95 *Missionary Register* (1813), 10–11.

96 'Call on British Females,' in *Missionary Register* (1815), 397–400.

97 'Appeal on behalf of the Native Females of British India' in *Missionary Register* (1820), 433–435.

98 Cf., Goodman, 'Languages of Female Colonial Authority'; C. Midgley, 'Can Women Be Missionaries? Envisioning Female Agency in the Early Nineteenth-Century British empire', *Journal of British Studies*, 45 (2006): 335–358.

99 Cf. *The first Report of the Ladies' Association for Native Female Education in Calcutta* (Calcutta: Church Mission Press, 1826). This society, chaired by Mrs Wilson (neé Mary Ann Cooke) supervised a network of Bengali girl's schools that had been connected to the CMS before. Another example for an independent, female-run association was the *Society for Promoting Female Education in China, India, and the East*, that took over tasks started by the *Ladies' Committees of the BFSS* in 1834. Cf. Midgley, 'Can women be missionaries', 339.

100 Cf. P. Chapman, *Hindoo Female Education* (London, 1839). Another important imperial educator, Hannah Kilham, also corresponded with and connected her work to the BFSS. Cf. Ferguson, 'Hannah Kilham'; A. Twells, '"Let Us Begin well at Home": Class, Ethnicity, and Christian Motherhood in the Writings of Hannah Kilham, 1774–1832' in E. J. Yeo (ed.), *Radical Feminity: Women's Self-Representation in the Public Sphere* (Manchester, 1998), 25–51.

101 Cf. C. Midgley, *Feminism and Empire. Women Activists in Imperial Britain, 1790–1865* (Routledge, 2007); idem (ed.) *Gender and Imperialism* (Manchester: Manchester University Press, 1998).

102 Tyrrell, Ian (1991): *Woman's World, Woman's Empire. The Woman's Christian Temperance Union in International Perspective, 1880 – 1930* (Chapel Hill: University of North Carolina Press), 5.

103 'Proceedings prior to the final Establishment of the Society, &c.', Appendix XIV in the 2nd report of the CSBS, p. 69; cf. also Basak, 'Origin and Role', 32–35 (emphasis orig.).

104 The reports published on account of the Benevolent Institution, the SNS as well as the CSBS include reports a considerable number of Bengali names among the subscribers. Also Robert May found generous patrons for several of his schools.

105 B. Hatcher, *Idioms of Improvement: Vidyasagar and Cultural Encounter in Bengal* (OUP 1996), 7–19.

106 T. Bhattacharya, *The Sentinels of Culture: Class, Education, and the Colonial Intellectual in Bengal* (OUP 2005).

107 Sen, *Scientific and Technical Education in India, 1781–1900* (New Delhi, 1991), 115–121; 2nd Report of the CSBS, especially 31–33, 97–100.

108 Speech delivered at the 16th Anniversary of the BFSS; cf. *Missionary Register* (1821), 197.

109 Bartle, 'Role', 20–21.

110 Nita Kumar suggests differentiating between three kinds of educational practices: formal teaching, apprenticeship, and mothering, whereby only the first one has been recognized as education by colonial observers. Cf. *Politics of Gender, Community, and Modernity*, 99–124.

111 D. Chakrabarty, 'The Difference-Deferral of a Colonial Modernity. Public Debates in Domesticity in British Bengal', in Cooper and Stoler, *Tensions of Empire*, pp. 373–403; M. Waligora, 'Empire and the Invention of a New Feminity. India and Europe in the Second Half of the Nineteenth Century', in *Südasien-Informationen* 12 (2007) [http:// www.suedasien.info/schriftenreihe/1763].

112 *The first Report of the Ladies' Association for Native Female Education in Calcutta* (Calcutta: Church Mission Press, 1826), 5.

113 Cf. J. Habermas, *Strukturwandel der Öffentlichkeit* (Frankfurt am Main: Suhrkamp, 1990 [1962]); N. Fraser, 'Rethinking the Public Sphere. A Contribution to the Critique of Actually Existing Democracy', in her *Justice interruptus. Critical reflections on the "postsocialist" condition* (New York: Routledge, 1997), 69–98.

114 For England, Thomas Laqueur has pointed out that working class demand was of crucial importance in the expansion and transformation of elementary education in early nineteenth century. T. Laqueur, 'Working-class demand and the growth of English elementary education, 1750–1850', in Stone, *Schooling and Society*, 192–205.

115 Cf. K. Kumar, *Political Agenda of Education: A Study of Colonialist and Nationalist Ideas* (New Delhi: Sage, 1991), 47–70.

116 3rd Report of the BNES (1827), 20; 22–24.

117 Report from Robert May (10 Oct 1816) in *Reports Connected with the Native Free Schools at Chinsurah*.

118 Carey, Marshman and Ward, 3rd Report of the SNS, 4–5.

119 Kumar, *Political Agenda of Education*, 47–70.

120 Report from Robert May (4 July 1815) in *Reports Connected with the Native Free Schools at Chinsurah*.

121 Letter by Reverend Addis, stationed at Tranvancore, reporting in *Quarterly Extracts of the Correspondence of the British and Foreign School Society*, 16 (1830).

122 Elaborating on a classificatory scheme suggested by Brian Hatcher, the missionaries were 'evangelical vernacularists' – which is true for Bengal, as well as for the Tranquebar Mission in the cases of Tamil and Telugu – while the 'Europeo-native institutions' followed an improving vernacularist approach; Cf. *Idioms of Improvement*, 45–60.

123 Cooper and Stoler, 'Between Metropole and Colony', 3–7.

124 Cf. S. Seth, *Subject Lessons: The Western Education of Colonial India* (Durham, London: Duke University Press 2007), 32; Tschurenev, *Imperial Experiments in Education*, 186–216.

Chapter Four

RECLAIMING SAVAGES IN 'DARKEST ENGLAND' AND 'DARKEST INDIA': THE SALVATION ARMY AS TRANSNATIONAL AGENT OF THE CIVILIZING MISSION

Harald Fischer-Tiné

'What, then, is my scheme? It is a very simple one, although in its ramifications and extensions it embraces the whole world'
—William Booth, *In Darkest England and the Way Out*, London, 1890

Introduction

It is by now a well established fact that transnational interaction and communication on a global scale is by no means a recent phenomenon. According to prominent historians, such as C. A. Bayly and Jürgen Osterhammel, the intensity of globalizing processes in modern times had reached a first peak by the end of the nineteenth century.[1] As they persuasively demonstrate, this holds true not only for the economic, political, and cultural level, but also for the emerging religious and philanthropic organizations that could be seen as forerunners of today's INGOs.[2] Some scholars have argued that this new type of internationalism carried by organizations and agents belonging to the realm of the civil society was important inasmuch as it was able to 'challenge state power',[3] and emphasize its inherent aspirations 'to a more peaceful and stable world order through transnational efforts'.[4]

Building on Kathleen Wilson's important insight showing that the British Empire provides us with a particularly striking example of interdependent sites that 'allow us to rethink the [...] historiographies of national belonging and exclusion',[5] the present case study tries to question such an hypothesis by analyzing the ideology as well as the practical endeavors of one of the most successful global philanthropic movements in a transnational context: the Salvation Army. Founded as a modest lay-missionary organization in 1878 in England, the Salvation Army was represented in more than 30 states by 1910. It entertained a flourishing network of schools, hospitals, reformatories, factories, publishing houses and other institutions almost all over the globe and was particularly conspicuous in British colonies and dominions. Complementing and partly challenging previous work that tended to study the movement in isolation, either in Western – mostly British and American[6] – or non-Western contexts,[7] I want to stress the close interrelation between the metropolitan and the imperial (and eventually global) dimensions of the Salvation Army's work that mutually influenced and informed each other in significant ways.[8] I argue that – in both arenas – the organization was engaged in projects that can be aptly described as civilizing missions. Mainly focusing on the Army's activities in Britain and British India, I would like to show that:

First, even when the Army's activities were largely confined to British or other European theatres, the epistemological base of Salvationist ideology was significantly shaped by what has been described as 'imperial technologies of knowledge-gathering'.[9] Britain's urban poor, the prime targets of the organization's reclamation activities, were constructed as 'heathens' or 'savages' in a rhetoric borrowing heavily from colonial surveys and imperial travel writing. It is evident that extra-European points of reference had become commonplace in late Victorian public debates, in a manner that led ultimately to the convergence of exclusionary discourses of 'class' and 'race'. Consequently, the Salvationists proclaimed a civilizing mission designed to bring about the moral purification and material uplift of both the domestic and colonial 'savages'.

Second, apart from this ideological entanglement, the movement's imperial dimension became very concretely visible in its scheme to eradicate urban poverty in Britain. The Army's program of Social Salvation was conceived on a global scale, as one of its features was the emigration of unemployed plebeian elements of British society to overseas colonies. Thus, not only the epistemological 'tools of empire' but also its infrastructure and the practical possibilities it offered were very much present in public debates and shaped what can, from that point on, no longer merely be called a metropolitan discourse.

Third, in the beginning, the Salvation Army had to cope with official suspicion, in the United Kingdom as well as in the British colonies and various other countries. During the first two or three decades after its inception it acted not only without any support from the state but often suffered outright repression by the state authorities. However, an exploration of the Indian example shows that the state attitude changed as soon as it was realized that the Salvation Army could be used as a helpful tool to control and 'reform' segments of the population that were deemed dangerous. Within a few decades, the role of the organization changed fundamentally. From being denounced as troublemakers raising the concern of the colonial administration, the Salvationists had been transformed into guardians of the empire by the second decade of the twentieth century. They supported the colonial state in various important projects concerned with inculcating 'civility' into the native population, thereby spreading the British/European standard of civilization[10] into a corner of the world regarded as half-civilized at best. Meanwhile, and arguably not entirely unconnected to its imperial usefulness, the organization had also won respectability at home after initially being attacked for decades from various constituencies including, as previously mentioned, government officials. One result of the eventual recognition by the establishment was that it could extend its services to other colonies and dominions of the British Empire and thus became a truly imperial force, active all over the globe.

The Emergence of Salvationism in Mid-Victorian England

Changing Religious Landscapes

The Salvation Army was a typical product of the economic, social, and intellectual cataclysms that took place in mid- and late Victorian England. The processes of industrialization and urbanization, with their endemic features of hunger, housing problems and unemployment had created two nations, not only in social and economic but also in religious terms.[11] They had alienated many members of the lower strata of British Society from the Church of England and even partly from the nonconformist sects, which had been very popular among the working classes in the eighteenth and early nineteenth centuries. The fact that the popularity of the conventional type of organized Christianity was 'receding in unprecedented rapidity'[12] became evident in the nationwide religious census conducted in 1851 that unmistakably showed 'how absolutely insignificant a proportion'[13] of the congregations was composed of members of the urban labouring classes. As a result, a whole wave of evangelist groups and individuals embarked on what became known as the Home Mission Movement from the late 1850s onward. It was their avowed aim to save Christianity – already under siege on a different level through the spread of scientific modes of explaining the world and man's place in it[14] – from further decline by reaching out for the working classes.

The Salvation Army has to be seen in the broader context of this religious revivalism that aimed to create a 'middle of the road Christianity', whose middle-class values could be adapted lower on the social scale. Conversion thus had not only a religious significance, it could also be used to contain a labouring population that – in the eyes of many upper-class observers – had grown more and more 'unruly', 'degenerate' and 'dangerous' by the 1880s.[15] That the process of downward diffusion of middle-class values through a large-scale re-Christianization was regarded as a viable method to counter such threats can be gathered from the report of a Salvationist officer dating from the 1890s. He observes with obvious relief that '[c]onversion has a wonderful effect on a man; he is very soon decently clothed; his home becomes better, and, although he remains a working man, outwardly he might pass with the clerks'.[16] New techniques of organization, mobilization and recruitment were used to convey this double message of spiritual and social uplift, and traditional congregational religion was being increasingly supported (and sometimes replaced) by large-scale public organizations combining religious interests with an agenda of social reform.[17] The Salvation Army was perhaps the most successful and doubtlessly the most original of these newly emerging bodies.

William Booth and the Rise and Growth of Aggressive Christianity

For what was to become a global movement, Salvationism had astonishingly narrow local origins. The movement's founder William Booth (1829–1912), originated from a humble working class family in Nottingham.[18] At the age of 15 he underwent a religious conversion experience and came under the influence of Methodism. He served for several years as a minister for a Methodist sect before he declared his independence in the early 1860s. Nonetheless, Methodism seems to have influenced his religious teachings in at least two important ways. His rather simplistic belief that eternal damnation was the inescapable fate of the unconverted that went in tandem with a strong conviction that personal salvation was possible in this world only due to the grace of the holy spirit, certainly bore traits of Wesleyan teaching. Undoubtedly his strong social commitment and concern for the 'poor and degraded' also has moorings in this tradition.[19] It was the combination of both factors that made him eventually settle down in the capital and found the East London Christian Mission in 1865.[20] After two years of preaching in tents or open air, a permanent headquarter of his mission was established in the Eastern Star, formerly a 'low drinking saloon'[21] on Whitechapel Road. This choice of place is significant, as the environs of Whitechapel were already infamous for being one of the most disreputable areas in the 'heart of the empire' even before they acquired Jack-the-Ripper-fame.[22] The symbolic message was unambiguous: in England – as in India later on – the outcasts of society were the main addressees of the Army's proselytizing.

From the very beginning William Booth and his wife Catherine, who played an important role in the movement and was later given the honorary title 'Mother of the Salvation Army',[23] made use of the print media to disseminate their message – a feature it shared with countless other modern religious movements and organizations all over the globe.[24] In addition to the impressive number of pamphlets that Booth had circulated from the inception of his career as a *homme public*, the *East London Evangelist* was published from 1868 as the first regular journal of his movement. Several other periodicals including the *Salvationist* (1878) and *The War Cry* (1879) – that was to become its most important mouthpiece – followed later. In spite of the extensive use of the mass-media available at the time,[25] the organization's rate of growth remained humble during the first decade of its existence. It was only during the years 1878–1880 that a major shift in matters of internal organization, strategy and public appearance changed the course of its history: the 'mission to the heathens of London'[26] became a quasi-military organization and was renamed Salvation Army. William Booth appointed himself as its General and introduced the complete range of military ranking for his fellow-Salvationists. The Army's brass bands parading through the streets of poorer urban quarters, together with the uniforms[27] and flags soon became one of the most powerful symbols of the restyled voluntary organization.

The adoption of military uniforms, terminology, music and modes of organization reflected an important broader tendency in late Victorian intellectual and religious life: a growing militarization.[28] Interestingly, the ground for this change of attitudes had partly been prepared by geopolitical developments of the 1850s, when the British Empire was shaken by the almost simultaneous outbreaks of the Crimean War and the Indian 'Mutiny'.[29] The feelings of vulnerability and anxiety provoked by these conflicts that involved heavy losses of life on the side of the British, also led to a subtle change in religious sensibilities. Traditional concepts of peacefulness and piety slowly gave way to ideals of aggressive self-assertion and missionary activities of which the conspicuous popularity of military rhetoric and imagery in Christian circles is but one index. As Peter Van der Veer and others have argued, the new concept of 'muscular Christianity', propagated by influential literary and public figures like Thomas Hughes and Charles Kingsley, must also be seen in this wider imperial connection.[30]

One result of these masculinizing tendencies was a widespread enthusiasm for the figure of the soldier-saint, construed as a defender of the faith who was pious and yet strong, godly and virile. By the middle of the 1860s, the phrase 'Christian soldier' was becoming commonplace as warrior-like qualities seemed to be best fitted to spread Christianity in an age regarded as godless and impious. This was not only obvious in the case of missionary work in Britain's various colonies that was pursued with renewed zeal from mid-nineteenth century onward,[31] but also in the crusade to win over the 'heathens' in the metropolis. In a seminal pamphlet, Catherine Booth justified the militarization of the former East London Christian Mission with the simple argument:

> [I]f you can't get them in by civil measures, use military measures. Go and COMPEL them to come in. It seems to me that we want more of this determined aggressive spirit. [...] Verily, we must make them look – tear the bandages off, open their eyes, make them bear it, and if they run away from you in one place, meet them in another, and let them have no peace until they submit to God and get their souls saved. This is what Christianity ought to be doing in this land.[32]

The advantages of an autocratic, army-like style of leadership for a religious outfit are outlined in even clearer terms by General Booth in a manual that was modeled after the British Army's 'soldiers' pocket-book and handed out to every new 'cadet'. After denouncing the uselessness of any democratic system of church government[33] Booth pointed out that:

> Only with this absolute power over men can there be regularity. [...] [W]ith people who are always under the same control, it is possible, no matter who the officer may be, for the services to be continued day after day, and year after year, without a break or hitch. This is militarism – a settled, absolute, regular system of using men to accomplish a common settled purpose.[34]

It was precisely the high degree of organization and discipline achieved through this 'militarism' that transformed the former 'Christian mission' into an authoritarian 'imperial structure'[35] able to 'overcome, conquer, subdue [and] compel all nations [...] to become the disciples of the son of god'[36] that later on made it an attractive partner for the common settled purpose of 'reforming' segments of the population viewed as degenerate and dangerous both in the metropolis and in the outposts of the empire.[37] Quite obviously, this scheme also fit in perfectly well with late Victorian society's more general obsession with regularity and national efficiency.[38] Whereas the attainment of a more effective style of leadership was thus the main goal of the organizational aspect of militarization[39] the expected results of its outward elements – the adoption of uniforms and other army paraphernalia – was threefold. First it was expected simply to 'attract attention'. Second, it was calculated to 'excite respect in the rowdy population'[40] whose souls were the prime targets of the Army's religious zeal. Third, it was supposed to clearly demarcate the Salvationists from other Christian missionaries, making them distinguishable as a lay civil society organization that had nothing in common with the established churches. The latter point is significant insofar as it did indeed appeal to the members of the working classes, many of whom were, as we have already noticed, strongly prejudiced against the congregational versions of Christianity.

Whichever aspect may have been decisive, the restructuring along military lines doubtlessly was a tremendous success. From the 31 branches existing in 1878 the movement's strength grew to 519 branches (now called corps) all over the United Kingdom by 1883.[41] In the following decades the Army's rise across Britain steadily continued, though at a somewhat slower pace: there were 1,507 corps by 1890 and 1,557 by 1900.[42] These impressive figures could easily mislead one to believe that the Army's growth was a neat and uncomplicated success story. Quite the reverse is true. From the outset, the Salvationists' catchy methods of spreading their gospel provoked what one author has called 'Salvophobism':[43] fierce opposition from various quarters.[44] Young workers formed skeleton armies and disturbed the public sermons and procession of the Christian revivalists. The clergy of the Church of England and other established denominations were often hostile, and the local authorities frequently regarded the zealous revivalists as troublemakers and had them arrested. It was only after the organization became significantly engaged in social service and philanthropic activities from the 1890s onward that things began slowly to change. By the turn of the century, the Army was increasingly recognized in official circles as an efficient agent of both social reform and social control.[45] George Bernard Shaw even saw it as a 'sort of auxiliary police' as it was 'taking off the insurrectionary edge of poverty'[46] thus 'preserv[ing] the country from mob-violence and revolution'.[47] The newly acquired official acclaim became most apparent in two symbolic acts. In 1904 General Booth was received by King Edward VII, and three years later he was even awarded an honorary doctorate from Oxford University.[48] Thus, by the end of the first decade of the twentieth century, there could no longer be a doubt about it: Salvationism had gone mainstream.

Long before such recognition by the establishment was even imaginable, the international expansion of the movement had begun. As early as 1880 the first branches were opened in other countries, by 1910 the Salvationists had 'seeded themselves'[49] in more than 30 countries (including British colonial territories)[50] and by the 1930s the movement had become an almost universal force, entertaining branches in 41 countries and territories spanning five continents.[51] Before we look more closely at the Army's actual activities overseas, it is worth exploring the ideological base of its social and philanthropic work in the metropolis, which eventually made the organization respectable in official circles. An analysis of this discursive dimension also demonstrates the importance of global (mostly colonial or exotic) metaphors and points of reference. On the basis of the conspicuous presence of imperial rhetoric in the core texts produced by leading figures of the Salvation movement, I would suggest reading the Army as a colonizing agency within the boundaries of the United Kingdom.

The Imperial Mission within 'Darkest England' and the Tools of Empire

In the first decade after the foundation of the Salvation Army, the organization's religious objective – 'saving' as many souls as possible – seems to have clearly outweighed its ambitions for social reform.[52] Soon it became evident that the targeted *Lumpen* elements of urban society would be hard to convince in terms of focusing their attention on their spiritual 'sanctification'[53] whilst they had to struggle with their utter material distress. Social reform thus appeared to be the first necessary step to realize the more ambitious goal of the 'the devil's children's'[54] spiritual regeneration.

The publication of William Booth's[55] controversial book *From Darkest England and the Way Out* in 1890 reflects this reorientation toward the material needs of the 'submerged tenth' of England's population.[56] *In Darkest England* is today rightly regarded as a classic of Victorian reform literature. Apart from being a tremendous commercial success (more than 300,000 copies were sold within one and a half years after its release),[57] the book provoked a vibrant public debate about poverty, philanthropy and the responsibilities of civil society, involving such prominent intellectuals as T. H. Huxley and George Bernard Shaw.[58] In spite of the fact that Booth focuses on England – almost all the examples he gives are taken from the London poor – the arguments brought forward in the book and in the ensuing debate reveal not only the omnipresence of imperial points of reference, they also show the extent to which Victorians were used to thinking in a global framework. The catchy title itself is a perfect illustration for this point. It capitalizes on the popularity of a book written by one of Britain's imperial heroes, brought out shortly before Booth's manifesto appeared: Henry Morton Stanley's *In Darkest Africa*.[59] Whereas Stanley describes his expedition through Central Africa as a voyage into the heart of a hostile, repulsive and dangerous wilderness, inhabited by uncivilized and degraded specimens of the human race 'nearly approaching the baboon',[60] Booth takes his readers to the poorer parts of London, the 'urban jungle' whose 'denizens' he describes in astonishingly similar terms:

> Darkest England like Darkest Africa reeks with malaria. The foul and fetid breath of our slums is almost as poisonous as that of the African Swamp. [...] Just as in Darkest Africa [...] much of the misery of those whose lot we are considering arises from their own habits. Drunkenness and all manner of uncleanness, moral and physical abound. [...] A population sodden with drink, steeped in vice eaten up by every social and physical malady, these are the denizens of Darkest England among whom my life has been spent and to whose rescue I would now summon all that is best in the manhood and womanhood of our land.[61]

A painstakingly detailed description of the slum areas in the heart of the empire and a meticulous categorization of its populace (the homeless, the out-of-work, the vicious, the criminals, etc.) follows.[62] The sociologist Mariana Valverde has persuasively argued that Booth's description of Darkest England and its 'degenerate' inhabitants is a typical example for the impact of imperial technologies of knowledge production on the emerging metropolitan discipline of urban social studies.[63] Cartographical mapping of 'spaces of disease and disorder' as well as taxonomic projects like the classification of human types (later on called ethnology or race science) had first been developed in an imperial context by explorers, surveyors, and 'scholar administrators'.[64] In a process Valverde describes as 'the dialectic of the familiar and the unfamiliar' hegemonic knowledge, based on metropolitan premises but produced in the colonial 'contact zone'[65] was re-imported into the metropolis to provide the attempts at categorization and hierarchization in the more familiar arena 'with scientific authorisation'.[66] Booth's tropicalization of London's East End – some of his contemporaries were indeed engaged in the drawing of an ethnographic map of the capital – shows that these imperial technologies of exploration, far from being objective scientific methods, were shot through with presumptions and laden with value judgments.[67] One certainly has to admit that General Booth had a genuine interest in the poor, and helped considerably in improving their material lot. Yet at the same time his 'benevolent despotism',[68] characterized by the constant use of the 'language of empire',[69] resulted in a widening of the gap between middle-class 'explorers' and the slum dwellers in England's industrial cities whose life-world was put under scrutiny.[70] Ultimately, the 'Sunken Millions'[71] of the urban poor were put on par with the savage 'natives', 'pygmies' and 'baboons' out there in the colonies. Such rhetoric compellingly demonstrates the impact of the powerful late Victorian trope of race and more specifically the fear of 'racial degeneration'.[72]

Booth was perfectly aware of the fact that the prevalence of excessive poverty and 'low life' in London and other English cities severely threatened the credibility of an imperial nation that boasted of spreading 'moral and material progress' over the globe and held it to be 'a satire [...] upon our Christianity and our civilization that these colonies of heathens and savages in the heart of our capital should attract so little attention!'.[73] He was convinced, however, that 'for Darkest England as for Darkest Africa, there [wa]s a light beyond'[74] in the form of responsible representatives of superior 'races' or individuals embarking on a civilizing mission 'to snatch from the abyss those who, if left to themselves, w[ould] perish'.[75]

Global Solutions for Domestic Problems

Booth's diagnosis of poverty in Britain was gloomy. According to his calculations no less than 3 million people, 10 per cent of the country's population, were living beneath the poverty line, but there were substantial differences between them even if the boundaries between the groups were fuzzy. According to Booth, Darkest England could be imagined as a territory demarcated by three concentric circles:[76] the outer was inhabited by the homeless and unemployed but honest poor; next came the vicious; and the innermost was the domain of the criminals. All of them were threatened by the constant temptation of the brothels and gin shops in their vicinity. Echoing a current stereotype,[77] Booth believed that moral weakness and particularly the affinity to drink was almost a natural character trait of the urban 'residuum'.[78] His program of 'social salvation' hence had two basic goals that could be aptly described in the imperial rhetoric of the time as 'material and moral improvement'.[79] Both were centered on the notion of work as a panacea for various kinds of evils and the ultimate key to salvation.[80] Work was not only seen as a key to self-help in the form of economic self-sufficiency, but also as a moralizing force.[81] It would inculcate virtues like regularity and self-discipline, encompassed in the Victorian omnibus term 'character'.[82] The actual instrument of uplift was to be a threefold scheme of self-sustaining communities, significantly termed 'colonies'. This scheme, Booth argued, should be entirely financed by donations and public subscriptions, thus setting an example for the self-healing capabilities of civil society. The 'city colonies' were supposed to be 'harbours of refuge' in the 'centre of the ocean of misery' and had the task of saving the 'poor destitute creatures'[83] from the most immediate forms of distress by providing shelter, food, and temporary employment in factories and industrial workshops.

Those who had passed a test 'as to their sincerity, industry and honesty'[84] could then proceed to the farm colony, situated a safe distance from the temptations of the city and the unhealthy and corrupting influences of urban life. Booth made it unmistakably clear that every person admitted into the settlement would not only be 'instructed in the needful arts of husbandry, or some other method of earning his bread' but also 'taught the elementary lesson of obedience'.[85] Drunkenness, falsehood and even the use of 'profane language' would be severely punished.[86] The rule that repeat offenders were to be expelled from the rural colony was designed to ensure that the 'scum of Cockneydom'[87] was sorted out and only the 'deserving', the refined products of this process of internal colonization, should reach the third and final stage in the Salvationists' regenerative scheme. For our present purpose the proposed establishment of New Britain or the colony overseas is certainly the most interesting aspect of Booth's ambitious plan. The General's awareness of the significance of recent improvements in transport and communication and the resulting intensity of ongoing processes of globalization was at the bottom of the whole project. His description of an Anglophone global village must strike today's readers:

> The world has grown much smaller since the electric telegraph was discovered and side by side with the shrinkage of this planet under the influence of steam and electricity there has come a sense of brotherhood and a consciousness of community of interest and nationality on the part of the English-speaking peoples throughout the world. The change from Devon to Australia is not such a change in many respects as merely to cross over from Devon to Normandy.[88]

Given his awareness of the global character of his age and the resulting possibilities, it seems to be logical for the founder of the Salvation Army to solve Britain's domestic problems of recurrent economic crises and unemployment by exporting surplus labor to other parts of the world. That this new type of expansion of England was only conceivable thanks to Britain's imperial expertise becomes evident when Booth assured that he would revise the details of his scheme according to the 'best wisdom and matured experience of the practical men of every colony in the empire'.[89] The importance of the existing imperial infrastructure comes out even more sharply when one considers the places Booth suggests for his proposed New Britain Colony: South Africa was his first choice but Australia and Canada were also considered suitable to establish similar settlements in the future. Borrowing again heavily from the imperial rhetoric of his times, the General made it a point that emigration did not mean a clean break with the motherland. Quite the reverse: the family ties would become even stronger through the diaspora situation:

> It will resemble nothing so much as the unmooring of a little piece of England, and towing it across the sea to find a safe anchorage in a sunnier clime. The ship which takes out emigrants will bring back the produce of the farms, and constant travelling to and fro will lead more than ever to the feeling that we and our ocean-sundered brethren are members of one family.[90]

The Salvationists' gravest concern seems to have been the right selection and adequate preparation of the would-be colonists for their new lives overseas. Booth was fully aware of the fact that sending colonists 'whose first enquiry on reaching a foreign land was for a Whisky shop'[91] could endanger the whole scheme. He therefore wanted to make sure, through a rigid training program, that only the most 'trustworthy characters' were eventually sent out. At the same time, he pointed to the necessity for the establishment of a 'strong and efficient government' in the colony and constant control and surveillance of the immigrants, as 'nothing less than the irresistible pressure of a friendly and stronger purpose' would constrain them to give up their old degraded ways.[92]

Another obstacle to overcome was the problem of transport.[93] Here, again, Booth was most anxious about the moral state of the passengers. Being onboard the ship for several weeks without an occupation could easily lead to the 'downfall' of female passengers and to the men 'contracting habits of idleness'. He therefore opted for the Army acquiring a ship of its own, wherein the female colonists would be compelled to engage in 'knitting, sewing, tailoring, and other kindred occupations' and the men could perform manual work on the ship. To ensure that unskilled men would be sufficiently occupied and the 'Salvation Ship' could indeed become both a 'floating temple' and a 'hive of industry', Booth recommended buying a sailing vessel rather than a steamer.

Anybody with even a cursory knowledge of the rhetoric of the British colonial civilizing mission[94] will see how closely the twin enterprises of imperial philanthropy and rescuing the lower classes in the metropolis were intertwined both on a discursive and practical level: England's regenerated jungle population would eventually contribute to the providential task of spreading the English version of civilization in the dark corners of the world. It should not come as a surprise, therefore, that the plan was received very warmly by the usual advocates of British imperialism, such as Rudyard Kipling, Henry

Rider Haggard,[95] Cecil Rhodes and Winston Churchill[96] as a useful strategy to foster imperial unity.[97] However, whereas Booth's appeal to pledge funds in order to finance the Darkest England Scheme was by and large a success, and both city and farm colonies soon became a reality, the proposed overseas colonies were 'destined to be still-born'.[98] Therefore, we have so far mainly been concerned with analogies, influences, and mutual borrowings between Christian revivalism and the forces of empire. In the concluding part of this chapter we see how the Army ultimately became an active *agent* of British imperialism. This can best be demonstrated by analysing the Salvationist engagement in Britain's oldest and most important colony: India.

The Imperial Mission Without

A Difficult Passage to India

In-house histories of the Salvation Army mention that the movement 'recognized its obligation to assume an international character'[99] immediately after it had been refashioned into a quasi-military body. The international expansion began in 1880 with the founding of a branch in the United States. Australia and several European countries (including France and Switzerland) followed almost immediately. India was thus only the sixth country to be 'invaded',[100] as the Salvationist rhetoric had it. Nevertheless, it is also emphasized that India was the army's first 'Missionary field in the East', and was hence regarded as a country of 'vast opportunities'[101] and a convenient bridgehead for the conquest of Asia's 'teeming millions'.[102]

It would be no exaggeration to say that the Indian campaign was in its initial phase a one-man enterprise, driven almost entirely by the missionary zeal of Frederick St George De Lautour Tucker (1854–1928), who had the vision 'to see the whole of India kneeling at the feet of Jesus.'[103] For a Salvationist – most officers came from the lower middle or 'respectable' working classes – De Lautour Tucker had a rather untypical 'gentlemanly' background.[104] A graduate of Cheltenham College and fluent in several Indian languages, he had served as magistrate in the Indian Civil Service, a highly paid and very prestigious post in British India. The legend has it that, after reading the Christmas 1880 issue of *The War Cry* while posted in the Punjab, he was so impressed that he took home leave to hear William Booth's sermons in London and immediately afterward offered his services to the General.[105] He resigned from his lucrative post, joined the Salvation Army, and became not only Booth's most loyal lieutenant but also his son-in-law a few years later.[106]

In September 1882, De Lautour-Tucker returned to India as the head of a small invading force consisting of merely four officers. In spite of the numerical insignificance of the expedition corps, both colonial officials and the Anglo-Indian public seem to have been extremely alarmed when it arrived in Bombay. Ironically, one British magistrate suggested dealing with them under the European Vagrancy Act, a law that allowed for the deportation of unemployed and distressed Europeans back to their country of origin.[107] Nobody would have imagined at the time that three decades later, the Salvation Army would become a state-financed agency to reclaim European vagrants. The reasons for this official distrust are obvious. First, the traumatic experience of the Indian 'Mutiny' had made the colonial government extremely sensitive toward a possible provocation of native religious sensibilities. The Queen's proclamation of 1858 had therefore stressed the absolute neutrality of the government of India in matters of religion.[108] In addition, it was well known that the Army's aggressive style of conveying its religious propaganda to the public had provoked controversies and outright disturbances even in England and some other European countries – much worse things could happen, it was feared, in the delicate religious landscape of India.[109]

Second, what was regarded by the Salvationists as the quintessential strategy for the successful evangelization of non-European races was considered a taboo in the extremely race- and class-conscious social environment of British India: 'going native'.[110] As with what happened later on in other Asian and African countries,[111] the complete assimilation of indigenous modes of dressing, eating, living and even the adoption of local names was attempted in India from the outset. De Lautour-Tucker (who changed his name to Booth-Tucker in 1888) thus became Fakir Singh. General Booth himself had instructed him before leaving Britain that 'to the Indians you must be Indian [...] in order that you may win them to your Master'.[112] Fully aware of the provocative effect, Fakir Singh even paraded his exotic dress through the streets of London a few years later when he led members of the Army's Indian division through the imperial metropolis on the occasion of the first International Salvation Congress in 1886.[113]

This transgression of the unwritten imperial law of keeping social distance toward the natives at any cost must have been even more disturbing because of Fakir Singh's biography. To see a former representative of 'the conquering race, the white aristocracy, the civilizing power'[114] travelling in third class railway compartments or walking around barefooted, begging for funds, wearing turbans and a long Indian *kurta* (shirt) could cause only the gravest concern of the British-Indian authorities.[115] Whether such a tactic of 'go[ing] down low enough to meet the lowest India on its own level'[116] indeed signified the denial of a fundamental racial or civilizational difference, as Jeffrey Cox has recently argued,[117] remains doubtful if one takes into account the heavily racialized language of contemporary Salvationist publications on India, not

Figure 4.1 and Figure 4.2 The steel-frame of the Raj 'gone native': Frederick Booth-Tucker as assistant commissioner (ICS) in the Punjab c. 1879 and as Commissioner 'Fakir Singh' 1919 (Source: Mackenzie, *Booth-Tucker*).

even to speak of the organization's aggressive strategies of proselytizing, which do not suggest a high degree of respect for cultural differences. The infamous 'boom marches', that were organized in rural areas of Southern and Western India from the 1890s, are particularly noteworthy in this respect. These huge processions involving horses and marching bands were calculated to intimidate the village population and sometimes resulted in the violent destruction of 'pagan temples and idols'.[118]

From Conflict to Cooperation

From the very beginning, the newly arrived invasion force was closely observed by the Bombay police. When Major De Lautour Tucker (*alias* Fakir-Singh) and his four subalterns tried to organize a musical procession, parading on 'war chariots' (converted bullock-carts) through the Bazaars of Bombay,[119] they were immediately arrested on the ground that their activities 'would be the cause of disorder and serious breaches of peace'.[120] Once again, it became obvious that the Army possessed a remarkable flair for publicity: Booth-Tucker's first arrest (several others followed) was stylized as 'martyrdom'[121] and brought the Army unprecedented sympathy from Europeans and declarations of solidarity from Indian elites. The Hindu reformer Keshav Chandra Sen, for instance, sent a memorandum to the viceroy complaining that 'the action of the government of Bombay against the Salvationists [...] has been most unjust, arbitrary, and improper and contrary to the enlightened policy of the Government'.[122]

Despite the growing popularity of Salvationism, the Bombay Presidency continued its hostile politics toward the religious body. Thus, Frederick De Lautour-Tucker was denied the right to solemnize marriages as a minister of religion in 1884. The central government – anxious to avoid another storm of protest – somewhat uneasily asked the Bombay authorities to reconsider their decision, reminding them that the Salvationists were 'as much a Christian sect as the Jumpers of Wales or a dozen of odd bodies that could be named'.[123] Nonetheless, the relationship between the Salvationists and colonial authorities remained a strained one in other provinces as well. In Punjab, for instance, W. M. Drysdale, an English police officer who had been converted to Salvationism during his home leave and started preaching to the natives and selling *The War Cry* in public places, was reported to his superiors as 'being both mad and a fool' by the district magistrate. Having refused to 'give up all interference with the religion of the Natives' he was eventually dismissed from service in 1891 for disobedience.[124]

Regardless of the continuing distrust of many colonial administrators, the Army managed to quickly extend its network from Bombay to other provincial cities and from there make inroads into the rural areas, getting increasingly engaged in what they termed 'village warfare'.[125] The pioneers were reinforced by scores of new officers from England, Sweden, Switzerland, Australia, the United States, Canada and other countries.[126] By 1889, Fakir Singh could boast of his 'devoted band of 170 officers gathered from all around the world' supported by 'more than 100 Indian officers [...] who have caught from them the real Army spirit'.[127] *The War Cry* started an Indian edition that was soon translated into several vernaculars.[128] Other periodicals and pamphlets followed. Salvationist popularity also benefited considerably from two visits by William Booth in the early 1890s. The General's rhetorical skills were proverbial and his brief Indian tours seem to have resulted in thousands of conversions, although most of them were from Christian communities.[129] In order to further widen its basis among the native population – the main attention was focused once again on the outcast[e]s of Indian society[130] – the organization's commitment to social service was also intensified. Educational institutions were established and many of the Salvationist Corps regularly engaged in philanthropic activities during famines and natural catastrophes.[131] In the early 1890s, rescue homes for 'fallen women' were opened in the red-light districts of Colombo, Calcutta, Bombay and Madras.[132] The year 1895 witnessed the inauguration of a medical institution in Travancore, South India and several other dispensaries and hospitals followed in other parts of the country[133] although the professional qualification of the Salvationists running these institutions was sometimes rather doubtful.[134]

Acting as a fully self-financed nongovernmental organization *stricto sensu*, the Army had made considerable progress. However, it had also become evident that a truly large-scale expansion would remain impossible without the approval and financial aid of the colonial state. This is probably the reason why the Army gave up its policy of strict autonomy and the first attempts to curry the favor of the colonial authorities began. In early 1907, 'Commissioner' Booth-Tucker asked the government of India for financial support to extend the Army's activities to the medical field.[135] The proposal was declined as the majority of the colonial officials were still of the opinion that hospitals run by the Army would 'tend to become […] instruments of religious propaganda'.[136] Some of the reports on which the government's refusal was based betray the continuing distrust toward an organization that was at times denigrated as a 'safe haven for the mentally disturbed',[137] even by fellow missionaries of other denominations. The assessment of one of the Salvationists' medical institutions in the Bombay Presidency by the responsible district collector is quite typical for the position of the colonial authorities. He states:

> I have the honour to report that the Salvation Army Hospital at Anand is a superfluous institution, founded for the purpose of competing for patients and possible converts with other Missions previously planted at the place. . . . Had they been guided by unmixed motives, whether philanthropic or even Christian, they could not have selected Anand for their centre […] I […] express my strong opinion against Government mixing itself up with any form of Missionary activity, and least of all with anything undertaken by the Salvation Army.[138]

The interests of the British-Indian Empire thus still seemed to be clearly at odds with the interests of the 'Kingdom of Christ' after more than two decades of the Salvationists' presence in India. Despite such discouraging reactions, Booth-Tucker and his fellow officers did not give up, and eventually the considerable ideological overlap in the common project of 'civilizing the native population' began slowly to be acknowledged by representatives of the colonial state. Education was one field where the Salvationists sought the recognition and financial support of the colonial government by bringing the imperial value of the Army's work to attention. By 1908 they had managed to establish more than 200 day-schools all over the subcontinent, daily attended by about 10,000 pupils without receiving any grants-in-aid.[139] In his effort to convince the highest representatives of the state[140] the Commissioner not only mentions that 'physical drills ha[d] been introduced' in these primary schools 'with great success';[141] he also tries bringing to bear the organization's worldwide experience. In connection with the appropriate language and script to be taught to transform the Indian populace into loyal citizens of the empire, he draws on his experience in the United States, where he had been working in the Army's headquarters from 1896–1903:[142]

> It seems to us further that an improvement might be made in these schools by an adoption throughout India of the Roman character. This would greatly simplify the teaching of the various languages, and would tend toward the unification of the country. A similar result would [...] be obtained by extending largely the study of the English language. [...] Having spent so many years in the United States, I should like to have an opportunity of explaining something of the general policy of that country with regard to that question. For instance the despatch of one thousand 'school marms' [sic!] to teach the Philippinos English probably did more for the pacification of those turbulent and many-languaged Islanders than could have been accomplished by fifty times that number of soldiers.[143]

With the government of India's eventual approval to integrate the primary day-schools run by the Salvationists into their grants-in-aid scheme, the 'imperial romance' of the organization had begun. It was going to last until the end of the Raj.

Reclaiming 'Savages', Brown and White

We have already discussed at length the homologies occurring in the Salvationists' (as in other Victorian reformers') discourse on the British working classes on the one hand and the 'heathens' or 'savages' on the other. The formula 'Soup, Soap and Salvation' coined by William Booth to describe the pillars of the Army's reclamation work[144] was believed to be applicable to savages worldwide – regardless of their color. As early as 1890, Commissioner Booth-Tucker had written a book entitled *Darkest India*, echoing General Booth's *In Darkest England*, in which he claimed that 'the gospel of social salvation, which has so electrified all classes in England can be adopted on this country almost as it stands'.[145] From about 1908 onward, more and more imperial administrators recognized that this potential as a civilizing agency made the Salvationists an ideal partner of the colonizing state. One could assume that the sudden change of attitude by representatives of the colonial state was facilitated by the growing influence of Indian philanthropic organizations that often combined their social agenda with nascent forms of nation-building and hence posed a serious threat to the legitimacy of colonial rule.[146] A joint venture with the Salvation Army promised to regain some of the lost ground in this particular situation.[147] It seems also likely that the general fear of losing grip over the Indian population has played a certain role – a fear that was prevalent among the British in the wake of the *Swadeshi* Campaign (1905–1907) and the first wave of 'terrorist' activities that accompanied it. Whatever may have been the exact reason for the government's conciliatory position, there is no doubt that the most spectacular cooperation between the Salvation Army and the British-Indian state was largely based on the official acknowledgment of the former's ability to teach 'the elementary lesson of obedience': the 'reclamation' of criminals and particularly of entire communities that were regarded as 'criminals by birth'.[148]

The so-called Criminal Tribes were itinerant groups of the rural Indian population whose uncontrolled mobility and 'predatory propensities' were seen as a threat to British authority and that were hence discriminated against as 'hereditary criminals'.[149] Two Criminal Tribes Acts were passed in 1871 and 1911 to provide for their confinement in segregated settlements and their gradual education to a sedentary lifestyle. Initially, the settlements had been run directly by the state. However, they soon turned out to be extremely costly and inefficient. The Salvation Army became the chief agency in this program, as it was believed that it could do a better and, more importantly, a cheaper job. In 1908 prominent government officials approached the Army offering them a grant to open a weaving school and industrial homes for the Doms, a low-caste community classed as 'criminal',[150] with a view of 'bringing them into discipline and subjection'.[151] A few years later the Indian edition of *The War Cry* would celebrate the way in which 'these poor despised off-scourings of the U. P.'[152] were adopted, civilized and evangelized by […] saintly Salvation Army Officers'.[153] Precisely how the civilizing process was applied to the Doms is apparent from the following description of the daily routine in the settlement:

> The Doms were housed, fed and put to work, some at weaving some at farming, some at forestry. Each evening they had to answer their names at the roll call, and if any was not there, he had to be searched for till he was found. After the roll call came a Salvationist meeting with plenty of music. Much care was given to the women and the education of the children was begun. The people were taught to keep themselves clean.[154]

Soon afterward the Lieutenant Governor of the Punjab entrusted the reeducation of ex-convicts from Lahore prison in state-financed reformatories to the Salvationists, and was obviously pleased with the results of the Army's work as 'prison sub-contractors',[155] described by one of his highest officers as 'unqualified success'.[156] In an effort to capitalize on the positive reaction of colonial officials, General Booth addressed India's Secretary of State, in person, to make a more far-reaching offer of cooperation. He suggested the introduction of a 'system of reformation and employment' for all the 'tribes to whom, by force of circumstance, criminality has become a hereditary occupation'.[157] That the program was apparently based on the Army's Social Salvation scheme developed for the 'savages' at home becomes clear when he explains the details of the proposed 'treatment':

> To carry out this scheme two kinds of treatment are essential: (*a*) Reformatory and kindly influences must be brought to bear on them which will appeal to their better instincts and [...] (*b*) they must not be allowed to wander about disposing of the products of their labour, as this will probably result in their relapsing into crime. Markets must be found and their produce must be sold for them. To the attainment of both these objects, our numerous agencies and extensive ramifications are favourable.[158]

To further strengthen his argument, Booth pointed to the success of the industrial homes and agricultural settlements already existing in the Punjab and the United Provinces. He apparently managed to overcome the initial skepticism of the colonial government, and the cooperation between the colonial state and what had been a nongovernmental social service organization was extended to an unprecedented scale. By 1919, the Army entertained 28 settlements (varying in size from 100 to 1,800)[159] for altogether 6,812 'Crims'[160] and had become a sort of a huge service business in social control. There can be no doubt that it played a crucial role in sustaining colonial rule. That the disciplinary aspect, which was so important to the colonial officials, was not neglected in the Army's benevolent work becomes evident from Booth-Tucker's writings. He reassures his readers, at least some of whom were apparently former ICS colleagues, that:

> The firm but kindly *control* of the Criminal should be an essential feature of a wise policy. A flip-flop shilly-shally wibble-wobble policy will not do. It has been well said that liberty is not license. It is not wise to trust to his voluntary efforts to be good and to pick himself up. His will power for good has become like broken or disjointed limb, and will need splints and plaster [...] for some time to come. This the strong hand of authority must supply.[161]

Figure 4.3 'The strong hand of authority': Booth-Tucker addressing inmates of the Lahore Borstal prison (Source: Mackenzie, *Booth-Tucker*).

The results of the reeducation processes were shown in quasi-imperial exhibitions, organized in Simla, British India's summer capital in the Himalayas, and displaying various agricultural and industrial goods produced by ex-criminals and 'reformed tribesmen'.[162] These products were also available in special shops run by the Army that provided a handsome extra income in addition to the government grants.

More important from an economic point of view than the sale of Crim products was the fact that the detainees in the Army's labour settlements were acquainted with the requirements of the capitalist mode of production. The work of Rachel Tolen and Meena Radhakrishna has shown in great detail that the transformation of 'very unpromising material' into 'decent, law-abiding citizens'[163] of the empire, living up to civilized standards of sedentariness, cleanliness and self-discipline and productivity, was at the core of the Army's reclamation work.[164] Booth-Tucker and other Army spokesmen promised that 'workshy *badmashes*' (scoundrels) were being transformed into a reliable workforce that could be easily made available for planters and industrialists. It is hence not all too surprising that the Salvation Army was popular with Indian capitalists and rulers of princely states that were otherwise not very receptive towards its religious message. Thousands of copies of the Gujarati *War Cry's* annual special edition on temperance were bought by local factory owners and distributed freely among their workers.[165] It is likewise certainly not by coincidence that the Indian entrepreneurial dynasty Tata and the reformist Maharaja of Travancore were among the most important patrons of the Christian organization.[166] Jamsetji Tata, the founder of the family's industrial empire, was even a close personal friend of Booth-Tucker's. The latter found ways to show his gratitude for the significant financial support he received from the Parsi entrepreneur: he put Jamsetji in touch with some steel magnates from Pittsburgh with whom he had been in close touch during his tenure in the United States.[167]

However, such occasional alliances should not distract from the fact that the colonial state remained a far more important partner than the Indian industrialist class. A particularly striking example of how the goals of the Salvation Army and the needs of the Raj converged can be gathered from their cooperation in wartime. During World War I, women of the Haburah tribe, 'whose entire character had […] undergone a radical change' under the firm tutelage of the Salvationists, were employed to make uniforms for the military department and actively supported the imperial war effort.[168] An even bigger contribution to Britain's warfare was the role the Salvation Army played in the recruitment of a Porter's coolie corps from among their 'depressed' clientele for service in Mesopotamia.[169] The successful conversion of some of the 'reclaimed' was, of course, another welcome side-effect.[170]

Figure 4.4 Booth-Tucker his wife and Indian converts, some of them ex-'Crims', c. 1919 (Source: *National Geographic* 72, 1 January 1920).

The cooperation with the colonial state was extended to several related fields, one of which, perhaps, deserves special mention, since it brings together the two areas of the Army's activity: the *domestic* and the *colonial* civilizing mission. The so-called 'European loafers' (mostly unemployed railway men or sailors and ex-soldiers), roaming all over the Indian subcontinent, often behaving in a way that was hardly suited to enhance the prestige of the 'ruling race', had become a major problem by the late 1860s.[171] As already conveyed, a special European Vagrancy Act was promulgated in 1869 to deal with the problem. But similar to the 'Crim' settlements run by the government, the workhouses opened in its wake proved to be expensive rather than effective institutions. Here opened another opportunity for the Salvationists who possessed matchless experience in 'reclaiming' members of the lowest classes at home. Frederick Booth-Tucker approached the government of Bombay with a scheme for running an industrial home for European vagrants in 1910. Pointing to the expertise tried and tested in similar fields in England as well as in India, the Commissioner promised to run the institution with the utmost efficiency:

> But the reformatory influence thus exercised is not limited to the 'deserving' men, who come within our reach. The undeserving and most degraded are frequently reformed. Cut off from their old associates, protected from those who often prey upon their weaknesses, surrounded with good and kindly influences, fed well, clothed well and found work of a not too repulsive and severe character, supplied with good wholesome literature, looked after during their leisure moments as well as when employed, with a firm, yet fatherly counsellor always at their side, thousands of them respond to the new atmosphere of hope and help.[172]

Booth-Tucker was allowed to proceed with his project and an industrial home for the deserving cases was opened with grand *éclat* by the Governor of Bombay in December 1910[173] in addition to the already existing government workhouse. The colonial authorities were so satisfied with the working of the King Edward Home[174] that the Salvation Army was soon asked to take over the government institution as well, which it subsequently did.[175]

Such was the official acclaim of the Army's achievement, that the government sponsored the establishment of two more industrial homes for stranded Europeans: a house called The Bridge was opened in Calcutta in November 1914, and in March 1915 the Chief Commissioner of Delhi inaugurated a branch of the Institution in the new capital of British India,[176] justifying his approval by stating that:

> the institution [...] is desirable in order to obviate the difficulties arising from the fact that Europeans and Eurasians of this class at present resort in some numbers to Delhi, and that their numbers are likely to increase rather than diminish in the future. [T]he Salvation Army offers an excellent agency for dealing with this class and the proposed terms appear to me very economical.[177]

The financial support of the government for the various Salvation Army projects was continually extended until the 1920s,[178] and the organization continued to blossom under the protection of the colonial state. By 1922, the Salvationists' British Indian detachment counted 3,700 officers and cadets as well as 100,000 soldiers in the rank and file. The Army had established more than 4,500 centers in India and developed into a 'well-organized fighting force, ready and eager to be led on to the attack on the millions of non-Christians who surround each Corps and institution'.[179]

Most Salvationists seem to have been proud of their newly acquired respectability within the empire framework. In an article in *The War Cry* one writer celebrates the Army as a 'regenerative force' of imperialism and asks the rhetorical question 'In what do the imperial services of the Army consist'? The answer he subsequently provides himself is revealing:

> In its endeavours to soften and remove the effect of extreme poverty, to raise the fallen to succour to the needy and assist the distressed, the products of a civilization which turns out an appalling proportion of waste products – paupers, prostitutes, criminals and lunatics in every class of society, and by this means to soften the conflict between the 'haves' and the 'have-nots' which constitute a fertile soil for the seeds of the rebellion that threatens the mother country.[180]

By the same time, Booth-Tucker, who had been arrested several times in the 1880s, came to be held in the highest esteem by the colonial authorities. He was regarded as *the* expert on the reclamation of criminal and dangerous segments both in the Indian as well in the white colonial society. In 1913, the prestigious *Kaiser-i-Hind* medal was conferred upon him for 'public services in India'[181] and a few years later he was asked to lecture on 'Criminocurology' – the Army's 'scientific' method of classification and treatment of people infected with the 'disease' of criminality – before an audience of high government officials including the Lieutenant-Governor of the Punjab.[182] He also published a book with the same title,[183] explaining in detail how to transform 'criminals' into 'productive and subjected bodies'.[184] With *Criminocurology*, the imperial taxonomic techniques that had shaped the understanding of the London poor had finally come back full circle to the environment from where they had originated: the colonial outposts of the British Empire.

Concluding Remarks

Our investigation into the history of the Salvation Army from a transnational perspective has thus produced some significant, if preliminary, results. First and foremost, the close entanglement of Britain and its empire in arenas not normally associated with imperialism has been made clear. Even civil society organizations and historical actors like the Salvationists who, at the outset, viewed themselves as distinctly apolitical and sometimes even anti-government, were marked by the imperial rhetoric and modes of knowledge production that were regarded as authoritative at the time: the imperial social formation heavily influenced the ways to look at and make sense of the world. The Salvationists' venture to map the 'swamps' and 'jungles' of Darkest England and 'rescue' their denizens by civilizing them through a paternal but rigorous course of training, have vividly illustrated this point. The fact that General Booth's plan to deport the 'sunken millions' to overseas colonies was seriously discussed (and partly realized through the practice of assisted emigration) shows the extent to which imperial thinking prevailed at the time under survey.

Most intriguing, perhaps, was the analysis of the Salvation Army's transformation from a Home Mission movement, based on traditions of lower middle and upper working-class religiosity and often viewed as disturbing by the authorities, into an imperial service business for social control. As we have seen, this transformation happened almost simultaneously in India and Great Britain and the developments on both sides mutually influenced each other. As a recent study on the role of the Salvationists in East Asia suggests, similar developments seem to have taken place in Meiji Japan, where Charles Booth was granted an audience with the emperor in 1907 and his organization was accepted as a 'useful handmaiden of the state'.[185]

The Army's metamorphosis in India was particularly spectacular. From a small band of idealists 'gone native' and placed under the constant surveillance of a colonial government anxious to avoid blurring the colonial boundaries, it developed into a powerful force whose high degree of organization, rigid discipline, experience in projects of disciplining and reforming 'unruly' segments of society and, last but not least, entrepreneurial skills, turned it into an attractive partner in empire-building. The knowledge gathered about 'criminals by birth' and other marginalized groups in British India then circulated back to England and onward to other parts of the world, including the United States, Scandinavia, Canada, Japan and Africa – together with the officers, who usually served only a limited time in one foreign field – and arguably played a role in further shaping the view on the 'waste products' of their respective home societies. In an article published in 1920 and entitled 'Around the World with the Salvation Army' Evangeline Booth emphasized the transnational character of the organization, proudly stating that 'it has been increasingly apparent that the faith which regenerates men recognizes no barrier of nationality or geographical limitation'.[186] While stressing the growing global importance the General's daughter resorted to a well-known imperialist metaphor, claiming that 'the story of the Salvation Army must be told as a history of a world-wide organization: Upon its flag the sun never goes down'.[187]

The Army's undeniable contribution to the softening of 'the effects of extreme poverty' helped sustain the existing asymmetrical power relations both in Europe and in the various colonies and dominions. The social activities of the movement were therefore ultimately welcomed by the establishment: the harbingers of global civil society had been hijacked, as it were, by the empire. Being aware of this ambiguous relationship between British imperialism and an important predecessor of today's INGOs, one would probably have to be cautious *vis-à-vis* the fashionable uncritical view that *a priori* postulates an 'epic struggle' between 'global civil society' and the 'forces of empire', extending back 'to the earliest human experience'.[188]

On a more general level, the present case study has produced results which help to better grasp the nature of civilizing missions at large. Most importantly, it has shown that civilizing missions were by no means synonymous with European colonialism nor were they geographically restricted to colonies and 'zones of influence' in the non-Western parts of the globe. The example of the Salvationists' activities in Britain and British India has shown that the attempt to spread 'civility' had a much more far-reaching character and encompassed the 'great unwashed' of the domestic working classes as well. Occasionally the two varieties of the civilizing missions were conflicting. As we have seen, the 'indigent Europeans' in the colonies, were particularly logical targets of the class-based internal civilizing mission that was implemented by the colonial state or by civil society outfits like the Salvation Army. In a way, it was even more urgent in a colonial setting than in the metropolitan domain to inculcate 'civility' into the deviant members of the small European communities than to apply the race-based civilizing mission to the Indian populace. The apparent 'savagery' of some representatives of the 'ruling race' blatantly undermined the civilizing pretensions held by the imperial elites towards the colonized population and thus endangered this larger imperial project. The civilizing of the white riff-raff had therefore to be done as discreetly as possibly so as not to raise doubts about the moral superiority of the self-styled European 'tutors' in the minds of the colonized population. Equally, it has also become evident that the two strands of the civilizing mission were not always easy to separate, as there was ample evidence of the manifold ways in which the rhetoric of class-based hierarchies could be and *was* translated into the language of race and *vice versa.*

Additionally, it has been shown that the institutions of 'reclamation', 'reform' and 'correction' in both domains – from Booth's 'city colonies' and 'salvation ships' to Booth-Tucker's 'Crim settlements' and 'homes for stranded Europeans' – were designed to inculcate the cardinal virtues of the age in white and brown savages: sedentariness, industriousness, time-thrift, austerity and control of 'lower impulses'. The underlying notion in these reform schemes about work having such healing capacities anticipated arguments made by the well-known Marxist historian E. P. Thompson in the 1960s: that the attempts to spread civility both horizontally and vertically through a quasi-military sense of discipline constituted a key element of modernity in the age of capitalism.[189] But one might also speculate that there was often a deeper cultural meaning attached to civilizing efforts. Civilizing others, it seems, might sometimes also have been used as a means to exorcise 'the savage within' that continued to haunt the Victorian society.

Appendix

Statistics on the Salvation Army's social, industrial, agricultural, educational and training work in British India in 1918:

28	Settlements for criminal tribes with population of	6,812
3	Homes for released prisoners and beggars	106
8	Industrial boarding schools for Crim children, inmates	246
4	Non-Crim colonies and farms	1,314
5	Women's industrial homes accommodating	110
2	Weaving and silk schools	100
5	Centers for nonresident workers, employing	960
2	Industrial homes for Europeans and Anglo-Indians accommodating	45
1	Military hospital for wounded soldiers, beds	100
10	Dispensaries, beds	45
3	General hospitals, beds	90
3	Naval and military Furlo homes accommodating	115

4	Hut and refreshment bars for troops	6
6	Depots for sale of institutions	
17	No-criminal hostels for boys and girls, inmates	775
14	Training garrisons for cadets	181
118	Institutions providing food, shelter, and employment for	11,059
550	Day schools for education for children	16,664
668	**Institutions caring for**	**27,723**

Source: *The War Cry*, 24, no. 10 (October 1918), 6.

Notes

Earlier versions of this chapter have been published in H. Fischer-Tiné, *Low and Licentious Europeans: Race, Class and White Subalternity in Colonial India* (New Delhi: Orient BlackSwan, 2009), 323–68, and as 'Global Civil Society and the Forces of Empire: The Salvation Army, British Imperialism and the "pre-history" of NGOs (ca. 1880–1920)', in S. Conrad and D. Sachsenmaier (eds), *Competing Visions of World Order: Global Moments and Movements, 1880s – 1930s* (New York: Palgrave-Macmillan, 2007), 29–67.

1 J. Osterhammel and N. Petersson, *Geschichte der Globalisierung Dimensionen, Prozesse, Epochen* (München: Beck, 2003), 60–70 and C. A. Bayly, *The Birth of the Modern World 1780–1914: Global Connections and Comparisons* (Malden: Blackwell, 2004), 451–87.

2 This point has been recently made in F. L. Lechner and J. Boli, *World Culture: Origins and Consequences* (Malden: Blackwell, 2005), especially 119–34. See also C. A. Watt, *Serving the Nation: Cultures of Service, Association and Citizenship* (New Delhi: Oxford University Press, 2005), 30–3; J. Boli and G. M. Thomas (eds), *Constructing World Culture: International Nongovernmental Organizations since 1875* (Stanford: Stanford University Press, 1999).

3 M. Walzer, 'The Concept of Civil Society', in Michael Walzer (ed.), *Toward a Global Civil Society* (New York: Berghahn, 1995), 7–27, 23–4. For a similar optimistic view see A. Iriye, *Global Community: The role of international organizations in the making of the contemporary world* (Berkeley-Los Angeles 2002) and T. Spybey, *Globalization and World Society* (Cambridge: Polity Press, 1996), chapter 7.

4 A. Iriye, *Cultural Internationalism and World Order* (Baltimore & London: Johns Hopkins University Press, 1997), 3.

5 K. Wilson, 'Introduction: Histories, Empires, Modernities', in K. Wilson (ed.), *A New Imperial History: Culture, Identity and Modernity in Britain and the Empire 1660–1840* (Cambridge: Cambridge University Press, 2004), 1–26. See also C. Hall, *Civilizing Subjects: Metropole and Colony in the English Imagination* (Chicago: University of Chicago Press, 2002), 10–19. Both authors, in turn, are drawing on the well-known models of the 'common analytical field' and the 'imperial social formation' as introduced by Cooper and Stoler, and Mrinalini Sinha respectively.

6 The most valuable newer research includes P. J. Walker, *Pulling the Devil's Kingdom Down: The Salvation Army in Victorian Britain* (Berkeley: University of California Press, 2001); R. Hattersley, *Blood & Fire: William and Catherine Booth and their Salvation Army* (London: Little, Brown, 1999); N. H. Murdoch, *Origins of the Salvation Army* (Knoxville: University of Tennessee Press, 1994); L. Taiz, *Hallelujah Lads & Lasses: Remaking the Salvation Army in America, 1880–1930* (Chapel Hill: University of North Carolina Press, 2001).

7 The only comprehensive work to date of the movement in a non-Western context is on Japan: R. D. Rightmire, *Salvationist Samurai: Gunpei Yamamuro and the Rise of the Salvation Army in Japan*, Pietist and Wesleyan Studies, vol. 8 (Lanham: Scarecrow Press, 1997). In her magisterial study on the emergence of the Salvation Army in Britain, Pamela Walker deplores that the imperial significance of the movement has only met with scant scholarly attention. Walker, *Pulling the devil's Kingdom Down*, 245, endnote 2. The only attempt so far to understand the Salvation Army in a transnational perspective has recently been undertaken by Peter Van der Veer. However, the army does not feature very prominently in his book on *Imperial Encounters*, as he devotes only four pages to the topic. See P. Van Der Veer, *Imperial Encounters: Religion and Modernity in India and Britain* (Princeton: Princeton University Press, 2001), 151, 153–5. Nevertheless, his stimulating but somewhat superficial exercise in 'interactional history' was the main inspiration to pursue this project.

8 A somewhat similar argument has been persuasively made by Laura Thorn with regard to earlier forms of missionary activity in Britain and its colonies. See L. Thorn, 'Missionary Imperialism and the Language of Class', in F. Cooper and A. L. Stoler (eds), *Tensions of Empire: Colonial Cultures in a Bourgeois World* (Berkeley: University of California Press, 1997), 238–62.

9 M. Valverde, 'The Dialectic of the Familiar and the Unfamiliar: "The Jungle" in Early Slum Travel Writing', in *Sociology* 30, no.3 (1996): 493–509. See also J. Marriott, *The Other Empire: Metropolis, India, and Progress in the Colonial Imagination* (Manchester: Manchester University press, 2003), 130–59.

10 For the western imperial concept of civilization cf. Aydin 'Beyond Civilization: Pan-Islamism, Pan-Asianism and the Revolt against the West', in *Journal of Modern European History* 4, no. 2 (2006): 204–23. See also Roland Robertson's interesting discussion of the political implications of Norbert Elias' concept of the 'civilizing process' in a global framework: R. Robertson, *Globalization: Social Theory and Global Culture* (London: Sage, 1992), 115–28.

11 The metaphor was famously introduced by Benjamin Disraeli in the 1840s to describe the growing gap between the rich and the poor. See D. E. Nord, 'The Social Explorer as Anthropologist: Victorian Travellers among the Urban Poor', in W. Sharp and L. Wallock (eds), *Visions of the Modern City: Essays in History Art and Literature* (Baltimore: Johns Hopkins University Press, 1987), 122–34, 123. For an exhaustive discussion of Victorian readings of poverty see also the two monumental volumes by G. Himmelfarb, *The Idea of Poverty: England in the Early Industrial Age* (New York: Knopf, 1984), especially 489–503; and G. Himmelfarb, *Poverty and Compassion: The Moral Imagination of the Late Victorians* (New York: Knopf, 1991). A more concise account can be found in G. Himmelfarb, 'The Colour of poverty', in H. J. Dyos and M. Wolff (eds), *The Victorian City: Images and Realities*, vol. 2 (London and Boston: Routledge & Kegan Paul, 1973), 707–38. For the late Victorian development of the 'two-nation theory' see D. Cannadine, *Class in Britain* (New Haven: Yale University Press, 1999), 112–3.

12 E. Hobsbawm, *The Age of Empire, 1875–1914* (London: Weidenfeld and Nicolson, 2000), 265. See also Himmelfarb, *Poverty and Compassion*, 150–2.

13 Quoted in K. T. Hoppen, *The Mid-Victorian Generation, 1846–1886* (Oxford and New York: Clarendon Press, 1998), 453.

14 G. S. Jones, *Outcast London: A Study in the Relationship between Classes in Victorian Society* (Harmondsworth: Penguin, 1976), 5.

15 *Ibid.*, 286–300; Marriott, *The Other Empire*, 171–81.

16 Quoted in V. Bailey, 'In Darkest England and the Way Out: The Salvation Army, Social Reform and the Labour Movement, 1885–1910', in *International Review of Social History* 29, no. 2 (1984): 133–71.

17 J. Harris, *Private Lives, Public Spirit: Britain 1870–1914* (London: Penguin Books, 1994), 163. As studies of continental countries indicate, this seems to have been a broader European trend. See, for instance, the essays in Collette Bec, Catherine Duprat, Jean-Noël Luc and Jacques-Guy Petit (eds), *Philanthropies et Politiques Sociales en Europe (XVIIIe-XXe Siècles)* (Paris : Anthropos, 1994).

18 For biographical details on Booth see Walker, *Pulling the Devil's Kingdom Down*, 13–22; The General of the Salvation Army (ed.), *The Salvation Army. Its Origin and Development* (London: Salvation Army, 1938), 1–15. The most comprehensive, though uncritical, treatment remains in H. Begbie, *Life of William Booth, Founder of the Salvation Army*, 2 vols. (New York: The Macmillan Company, 1920).

19 See also Murdoch, *Origins of the Salvation Army*, 21–39.

20 A more comprehensive account on the background and early years of the Salvationist movement can be found in G. K. Horridge, *The Salvation Army: Origins and Early Days, 1865–1900* (Godalming: Ammonite Books, 1993).

21 Salvation Army (ed.), *The Salvation Army. Its Origin and Development*, 20. This choice is typical for the Army's strategy of consciously 'capturing' places associated with leisure activities of the working classes that were regarded as corrupting, like pubs, music-halls, theatres, etc. Walker, *Pulling the Devil's Kingdom Down*, 188. See also R. Sandall, *The History of the Salvation Army*, vol. 1 *(1865–1878)* (London: Nelson, 1947), 150–1, 220.

22 See P. Keating, 'Fact and Fiction in the East End', in H. J. Dyos and M. Wolff (eds), *The Victorian City*, 589–93. See also J. R. Walkowitz, *City of Dreadful Delight: Narratives of Sexual Danger in Late Victorian London* (Chicago: University of Chicago Press, 1992), 30.

23 Salvation Army (ed.), *The Salvation Army Year Book. 1939, Thirty Fourth Year of Issue* (London,:Salvation Army, 1938), 39.

24 Bayly, *Birth of the Modern World*, 357–9.

25 In the early twentieth century, the organization also played a pioneering role in using film and radio as media for religious propaganda. See J. Cox, *Imperial Fault Lines: Christianity and Colonial Power in India, 1818–1940* (Stanford: Stanford University Press, 2002), 238; and Salvation Army, *The Salvation Army Year Book. 1939*, 7–10.

26 Christian Mission Report 1867, quoted in Horridge, *The Salvation Army*, 17. See also the programmatical statements in W. Booth, *Heathen England: Being a Description of the Utterly Godless Condition of the Vast Majority of the English Nation, and of the Establishment, Growth, System and Success of an Army for Its Salvation Consisting of Working People etc.*, 3rd ed. (London: 1879, passim).

27 The uniforms made out of plain simple dark blue cloth, trimmed with red braid, and marked with the letter 'S' on the collar, were worn by both male and female members of the organization, which was regarded as repulsive by quite a few contemporaries.

28 The following is based on O. Anderson, 'The Growth of Christian Militarism in mid-Victorian Britain', in *The English Historical Review* 86, no.338 (1971): 46–71. See also Walker, *Pulling the Devil's Kingdom Down*, 60–3.

29 Anderson, 'The Growth of Christian Militarism', 46–52; B. Stanley, 'Christian Responses to the Indian Mutiny', in W. J. Shiels, *The Church and War, Studies in Church History*, vol. 20 (Oxford: Blackwell, 1983), 277–99. See also V. Bailey, 'Salvation Army Riots: The 'Skeleton Army' and Legal Authority in a Provincial Town', in

A. P. Donajgrodzkij (ed.), *Social Control in Nineteenth Century Britain* (Totowa: Rowman and Littlefield, 1977), 231–53, 236–7.

30 Van Der Veer, *Imperial Encounters*, 83–94. See also H. J. Field, *Toward a Programme for Imperial Life: The British Empire at the Turn of the Century* (Westport: Greenwood Press, 1982). For a thorough discussion of 'Muscular Christianity' see also N. Vance, *Sinews of the Spirit: The Ideal of Christian Manliness in Victorian Literature and Religion* (Cambridge: Cambridge University Press, 1985); D. Hall (ed.), *Muscular Christianity: Embodying the Victorian Age* (Cambridge: Cambridge University Press, 1994).

31 Hoppen, *The Mid-Victorian Generation 1846–1886*, 454.

32 Mrs [i.e. Catherine] Booth, 'Aggressive Christianity', in C. Booth, *Papers on Aggressive Christianity* (London: 1891), 13. Emphasis in the original text. See also The Salvation Army (ed.), *All about the Salvation Army* (London: The Salvation Army, 1882), 4–5.

33 'Now surely the least-witted person can see that it cannot be possible to do a great spiritual work for the deliverance of people from what is wrong about them by a system under their own direction!' W. Booth, *Orders and Regulations for the Salvation Army*, Pt. I. (London: ca. 1880), 3.

34 *Ibid.*, p. 5. See also Horridge, *The Salvation Army*, 52–9.

35 Murdoch, *Origins of the Salvation Army*, xi.

36 W. Booth, 'The Salvation Army', in W. Booth, *Salvation Soldiery. A Series of Addresses on the Requirements of Jesus Christ's Service* (London: S. W. Partridge & Co., 1882), 27–33.

37 A Salvationist pamphlet published in 1882 states that 'We have 300 officers and thousands of the rank and file, who are so far disciplined as to regularly discharge their duty, or who are willing to go to any part of the world simply at the word of command'. The Salvation Army (ed.), *All about the Salvation Army*, 23.

38 See G. R. Searle, *The Quest for National Efficiency: A Study of British Politics and Political Thought, 1899–1914* (Berkeley and Los Angeles: University of California Press, 1971).

39 When the adoption of a military strategy was discussed in the autumn of 1877, the General's entourage was convinced that 'if we can only drill and mobilize fast enough, we can overrun the country before Christmas'. Letter of G. S. Railton to W. Booth (October 11, 1877), cited in Sandall, *History of the Savation Army*, vol. 1, 225.

40 Booth, *Orders and Regulations for the Salvation Army*, 11–12.

41 Horridge, *The Salvation Army*, 38.

42 P. A. Clasen, *Der Salutismus: eine sozialwissenschaftliche Monographie über General Booth und seine Heilsarmee, Schriften zur Soziologie der Kultur*, vol. 2, Jena, E. Dierichs (1913), 322.

43 F. Booth-Tucker, *The Short Life of Catherine Booth the Mother of the Salvation Army*, 2nd ed. (London: The Salvation Army, 1895), 332–41.

44 For the following see Walker, *Pulling the Devil's Kingdom Down*, pp. 206–34; Bailey, 'Salvation Army Riots', 241–49; and Horridge, *The Salvation Army*, 101–13.

45 The 'social control' argument has been brought forward most clearly in Bailey, 'Salvation Army Riots.' Bailey, however, later revised his thesis somewhat by pointing to the similarities between the socialist workers' movement and the army's work. For a critical general discussion of the concept of social control see also K. Williams, *From Pauperism to Poverty* (London: Routledge & Kegan Paul, 1981), 136–39.

46 Cited in M. Radhakrishna, *Dishonoured by History: 'Criminal Tribes' and British Colonial Policy* (New Delhi: Orient Longman, 2001), 78.

47 Cited in Bailey, 'Salvation Army Riots', 236.

48 Walker, *Pulling the Devil's Kingdom Down*, 242.

49 Salvation Army, *The Salvation Army Year Book. 1939*, 28.

50 Clasen, *Der Salutismus*, 322.

51 Salvation Army, *The Salvation Army. Its Origin and Development*, 29, 41–50.

52 Bailey, 'In Darkest England and the Way Out', 136.

53 W. Booth, *Holy Living: Or What the Salvation Army Teaches about Sanctification* (London: ca. 1880, passim).

54 W. Booth, *Sociales Elend und Abhülfe. Vortrag gehalten in der Schweiz etc.* (Bern: 1896), 21.

55 For the sake of convenience, I refer to William Booth as the author. It is almost certain, however, that the book was not the product of Booth's limited literary talent, but at least partly ghost-written by the investigative journalist and social reformer W. T. Stead of the *Pall Mall Gazette*. See J. McLaughlin, *Writing the Urban Jungle: Reading Empire in London from Doyle to Eliot* (Charlottesville: University Press of Virginia, 2000), 209, endnote 6.

56 After being largely neglected for a long time, *In Darkest England* has only in recent decades received some critical scholarly attention. The most insightful treatments are: Bailey, 'In Darkest England and the Way Out'; McLaughlin, *Writing the Urban Jungle*, 79–103; and Valverde, 'The Dialectic of the Familiar and the Unfamiliar', passim.

57 McLaughlin, *Writing the Urban Jungle*, 94.

58 For a detailed account of the debate between 'Boothites' and 'anti-Boothites' see H. Ausubel, 'General Booth's Scheme of Social Salvation', in *American Historical Review* 56, no. 3 (1951): 519–25.

59 H. M. Stanley, *In Darkest Africa, or the Quest, Rescue and Retreat of Emin, Governor of Equatoria* (London: S. Low, Marston, Searle, and Rivington, 1890).

60 Cited in Booth, *In Darkest England and the Way Out*, 11.

61 *Ibid.*, 14–5. For a similar powerful example of Booth's rhetoric see W. Booth, 'Getting Rid of the Filth', in W. Booth, *Salvation Soldiery*, 34–40.

62 Booth, *In Darkest England and the Way Out*, 24–66.

63 Valverde, 'The Dialectic of the Familiar and the Unfamiliar', 495–500.

64 S. Sen, *Distant Sovereignty: National Imperialism and the Origins of British India* (New York and London: Routledge, 2002), 57–84; B. S. Cohn, *Colonialism and Its Forms of Knowledge: The British in India* (Princeton: Princeton University Press, 1996), 3–5; and Marriott, *The Other Empire*, 130–59. See also M. Waligora, 'What Is Your Caste?' in H. Fischer-Tiné and M. Mann (eds), *Colonialism as Civilizing Mission: Cultural Ideology in British India* (London: Anthem Press, 2004), 141–62 for categorization of human 'tribes' and I. J. Barrow, *Making History, Drawing Territory: British Mapping in India, c. 1756–1905* (New Delhi: Oxford University Press, 2003), as well as M. H. Edney, *Mapping and Empire: The Geographical Construction of British India, 1765–1843* (Chicago: University of Chicago Press, 1997) for the imperial relevance of topographical mapping. For a concise general discussion of colonial knowledge production, see T. von Trotha, 'Was war Kolonialismus? Einige zusammenfassende Befunde zur Soziologie und Geschichte des Kolonialismus und der Kolonialherrschaft', in *Saeculum* 55, no. 1 (2004), 49–95, 81–6.

65 M. L. Pratt, *Imperial Eyes: Travel Writing and Transculturation* (London and New York: Routledge, 1992).

66 Valverde, 'The Dialectic of the Familiar and the Unfamiliar', 494.

67 For an analysis of the symbolical meanings of such value judgments see also P. Stallybrass and A. White, *The Politics and Poetics of Transgression* (London: Methuen, 1986), 125–48.

68 The term, perhaps most frequently used by contemporaries to describe the nature of British rule in India during the later nineteenth century, is employed by Anthony

Wohl to describe the social philosophy coupling material improvement with moral reformation that was underlying much of the philanthropic efforts in Victorian England. See A. S. Wohl, *The Eternal Slum: Housing and Social Policy in Victorian London* (New Brunswick: Transaction Publishers, 2002), 179–99.

69 Walkowitz, *City of Dreadful Delight*, p. 28. See also McLaughlin, *Writing the Urban Jungle*, 80.

70 For the diverse motives and contradictory effects of Victorian urban philanthropy see also S. Koven, *Slumming: Sexual and Social Politics in Victorian London* (Princeton: Princeton University Press, 2004), particularly pp. 3–14, and A. McClintock, *Imperial Leather: Race, Gender and Sexuality in the Colonial Contest* (New York and London: Routledge, 1995), 75–100.

71 Booth, *In Darkest England and the Way Out*, 40.

72 For a further exploration of this impact see P. Brantlinger, *Dark Vanishings. Discourse on the Extinction of Primitive Races, 1800–1930* (Ithaca and N.Y.-London: Cornell University Press, 2003); S. Ledger, 'In Darkest England: The Terror of Degeneration in *fin-de-siècle* Britain', in *Literature and History* 4, no. 2 (1995): 71–86; K. Malik, *The Meaning of Race: Race, History and Culture in Western Society* (Basingstoke: Macmillan, 1996), 91–100; D. Pick, *Faces of Degeneration: a European Disorder ca. 1848–1918* (Cambridge: Cambridge University Press, 1989), 189–203; and T. Barringer, 'Images of Otherness and the Visual Production of Difference: Race and Labour in Illustrated Texts, 1850–1865', in Shearer West (ed.), *The Victorians and Race* (Aldershot: Scholar Press, 1996), 34–52.

73 Booth, *In Darkest England and the Way Out*, 16.

74 *Ibid.*, 15.

75 *Ibid.*, 43.

76 See also the analysis of Booth's scheme in Clasen, *Der Salutismus*, 237–9.

77 See for instance J. Briggs et al., *Crime and Punishment in England: An Introductory History* (London: UCL Press, 1996),194.

78 Interestingly, the term 'residuum', frequently used by Booth, was soon employed by the advocates of eugenics. See P. M. H. Mazumdar, 'The Eugenicists and the Residuum: The Problem of the Urban Poor', in *Bulletin of the History of Medicine* 54, no. 2 (1980): 204–15.

79 For a discussion of the Salvation Army's program of 'religious colonization' of the working classes see Himmelfarb, *Poverty and Compassion*, 228–30. For the twin aim of moral and material improvement in a colonial setting see also M. Mann, 'Torchbearers upon the Path of Progress', in H. Fischer-Tiné and M. Mann (eds), *Colonialism as Civilizing Mission*, 1–26.

80 Booth, *Sociales Elend und Abhülfe*, 18.

81 That similar discourses existed in continental Europe is evident from recent work on the policies of 'education to work' in late-nineteenth-century Germany and the German colonies in Africa. See S. Conrad, 'Education to work in colony and metropole: The case of Imperial Germany', in: H. Fischer-Tiné and S. Gehrmann (eds), *Empires and Boundaries: Rethinking Race, Class and Gender in Colonial Settings* (New York and London: Routledge, 2009), 23–40.

82 S. Collini, *Public Moralists: Political Thought and Intellectual Life in Britain, 1850–1930* (New York: Oxford University Press, 1991), 92–118, and Richard Bellamy, *Liberalism and Modern Society: A Historical Argument* (Cambridge: Polity Press, 1992), 9–14.

83 Booth, *In Darkest England and the Way Out*, 92.

84 *Ibid.*

85 *Ibid.*, 134.

86 *Ibid.*, 137–8.

87 *Ibid.*, 129. In spite of quoting this phrase, Booth places emphasis on the fact that most of the urban poor were not 'real' Cockneys but country dwellers who had moved to the capital only recently, and hence it could be expected that they proved useful in the farm colony. He thus implies that 'the real Cockney' was a lesser species, unfit for rural life.

88 *Ibid.*, 143.

89 *Ibid.*, 149.

90 *Ibid.*, 152. This idea of a global 'Greater Britain' had earlier been formulated in C. W. Dilke, *Greater Britain: A Record of Travel in English- Speaking Countries During 1866 and 1867*, 2 Vols. (London: 1869).

91 *Ibid.*, 145.

92 *Ibid.*, 146 and 157. See also F. Booth-Tucker, *The Short Life of Catherine Booth*, 515.

93 For the following see Booth, *In Darkest England and the Way Out*, 152–55.

94 For a general discussion and case studies of the concept's application see B. Barth and J. Osterhammel (eds), *Zivilisierungsmissionen. Imperiale Weltverbesserung seit dem 18. Jahrhundert* (Konstanz: UVK Verlag, 2005), passim.

95 Agricultural reformer Sir Henry Rider Haggard, better known for his adventure novels like *King Solomon's Mines* or *She*, was appointed as the head of an inspection committee by the Colonial Secretary to evaluate the Army's farm colonies in Britain and the United States. He recommended them as an appropriate means to stop the 'racial degeneration' supposedly resulting from urbanization. See H. R. Haggard, *The Poor and the Land: Being a Report on the Salvation Army Colonies in the United States and at Hadleigh, England* (London: Longmans, Green & Co., 1905). See also J. Harris, *Unemployment and Politics: A Study in English Social Policy, 1886–1914* (Oxford: Clarendon Press, 1972), 130.

96 Clasen, *Der Salutismus*, 273, and Murdoch, *Origins of the Salvation Army*, 163, 213, endnote 34.

97 See McLaughlin, *Writing the Urban Jungle*, 211, fn. 37.

98 Hattersley, *Blood & Fire*, 370. The Salvation Army did, however, support schemes of aided emigration, especially to Canada, see Clasen, *Der Salutismus*, 272–73; M. Harper, 'British Migration and the Peopling of the Empire', in A. Porter (ed.), *The Nineteenth Century: The Oxford History of the British Empire*, vol. 3 (Oxford: Oxford University Press, 1999), 75–87, 82; Harris, *Unemployment and Politics*, 131–2; and Desmond Glynn, '"Exporting Outcast London": Assisted Emigration to Canada, 1886–1914', in *Social History* 15, no. 29 (1982): 209–38.

99 Salvation Army, *The Salvation Army. Its Origin and Development*, 41.

100 Booth-Tucker, *The Short Life of Catherine Booth*, 374.

101 Clasen, *Der Salutismus*, 89. See also Salvation Army, *The Salvation Army. Its Origin and Development*, 41, 45.

102 *India's Cry: A Monthly Record of the Spiritual and Social Operations of The Salvation Army in India and Ceylon* 1, no. 2 (May 1896): 1.

103 S. Smith, *By Love Compelled: The Salvation Army's One Hundred Years in India and Adjacent Lands* (London: Salvationist Pub. & Supplies, 1981), 9.

104 See H. Williams, *Booth-Tucker: William Booth's First Gentleman* (London: Hodder & Stoughton Ltd., 1980). Other biographical monographs include M. Unsworth, *Bridging the Gap: Frederick Booth-Tucker of India* (London & Edinburgh: Eagle Books, 1944); and F. A. Mackenzie, *Booth- Tucker: Sadhu and Saint* (London: Hodder & Stoughton Ltd., 1930).

105 Hattersley, *Blood & Fire*, pp. 289–90; and Clasen, *Der Salutismus*, 85–6.

106 *Ibid.*, 300.

107 For details see D. Arnold, 'European Orphans and Vagrants in India in the Nineteenth Century', in *Journal of Imperial and Commonwealth History* 7. no.2 (1979): 104–27, especially 119–21, and A. Ganachari, 'White Man's Embarassment: European Vagrancy in 19th Century Bombay', in *Economic and Political Weekly* 37, no. 2 (2002): 2,477–85, especially 2,481–4.

108 Reprinted in A. B. Keith (ed.), *Speeches and Documents on Indian Policy,1750–1921*, vol. 1 (London: H. Milford, Oxford University Press, 1922), 370–86.

109 Williams, *Booth-Tucker*, 71.

110 See, for instance, K. Ballhatchet, *Race, Sex and Class under the Raj: Imperial Attitudes and Policies and Their Critics, 1793–1905* (London: Weidenfeld & Nicolson, 1980), passim. See also H. Fischer-Tiné, *Low and Licentious Europeans: Race, Class and White Subalternity in Colonial India* (New Delhi: Orient BlackSwan 2009), 54–60 and E. M. Collingham, *Imperial Bodies: The Physical Experience of the Raj, ca. 1800–1947* (Cambridge: Polity Press, 2001), particularly chapter 4. For an interesting compilation of insiders' accounts see C. Allen, *Plain Tales from the Raj: Images of British India in the Twentieth-Century* (London: Futura Publications, 1999).

111 The 'native policy' proved to be counterproductive in Japan, where people 'roared with laughter' at the sight of the Salvationists wearing night kimonos they had erroneously bought in Hong Kong as typical 'native dress'. Rightmire, *Salvationist Samurai*, 16–7.

112 Quoted in Smith, *By Love Compelled*, 3.

113 For details see H. Fischer-Tiné, ' "Meeting the lowest India on its own level": Frederick Booth Tucker und die Anfänge der Heilsarmee in Britisch-Indien', in M. Mann (ed.), *Aufgeklärter Geist und evangelische Mission in Indien* (Heidelberg: Draupadi-Verlag, 2008), 177–9.

114 According to a typical British self-representation in a contemporary weekly journal for Europeans: *The Friend of India* 24, no. 5 (1866): 607.

115 On a completely different level, the Salvationists also transgressed cultural and 'civilizational' boundaries by arranging their pious songs in the style of traditional Indian music and playing them with Indian instruments. See e.g. Salvation Army (India), *Salvation Army Songs*, rev. and enl. ed. [in Kannarese] (Bapatla: The Salvation Army, 1918).

116 Anonymous, *Catherine Bannister. Given for India* (London: The Salvation Army's Miniature Biographies no. 10, 1930), 10.

117 Cox, *Imperial Fault Lines*, 236–7.

118 Further details can be found in H. Fischer-Tiné, '"Meeting the lowest India"', 177–9.

119 *The War Cry*, 25. no. 10 (1919): 5, and Williams, *Booth-Tucker*, 220.

120 F. Booth-Tucker, *Muktifauj, or, Forty Years with the Salvation Army in India and Ceylon* (London: Salvationist Publishing & Supplies, 1923), 14.

121 National Archives of India, Government of India Home Department Proceedings [hereafter quoted as NAI, GoI, Home Dept Progs], Public A—201–202 (October 1882), 'Viceroy Lord Ripon to members of the Viceregal Council' (October 25, 1882).

122 NAI, GoI, Home Dept Progs, Public A—202, 'Petition of the inhabitants of Calcutta protesting against the treatment of some members of the Salvation Army'.

123 NAI, Home Dept Progs, Ecclesiastical, A—19–30 (September 1884), Letter No. 158, dated Simla (September 15, 1884), A. Mackenzie, Secretary to the Government of India to the Government of Bombay.

124 Oriental and India Office Collection, India Office Records [hereafter quoted as OIOC, IOR]: L/PJ/6/411, File No. 2249, 'Letter of W.G. Drysdale to William Booth'.

125 *India's Cry (Special Self-Denial Number)* 11, no. 11 (November 1906): 5.

126 Smith, *By Love Compelled*, 34–5, 39.

127 Quoted *Ibid.*, 43.

128 *Ibid.*, p. 44 and Salvation Army, *The Salvation Army Year Book (1939)*, 92. The journal was renamed *India's Cry* between 1896 and 1908.

129 Murdoch, *Origins of the Salvation Army*, 138. See also Booth-Tucker, *The Short Life of Catherine Booth*, p. 376. For a more detailed account of Booth's visits see Booth-Tucker, *Muktifauj*, 140–8.

130 Williams, Booth-Tucker, 100–8. The pragmatic reasons for this were made plain by Fakir Singh in 1891: 'Religious by instinct, obedient to discipline, [...] inured to hardship, and accustomed to support life on the scantiest conceivable pittance we cannot imagine a more fitting object for our pity, nor a more encouraging one for our effort, than the members of India's submerged tenth'. F. Booth-Tucker, 'Preface', in F. Booth-Tucker, *Darkest India: A Supplement to General Booth's In Darkest England and the Way Out* (Bombay: Bombay Gazette Steam Printing Works, 1891), 5–6. See also *The War Cry*, 14, no. 3 (March 1910): 6.

131 See for instance *India's Cry* 1, no. 6 (September 1896): 4; 1, no. 9 (December 1896): 1–2; 2, no. 1 (April 1897): 1–6; 2, no. 3 (June 1897): 3–6, 11–13; 5, no. 7 (July 1900): 1–2. See also Smith, *By Love Compelled*, 71–72.

132 *India's Cry* 1, no. 6 (September 1896): 5; 1, no. 7 (October 1896): 1; 2, no. 4 (July 1897): 1–2; 2, no. 3 (September 1897): 3. See also Salvation Army, *A Year's Advance: Being the Eleventh Annual Report of the Salvation Army in India and Ceylon 1892–93* (Bombay: 1893), 47–8; *The Bombay Guardian* (March 8, 1890), 10; M. Hatcher, *The Undauntables: Being Thrilling Stories of the Salvation Army's Pioneering Days in India* (London: Hodder & Stoughton, 1933), 133–4; and *The Sentinel. Organ of Movements for Social Purity and National Righteousness* 17, no. 10 (October 1895): 145. See also F. Booth-Tucker, *Darkest India*, 94.

133 Salvation Army, *The Salvation Army Year Book (1939)*, p. 91. See also Smith, *By Love Compelled*, 77–79.

134 OIOC. IOR: L/PJ/6/544 File No. 1291. 'Salvation Army Headquarter's Enquiries Regarding the Practice of Medicine in India by Persons Not Having the Legal Medical Qualifications Required in Great Britain'.

135 NAI, GoI Home Dept Progs, Medical, A—19–21 (July 1907).

136 NAI, GoI Home Dept Progs, Medical, A—14–19 (June 1908), 'Offer Made by the Salvation Army to Cooperate with the Government in Supplying Medical Assistance to the People of India'.

137 Cox, *Imperial Fault Lines*, 228.

138 NAI, GoI Home Dept Progs, Medical, A—15 (June 1908), Letter No. 4424, Arthur Wood, ICS, Collector of Kaira to the Commissioner, Northern Division, dated Kaira (September 25, 1907).

139 NAI, GoI Home Dept Progs, Educational, A—48 (July 1908), Letter No. 596, dated June 18, 1907, E. D. Maclagan, Chief Secretary to the Govt Of Punjab to the Director of Public Instruction, Punjab, 'Forwarding extracts of a letter dated 19-2-1907 from Mr. F. de L. Booth Tucker, Commissioner, Salvation Army'. Three years later the figures in *The War Cry*, 17, no. 11 (November 1911): 6, mention even 400 day schools.

140 Booth-Tucker was granted interviews by Lord Minto, Viceroy of British India and Herbert Hope Risley, one of the most influential members of his Council on February 5, 1905. He was also in contact with John Morley, the Secretary of State for India in Whitehall.

141 NAI, GoI Home Dept Progs, Educational, A—48 (July 1908), Letter No. 596, 'Forwarding extracts of a letter dated 19-2-1907 from Mr. F. de L. Booth Tucker, Commissioner, Salvation Army'. To impart 'English Drill' was indeed one of the most prominent features of the Salvationists schools. See *India's Cry*, 1, no. 11 (February 1897): 3.

142 Walker, *Pulling the Devil's Kingdom Down*, 236. Interestingly, Booth-Tucker had been engaged in the United States amongst other places in the founding of 'farm colonies', an experience that would prove valuable for his later work in India. For an account of his American career see Taiz, *Hallelujah Lads & Lasses*, 108–30.

143 NAI, GoI Home Dept Progs, Educational, A—48 (July 1908), Letter No. 596, 'Forwarding extracts of a letter dated 19-2-1907 from Mr. F. de L. Booth Tucker, Commissioner, Salvation Army'.

144 See *The War Cry*, 22, no. 5 (May 1916): 6.

145 Booth-Tucker, 'Preface', in Booth-Tucker, *Darkest India*, 3.

146 See Watt, *Serving the Nation*, 2–13. passim. I am grateful to Carey Watt for guiding my attention to this likely interconnection. Before drawing final conclusions, however, further research on this point is required.

147 For the context of the *Swadeshi* movement and Indian 'terrorism' see P. Heehs, *The Bomb in Bengal: The Rise of Revolutionary Terrorism in India, 1900–1910* (Delhi: Oxford University Press, 1993); S. Sarkar, *Modern India, 1885–1947* (Madras, New Delhi: Macmillan India, 1983), 111–47 and R. K. Ray, *Social Conflict and Political Unrest in Bengal, 1875–1927* (Delhi: Oxford University Press, 1984), 160–206.

148 As this particular aspect has received some scholarly attention recently I will confine myself largely to a brief summary. For a more exhaustive treatment of the Salvation Army's work with the 'Criminal Tribes' see also Radhakrishna, *Dishonoured by History*, and the same author's 'Surveillance and Settlements under the Criminal Tribes Act in Madras', in *Indian Economic and Social History Review* 29, no. 2 (1992): 171–98, as well as Andrew J. Major, 'State and Criminal Tribes in Colonial Punjab: Surveillance, Control and Reclamation of the "Dangerous Classes"', *MAS* 33, no. 3 (1999): 657–88 and R. Tolen, 'Colonizing and Transforming the Criminal Tribesman: The Salvation Army in British India', in Jennifer Terry and Jacqueline Urla (eds), *Deviant Bodies: Critical Perspectives on Difference in Science and Popular Culture* (Bloomington: Indiana University Press, 1995), 78–108.

149 There is a vast body of literature on 'hereditary criminality' in colonial India. For some recent general accounts see, for instance, M. Fourcade, 'The So-Called Criminal Tribes of India: Colonial Violence and Traditional Violence', in D. Vidal, G. Tarabout and E. Meyer (eds), *Violence/Non-Violence. Some Hindu Perspectives* (New Delhi: Manohar, 2004), 143–73. M. Brown, 'Race, Science and the Construction of Native Criminality in Colonial India', in *Theoretical Criminology* 5, no. 3 (2001): 345–68. M. Brown, 'Ethnology and Colonial Administration in Nineteenth-Century British India: The Question of Native Crime and Criminality', in *British Journal of the History of Science* 36, no. 2 (2003): 201–19; Major, 'State and Criminal Tribes in Colonial Punjab''; S. B. Freitag, 'Crime in the Social Order of Colonial North India', in *Modern Asian Studies* 25, no. 2 (1991): 227–61; J. Pouchepadass, 'Criminal Tribes of British India: A Repressive Concept in Theory and Practice', in *International Journal of Asian Studies* 2, no. 1 (1982): 41–59.

150 Booth-Tucker, *Muktifauj*, p. 164; Smith, *By Love Compelled*, 103–4; Cox, *Imperial Fault Lines*, p. 240; and Radhakrishna, 'Surveillance and Settlements', 179.

151 *The War Cry*, 16, no. 4 (April 1910): 13.

152 United Provinces: One of the British Presidencies in Northern India.

153 *The War Cry*, 25, no. 11 (November 1919): 6. See also C. R. Henderson, 'Control of Crime in India', in *Journal of the American Institute of Criminal Law and Criminology* 4, no. 3 (1913): 378–401.

154 Mackenzie, *Booth-Tucker*, 221.

155 Tolen, 'Colonizing and Transforming the Criminal Tribesman', p. 94. See also NAI, GoI Home Dept Progs, Jails, A—35–36 (April 1914), 'Report on the Experimental Salvation Army Settlement, Lahore for the Reclamation of Juvenile Criminals'.

156 The OIOC, IOR: P/9453, GoI, Home Dept, Jail Progs, 1914, Letter No. 364 G.I., Lieut.-Col. G.F.W. Braide, IMS, Inspector-General of Prisons, Punjab to the Revenue Secretary to the Government of Punjab (January 30, 1914).

157 NAI, GoI Home Dept Progs, Police, A—102–03 (November 1910), 'Letter from General Booth of the Salvation Army Making Certain Proposals in the Connection with the Reclamation of Criminal Tribes'.

158 *Ibid.*

159 Commissioner Booth-Tucker, *India's Millions: Being a Summary of a Lecture on the Work of the Salvation Army in India* (London-Edinburgh: Marshall Bros., 1923), 13.

160 *The War Cry*, 25, no. 11 (November 1919): 6.

161 F. Booth-Tucker, *Criminocurology or the Indian Criminal and what to do with him: being a review of the work of the Salvation army among the prisoners, habituals and criminal tribes of India*, 4th ed. (Simla: Liddell's Printing Works, 1916), 33.

162 'Address Presented to his Excellency the Viceroy by Commissioner Fakir Singh. At the Industrial Exhibition and Sale of Work at Simla', *The War Cry* 21, no. 7 (July 1915): 2; and Booth-Tucker, *Muktifauj*, 212–3.

163 See Radhakrishna, *Dishonoured by History*, chapter 3; and Tolen, 'Colonizing and Transforming the Criminal Tribesman', 94–9.

164 *The War Cry* 17, no. 7 (July 1911): 1; 21, no. 7 (July 1915): 1–4; Cox, *Imperial Fault Lines*, 241; and Booth-Tucker, *Muktifauj*, 163–4. See also *The War Cry* 22, no. 1 (January 1916): 5–7.

165 Booth-Tucker, *Muktifauj*, 49.

166 K. Kawashima, *Missionaries and a Hindu State: Travancore 1858–1936* (Delhi: Oxford University Press, 1998), 136 and Radhakrishna, *Dishonoured by History*, 78.

167 Mackenzie, *Booth-Tucker*, 207.

168 'Address Presented to his Excellency the Viceroy by Commissioner Fakir Singh. At the Industrial Exhibition and Sale of Work at Simla', *The War Cry* 21, no. 7 (July 1915): 2; and Booth-Tucker, *Muktifauj*, 212–3.

169 In 1916, two corps consisting of 800 'coolies' each were sent to the Persian Gulf under the command of European Salvation Army officers; they served in loading and unloading ships. *The War Cry* 22, no. 10 (October 1916): 11 and *The War Cry* 24, no. 8 (August 1918): 1.

170 Salvation Army, *The Salvation Army. Its origin and development*, 61–2. Quite astonishingly, a critical evaluation of the army's role in the reeducation of the so-called Crims seems not to have taken place, as the reclamation work it is still described as 'one of the greatest and most successful enterprises in the history of the Salvation Army in India' in semiofficial accounts published in the 1980s. See Smith, *By Love Compelled*, 103, and Williams, *Booth-Tucker*, 178.

171 For the following see also Harald Fischer-Tiné, 'Britain's Other Civilizing Mission: Class Prejudice, European Loaferism and the Workhouse-System in Colonial India', in *Indian Economic and Social History Review* 42, no. 3 (2005): 295–338, 323–26. Maharashtra State Archives, Government of Bombay, Judicial Dept Progs,Vol. 134 (1910), 'The Loafer Problem in Bombay', Memorandum by F. Booth-Tucker, Salvation Army.

172 Maharashtra State Archives, Government of Bombay, Judicial Dept Progs, Vol. 134 (1910), 'The Loafer Problem in Bombay', Memorandum by F. Booth-Tucker, Salvation Army.

173 *The War Cry* 17, no. 1 (January 1911): 6, 9; OIOC, IOR: P/8599, Government of Bombay Judicial Progs, September–December 1910 A—30 November 1910, 'Opening of the Industrial Home for Europeans Vagrants in the City of Bombay'. OIOC, IOR: P/9851, Government of Bombay, Judicial Progs, 1915, Letter No. 13538–6, December 10, 1914. S. M. Edwardes, Commissioner of Police, Bombay, to Under Secretary, Judicial Dept., Bombay A-24, January 1915, 'Report on the Working of the European Vagrants Labour Home, Managed by the Salvation Army', and NAI, GoI, Home Dept Progs, Police, A—141–52, April 1915, 'Despatch from the Secretary of State for India (Public) No. 56 to the Governor General of India in Council' (March 12, 1915).

174 OIOC, IOR: P/9851, Government of Bombay, Judicial Progs, 1915, Letter No. 13538–6 (December 10, 1914). S. M. Edwardes, Commissioner of Police, Bombay, to Under Secretary, Judicial Dept., Bombay A-24, January 1915, 'Report on the Working of the European Vagrants Labour Home, Managed by the Salvation Army', and NAI, GoI, Home Dept. Progs., Police, A—141–52, April 1915, 'Despatch from the Secretary of State for India (Public) No. 56 to the Governor General of India in Council' (March 12, 1915).

175 OIOC, IOR: P/10054 Government of Bombay, Judicial Progs (A-5, March 1916, Letter No. 1476, March 6, 1915. Secy. to Government of Bombay to Commissioner Booth-Tucker of the Salvation Army, 'Proposal to Transfer to the Salvation Army the Management of the Government Workhouses in Bombay and the Erection and Provision of New Buildings for the Male and Female Workhouses'. See also 'The Salvation Army (Western India Territory)', *Reclamation. A Review of the Salvation Army's Social and Medical Activities*, Bombay, n.d. [ca. 1927], 14.

176 *The War Cry* 21, no. 4 (April 1915): 18; 21, no. 7 (July 1915): 8. See also NAI, GoI Home Dept. Progs., Judl., A 28–29, February 1915, 'Establishment by the Salvation Army of a Labour Home for Indigent Europeans and Eurasians at Delhi'.

177 *Ibid.*, Prog. 28, Letter No. 8854, W. M. Hailey, Chief Commissioner of Delhi, to GoI, Home Dept (December 14, 1915).

178 See for instance NAI, GoI Home Dept Progs, Judicial, A—61–62, July 1912, 'Further Continuance of the Scheme Relating to the Establishment of a Labour Home for European Vagrants, by the Salvation Army, Bombay', NAI, GoI Home Dept Progs, Police, A—36–50, November 1912, 'Reclamation Of Criminal Tribes Through the Salvation Army and Grant to the Salvation Army of a Plot of Land in Madras Presidency'; NAI, GoI Home Dept. Progs., Jail, A—62–63, March 1918 'Proposal to Increase Grants to the SA in Madras for Reclamation Work'.

179 Commissioner Booth-Tucker, *India's Millions*, 9.

180 *The War Cry* 17, no. 1 (January 1911): 14.

181 At least four other Salvation Army officers (Col. E. Sheard, Brig. S. Smith and W. Francis and Maj. L. Gale) engaged in the reclamation of 'Crims' later received the same award. See also Smith, *By Love Compelled*, 110.

182 Cox, *Imperial Fault Lines*, 240.

183 F. Booth-Tucker, *Criminocurology*.

184 Tolen, 'Colonizing and Transforming the Criminal Tribesman', 98.

185 Cited in Rightmire, *Salvationist Samurai*, 111.

186 E. Booth, 'Around the World with the Salvation Army', in *National Geographic* 72, no. 1 (1920): 351.

187 *Ibid.*, 363.

188 D. C. Korten, N. Perlas and V. Shiva, 'Global Civil Society: The Path Ahead', (http://www.pcdf.org /civilsociety/path.htm), retrieved 1 February 2005.

189 See, for instance, E. P. Thompson, 'Time, Work-discipline, and Industrial Capitalism', *Past & Present* 38 (1967): 56–97.

Chapter Five

MEDIATING MODERNITY: COLONIAL STATE, INDIAN NATIONALISM AND THE RENEGOTIATION OF THE 'CIVILIZING MISSION' IN THE INDIAN CHILD MARRIAGE DEBATE OF 1927–1932

Andrea Major

When discussing the attitude that the Government of India should take to the Hindu Child Marriage Restraint Bill, proposed by Rai Sahib Harbilas Sarda in February 1927, Home Member Sir James Crerar commented that they should regulate child marriage through a Government measure, rather than a Private Member's Bill, because 'Governments are invariably held responsible in the end for all legislation, whether they have promoted it themselves or merely acquiesced in it. If any odium is incurred it will inevitably fall on the Government and we may as well have the merit'.[1] Crerar's remarks epitomize the ambivalent relationship between colonial state and social reform in early twentieth century India, encapsulating both the desire to legitimize imperialism through 'improvement', and the need to reconcile, and even subordinate, reformist projects to political expediencies. Such tensions between justificatory discourses and pragmatic considerations shaped the colonial state's engagement with social reform in the nationalist era; Sarda's Bill existed at an ideological intersection between emergent discourses of Indian nationalism, colonialism as 'civilizing mission' and the survival strategies of a colonial state under growing social and political pressure. Its history reflects the ambivalent role of the colonial state as it attempted to mediate impulses for and against reform, from Indian society, the international community and its own regional representatives. The result was a more complex colonial engagement with social change than is usually allowed in the dichotomy of reform or reaction that epitomizes traditional and revisionist accounts respectively.

The colonial state's engagement with social reform has conventionally been articulated through the concept of 'civilizing mission', a justificatory discourse that rationalized colonial domination by emphasizing the social, political and infrastructural benefits of British rule. Drawing upon popular themes of evangelism and utilitarianism, as well as Enlightenment ideas about the evolution of civilized societies, it assumed that civilizations could be evaluated and ranked, with the domination of the superior justified in terms of the dissemination of 'civilized values'. Various indicators determined a country's level of civilization, including its political institutions, spread of education, technological advancement and, especially, the status of women. In the colonial imagination, the civilizing mission was a unidirectional process, emanating from the imperial centre outwards, implemented by a colonial state that was a catalyst for unprecedented change in the subject society. Revisionist historians have long since undermined this interpretation of colonial state as committed social reformer. As Tanika Sarkar points out, British non-interference in religious and cultural practices left little room for meaningful social legislation,[2] especially after 1858, when the Queen's Proclamation re-enshrined religious neutrality as official policy. The disjuncture between justificatory discourse and actual implementation was evident even during the so-called 'Era of Reform', the period most closely associated with the ideological formulation and practical execution of the civilizing mission. As the two decades of political prevarication, and the tortuous redefinition of its 'traditional' status that preceded the prohibition of sati in 1829 demonstrate, the implementation of the civilizing mission was rarely unproblematic.[3] In the late colonial period, although the British still justified the imperial project in terms of India's 'Moral and Material Progress', they retreated from overt interventions in Indian socio-religious practice and measured their contribution to Indian modernity in terms of developments in infrastructure, technology and the maintenance of law and order. Even after the institution of the Indian Legislative Assemblies in 1919, a private Indian member proposing a bill affecting religious practice had to obtain prior sanction from the Viceroy. Interventions in issues of indigenous conjugality were deemed doubly dangerous, encroaching on both religion and femininity at a time when women's issues were increasingly imagined as belonging to the domestic realm – an uncolonized space guarded jealously against real or perceived incursions by the colonial state.[4] The controversy surrounding the Age of Consent Act of 1891 underlined the explosiveness of such issues for the colonial administrator, who was increasingly advised to 'stay off the woman question'.[5] The early 1920s saw the Government of India repeatedly oppose bills on marriage or consent issues, demonstrating itself reluctant to deal with such controversial subjects, or even allow individual Indian reformers to do so.[6] Such behaviour gave credence to the accusations that far from being an instrument of progress, the colonial state manifested reactionary tendencies, supporting the orthodox 'status quo' over the forces of social advance.

Recent revisionist interpretations of British involvement with the Child Marriage Restraint Act of 1929 reinforce the assumption of colonial conservatism, downplaying any state support and suggesting instead that Government actually sought to block the bill. Mrinalini Sinha echoes the criticism of Indian women's organizations and nationalist reformers, that the Government of India paid lip service to the ideal of social reform while actually employing dilatory tactics to kill the bill. She represents the colonial state as invariably hostile, and the bill's eventual passage as a victory for the incipient Indian women's movement and emergent nation state.[7] Such an indictment of the colonial state's role is an important corrective to laudatory colonial histories. The assumption of homogenous colonial opposition to the measure simplifies the state's position, however. The abstract entity of 'colonial state' was constituted of individuals at various levels of the bureaucracy, who manifested a range of moral and practical attitudes to reform. Nor was the colonial position static; it shifted with the permutations of the debate, as the bill changed shape and different protagonists entered the arena. Most recent studies have contextualized the Sarda Act it in terms of its contribution, real and symbolic, to wider developments in women's rights or Indian nationalism.[8] As a result the complexity of the role of the colonial state is often lost and British engagement with the issue appears one-dimensional and static, impacting upon, but not engaging with, wider developments. In fact, the Government negotiated and reacted to a number of often-conflicting imperatives – moral, ideological and practical – in the regions, the centre and the metropole. This is not to advocate a rehabilitation of the reputation of the colonial state, which, civilizing mission notwithstanding, consistently put imperial stability over any ideological commitment to reform. Rather, it is to seek a better understanding of the survival strategies of the colonial state and the interaction between these and the practical, moral and ideological imperatives that informed its (re)negotiation of the concept of 'civilizing mission' in late colonial India.

Child Marriage, Colonialism and the 'Civilizing Mission'

The social and scriptural origins of Hindu child marriage were hotly contested in the early twentieth century. While orthodox opponents of marriage reform cited both religious texts and popular practice in defence of its authenticity, Indian reformers maintained that during the Vedic period marriage was performed when both parties were mature, suggesting that child marriage was only adopted when medieval invasions made early marriage necessary to protect pubescent girls.[9] While agreeing that child marriage was rare in Vedic India, contemporary scholars like Young and Chakrovarty attribute it instead to the development of Brahmanical Hinduism in the early centuries AD.[10] In this tradition, a woman's status depended on successful reproduction and conjugal fidelity. Marriage was a sacred duty, and the provision of a suitable husband in a hypergamous marriage market was a binding parental responsibility. Early marriage lengthened the girl's reproductive life, protected her chastity, reduced the chance of romance and relieved the natal family of the cost of her support, the threat of her misbehaviour and the potential stigma of having an unmarried daughter. A young bride was also considered more malleable and easily socialized into her new family.[11] As a result pre-puberty marriage became the norm in many high castes and some aspiring lower ones. It is no coincidence that areas of high child marriage were those where Brahmanical Hinduism predominated – Bengal, the Indo-Gangetic plain, Bombay and among high caste communities in Madras[12] – and while child-marriage was far from universal, for those who practiced it, it was underpinned by both religious belief and socio-economic imperatives.

British awareness of child marriage in India is observable from the seventeenth century, as several early European travellers reported that high caste Indians married their children in infancy.[13] Unconcerned with the justification of empire, these travellers had no need to reconstruct child marriage (not unknown in Europe at the time) as an indicator of Indian backwardness and as a result rarely presented it as an evil; indeed some actually praised the conjugal fidelity it engendered.[14] Their lack of censure underlines the extent to which negative constructions of Indian social customs were embedded in a later colonial discourse of civilizing mission that utilized the status of Indian women, and especially Indian widows, in its justification of empire. Child marriage first became a cause for colonial concern in the context of debates on Hindu widowhood and its sensational corollary, sati. Sati was a *cause celebre* in the early nineteenth century and its prohibition in 1829 is often cited as the prime example of the civilizing mission in action. Colonial motivations for outlawing sati remain controversial, however, and recent studies demonstrate the complex interaction between civilizing mission and the political imperatives of the colonial state.[15] The sati debate set a precedent for colonial reform, demonstrating both the possibility for and complexity of colonial interventions in socio-religious issues. After sati, British and Indian reformers turned their attention to the condition of child widows, culminating in the legalisation of widow remarriage in 1856. The 1929 legislation against child marriage completed a triumvirate of social reform legislation relating to Hindu widowhood, striking at the perceived cause of the disproportionate number of widows in Indian society. The poignant image of the child widow was emphasized in all three movements. Anti-sati campaigners emphasized the fact that even children were coerced into the rite; William Ward, for example, recited the story of one eight year old sati who, when the news of her husband's death arrived, was 'playing with the other children at a neighbour's house'.[16] This image of young life cut short was shared by the discourses on ascetic widowhood, as both British and Indian reformers concentrated on the child left widowed before reaching physical or sexual maturity. Such a focus both had emotive appeal and circumvented patriarchal gender norms, which problematized the remarriage of mature, sexually experienced widows. Child marriage reform was thus embedded in a pre-existing discourse on Hindu widowhood; Sarda himself lamented that 'No country in the world except this unhappy land presents the sorry spectacle of having in its population child widows',[17] stating this as the main motivation for his bill. By doing so he situated it within a longer tradition of colonial social reform, underlining the potential of the colonial state to intervene and linking child marriage to a widely accepted evil.

Concern with child marriage was not restricted to issues of widowhood. From the late nineteenth century, it was also presented as an evil in itself. Sensational cases such as those of Rukhmabai and Phulmani Debi highlighted the iniquities of non-consensual, indissoluble infant marriage and premature consummation, focussing attention on the fate of the girl-wife, whose childhood was severed by untimely removal from her natal family, premature sexual activity and maternity. Indeed, the image of the wretched child bride, popularized by missionary and other tracts purporting to describe the position of Indian women, gained a status similar to that of sati as an indicator of Indian 'backwardness', prompting journalist Mary Francis Billington to warn her readers in 1895 that:

Inaccurate sensationalism reaches its climax over the system of child marriage. The assiduously circulated idea of missionary reports and social grievance seekers is that the wretched girl-infant is married at about five or six years of age, generally to someone vastly older than herself, who takes her away whenever he pleases, and exercises whatever violence of brutal lust he cares for.[18]

Many accounts by British, and later American,[19] authors gave the impression that infant marriage and pre-pubescent consummation was the norm, yet Britain's own figures, recorded in the decennial Indian censuses, showed that this was not the case. According to the 1921 census, less than 1.5 per cent of 13.5 million Hindu girls under the age of five were either married or widowed. The figure rose to 12 per cent for girls between the ages of five and ten and 46 per cent for girls between ten and fifteen. Thus even before the 1929 reforms, more than half of Hindu girls were married at the age of 16 or above. Moreover, these figures, which represent national averages, disguise significant regional variations. In Bengal, Bihar, Orissa, the Central Provinces, Berar, the United Provinces and Bombay between 10 per cent and 20 per cent of Hindu girls were married by the age of ten, and between 50 per cent and 60 per cent by the age of fifteen. In Punjab, Assam, Madras and the North West Frontier Provinces, only 1 per cent to 5 per cent of Hindu girls under ten were married and between 20 per cent and 35 per cent of girls under fifteen.[20] My intention here is not to belittle the problem, or undermine the individual tragedies of the many girls who were married, and sometimes widowed, before reaching adulthood, but rather to emphasize both its regional diversity and the distortions imposed by a justificatory colonial discourse that pressed certain social evils into its service.

Indians also focussed on child marriage as a subject for reformist activity in the late nineteenth century. Men like Behramji Malabari, Mahadev Govind Ranade and Ramakrishna Gopal Bhandarkar lobbied for a change in the law to restrain child-marriage and prevent precipitous consummation, while progressive societies such as the Arya Samaj and Brahmo Samaj, as well as some caste associations,[21] outlawed the practice for their members. Such moves reflected a desire to reform controversial aspects of Hinduism in line with an idealized image of the Vedic past, as part of a 'self-civilizing mission' designed to counter negative colonial representations of Indian society and prepare the Indian nation for self-determination. By the late nineteenth century domesticity had become a central trope in discourses of 'civilizing mission', with western ideals of conjugality and companionate marriage acting as markers for advanced behaviour.[22] In response to this, as Charu Gupta points out, Indian reformers constructed an ideology of respectable Hindu domesticity, in which 'the discursive management of female bodies was essential to project a civilized and sectarian Hindu identity and a new nation'.[23] Reform of marriage laws was implicated in a discourse that sought to invert colonial constructions about Indian sexuality and reassert Hindu morality as epitomized by an idealized conjugality.[24] To some extent reformers and revivalists shared this project, although where reformers sought to 'modernize' or 'civilize' Hindu marriage practices in line with global developments and ideas, revivalists emphasized the superiority of existing Hindu customs. Judy Whitehead describes the ideal woman espoused by reformers and women's organizations as 'an educated mother aware of home science and hygiene' who 'combined the self-sacrificing traditional mother image, the education autonomy of the Vedic woman, and hygienically informed 'modern' motherhood'.[25] The orthodox community, on the other hand, took a 'status-quoist position',[26] glorifying the very customs that liberals sought to reform and representing them as indicative of the moral superiority of Hindu civilization. They defended child marriage as engendering pure and virtuous conjugality that reflected the particular excellence of Indian women and their culture. Tanika Sarkar cites the following description of a child bride:

> People in this country take great pleasure in infant marriage. The little bit of a woman, the infant bride, clad in red silk [...] Drums are beating and men women and children are running in order to have a glimpse at that lovely face. From time to time she breaks forth into little ravishing smiles. She looks like a lovely little doll.[27]

Sarkar emphasises the way in which such sensualized descriptions of the child bride subsume the trauma of patrilocality and non-consensual, indissoluble infant marriage in the rhetoric of idealized Hindu conjugality.

Nationalism, Feminism and the 'Self-Civilizing Mission'

The 1927–1930 child marriage debate was thus implicated in wider discourses presenting the Hindu girl-child as an icon (positive or negative) of Hindu civilization. It was also deeply embedded in the social and political context of late 1920s India. As Mrinalini Sinha has pointed out, the passage of the Sarda Act took place at a moment of social and political disjuncture that created space for an otherwise unremarkable bill.[28] Against the backdrop of growing Indian nationalism, the independent women's movement and a crisis of confidence in the colonial state, the publication of Katherine Mayo's pro-imperialist diatribe *Mother India* represented a transformative moment.[29] Mayo's vitriolic and often disingenuous attack on social conditions in India, including child marriage, was meant to bolster the position of the colonial state by emphasizing the physical and moral degeneracy of the aspiring Hindu nation, but it also, perhaps inadvertently, highlighted the failures of two centuries of 'civilizing mission'. The book caused a major controversy, providing impetus for a reintegration of social reform and nationalist rhetoric, articulated as 'self-civilizing mission' in the service of Indian social and political modernity. Child marriage was an apposite issue for such a project. Not only was it Mayo's main line of attack, but it also resonated with wider international developments in maternal health, hygiene, child welfare, scientific advances in pre- and postnatal care, fashionable ideologies like eugenics and social Darwinism and emerging ideas about universal human rights,[30] all of which were recognized indicators of social modernity.[31] As Geraldine Forbes points out, by supporting child marriage reform, and linking it with the physical and political vitality of the aspiring nation, Indian nationalists demonstrated their commitment to modernity and to securing India's place within the global framework of competing nations.[32] Sarda called his bill 'a very modest attempt to recognize that female children, even among Hindus, have certain inalienable rights and that the State with any pretensions to civilization will deem it its duty to protect them, without heeding the vagaries that masquerade in the guise of social customs'.[33] Reform of child marriage allowed India to align itself with global advances, stake its claim as an advanced nation and challenge the colonial state to apply universal 'civilized' principles to India, regardless of the pressure of orthodox opinion. Indeed, Mrinalini Sinha suggests that in this debate, Indian nationalist reformers publicly divested the colonial state of its claim to be the instrument of modernity in India, assuming that mantle for themselves[34] and exposing what Partha Chatterjee has termed 'the rule of colonial difference' – the inability of the colonial state to allow subject people to fully attain the modernity it purports to bestow.[35] The *Modern Review* invoked the image of 'civilizing mission' grinding to a halt in the face of sinister imperial imperatives, saying:

The abolition of child marriage and child mortality and the raising of the age of consent within and outside marital relations would tend to make Indians a physically, intellectually and morally fitter nation. But British bureaucrats have all along been very unwilling to help Indian social reformers in affecting these reforms by direct and indirect legislation. They had no objection to abolish suttee, probably because it was mainly a question of humanity; – the abolition of suttee was not expected to promote the building up of a stalwart nation. But the abolition of child marriage is indirectly and almost directly, a political as well as a social remedy. So in these matters our British bureaucrat friends fall back on the cant of neutrality and non-interference in religious and socio-religious matters. As if suttee, hook swinging, etc., were not such things, which the British Government have stopped by legislation.[36]

For Sarda, a 'self-civilizing mission' was integral to the success of nationalism. A staunch Arya Samajist and author of *Hindu Superiority: An Attempt to Determine the Position of the Hindu Race in the Scale of Nations* (1906), Sarda used a Western evolutional and civilizational framework to expound both his belief in the superiority of Hindu Vedic culture and his commitment to reforming aspects of social practice that deviated from the Vedic ideal and undermined India's standing in global terms.[37] 'Progress is unity', he declared 'and if we are to make any advance, and if we are to come into line [...] with the progressive countries of the West or to be completely free from their domination, a programme of social reform of a thorough going character […] must be taken in hand along with the pursuit of political reform'.[38] Such reforms, he argued were vital if India was to 'hold our own in the international conflict of interests, the clash of colour and the struggle for life, which is raging all over the world' because 'so long as these evils exist we will have neither the strength of arm nor the strength of character to win freedom'.[39]

Thus although ostensibly a social reform designed to prevent child widowhood, Sarda's bill very quickly became a vehicle for a political debate over the well being of the Indian nation, physically and metaphorically. Sarda and his supporters emphasized that such 'self-civilizing' was compatible with Hinduism; as S. Srinivasa Iyenagar put it, 'we who stand up for Hinduism have a duty to see that Hinduism promotes the growth of a virile race of men and an efficient race of girls who will become the mothers of a greater India'.[40] Both Indian nationalists and the British government knew that the eyes of the world were upon this debate. Sarda warned 'The world is watching if the members of this house possess the necessary self-restraint, the capacity and the liberal mindedness to appreciate the rights of those who are at their mercy'.[41] Even Gandhi, who opposed cooperation with the Legislative Assemblies on political grounds, urged the members to vote for the bill as a matter of national duty.[42] Outside the Assembly, protesters held placards warning 'If you oppose Sarda's Bill, the world will laugh at you'.[43] Civilizing Hindu marriage customs was thus inextricably linked to political progress and to positioning India as an equal among 'civilized' nations. In adopting the rhetoric of modernity, supporters of Sarda's bill were simultaneously undermining and appropriating the colonial discourse of 'civilizing mission', refashioning the justificatory discourse of the colonial state into one of their own. The reformist/nationalist elites' desire to 'bestow' social progress on the 'dumb millions of India' represented an attempt to legitimize their own political aspirations as future rulers of India, just as British interventions in issues like sati had been used to validate imperialism. As Geraldine Forbes points out, the flaws in the final bill and the failure of nationalists to commit to its enforcement suggests that they were more committed to its symbolic utility than to actually improving women's lives.[44]

Not everybody was prepared to adhere to discourses of 'western' modernity, of course. Opponents of the bill made religious freedom their central argument, claiming that scriptural authority and popular usage made marriage before puberty a binding religious duty for some communities. They did this in the context of 'modern', 'universal' rights to freedom of conscience, contesting the right of a civilized state, colonial or Indian, to penalize the pious in their pursuit of their religious beliefs.[45] They denied the evil of child marriage, emphasizing instead its contribution to a perfected Hindu version of monogamous and companionate marriage. Acharya cited 'scientific' evidence refuting the evil consequences of early cohabitation and emphasized the moral and practical benefits of such a system.[46] Child marriage, he argued, was the only humane way of ensuring sexual morality and was the best way of producing conjugal happiness: 'blessed are they who will help to bring their little children together unconsciously into those life long unions which probably know no end even when the body passes away; for, according to man's higher view, love is immortal, love is divine'. 'Yet', Acharya lamented, 'this Legislature will intervene to take away the girl of 11 from the boy of 18, and the boy from the embrace of his married wife and send him to jail. Can you think of a greater horror?'[47] Such positions sought to invert the traditional assumptions underpinning the civilizing mission and, as Charu Gupta points out, 'revealed the oppressive and aggressive nature of Hindu patriarchy, but were camouflaged in the language of love'.[48] Such arguments invoked an alternate interpretation of 'civilized values', making Hindu domestic norms superior and pressing the colonial state to adhere to the 'civilized values' of religious tolerance and freedom of conscience. M. S. Sesha Ayyangar complained that to punish a form of marriage considered by many to be 'valid in law, ordained by religion and sanctified by immemorial usage' was a violation that had no parallel anywhere in the 'civilized world'.[49] A 'self-civilizing mission', some opponents of the bill argued, did not have to reproduce the westernizing mission of the colonialists; it could mean perfecting superior Hindu institutions. Amar Nath Dutt warned the Assembly not to be 'misled by the hypnotism of words such as "progress", "advance", "emancipation" and "twentieth century" into thinking that the path of civilization must follow in the footsteps of the western nations'.[50] India's superior civilization rested upon perfected Hindu tradition and this bill was guilty of 'setting at naught our ancient ideals of marriage'. Indeed, he commented on the irony that Sarda, who in his book *Hindu Superiority* had sought to show that Hindu civilization could be ranked as high as any in the world, should 'now give up his respect for the ancient ideals'[51] and align himself with the 'westernizers' in an attempt to foist a false modernity on India.

The idea of Hindu child marriage as the epitome of conjugal felicity was imbedded in a patriarchal constructions of Hindu society that spoke 'as if there were only one sex in the world',[52] ignoring the views of women themselves. Although organized Indian women's voices against child marriage only emerged in the 1920s, indications of women's dissatisfaction with the system predate this. Tanika Sarkar cites eighteenth century devotional poetry, Agamani songs, lullabies and folk songs as depicting the bleakness of the young bride's experience of patrilocal marriage and the joint family system – 'the son of a stranger is coming to take me away and I shall never play again'.[53] This dissatisfaction was expressed in the late nineteenth century in tracts and books by Indian women, and in the early twentieth century through varieties of print media and by the organization of women's groups and platforms. As Mrinalini Sinha has argued, the child marriage debate of the 1920s was the first time that women entered the discourse as autonomous agents and rights bearing subjects,[54] for although the use of the term 'Consent' in 1891 suggested an incipient sense of women's individual humanity and rational agency, women were not yet seen 'to be in possession of individuated identity or self – separable from the family-kin-community nexus – to which rights could adhere'.[55] In the 1920s, while male politicians were debating this bill in the Legislative Assembly, women's organizations across India were rallying support for legislation against child marriage. The Women's Indian Association championed the bill in its journal *Stri Dharma*, aligning child marriage with issues such as child and maternal welfare work and female education.[56] As well as passing resolutions in organized meetings and petitioning government, women gathered outside the assembly during debates, bearing placards supporting the bill. Significantly, where male reformers discussed child marriage in terms of a wider nationalist agenda of improving the race and civilizing the nation, women's groups, while not immune to nationalist rhetoric, stressed the intrinsic benefits of reform for women in terms of carefree childhoods, better education and improved prospects of happiness within marriage, lamenting the child bride who, 'robbed of her own girlhood and youth, is almost unaware of the many happinesses of a cultured life'.[57] Indian women's support for the bill was problematic for its opponents, who needed to present 'traditional' Hindu conjugality as both civilized and superior. M. S. Sesha Ayyanagar cited meetings of conservative women in Kumbakonam, Madras and Benares against the bill, while also declaring that female supporters of the bill were 'ladies strayed out of the ancient Indian manner of feminine ideal and conduct'.[58] 'True' Hindu woman's voices, he argued, were not heard because they had not divested themselves of their modesty by entering the public arena. By thinking 'only of the pleasures of this life', organized women only emphasized their unfitness to speak for Hindu womanhood.[59] Yet as the volume and vociferousness of women's support for the bill attests, the organized women's movement was moving beyond the constraints of traditional patriarchy and taking many ordinary women with them on this issue. Women, it seems, did not accept that 'tradition' equalled superior civilization. As Sarda himself put it, 'the women of India do not talk of Shastra; they do not bother themselves about the effect of marriage on their prospects in the next world. They are practical and think of this world, and they want that their sufferings in this world should come to an end'.[60] When told that the Shastras enjoined child marriage, one woman, Kamala Lakshman Rao, responded 'we want new Shastras'.[61]

British women also joined the campaign against child marriage, led by Eleanor Rathbone, who used the suffragist organ *Women's Leader and Common Cause* to remind them of their 'duty' towards their Indian sisters, the improvement of whose condition she believed was 'vital to our own self respect and to the success of every women's movement'.[62] The position of Rathbone's movement closely resembled the traditional discourse of civilizing mission, invoking social reform as a moral obligation of the legitimate colonial state. The difficulties that Rathbone faced engaging with the Indian women's movement reflects the ambivalent position of British women within the colonial project; on the one hand critical of the Government of India's failure to act decisively in favour of social reform, while simultaneously unable to escape the tendency to 'bestow' solutions on Indian subjects.[63] As a result of this paternalism (maternalism?), the relationship between Rathbone and the Indian feminists was problematic, with women like Dhanvanthi Rama Rau contesting the right of British women to speak for their Indian sisters.[64] Despite this, *The Woman's Leader and Common Cause* actively supported the Sarda Bill and openly criticized Government inaction and the 'sinister combination' of government with Hindu orthodoxy on social reform issues.[65] Rathbone repeatedly harried the Secretary of State for India on the issue in Parliament, both before and for some years after the Act came into force, arguing that it was the duty of the colonial state to facilitate and enforce such obviously beneficial reforms. As had the sati debate a century earlier, the child marriage controversy caught the imagination of British reformers partly because of sensational coverage of the issue, and partly because its themes resonated with prominent domestic concerns including maternal health, hygiene and child welfare. The uplift and training of working class mothers in Britain and young mothers in India were both part of an emerging feminist discourse of civilizing mission, expressed in medical rather than moral terms, which stressed the universal value of 'modern' maternity.[66] In an interesting example of the bi-directionality of the colonial experience, the Indian child marriage debate also prompted British feminists to successfully lobby Government to raise the age of marriage in Britain to sixteen, on the basis that 'it is impossible to ask for a higher marriage age in India until our own house is set in order'.[67] Of course, not all British public opinion backed the Sarda Bill and there was a significant seam of support for non-interference in socio-religious issues. Dhanvanthi Rama Rau was famously disillusioned when the wives of British officials in Simla refused to support her campaign for the Sarda Bill because it would contravene the Queen's Proclamation. Others detached opposition to this particular measure, which they saw as deeply flawed and unenforceable, from a wider engagement with social reform.[68]

Pragmatism, Principle and the Colonial State

The role of the colonial state in the Sarda Bill debate has received much criticism, both at the time and subsequently. Mrinalini Sinha even suggests that the Government, faced with the unenviable dilemma of supporting the bill and alienating Hindu orthodoxy or opposing it and appearing reactionary, first tried dilatory tactics to kill it prematurely then, when this failed, opposed it openly, relenting only on the eve of its passing in September 1929.[69] Analysis of the debate from the colonial perspective, however, reveals a more complex engagement with the measure. The controversy over *Mother India* forced the colonial state to renegotiate its own relationship with social reform in a climate where conservative 'neutrality' would be read as reactionary obstructionism, while impending nationalist agitation increased the need for political pragmatism. Rather than uniformly opposing the bill, the Government's position and tactics shifted between active support, deferment and opposition as the shape of the bill and the political considerations connected with it evolved through the different stages of the bill's three-year legislative journey.

The bill introduced by Sarda in February 1927 bore little resemblance to that finally passed in September 1929. Sarda's initial bill sought to regulate Hindu marriages by invalidating those involving girls below 12 years and boys below 14 years, allowing for the marriage of girls of 11 in exceptional circumstances. As such, despite the controversy that would rage over its final form, the bill was not particularly contentious. Fixing the age at 12 (potentially 11) satisfied significant segments of Hindu orthodoxy, which required only that girls be married on or before puberty, an event rarely conceived to occur before 12 years. Even staunch Sanatanists Acharya and Madan Mohan Malaviya were prepared to accept the premise of regulating pre-pubescent marriage.[70] Reformers and women's groups were prepared to accept Sarda's Bill as a first step, while most Muslims had no objection to a measure that did not apply to their community. There were significant concerns about the actual terms of the bill, especially the invalidation of marriages, but the principle received widespread approval and significant pressure was put on the colonial state to support the measure.

Despite this pressure, the British followed their usual policy by moving for circulation when the bill was first debated in September 1927. While declaring that he had a 'large measure of sympathy' with the principle of the bill, Home Member Sir James Crerar invoked the customary excuse that the Government had a duty to consult 'all legitimate interests and legitimate opinion'. Significantly, he also stressed the need to ensure that 'such measures as are proposed are really conducive to the ends to which they are directed' – a direct reference to the flawed construction of the bill.[71] Support for circulation among orthodox members of the house,[72] combined with the hostile position taken by the former Home Member (Sir Alexander Muddiman) led to circulation being understood as a dilatory measure, eliciting criticism from both the bill's supporters within the Assembly and women's groups outside it. M. R. Jayakar, for example, accused the government of 'ignorance and timidity' where religion was concerned, asking whether circulation was necessary to 'ascertain that the proper place for a child under 12 is the nursery and not the marriage bed'.[73] *Stri Dharma* criticized the motion as revealing a desire to 'delay action on the whole question'[74] and repeatedly called on the government to adhere to its policy of 'neutrality' by remaining aloof from the divisions in the house.[75] It is not clear, however, that the Government had actually decided its position at this stage. Muddiman had advocated dilatory tactics,[76] and circulation would certainly have afforded the Government valuable time, but it was also usual practice for private members' bills. Crerar himself stated that circulation was desirable 'so that the attitude to be adopted to the bill in its further stages may be decided',[77] suggesting that he was not yet committed to following his predecessor's proposed policy of obstructionism. Indeed, he declared his support for the bill in principle, although at the same time pointing out its 'obvious defects'[78] in terms of practical implementation.

The government measure for circulation was defeated in the Assembly and the bill was referred to a select committee, scheduled to meet in the Spring session of 1928. Still keen to ascertain public and local government opinion, Crerar used the intervening period to have the bill circulated by executive order. A range of opinions were collected from individuals and organizations across British India. Attitudes were mixed, both among Indian and British respondents. Supporters of the bill, including the major women's groups, warmly endorsed the principle, although some called for an age of 14 or even 16 for girls. Its opponents, on the other hand, including staunchly orthodox groups such as the Marwari Association of Bengal, refused to acknowledge any evil consequences arising from infant marriage and opposed any interference in their domestic relations.[79] Others accepted a minimum age, but wanted it set at eight or ten years. Some British officials, like the Governor of Madras, supported the principle of reducing child marriage, but opposed any legislative intervention in social issues, preferring to trust to the (less disruptive) influence of time and public opinion.[80] Others, like the Government of Bihar and Orissa (a state with very high levels of child marriage), feared the bill would do little except stir up anti-British feeling.[81] The Punjab Executive Council found itself split on the issue, while the Commissioner of Sind and Governor of Bombay actively supported the idea of legislation and encouraged the Government to uphold the well-intentioned aims of the reformers.[82] J. A. Shillady, the secretary to the Government of India, agreed with this latter position, advising that

> Realising to the full the disturbance that may be caused, and the agitation that may be set on foot by malicious representation, the evil is such and the effects on the people so great, while the advance of public opinion is so slow, that I feel the risk…should be run in an endeavour to support those who would take a step forward at the present time.[83]

He advocated giving the bill their 'warm support', adding that he found it difficult 'to accept with complacency the argument that matters are progressing and that we should trust to time and enlightenment […] the question is one that requires Government's aid, and without such aid little progress will be made'.[84] As a result the Executive Council decided to support the reform, with the caveat that the clause invalidating child marriages be exchanged for one that penalized the adults who arranged them.[85]

The invalidation of marriages was raised as a problem by reformist and reactionary respondents alike. Not only did it transgress the ideal of Hindu marriage as an indissoluble sacrament, but a compelling argument was also made that invalidation would penalize the very children the reform was designed to protect. Indians and Europeans alike feared that if complaints were made after the event, in the eyes of the community the girl would be married, legal interpretations notwithstanding. If there was significant delay, the marriage might even have been consummated and children born, who would be rendered retrospectively illegitimate. Declaring such marriages invalid would not punish the adults who orchestrated the unions, but would render the wife a *de facto* widow; legally single, bereft of marital protection and unlikely to find another husband. Given that the bill's very rationale was to prevent child widowhood, such an outcome was obviously counterproductive. On this basis, Crerar declared that 'The actual provisions of the bill are irredeemably bad and must be strongly opposed'.[86]

The subsequent change from invalidation to penalization of under age marriages has been viewed retrospectively as weakening the measure. Whatever the eventual impact, suffice here to say that Government opposition to the original bill was based on a practical assessment of its workability, rather than ideological opposition to the principle of reform. That this was more than simply a pretext for inaction is reinforced when we consider that invalidation was also a key sticking point for the 1929 Age of Marriage Act in Britain; the *Women's Leader and Common Cause* worried that invalidation would mean 'the man could not be required to maintain the wife, nor could any child be legitimated',[87] while the House of Lords delayed the passage of the bill in

March 1929 to debate whether underage marriages should be automatically void, or simply be voidable, because of unease about illegitimacy.[88] In India such concerns were exacerbated by accepted socio-religious ideals of indissolubility of Hindu marriage, leading the Government decided that, unless it was suitably amended, they would have to oppose the bill if it came to a vote.[89] The Government of India thus found itself needing to oppose the unworkable provisions of the bill without appearing unsympathetic to social reform, 'the necessity of which', it admitted, 'cannot be disputed'.[90] Crerar proposed that the Government should oppose Sarda's bill, but only on the basis of presenting its own bill, in which child marriages would be penalized by a fine or prison sentence for the adults involved. Making the bill a government measure would be a means of reaffirming British commitment to its 'civilizing mission'. It was also a way of making the best of a bad situation. As we noted at the beginning of this chapter, Crerar believed that 'If any odium is incurred it will inevitably fall on the Government and we may as well have the merit'.[91] Other members of the Executive Council were concerned, however, that even such qualified opposition would make the Government liable to 'adverse but merited criticism for adopting obstructivist tactics',[92] which would foster the misconception that the Government opposed the principle, not just the terms, of the bill. It was eventually deemed 'tactically advantageous' to persuade Sarda to present a revised measure along the lines proposed by the Government and a draft bill penalizing the celebration of marriages of girls under 12 and boys under 15 was accordingly prepared by the Legislative Department.[93] Thus rather than attempting to block the bill, at this stage at least, the Executive Council actually supported a legislative measure to restrict child marriage and was actively engaging in ways to make this a plausible reality.

The bill that emerged out of the Select Committee in March 1928 was a penal measure, applicable to all religious communities, which set the legal age of marriage at 14 for girls and 16 for boys. The first two alterations were incorporated at the express wish of the Government, which now changed its position to one of unequivocal support for the bill. Even Sarda accepted that the Government was 'committed to legislative action on the question of child marriage' and had 'given all possible assistance to the passage of the bill'.[94] Crerar confirmed this position, saying it had his 'cordial support'. He stressed that the bill opposed by Muddiman 'was a very different measure from that which has now emerged' which was 'a measure along sound lines'.[95] The changes in the bill did not please everyone, however. M. K. Acharya, who had surprised some by supporting the original bill, came out in strong opposition to the new penal measure, saying 'It is a matter of principle with me that the state ought not to penalise the views of those who honestly believe [...] that the line they are pursuing is the right line of conduct'.[96]

Because the amendments to the bill were significant, the Select Committee asked that the newly framed bill be re-circulated for opinion. When the new opinions were received in September 1928, standard procedure was to refer the bill back to the Select Committee, although Sarda requested that this be suspended and the bill taken into consideration immediately. The Government refused on the basis that new opinions needed 'careful consideration'.[97] Such a postponement was frustrating for Sarda, and was the first indication of a further shift in the position of the Government, which was worried by the significant opposition the new bill had engendered. The orthodox community attacked it vociferously, claiming that the change in age from 12 to 14 was an infringement of *shastric* injunction. On 18 September 1928 the Viceroy received a deputation of orthodox Hindus led by the Maharaja of Dharbhanga and M. K. Acharya, who claimed the proposed measure was an infringement of their religious rights and would 'set millions in rebellion against Government'.[98] On 21 September 1928 the Home Member placed on file a memorandum signed by thirty members of the Legislative Assembly, Hindu and Muslim, asking that the Government oppose the bill on the grounds that it struck 'at the root of the most cherished and sacred institution of Hindus and Muslims and penalized what is lawful under the personal law of Hindus and Muslims'.[99] The extension of the bill to the Muslim community had caused a wave of opposition, manifested in the tabling of several amendments exempting Muslims from the scope of the bill. The Government had not foreseen a major problem with the Muslim community, believing child marriage to be a Hindu issue and any opposition by Muslims to be 'more or less sentimental […] for the simple reason that child marriages are rare in that community'.[100] In fact, a significant proportion of Muslims especially in Bihar and Orissa and the United Provinces did practice child marriage, but opposition was based not on the popularity of the custom, but on the principle that marriage customs were covered by Sharia Law and state interference with them was an infringement of Muslim minority rights. In the light of an alliance between orthodox Hindu and some Muslim members, the Government believed the bill might be defeated if Sarda pursued his intention to have it taken into consideration at that time.[101]

The Government found itself caught between growing pressure from the reformers and international public opinion[102] on one side and the wishes of the Hindu orthodoxy and Muslim communalists on the other. These latter two groups formed the colonial state's natural constituency of support and their conciliation was certainly politically desirable. Discussions about the 'tactical problem' posed by the whole child marriage issue were ongoing at the highest level, with the Viceroy among others suggesting ways to 'reconcile our duty of encouraging reform with the desirability of having a reasonable regard for average public opinion'.[103] Suggestions included distinguishing between betrothal (especially the Muslim *nikah* ceremony) and marriage, or making the legislation a permissive bill that provincial governments could enforce at their discretion. Both these suggestions were aimed primarily at placating the Muslim community; the latter in particular allowing non-implementation in Muslim majority areas such as North West Frontier Province and Punjab, which were more prone to political disturbance than to child marriage. These suggestions, which reflected both the pragmatic orientation of the colonial state and an appreciation of the regional diversity of child marriage as a problem, were, however, not ultimately considered plausible, leaving the Government with the following options: to change tack and oppose the bill; to pass the bill, but to also allow amendments exempting the Muslim community; to remain neutral; to use their voting power to pass it, alienating the orthodox Hindu and Muslim communities; or to seek a delay by waiting for the report of the Age of Consent Committee, with the hope that in the meantime a compromise could be reached. While most agreed that the first three were all now impossible, there was some debate about the relative merits of remaining two courses. B. L. Mitter advocated passing the bill and taking the consequences, while G. Schuster considered that delaying in order to allow further discussion, not of the principle but of the terms of the bill, would be the best way forward, with the Government adopting 'the attitude of an independent and impartial arbiter, as between opposing views'.[104] At this stage the colonial state's commitment to reform had been overtaken by the political expediencies of the moment, and it seems apparent that only fear of a public relations disaster prevented them from actively opposing the bill.

Having decided to try and delay the bill, but still hopeful of finding a solution to their predicament, the Home Member wrote to Sarda suggesting that he defer consideration of his bill in order to allow a compromise to be reached. Sarda was very much opposed to the delay, however, and determined to move the bill on 29 January 1929 as intended. At this debate the Government, while still claiming to support the bill in principle, forced a postponement by backing Acharya's motion to wait for the Age of Consent Committee Report. This strategy backfired, however; no compromise was ultimately reached and its actions in delaying the issue gave rise to widespread accusations that it was deliberately impeding the passage of the bill. Annie Besant vociferously attacked the Government's action in the pages of *New India*, *Stri Dharma* was hotly critical, and Sarda himself also hit out at the obstructionist actions of the state. The *Women's Leader and Common Cause*, hit the nail on the head when it commented that 'On the face of it – and from a publicity point of view – the Government action appears a deplorable mistake. Any delaying action of the kind that may be tactically necessary [...] should be carried through with some show of positive intention'.[105] As a result of this popular backlash, the

Government of India eventually felt that it had little choice but to support the bill, even in the face of growing Muslim and orthodox Hindu opposition and it was eventually passed in September 1929. The colonial state continued to seek ways of mitigating the impact of the Act on their relationship with the orthodox and Muslim communities, however, insisting on a six month period of grace before the bill was enforced and allowing (but not supporting) the tabling of a number of amendments to exclude Muslims from the operation of the bill on the grounds that 'It would be a serious tactical error to refuse to permit discussion [...] however embarrassing it may be to Government. The Muhammadans cannot be muzzled'.[106]

The Aftermath

British engagement with the passage of the Sarda Act was more complicated than simple obstructionism, involving the negotiation of a variety of issues and concerns. The relative toothlessness of the final act and the Government's failure to rigorously enforce it has rightly led to criticism of its commitment to implementing social reform. It is clear that from the outset the Government considered that the impact of the act would be primarily educative and that the associated penalties should not be too severe as 'it is advisable to make a modest beginning in social legislation'. Crerar even admitted that 'It was never our intention that there should be a vast mass of prosecutions so as to enforce strictly the operation of this Act [...] It was definitely a cautious Bill, not intended for wholesale execution'. The failure to include a provision for the registration of births and marriages was a glaring hole in the legislation, making it difficult to prove violations. Prosecutions under the act were rare; between the act coming into force on 1 April 1930 and 31 August 1932 there were 473 prosecutions and only 167 convictions.[107] In the light of widespread agitation against the reform, the Government was prompted to warn that 'care should be taken to ensure that the introduction of the act is not made the signal for numerous and sensational prosecutions'.[108] Such timidity in terms of the enforcement of the Act has rightly engendered criticism, but the extent and nature of the Act's implementation, or otherwise, must also be understood in terms of the political climate of the time. A delay of six months between the passing and the implementation of the bill was designed to allow passions on the matter to subside. In the intervening period, however, there was a sharp increase in child marriages, as parents hastened their children's nuptials in order to circumvent the provisions of the Act, while the voices of women's movements in Britain and India calling for its strict enforcement, were drowned out by a wave of protest meetings, petitions and amendments tabled in the Legislative Assembly. Moreover, the coming into force of the

Sarda Act coincided with Gandhi's Salt March to Dandi and the launching of civil disobedience in March/April 1930. With the country once again on the brink of major social and political unrest, it is hardly surprising that enforcing a controversial social reform slid down the Government's list of priorities. The nationalist reformers who had supported the act were now engaged in anti-colonial activities and there was even suggestion that Congress workers were stirring up agitation against the Sarda Act in a capricious attempt to harness it to the nationalist cause. Such accusations were hotly denied by Congress, and were probably the product of imperial paranoia, but the Act also involved very real unrest that could not have come at a worse time for the colonial state. Previously loyal orthodox communities threatened 'satyagraha' against the reform, while some Muslim groups made opposition to it a matter of political principle at a time of growing Hindu-Muslim tensions. As Fazal Ibrahim Rahimtoolah, the secretary for the All India Muslim Conference put it: 'What Muslims feel is that by accepting the Sarda Act as law they will be accepting the principle of the right of the legislatures to decide by a majority inter-communal questions without consulting the community affected thereby. Muslims are not prepared to subscribe to this principle at this critical juncture when the relations between them and the Hindus are strained'.[109] *The Times of London* reported that the whole Afghan border had been 'saturated with propaganda about the Sarda Act' causing great excitement and resentment among Muslim tribes, and adding to the already endemic instability in that region at the time.[110] That the Act was made emblematic of local fears and discontents with colonial rule and with the prospects for Muslim position in any independent India is underlined by the fact that child marriage itself was practically non-existent in the North West Frontier Province, where the worst Muslim agitation took place. In this hostile social climate the Viceroy told the Secretary of State that they were not going to take special measures to enforce the Act because they were 'anxious for it to come into operation as quietly as possible in the hope that agitation against it may quietly subside [...] Possibilities of embarrassing agitation are by no means negligible, especially in the Punjab'.[111] In London Eleanor Rathbone continued to press for the implementation of the measure although even she rallied to the cause of imperial stability, saying 'so long as the reforming and emancipated section of Indians, both men and women, are wholly absorbed in the political struggle and willing – many of them – to use any weapon to stir up the orthodox against the existing authorities, the difficulties and dangers of enforcing this and other social reforms are too great'.[112]

The Sarda Act thus became a dead letter in practical terms, as the colonial government put its own stability ahead of the implementation of reform, while Indian nationalists were once again distracted by the political struggle for independence. In both cases the symbolic value of the reform was quickly overtaken by pragmatic political considerations and priorities. The tempering of the colonial civilizing mission with the political considerations of the moment was hardly a new departure; the implementation of social reform had always been second to the pragmatic expediencies of government. By its very nature the civilizing mission had to be subordinated to imperial survival. Bentinck himself in his famous minute on sati had explicitly stated that the stability of colonial rule must come before social reform. In 1829 the threat of instability was largely in the colonial imagination. In 1930 it was very real as the agitation against the Sarda Act became entwined with the wider agitations against British rule. The nature of the anti-Sarda Act demonstrations underlined the extent to which social reform had become politicized within the broader discourses of imperialism, nationalism and communalism that dominated the Indian scene in the late 1920s. The Act and its meanings were manipulated by all sides to suit the political imperatives of the moment and while the precedent that it set as the first piece of legislation to regulate marriage customs across religious divisions makes it emblematic for a united, secular state, in practice it did little more than 'prove that the heart of Mother India is in the right place'.[113] Significantly, it also emphasized the extent to which, even though now actively engaged in the debate, women's voices remained on the political margins, while their symbolic being was appropriated by the justificatory discourses of a patriarchal colonial state and emergent Indian nation. The 'civilizing mission', once seen as a process emanating from the imperial centre outwards, had been refashioned as a 'self-civilizing mission' in the service of a predominantly upper class/caste and male dominated Indian nationalism. Yet in both cases the implementation of 'civilizing' reforms was predicated as much on immediate political and pragmatic considerations as on any over arching moral project. The role of the colonial state in reform initiatives was complex. It had to mediate a number of often competing considerations as it sought to renegotiate its own relationship with Indian modernity.

Notes

1 Home Department, Judicial, National Archives of India (Henceforward HD-J) 1024, 8 – Crerar, 24/1/28.

2 T. Sarkar, *Hindu Wife, Hindu Nation* (Delhi: Permanent Black, 2001), 230–1.

3 See L. Mani, *Contentious Traditions: The Debate on Sati in Colonial India* (Berkeley: University of California Press, 1998) and A. Major, *Pious Flames: European Encounters With Sati, 1500–1830* (Delhi: Oxford University Press, 2006).

4 See P. Chatterjee, *The Nation and Its Fragments* (Princeton: Princeton University Press, 1993).

5 K. Jayawardena, *The White Women's Other Burden: Western Women and South Asia During British Rule* (London: Routledge, 1995), 101.

6 G. Forbes, 'Women and Modernity: The Issue of Child Marriage in India' in *Women's Studies International Quarterly*, vol. 2 (1979): 412.

7 M. Sinha, *Specters of Mother India: the Global Restructuring of an Empire* (London: Duke University Press, 2006).

8 See Forbes, 'Women and Modernity'; B. Ramusack, 'Women's Organisations and Social Change' in N. Black and A. Baker Cotrell (eds), *Women and World Change: Equity Issues in Development* (London: Sage, 1981); M. Sinha, 'The Lineage of the Indian Modern: Rhetoric, Agency and the Sarda Act in Late Colonial India' in A. Burton (ed.), *Gender, Sexuality and Colonial Modernities* (London: Routledge, 1999); Sinha, *Specters of Mother India.*

9 Such interpretations were rejected by Muslim reformers, who objected to once again being blamed for the ills of Hindu India. Maulvi Mahommed Yakub, for example, called it 'part of the mischievous propaganda which is being carried on in the country to attribute all sorts of evils and vices to the Mussalmans in order to create and intensify hatred towards them', *The Star* (9 September, 1929), 8.

10 K. Young, 'Hinduism' in A. Sharma (ed.), *Women In World Religions* (Albany: State University of New York Press, 1987), pp. 65–67, U. Chakrovarty, 'Beyond the Altekarian Paradigm' in K. Roy (ed.), *Women in Early Indian Societies* (Delhi: Manohar, 1999), 75.

11 Young, 'Hinduism', 81–83.

12 Differing social systems, including cross-cousin marriage, made child marriage less common in South India (see A. Good, 'The Female Bridegroom' in *Social Analysis* vol. 11 (1982)), while among lower castes in the north, economic considerations often undermined *Shastric* injunctions informing marriage customs. The importance of women to the agrarian economy in Haryana and Punjab made older brides more desirable for all but the highest castes. P. Chowdhury, *The Veiled Women* (Delhi: Oxford University Press, 1994), 63–64.

13 See Jan Huygen Van Linschoten, *Voyage of Linschoten to the East Indies* (London: Hakluyt, 1885), 249; J. Burnell, *Bombay in the days of Queen Anne* (London: Hakluyt, 1933); John Ovington, *A Voyage To Surat In The Year 1689* (Delhi: Asian Educational Services, 1994), 189–90.

14 See Ovington, *A Voyage To Surat*, 189–90.

15 See Mani, *Contentious Traditions* and Major, *Pious Flames.*

16 W. Ward, *View of the History, Religion and Literature of the Hindus* (Madras: J. Higginbotham, 1863), 242.

17 Indian Legislative Assembly Debates (Simla: Government of India Press, 1927–30) (henceforward LAD), 4–1927, 4405.

18 M. F. Billington, *Women in India* (London: Chapman and Hall, 1895), 58.

19 Most famously, but not uniquely, K. Mayo, *Mother India* (London: Jonathan Cape, 1927).

20 Indian Census, 1921.

21 See S. Bandyopadhyay, *Caste, Culture and Hegemony: Social Dominance in Colonial Bengal* (Delhi: Sage, 2004), 166.

22 J. Walsh, *Domesticity in Colonial India: What Women Learned When Men Gave Them Advice* (Lanham: Rowman & Littlefield, 2004).

23 C. Gupta, *Sexuality, Obscenity and Community: Women, Muslims and the Hindu Public in Colonial India* (Palgrave: New York, 2002), 124.

24 *Ibid.*

25 Judy Whitehead, 'Modernising the Motherhood Archetype' *Contributions to Indian Sociology*, 29:1–2 (1995), 188.

26 Sarkar, *Hindu Wife*, 192.

27 *Ibid.*, 41.

28 Sinha, *Specters of Mother India.*

29 *Ibid.*

30 The Geneva Declaration of the Rights of the Child outlined universal and inalienable rights of minors for the first time in 1924.

31 See Judy Whitehead, 'Modernising the Motherhood Archetype', 189–90.

32 Forbes, 'Women and Modernity', 417.

33 LAD 4–1927, 4406.

34 M. Sinha, 'The Lineage of the Indian Modern', 207.

35 Chatterjee, *The Nation and Its Fragments*, 10.

36 *Modern Review*, cited in LAD 4–1927, 4409.

37 Christophe Jaffrelot notes that Sarda's reformist discourse was typically 'Arya Samajist' in that some issues, such as inter-caste marriage, remained taboo. C. Jaffrelot, *Hindu nationalism: a reader* (Princeton: Princeton University Press, 2007), 51.

38 *Ibid.*, 4407.

39 *Ibid.*

40 *Ibid.*, 4437.

41 *Ibid.*, 4407.

42 Sinha, *Specters of Mother India*, 153.

43 Sinha, 'Lineage of the Indian Modern', 215.

44 Forbes, 'Women and Modernity', 417.

45 LAD 1–1929, 259–262.

46 LAD 4–1927, 4450.

47 LAD 3–1928, 358.

48 Gupta, *Sexuality, Obscenity and Community*, 129.

49 LAD 1–1929, 264.

50 *Ibid.*, 261.

51 *Ibid.*, 268.

52 LAD 1–1928 (henceforward LAD 1–28), 1974.

53 Sarkar, *Hindu Wife*, 45

54 Sinha, *Specters of Mother India.*

55 Sarkar, *Hindu Wife*, 227.

56 Likewise the All Indian Women's Conference after it was formed in 1927.

57 *Stri Dharma*, December 1927, 22.

58 LAD 1–1929, 262.

59 LAD 1–1929, 262–263.

60 LAD.

61 Sinha, *Specters of Mother India*, 183.

62 *Women's Leader and Common Cause* (henceforward *Leader*), 11 March 1927, 34.

63 Criticism was levelled, for example, at Rathbone's decision to hold a conference on the 'plight of Indian women' in London made up of many delegates who had never even been to India.

64 Rathbone's initial interest in the issue was prompted by Mayo's book, which led her to be viewed with suspicion by Indian women reformers.

65 *Leader*, 29 June 1928, 1.

66 See, for example, the call for the formation of a 'World League of Motherhood' promoting 'modern' motherhood as a 'dynamic power in evolution and civilization' in *Stri Dharma*, September 1927, 166. For more on reforms in pre and postnatal care in Britain see J. Lewis, *The Politics of Motherhood: Child and Maternal Welfare in England, 1900–1939*. For an excellent discussion of the Sarda Act in the context of developments in maternity and public health models see Whitehead, 'Modernising the Motherhood Archetype'. For more on the role of British women's movements see Ramusack, 'Women's Organisations and Social Change'.

67 *Leader*, 20 January 1928.

68 *Times*, 14 September 1932, 6.

69 Sinha, *Specters of Mother India*, 159.

70 LAD 4–1927, pp. 4439–4446, 4450–51.

71 *Ibid.*, 4417.

72 D. V. Belvi, for example invoked the Queen's Proclamation of 1858, arguing that social advance should not be achieved by legislative intervention. Others, such as M. S. Aney supported circulation on practical grounds. Malaviya, while declaring himself in sympathy with aim of preventing marriages at 'very tender ages', called it a 'drastic measure' that had to be circulated for opinion. Like many others he was particularly worried about the clause that invalidated child marriages.

73 *Ibid.*, 4423.

74 *Stri Dharma*, October 1927, 1.

75 See *Stri Dharma*, November 1927, 1.

76 See Sinha, *Specters of Mother India*, 159.

77 HD-J 1024, 3 – Crerar, 21/9/27.

78 *Ibid.*, 3 – Crerar, 21/9/27.

79 *Ibid.*, 4 – Shillady, 18/01/28.

80 *Ibid.*, 9 – Government of Madras, 12/12/27.

81 *Ibid.*, 5 – Shillady, 18/01/28.

82 *Ibid.*, 20 – Government of Bombay, 18/01/28.

83 *Ibid.*, 5 – Shillady, 18/01/28.

84 *Ibid.*, 5 – Shillady, 18/01/28.

85 *Ibid.*, 8 – Crerar, 24/1/28.

86 HD-J 1024, 7 – Crerar, 24/1/28.

87 *Leader*, 10 June 1927, 143.

88 See *Leader*, 8 March 1929, 1.

89 HD-J 1024, 8 – Crerar, 24/01/28.

90 *Ibid.*, 8 – Crerar, 24/1/28.

91 *Ibid.*, 8 – Crerar, 24/1/28.

92 *Ibid.*, 8 – Mittra, 29/1/28.

93 *Ibid.*, 14 – Crerar, 23/2/28.

94 LAD 1–1928, 1967–1968.

95 *Ibid.*, 1968.

96 *Ibid.*, 1969.

97 *Ibid.*, 17 – Shillady, 1/9/28.

98 See *Ibid.*, 23–4.

99 *Ibid.*, 24.

100 *Ibid.*, 34 – Mitter, 16/1/29.

101 *Ibid.*, 33 – Shillady, 7/1/29.
102 On 13 September the *Times of London* carried a letter in which representatives from a range of liberal, feminist and missionary groups pressed for the whole weight of Government to be thrown into the scale on the side of reform, for 'the good of India and the credit of Great Britain'. *Leader*, 20 September 1929, 249.
103 HD-J 1024, 29 – Irwin, 21/12/28.
104 *Ibid.*, 32 – Schuster, 8/1/29.
105 *Leader*, 28 February 1929, 2.
106 HD-J 946.
107 HD-J 563/33.
108 HD-J 908/34.
109 *Times of London*, 19 May 1930,13.
110 *Times of London*, 19 May 1930, 13.
111 HD-J 304/30.
112 *Times of London*, 24 September 1930, p8.
113 Sinha, 'The Lineage of the Indian Modern', 207.

Part Three

INDIAN 'SELF-CIVILIZING' EFFORTS c. 1900–1930

Chapter Six

'CIVILIZING SISTERS': WRITINGS ON HOW TO SAVE WOMEN, MEN, SOCIETY AND THE NATION IN LATE COLONIAL INDIA[1]

Shobna Nijhawan

The early twentieth century witnessed a diversity of social and religious reforms as well as nationalist efforts to 'elevate' segments of Indian society to a supposedly 'higher' stage of civilization. In 'civilizing' discourses of this time period, the degradation of women in Indian society featured central not only amongst colonial rulers and missionaries; it also inserted itself into the consciousness of indigenous elites and the emerging middle classes, including elite and middle-class women. This chapter explores the interventions of Hindi women's periodicals in colonial and nationalist 'civilizing missions' of the late 1910s. More precisely, it analyses how contributors to women's periodicals examined the arguments brought forth by agents of the British civilizing mission such as James Mill, James Tod and Herbert Spencer. It also addresses (male) social reformist and nationalist positions on the topic of the woman question. Most importantly, though, it presents examples of women writers and activists proffering their very own civilizing missions. The central question of such contributors revolved around the implications of 'improvement' and 'development' for Indian middle-class women. The contributors also assessed notions of 'civilization' both in theory and in practice, specifically considering what could be in the best interest of women (as defined by both women and men). Some contributors suggested that more attention be turned towards a presumed ideal Hindu past and women's revered status therein. Others called for a break with tradition and a redefinition of gender roles. Tied into such writings was a call for action that was often phrased in nationalist idioms of awakening (*jagaran*) and service (*desh seva*). Moreover, as

I show in this chapter, new scales against which to 'measure' Indian society *from within* became instrumental to reformist and nationalist agendas of Indian women and men who ultimately desired to prove their cultural superiority over their Western counterparts.

I

In 1917, the male writer Raj Bahadur Pandey commented on the topic of women and patriotism in the women's periodical *Stri Darpan:*[2]

> Nowadays, I see my sisters and mothers emerge from ignorance and deep blindness breaking evil chains such as *parda*, editing newspapers, delivering speeches at common places, and working in social and national associations. There is certainly hope that if even more women invest their energy in this manner, there will soon be salvation and Mother India will be released from the bonds of subjugation.[3]

Pandey was appreciative of women's involvement as reformers and editors in different institutions of the Hindi public sphere. He held that it was them who would ultimately break free of colonial and patriarchal bondage and 'release' their country by reforming it. In this chapter I look at precisely those women mentioned by Pandey who 'invested their energy' into writing and giving speeches for the benefit of their country. I have thus chosen a perspective that focuses on Indian actors' opinions on how their country could 'progress', rather than on British efforts to 'civilize' India. 'Civilizing missions' were hardly a one-directional enterprise conducted by British colonialists and missionaries; rather, they constituted vibrant discussions in vernacular public spheres and, in the process, formed new trajectories that were also qualified by the colonial encounter. I look at such engagements with 'civilizing' discourses through a specific vernacular genre, the Hindi women's periodical. From the publications in this genre it becomes apparent that 'civilizing missions' had not only been a matter of concern for missionaries, British administrators and Indian social reformers; the contributors to women's periodicals also partook in such debates when responding to, as well as creating new, points of discussion that pertained to the improvement and development of middle-class women's lives. In this chapter I wish to outline the interconnections of colonial discourses on civilization, Indian nationalism (as performed by middle-class and elite women) and debates on social reform. While I focus on the Hindi heartland with Allahabad as the centre for literary and nationalist activities in the early twentieth century, I also make reference to colonial discourses on Indian womanhood from the second half of the nineteenth century. Uma

Chakravarti, who has analysed such discourses, has shown that Indian actors were very much a part of Orientalist and Anglicist discourses on Indian civilization and that they disseminated a 'reconstructed past' in the vernacular press.[1] She situates her research at a specific historical juncture, at which 'the sense of history may be heightened and the past may be dramatically reconstituted, bringing into sharp focus the need of a people for a different self-image from the one they hold of themselves'.[5] The early twentieth century, I add, formed yet another juncture, at which 'the "burden" of the present'[6] featured central. Evidence presented in the primary sources discussed here demonstrates that the low status of women, and the implications thereof for the 'level' of civilization of a society, was an issue that was also being tackled in the Hindi public sphere by Indian women.

Women's periodicals emerged in the Hindi public sphere several decades after the first Hindi political and literary periodicals had been launched. Titles such as *Stri Darpan* (Women's Mirror),[7] *Grihalakshmi* (*Lakshmi* of the Home),[8] or *Arya Mahila* (Arya Woman)[9] indicated that the periodicals were self-proclaimed women's periodicals addressing a primarily female readership. They were edited either solely by women (*Stri Darpan*, *Arya Mahila*) or in joint ventures with men (*Grihalakshmi*). Hindi women's periodicals of the first decade of the early twentieth century also emerged at the historical conjuncture that was marked by a shift in mainstream north-Indian discourse from social reform to nationalism. While they preceded the nationalist mass movements and women's mobilization under the leadership of Mohandas K. Gandhi, women's periodicals were essential to establishing a network of feminist-nationalist enunciations in a period of social transition and political emancipation.[10] They became a medium for elite and middle-class women to express themselves in idioms of literary and political discourses and to communicate across familial forms of connectedness. Women's periodicals not only provided a forum for those women writers and readers who were already involved in public activities; they also appealed to an educated, upper-class, Hindu women's community, urging them to involve themselves in the cause to liberate women from oppressive social customs. Throughout the 1910s and 1920s, contributions in women's periodicals scrutinized the causes for women's subjugation and suggested areas of activity for women and men that went beyond the mainstream nationalist political agenda. In fact, the contributors expressed discontent with the (mostly male) nationalist resolution of the woman question that relegated women's issues to institutions like the National Social Conference or tied them into the nationalist agenda of restoring a homogenized perception of Indian culture.[11] Many of the female contributors rejected being relegated to a private or spiritual sphere from which they were supposed to signify an essentialized Indian-*ness*. Correspondingly, women's periodicals investigated gender roles as well as women's responsibilities in light of the colonial civilizing mission. The mainstay of such writings was nationalism's larger cause: the promotion of self-government.

Many writings in women's periodicals expanded the liberal presumption that women (and men) were educable. For example, by receiving domestic advice, women could hone their skills (and so could men). Apart from very practical guidance on how to properly manage the household and nourish a joint family, these writings attempted to convince Hindu men from upper castes and middle-classes that the (then) current low status of women was no longer acceptable. While legislation associated with the colonial civilizing mission had abolished so-called disdainful practices such as the immolation of widows on the funeral pyre of their husbands (*sati*) and certain marriage practices such as child marriage, 'real' social change in the lives of women still lagged behind. The contributors to women's periodicals were not in denial of the contemporary state of women. When describing women's suffering they often spoke in idioms of slavery, as demonstrated in the following two quotations.

> Like a slave or servant her duty is limited to cooking, working on the grindstone and doing the dishes. She has neither the desire to progress, nor the energy.[12]
>
> To obey the commands of the husband whether they be justified or not – in short, to live in slavery – , this is the position of Indian women even today.[13]

Regardless of whether the female reader was immediately affected by the descriptions of the plight of women, she was able to recognize herself in the kind of subject that was portrayed in the texts. It was a characteristic of women's periodicals that women publicly expressed themselves as women. What was important to them was that the reader *felt* the plight of women, which would eventually lead to the conviction that the status of women was less than ideal. In this context, it was also the responsibility of women to 'awaken' and make it their personal goal to achieve change. The metaphors of imprisonment and enslavement went hand in hand with the metaphors of emancipation and liberation.

While many contributors acknowledged those men in favor of women's education, many others denounced and blamed them. Not only were they responsible for the systematic subordination of women, they also used woman's fallen position as means to legitimate systemic humiliation and exploitation. It is inevitable to bring nineteenth-century British arguments of civilization into the discussion: whereas the British claimed to be bringing the moral and material progress of civilization to the subcontinent to gain political and economic power, the contributors to women's periodicals called for improvement in an explicitly gendered manner: also to gain power, but first and foremost to gain respect and claim women's birthright to education and citizen rights. This was their mission and it also meant that men had to be 'civilized'.

So, campaigns for the social and political emancipation of women continued especially in women's periodicals, where women were asked to awaken and recognize their fallen state before they set out to ameliorate it. Men, who were often identified as the ones reinforcing the oppression of women, were urged to end hypocritical attitudes and practice (not merely preach) the uplift of the status of women. Criticism directed at men's treatment of women was voiced by male and female writers, as evinced by the following three passages, all of which were published in *Stri Darpan*. In the first, Matadin Shukla uses poetry to describe the systematic oppression of women by men who themselves were 'fallen' (*patit*):

He keeps you illiterate but then calls you a fool.
He himself is unjust and on the wrong path.
He cuts the roots of the tree, from which he expects care.
This is how he falls into darkness and suffers. (3)

He considers you the scum of the earth and humiliates you.
As if in this world you were living half of your life as an animal.
Can the shoes and scum of this world ever give birth to precious sons?
Can they ever be wise, become queens, heroines or ascetics? (4)[14]

Kumari Chandravati Gupta, in an essay from which the following extract is taken, calls attention to the need for women's education so that women may eventually speak out against their oppression:

If there were not ignorance [amongst women], menfolk would not deprive us of our rights and independence. Men would not arbitrarily be atrocious, keep us as slaves and for their sexual pleasures. The way men of today treat women is worse than the way animals are treated. Animals roam around the entire day and have a shelter for the night. But the poor women have no place to go.[15]

A writer named Gyandevi was very straightforward about men's unjustified political demands. She referred to the political term 'Home Rule' as it had been coined by Annie Besant in 1916 in a move to advocate political self-rule. Gyandevi provokingly questioned what allowed men to make grand political demands while they were readily engaged in the practice of oppressing women:

> You do nothing but will readily accept Home Rule
> You debate in assemblies with an air of importance
> But you cannot live in peace. Yet you want Home Rule. [...]

> You yourself have earned MA degrees and keep us as fools
> To obtain independence you want Home Rule?

> You marry early and leave behind many widows
> Upon whom you do not show mercy, and you want Home Rule?[16]

The preceding citations suggest that women and men were in the process of developing a civilizing agenda not only for women, but also for Indian men, as 'improvement' was also contingent upon a change of mind in men. Women's periodicals furthermore made numerous calls for education and women's political involvement. Though the appropriated definition of the term 'political' was broad and did not necessarily imply women's involvement as politicians and activists in the public sphere, the articles printed in women's periodicals shared the assumption that women were responsible for shaping their own lives and working towards the wellbeing of their families, society and the nation. In women's periodicals, women were no longer conceptualized as being merely the beneficiaries of reforms engineered by British and Indian men. They were expected to instigate reforms according to their own needs. In this process, civilizing discourses were appropriated by women who utilized feminist-nationalist modes of argumentation. I discuss these issues further below.

II

Indian writings on the state of Indian society contained numerous reference points to British discourses on Indian civilization. Unlike late eighteenth century Orientalist writings, such as those undertaken by William Jones and H. T. Colebrooke, which exalted a Vedic past and an ancient Hindu civilization, the Anglican and Utilitarianist James Mill (1773–1836) was convinced that India lacked a clearly-defined concept of human civilization. Mill claimed, in his *History of British India*, British superiority over the 'people of Hindustan' in nearly all aspects of life: religion, philosophy, arts, architecture, poetry, as well as in government, law, agriculture and the military.[17] His claim of Western superiority was central to the direction that the historical consciousness would take for a century to come.[18] Mill also claimed that the position of women was one of the most appropriate standards of measurement in terms of judging the extent to which a society was 'advanced'. He articulated this position in a blatant manner: 'Among rude people they are generally degraded; among civilized people they are exalted'.[19] As for Indian women, Mill observed that they were being kept in a state of 'extreme degradation', excluded from education, property rights and the right to remarry. Mill was not alone in this assessment. A majority of his contemporaries in Britain as well as colonial administrative officers and Christian missionaries in India shared this position.

The critique forwarded in civilizing discourses, especially in accounts concerning the status of Indian women, inserted itself into the consciousness of those groups who were in contact with the colonialists and missionaries: the indigenous elites and emerging middle classes. Throughout the nineteenth and twentieth centuries, the colonial discourse on women featured centrally in the writings of Indian social reformers and nationalists.[20] As late as 1927, a contributor to the women's periodical *Stri Darpan*, opened an essay on the status of Indian women with a reference to writings on civilization from Mill's times.[21] The contribution, which will be discussed further below, was one of several three- to six-page essays on social reform, which appeared in the periodical's common section rubrics titled *stri jagat* (woman's world), *stri sudhar* (woman's reforms), *stri shiksha* (woman's education), or *stri jivan* (women's life). Though this is not certain, the author Ramchandra seems to have been a female writer publishing under a male penname (I therefore use both, masculine and feminine pronouns together, when referring to this author). This can be gleaned from the use of grammatical gender and the ways Ramchandra speaks of the women community in an inclusive way. The author commenced her/his contribution with a reference to two influential British scholars of the nineteenth century: James Tod who had published the *Annals and Antiquities of Rajasthan* (1829), a book about the customs and lore of the Rajput states; and the philosopher and sociologist Herbert Spencer, whose evolutionist writing on 'the survival of the fittest' also had had reverberations in Indian reformist circles.[22] Ramchandra reminded the readers that these scholars had established the status of women as an indicator of a country's civilization and s/he assumed this position:

> Colonel Tod writes in his book titled 'Rajasthan' that, 'the touchstone of a nation's greatness is the status of its women'. If the women of that nation enjoy a high status it can be inferred that the nation is of a high civilization. And England's famous metaphysician Mister Herbert Spencer is of the same opinion.[23]

Ramchandra, furthermore, intended to demonstrate that women had once held a *high status* in Indian society. Such a move was representative of many writers of the time who were eager to reconstruct a past in which women were educated and respected. For this purpose, they generously drew on the writings of European scholars, the most prominent of which were Orientalist. Credibility was also sought through a medley of other authoritative sources that ranged from the publications of Western thinkers (mostly utilitarian and evangelical) to Indian scholars of Sanskrit. Furthermore, orally transmitted sources of popular knowledge were blended into the texts. Vernacular sources and translations thereof, whenever available, also added to the perceived level of knowledge of the contributions. Ramchandra, for example, was likely to have drawn on Romesh Chandra Dutt's *History of Civilization* (1890), a rebuttal of Mill's arguments about the nature of Indian civilization. India, Ramchandra claimed, was not only the most ancient civilization, it was also highly civilized.[24] Adhering to scriptures referenced in Orientalist scholarship the author states: 'Since it has been proven that the Indian civilization is the oldest, finding evidence of the very best conditions of women will be the most splendid example of the high status of this culture'.[25] Ramchandra sought to reconstruct an image of women in the past, not necessarily to offer a model for the present. While making 'woman' the scale of measurement, the author ventured into a comparison of the status and achievements of Indian and Western women in three different regards. First, s/he argued that Western women had not given birth to as distinguished male heroes as had Indian mothers. In this argument, the conception of 'woman' is reduced to her reproductive role and to her relationship to her male offspring. Secondly, s/he argued that Indian women could be deemed superior to Western women by virtue of their faithfulness, chastity, self-sacrifice and devotion to their husbands. Ramchandra ascribed such virtuous comportment to the special conjugal bond created by the Indian system of arranged marriage. S/he also juxtaposed such an arrangement to Western love marriages. Third, Ramchandra compared Indian women of ancient, medieval and contemporary times to women from around the world and argued that Indian women had been learned and heroic, and thus revered:

No woman on the globe is comparable to worthy [female] scholars of the *shastras* such as Vidyottama, Mandalsa and Gargi, or to the mathematician Lilavati and to the learning of Visharda. Even in these unfortunate times, India has had Ahilya Bai, Tara Bai and the heroic queen Lakshmibai of Jhansi as politicians and great warriors who, like Durga, have conquered their foes. Their valor is sung aloud by friends and foes alike. In this manner, numerous female warriors and Devis have protected their country and community.[26]

In describing the roles and status of women as mother, wife, scholar and warrior, Ramchandra was reconstructing a supposed Vedic past in an Orientalist manner. S/he was also responding to utilitarian and evangelical criticisms of the low status of Indian women, comparing the contemporary lives of women in Britain to those of Indian women of the past. This was not an uncommon mode of argumentation. Nationalist writers of the nineteenth century had commonly constructed an ideal image of Indian womanhood that sharply contrasted the low status of women during their own time.[27] They asserted that Indian women had once not been inferior, neither to men nor to women of other civilizations. Ramchandra also created hierarchies that were rooted in a mythological past. S/he did not mention contemporary female politicians, activists and writers such as Sarojini Naidu and Rameshwari Nehru, nor did s/he refer to an earlier generation of pioneers from other British Indian provinces such as Pandita Ramabai from Maharashtra or Sarala Debi from Bengal. This absence may be surprising, but it is to be read as a choice on the author's part rather than as a reflection of women's periodicals as a whole, since the writings of eminent female politicians and activists were a regular feature in women's periodicals.

Ramchandra's engagement within the popular rhetoric of civilizing discourse was probably not the way Mill would have imagined it: Ramchandra based her/his confidence on the once *high* status of Indian women. Western society remained a reference point albeit one with new criteria of 'measurement': comparing the status of Indian women in the past to contemporary Western women, Ramchandra writes, 'the Shastras have given women rights of which Western women do not even dare dream of'.[28] Such comparisons were commonly used by writers who wanted to prove India's cultural superiority over the West. In this context, notions of superiority were established by assessing the rights that women had once enjoyed. Ramchandra touched upon the various virtues for which women in the past had been highly regarded: their participation in religious activity and ritual, motherhood, faithfulness, learning and heroism. Ramchandra also investigated British notions of domesticity, according to which the separation of spheres into public and private relied on innate biological differences of the sexes. Providing both historical and mythological examples, s/he questioned whether women's bodily constitution and mental disposition necessarily made her passive, emotional and fragile. S/he attributed so-called masculine virtues of activity, self-control and heroism to Indian women. In his/her logic, women could protect themselves and 'save' others from bondage without having to rely on Indian men and British men or women:

> Today, the duty of women is to take the form of Padmavati and Durga and to be prepared to protect themselves so that no power in the world will ever be able to defeat them. Then, she will be the one who gives

birth to children and who will enable them to finally end the suffering of oppressed Mother India.[29]

Women were elevated to the status of goddesses and were portrayed as virtually invincible. At the same time, though, their primary role was to mother future leaders of the country. The gender of such future leaders was not specified.

III

I now turn from writings on women as 'the touchstone of a society', as Ramchandra phrased it, to the ways in which it was suggested in women's periodicals that women's lives could be 'improved'. It becomes evident in such writings that women were asked to take a much more active role than that of a 'merely' revered goddess. Rather than awaiting reverence in a niche, the impersonated *active* goddess would be required to assume more public roles, a demand that was established by the nationalist atmosphere of the early twentieth century. It was at this point that women began to physically emerge on the political scene and in other fields of social activity.[30] It was, however, not before the non-cooperation movements of the 1920s and the civil disobedience movements of the 1930s that women's political participation was established as an accepted and respected activity for a steadily increasing number of women, and even then, this participation remained contingent upon male approval.[31] In women's periodicals, those women who faced impediments to their social and political progress could reprocess knowledge production and contestation by means of writing. Editors, along with eminent and lesser-known authors within Hindi literary and political establishments, as well as a large number of subscribers, were all part of the making of women's periodicals. The laywriters did not partake in creative writing or journalism as a profession, but occasionally contributed to debates in these periodicals – such as those regarding social and political progress – or broached topics of their own interest. The unrestrictive form of the periodical made such participation possible.

A central difference between Orientalist and nationalist writings of the turn of the century centered on assigning liability for the ruinous state of women: contributors to women's periodicals often held *women* responsible for their own plight (*apne nash ka karan*). Female authors in particular emphasized the importance for women to awaken and grapple with oppressive structures encountered in the family and in society, rather than to wait for others to do it for them. Certainly, such a call came from an arguably negligible 2–3 per cent of women from the upper middle classes who considered themselves awakened by virtue of being educated. Their interest to awaken Indian women from sleep and torpor was articulated forcefully in women's periodicals. In scrutinizing practices that fell under the umbrella of tradition, women writers called for women to not only reform, but to destroy oppressive customs and evil practices. A certain Miss Pal was critical about the way the past had been internalized by Indian middle-class society. Of what use was a golden past, she asked in 1917, when the present was wrought with oppression?

> I will say that women need to be prepared to eradicate the present misery that Indian women have had to endure far too long in the name of tradition. We speak with great pride about our past and tell great stories about it. We say that in those times our position was the best in the world. Some eminent people even boast about our present state. It is possible that in some respect our status is and has been a good one. But the situation of Indian women is steadily becoming worse, and every Indian citizen should feel ashamed.[32]

While not denying the revered position of women in a supposedly golden Vedic past, Miss Pal drew attention to the unjustified degradation of Indian women in contemporary society. Other writers used the metaphor of a well to describe women's helpless position. The following quotation from a contribution to *Grihalakshmi* uses the well not to describe saviours removing women therefrom, but to emphasize that it was the prerogative of women to liberate their sisters. Like Miss Pal, Hukmadevi, who was the principal of the Girls' School in Dehradun, appealed to women to reach out and accept help.

> [T]he women community has to herself attempt to find a way out of the pond of ignorance. If a person falls into a deep well, people try to pull him out with ropes. But it needs to be remembered that as long as the person who has fallen into the well does not want to be rescued, those who wish to help will not succeed. Correspondingly, if the women community does not, on its own, attempt to be rescued from the well of ignorance, if women do not insist on a rescue operation from the atrocities imposed upon them by men, no success can be obtained. It will remain difficult for the women community to progress.[33]

Recognizing their abilities and responsibilities vis-à-vis the country's state of civilization was only possible once women developed an awareness of their own positions and those of fellow women. A call for more education featured central and was frequently encountered in women's periodicals of the late 1910s. This call for personal and social progress quickly led to calls for political advancement. In a speech given at the Women's Assembly in Allahabad, reprinted in *Stri Darpan* in February 1917, the well-known female politician Sarojini Naidu[34] questioned whether or not *men* were at all equipped for the nationalist struggle. Whereas writers such as Ramchandra emphasized a historical and mythological superiority of Indian women (to those in the West), Hukmadevi and Miss Pal called for women to awaken (themselves and each other), directing their own civilizing missions at women. Sarojini Naidu, similar to Gyandevi's criticism, redirected attention from women's responsibilities to questioning the extent to which men were capable of engaging in any type of struggle for independence. It can be gleaned from such contributions that Hindi women's periodicals not only played an important role in discourses on Indian womanhood; they, in fact, helped to redefine gender roles and, in so doing, paved the way for women's involvement in the Indian nationalist movement.

While it was uncommon, difficult and not necessarily desirable for women to aspire toward leading positions in politics, Naidu, whose own experiences hardly resembled the advice she proffered in the quotation that follows, emphasized women's responsibility in the nationalist struggle by calling attention to the importance of their domestic duties.

> Not everyone amongst us can become a Gandhi, Tilak or Gokhale. But, all women have some strength. All of them have a home from where they can contribute to the country's cause by educating the children, removing the sorrow of the unhappy and helping the needy people. That is how they can serve the country and fulfill their duty.[35]

This part of the speech went hand in hand with social reformers' and nationalist politicians' ideas on women's roles and responsibilities towards the family, which was conceptualized as 'embryonic' of the nation.[36] However, Naidu also appealed to women to pursue those tasks that men had not been able to achieve. Men, she argued, had been enslaved and were entangled in a web of power relationships. Women's duty lay in freeing them.

> Men are tired of constantly complaining for all these years. They have not been able to achieve anything. They keep demanding alms from the government in that they ask for several rights, but they are unsuccessful. Sisters, show them that it is possible to accomplish what they have not been able to achieve until now. Give them the reason to say 'what we have not been able to achieve has been accomplished by our mothers and sisters' [...] Your men are enslaved. They are caught in the chains of bondage. They have handcuffs around their hands and their feet are in fetters. The keys are in your hands, but you are not reacting. You are

capable of breaking the chains, but you are not doing it. You can free them, but you are not.[37]

Naidu urged women to overcome the twofold subordination they experienced through patriarchy and colonialism, stressing that women were more capable than men and able to engage with supposedly male spheres in order to realize pending political demands. Such a call for immediate action allotted women an active role in the nationalist movement of the 1920s. With regard to the question of how women could serve their country, Naidu tempered her radicalism by referring to virtuous and heroic mythological figures, similar to the discourse propounding a golden Vedic past. 'Like Sita, women shall bear the pain and share man's plight. Like Savitri, they shall fight against Yamaraj and save men's lives.'[38] She also promoted motherhood with educated, sensible and truly loving mothers.

> Like me, you are all also mothers. We are familiar with the love a mother feels [for her children]. There is amongst us no one whose heart is not filled with the love towards a child. Which mother does not herself experience pain on seeing her child suffer? But what is the use of this love alone? As long as you cannot tell your children, "I am your best friend, I will make you understand whenever you have been forgetful, I will always lead you to the right path"; as long as you cannot teach them to have trust in you [...], – so long our love will remain fruitless.[39]

This rhetoric was not surprising considering the nationalist sentiment at the time. It was also not uncommon for women writers to portray ideal social realities either in the past or in the colonial present.[40] Contributors to women's periodicals intended to provide Indian women with a unique path, one that was progressive *and* traditional, rather than overtly Western.

Naidu's speech took many unexpected turns. While she began with what would certainly then have been considered a daring move juxtaposing women's energy and capacity with men's weakness, she returned to women's self-sacrificial role as mothers. Naidu was convinced that women had a special responsibility for uplifting society and creating the Indian nation. If men dominated women and were in turn dominated by colonial rule, Sarojini Naidu implied that a woman's role was to free men and, thereby, the nation. The imagery still drew on the supposed golden past, but now women's responsibilities had nationalist reverberations.

The redefined gender roles and responsibilities that were assumed to be better suited to accommodate nationalist demands went hand in hand with demands for women's rule. Rameshwari Nehru, the editor of *Stri Darpan*, for example, demanded 'women's right to rule [*rajya karna*] besides serving [*seva karna*]. We need to be in a position to give orders as well as to take them.'[41] Sarojini Naidu had already called into question the metaphor of the cart that could not move without two wheels (i.e. man and woman) complementing each other. Other writers, too, used this metaphor in their calls for equality in conjugal life or to condemn the remarriage of widowers to young girls. Rameshwari Nehru described women as the mute cattle pulling a damaged cart. Granting women more rights would allow them to free men and the country, thus her message. Hukmadevi described man and woman as two horses of different ages who would never reach their goal since they were pulling the cart with imbalanced forces:

> A wealthy man was committed to make stout and robust the foal of a mare. He had a beautiful cart made for him, studded with jewels. A second horse of age, old and weak, was tied to the cart. This is the place to reflect whether this old horse will thrive next to the young one and whether he will be able to complete the journey. What would any spectator think about such a cart? Can his master be called wise? Just as this cart is not in equilibrium, so too are marriages in which a great age gap separates the two. A man married for a second time to a young girl cannot obtain peace in his life. Sisters! If you asked yourself, completely unbiased, you would certainly receive the answer that the best match for a young horse is another young horse.[42]

While the rhetoric of Hukmadevi, Rameshwari Nehru and Sarojini Naidu could still be considered social reformist, these authors forwarded the idea that men and society as a whole were in need of help, not just women.

I now return to writings on Indian womanhood and ways in which they were situated within larger authoritative colonial, social reformist and religious discourses. Indigenous actors had access to a variety of authoritative sources, pre-colonial and colonial alike, and made frequent use of them when investigating the positions of Indian women. Ram Mohan Roy (1772–1833) for example, one of the first Indian social reformers and advocate of reforms for women, referenced the well-known Maitreyi-Yajnavalkya story from the Brihadaranyaka Upanishad for his rebuttal of *sati*. He intended to provide evidence that women such as Maitreyi had received complex 'divine' knowledge and were thus not barred from Sanskrit learning. Uma Chakravarti has read this move as an effort of Ram Mohan Roy to prove 'that women *had* pursued the highest goal of Hindu religion and in his view, it was the "wicked" pandits who distorted the Shastras in subsequent times'.[43] Roy consulted the original Sanskrit text and Orientalist renderings of this story, subsequently setting new parameters for debates in which Indian men were held responsible for the degradation of women.[14] Contributors to women's periodicals also approached the sources with a range of objectives in mind and, often, with wit. They acknowledged the favorable observations made by male authorities about the treatment of women even if this was at the risk of reinforcing patriarchal structures. The law books of Manu, the (*Manava*) *Dharmashastras*, for example, composed around 500 BCE, were not only referenced by Orientalists and social reformers in support of patriarchal ideology; they were also cited by women. In a public speech, originally given at a women's organization in Dehradun and then reprinted in *Grihalakshmi*, Hukmadevi asked:

> What does *Maharaja* Manu have to say on the topic of women? The Gods dwell at a place where women are respected and honoured; everything becomes fruitless where women are not respected.[15]

Hukmadevi's speech was impudently titled 'How long will the women community remain satisfied in being the shoes'. She chose an authoritative quote from the *Dharmashastras*, and then redirected attention to contemporary misogynistic attitudes and general maltreatment of women. Her witty speech severely criticized the cruelty women were experiencing in the hands of men. The parallels to colonial rule cannot escape notice:

> Duteous men have openly begun to tyrannize women, snatching all rights of women and considering them the shoes of their own feet. It is a common fact that a community, a country or a society floating in the stream of ignorance easily becomes subjected to others imposing rights on them and trampling them with the sole of the foot.[16]

Authors like Hukmadevi and Ramchandra drew on authoritative Sanskrit sources when setting their terms for the position of women. In the process of laying out their claims for social reform, both authors also drew on British colonial discourse claiming a direct relationship between the social and political position of women and the status of a nation and its people. The woman question thus became a figure upon which hinged various processes of cultural translation: the translation of modern ideas into indigenous ones, the translation of various Hindu customs and practices into a modern context and the translation of notions of subjecthood that seemed alien to the pre-modern environment. Those debating the woman question thus constructed an interpenetration of different discourses: Orientalist, colonial and social reformist. This created what Vasudha Dalmia, drawing upon Ranajit Guha's political use of the term, has called the 'third idiom' of colonial modernity in South Asia.[47] This indigenous 'third idiom' explored by women writers consolidated Western and ancient concepts in light of an emerging and complex Indian modernity.

Conclusion

This chapter has demonstrated how concepts of civilization were not only appropriated in women's periodicals, but were transformed in order to serve a civilizing mission that was nationalist-feminist in scope. All the writings referred to in this chapter considered women's rights and active citizenship to be a *precondition* rather than a logical consequence of the Indian independence struggle. The writers stressed the necessity of changing and expanding the roles of women from submissive and obedient housewives to more active roles in both public and private spheres. At times they even questioned men's capabilities in the nationalist struggle. In their descriptions of the plight and suffering of women, parallels to British reasoning on civilization and improvement are visible. But while the British discourse was primarily directed at maintaining colonial power, women were seeking respect, education and citizenship rights, all for a more humane society.

Women's periodicals were particularly important in investigating and redefining gender roles and responsibilities from the vantage point of middle-class women's quotidian lives. Gender roles as defined in civilizing, social reformist and nationalist discourses had mostly operated within binaries of the strong male sex and the weak female one. Such assumptions had also served as grounds for the colonial project to protect and save Indian women from the supposed clutches of the men in their lives. As I have shown in this chapter, writers in women's periodicals attempted to refute this argument in a number of ways: (1) Since it was claimed that Indian women had once upon a time not been degraded by men, but rather held in high esteem, writers forwarded an image of empowered women in a golden Vedic age and demanded a return to this ideal after it had been *adjusted* to modern times. So, while the greatness of India could indeed be measured by reference to the status of its women, the emphasis had to be placed on their status and role in the present day. (2) In addressing their own victimization, many contributors to women's periodicals asserted that improvement could not be a gift, but had to be reclaimed *by women*. In their resistance towards female passivity and subjectivity, writers also sought alliances with Indian men for the sake of the larger cause of home rule, looking to be considered as actors in the Indian public sphere (as opposed to mere victims of crude patriarchal practices). (3) Women writers and activists – both local actors such as Ramchandra, Hukmadevi and Miss Pal as well as players on the national political platform such as Sarojini Naidu – considered their activism not only in the light of the (social reformist) woman question; they propelled a nationalist message and conceptualized women as future subject citizens.

Tied into the contributors' 'missions' were notions of civilization and reform that first appropriated and then disregarded the commonly held idea that men would be required to rescue women. Oppressive patriarchal structures and even men's abilities were openly questioned by women and men. Recourses to Hindu mythological figures were common. In invoking the names of Sita and Savitri, a writer and activist such as Sarojini Naidu was subverting terminologies in that she emphasized the goddesses' strength and action, and not necessarily passive and subservient virtues of women. In this manner, women contributors to periodicals resisted the notion that women were emblematic of tradition and instead refuted (male) social reformist and British colonial attempts of civilizing women by speaking for them and defining their best interests. By virtue of their skills and intelligence, women had the capability of serving their families, society and the nation.

Uma Chakravarti has claimed that the myth of the lost glorious golden Vedic age of Indian womanhood was also a burden, particularly for women, as it 'led to a narrow and limiting circle in which the image of Indian womanhood ha[d] become both a shackle and a rhetorical device that nevertheless function[ed] as a historical truth.'[48] As I show by analysing discourses on Indian womanhood, women's reconstructions of the past opened up new arenas for women's intervention and participation. During the nationalist period, women had temporarily been able to break proverbial shackles. To demonstrate this, I consulted essays and speeches on the topic of women's roles and responsibilities in various programs for civilizing women. In combination with the other contributions in women's periodicals – fiction, biography, poetry, advice, political news, editorials and readers' letters – the argument that I have developed around female agency and mobilization is intensified. The aim of these writings in their entirety was to expose colonial and patriarchal oppression and to (re-)gain self-esteem in order to contribute to the accomplishment of the larger goal at the time: political independence with women as active subject citizens of the nation-to-be.

Appendix. The Life of Women: Women's Place in Ancient Times

By Ramchandra, BA.[49]

Colonel Tod writes in his book titled *Rajasthan* that 'the touchstone of a nation's greatness is the status of its women'. If the women of that nation lead a life in which they enjoy a respectable status it can be inferred that the nation is civilized. England's famous metaphysician Mister Herbert Spencer is of the same opinion.

Today, it is a well acknowledged fact that the Indian civilization is the most ancient of civilizations, and many great Western thinkers seem to agree. Writing about the four eras of the Hindus, a Western thinker says that in comparison to these ancient eras, the coming of Moses seems to have occurred just yesterday. Hundreds of communities evolved and perished, great empires were established and have fallen; but the Vedic civilization has witnessed the rise and fall of them all. Despite numerous obstacles, it continues to exist. None of the world's nations can equal the antiquity of the Vedic religion and the Vedic civilization. Since it has been proven that the Indian civilization is the oldest, finding evidence of the very best conditions for women will be the most splendid example of the high status of this culture. It is amazing to see the ideals put forth to us women by the men of *Bharatvarsha*. The way they honored us women seems an unreal impossibility today; many do not even believe that those great men conducted themselves so. It was this Mother India that had the fortune of witnessing the births of Munishwar Manu and Yagyavalkya, the knowers of the *Dharmashastras* just like Gautam and Vashishtha; of eminent poets such as Puru, Bharat, Raghu, Ram, just like Valmiki and Vyas; and also of Yudhishtir, the protector of mankind; of Krishna, the great politician and of Vidur, the highly learned man. No person from another country can be compared to such great men.

In a similar vein, in ancient India, the goddesses of this country gained reputation by virtue of erudition and devotion. The women were true goddesses who cared for their husbands with their body, heart and wealth. They held the scepter of Mother India high and showed both the Eastern and Western world that they possessed rights equal to those of men and that men had protected and honored these rights. The idea that women were the servants of men was completely foreign. Many sections of the *Manusmriti* support this account and claim that women's speech is inherently pure in every respect. It is said that the Gods dwell where women receive their due reverence and that, where women are disrespected, all deeds remain fruitless. A woman is a man's *ardhangini*, the other half of his body. She is also his best friend. It is a woman who can help a man experience *dharma*, *artha*, *kama* and *moksha*. The *shastras* have bequeathed upon women rights of which Western women cannot even dream of. Their education trained them to care for their communities. This education would also promote their own personal development and enable them to give birth to children incomparable in intelligence, vigour and conduct.

A woman is called a man's *ardhangini*. Throughout her life she is a part of man, who cannot perform any deed without her. After marriage she becomes one with man and man remains incomplete without her. As such is the case, it cannot be concluded that a woman's state is in any form inferior to that of man (as it is nowadays often erroneously proclaimed).

It is well known that the rituals of Hindus remain incomplete if they are not performed jointly by man and woman. This holds as true for the Vedic horse sacrifice as it does for the holy bath in the Ganges. In fact, it holds true for every religious act. During the marriage ritual when it is time for the *kanyadan*, the bride's mother and father both hold the knot [that binds husband and wife] and perform the rite of giving away their daughter. In all such rites tying the knot is undertaken jointly.

Having man and woman perform deeds together is a sovereign principle. The creation of such an immense universe has also occurred through the union of man and Mother Nature. Man represents the *Positive Power* (*tej shakti*) and woman the *Negative Power* (*rajah shakti*).[50] Without the support of these energies nothing can ever be accomplished. The Western civilization has been opposing and resisting these principles. Apart from one or two tasks, men and women [in the Western world] lack a uniting principle. Both take care of their personal tasks only. There, the bride's father gives the bride away ceremonially all by himself. The bride's mother does not take part in it and nobody considers this to be necessary. European women do not have those rights that the women of ancient India enjoyed. The social organization in Europe has not yet reached this high stage and major changes are required for European society to compete with Hindu society.

The deep appreciation for domestic life – prominent in ancient times, but also found in these fallen days – is completely absent in Europe. There, husband and wife quarrel in most of the homes because amongst them love comes prior to marriage. In what kind of a wedding do husband and wife omit taking mutual vows? It is merely by holding each other's hands together that the marriage rites are performed! The wedding tie is so fragile and unstable that a slight knock can tear it apart. So, how can there be eternal love? Love borne of youthful desire disappears with youth and fades like a wave that reaches the shore. Merely hoping for domestic happiness is futile. In India, the situation is completely different. Here, love develops only after marriage. The significance of the marriage rites and the vows taken at that time imprint a mark in the hearts of both, man and woman, the effect of which assures everlasting love between both individuals. The marriage bond is so strong that nobody can ever break it. Man and woman are tied to one string and the bond urges them to love each other. This is why sages had claimed that the happiness of married life could not be obtained even in heaven.

This glimpse into the ancient times provides evidence that women were the true gems of this community, religion and country. Mother Vidula encouraged her indecisive son, prince Sanjay, to again step into war. Sumitra sent her beloved son Lakshman to accompany Ram for 14 years to the forest. No consideration was made of her new daughter-in-law. Savitri, by virtue of her faithfulness rescued her deceased husband from the clutches of death. Her insistence on protecting king Nala made the dutiful wife Damayanti accompany her husband from one forest to another. The wife of the blind Dhritarashtra did not enjoy the pleasure of her eyesight [and willingly covered her own eyes] because her husband was blind. This group of faithful wives was born on Indian soil. Compared to their mighty energies, the Sun God's energies appear meek. No woman on the globe is comparable to worthy [female] scholars of the *shastras* such as Vidyottama, Mandalsa and Gargi, or to the mathematician Lilavati and to the learning of Visharda. Even in these unfortunate times, India has had politicians and warriors like Ahilya Bai, Tara Bai and the heroic queen Lakshmibai of Jhansi, who, like Durga, have conquered their foes. Their valor is sung aloud by friends and foes alike. In this manner, numerous female warriors and Devis have protected their country and community. Whenever they realized they would not be able to succeed in their duty, they readily sacrificed their delicate bodies on the blazing pyre. Who has not heard of the success story of Padmavati, the great queen of Chittaur? These are the auspicious biographies of our great female warriors of the past. Today, the duty of women is to take the form of Padmavati and Durga and to be prepared to protect themselves, so that no power in the world will ever be able to defeat them. Then, she will be the one who gives birth to children and who will enable them to finally end the suffering of oppressed Mother India.

Notes

1 The author wishes to thank Carey Watt and Balraj Persaud for their encouragement and careful reading of an earlier version of this chapter.

2 Raj Bahadur Pandey. 'Striyam aur deshbhakti' [Women and patriotism], *Stri Darpan* (January 1917): 12–15.
All translations from the Hindi women's periodicals are mine.

3 Pandey, 'Striyam aur deshbhakti' [Women and patriotism], 12.

4 Uma Chakravarti. 'Whatever Happened to the Vedic *Dasi*? Orientalism, Nationalism and a Script for the Past', in *Recasting Women*, ed. K. Sangari and S. Vaid (Delhi: Kali for Women, 1989): 27–87. See 32.

5 *Ibid.*, 27.

6 *Ibid.*, 28.

7 *Stri Darpan* [Women's Mirror] was one of the first Hindi women's periodicals edited by women. First published in 1909 at the Law Periodical Press in Allahabad, the chief editor Rameshwari Nehru along with other members of the politically affluent Nehru family developed *Stri Darpan* into one of the most influential instruments of the women's movement in the Hindi speaking provinces; see V. B. Talwar, *Rashtriya Navajagaran aur Sahitya. Kuch Prasang. Kuch Pravrittiyam* (Delhi: Himacal Pustak Bhandar, 1993). *Stri Darpan*

became the mouthpiece of the *Prayag Mahila Samiti* [Women's Assembly Allahabad] that Rameshwari Nehru had founded in 1909. The monthly ran fifty-five to sixty pages in length. An issue was roughly divided into four sections. First, an editorial informed the reader about current events at local, national and international levels with a special emphasis on women's topics. A second section consisted of informative texts and essays on a variety of social, cultural, historical and political topics. Professional writers and eminent public figures – both male and female – contributed to this section. A third, literary section consisted of serialized novels, short stories, biographies, poems and prayers. Miscellaneous items, letters to the editor with responses and book reviews constituted the fourth section. Under the editorship of Rameshwari Nehru, men and women contributed in equal shares to the periodical.

8 *Grihalakshmi* [*Lakshmi* of the Home] was first published in 1909 in Allahabad by Pandit Sudarshan Acarya and his wife Shrimati Gopaldevi. Along with *Stri Darpan*, the periodical was one of the earliest Hindi women's periodicals with women on the editorial board. In the first year of its publication, *Grihalakshmi* counted the remarkable number of 4,000 subscribers, which decreased in the subsequent years to approximately 1,000–2,000 readers. *Grihalakshmi* promoted an ideal of the educated (*sushikshita*) homemaker, whose domestic sphere was acknowledged as an equally important area of activity as the public sphere, in which men operated. Linking 'Lakshmi' to the metaphor of the home was a move predicated on the construction of an indigenous domestic sphere that, while adapting to Victorian values regarding domesticity, did not eliminate Hindu spiritual-devotional duties of women. Naming a women's periodical *Grihalakshmi* reflects the debates of the 'different yet dominated discourse' of colonial modernity including the efforts of constructing a model woman on the lines of a 'modern but not Western' woman – a 'modern Lakshmi'. See Dipesh Chakrabarty, 'The Difference-Deferral of a Colonial Modernity: Public Debates on Domesticity in British India', in *Subaltern Studies VIII. Essays in Honour of Ranajit Guha*, ed. D. Arnold and D. Hardiman (Delhi: Oxford University Press, 1994): 50–88. And yet, the message delivered to women in *Grihalakshmi* cannot be simplified to a single coherent and monolithic domestic woman's ideal. The contributions offer themselves to flexible definitions on what constituted the ideal woman.

9 *Arya Mahila* [Arya Woman] was first published in 1917 from the Shri Mahamandal Bhavan in Benares. The editor of this quarterly (and later monthly) periodical was Surath Kumari Devi (1866–1936). *Arya Mahila* was the official periodical of the Shri Arya Mahila Hitkarini Mahaparishad (Society for the Welfare of Aryan Women). A review of the periodical praised it as the first monthly to provide women a sound religious education in the tradition of *sanatana dharma* [eternal dharma]. As a self-proclaimed periodical for the Arya woman, *Arya Mahila* aimed at the re-establishment of a formerly ideal state of society, in which women were revered and respected. The preservation of *varnashrama dharma* was central to this project, which also stood close to the religious and educational teaching of Swami Vivekananda.

10 Shobna Nijhawan, *Nationalism, Creativity and the Hindi Public Sphere: Women's Periodicals in the Early Twentieth Century* (Delhi: Oxford University Press, forthcoming 2011).

11 Partha Chatterjee, 'The Nationalist Resolution of the Women's Question', in *Recasting Women*, K. Sangari and S. Vaid (eds) (Delhi: Kali for Women, 1989): 233–253.

12 Vishveshwar Dayal, 'Ham ko kya kya dukh hai' [Our Troubles], *Stri Darpan* (July 1917): 30–36. See 34.

13 R. P. Pal, 'Striyom ko pahile "hom rul" dijiye' [First Give Women 'Home Rule'], *Stri Darpan* (February 1917): 73–76. See 74.

14 Matadin Shukla, 'Mahilaom se nivedan' [A Plea to Women], *Stri Darpan* (March 1917): 132–133.

15 Kumari Chandravati Gupta, 'Striyam aur samajik svatantrata' [Women and Social Independence], *Stri Darpan*, (December 1918): 306–307. See 307.

16 Gyandevi, 'Kya hom-rul loge?' [You Want Home Rule?], *Stri Darpan* (December 1918): 288.

17 James Mill, *The History of British India*. (Delhi: Associated Publishing House, 1975 [1817]): 246–247.

18 Chakravarti, 'Whatever Happened to the Vedic *Dasi?* Orientalism, Nationalism and a Script for the Past', 37.

19 Cited in Tharu and Lalita (eds). *Women Writing in India. 600 BC to the Present*. (Delhi: Oxford University Press, 1991): 46.

20 Chakravarti, 'Whatever Happened to the Vedic *Dasi?* Orientalism, Nationalism and a Script for the Past'.

21 A full translation of this essay on the life of Indian women by Ramchandra appears in the appendix.

22 Harald Fischer-Tiné, *Der Gurukul Kangri oder die Erziehung der Arya Nation: Kolonialismus, Hindureform und 'nationaleBildung' in Britisch-Indien (1897–1922)* (Würzburg: Ergon-Verlag 2003): 239.

23 Ramchandra, 'Nari-jivan: pracin kal mem striyom ka sthan' [The Life of Women: Women's Place in The Olden Days], *Stri Darpan* (April 1927): 98–103. See 98.

24 *Ibid.*, 98.

25 *Ibid.*, 99.

26 *Ibid.*, 100.

27 Chakravarti, 'Whatever Happened to the Vedic *Dasi?* Orientalism, Nationalism and a Script for the Past', 30.

28 Ramchandra, 'Nari-jivan: pracin kal mem striyom ka sthan' [The Life of Women: Women's Place in The Olden Days], 100.

29 *Ibid.*, 103.

30 Geraldine Forbes, *The New Cambridge History of India, Vol. IV.2: Women in Modern India.* (Cambridge: Cambridge University Press, 1998): 126.

31 *Ibid.*, 121.

32 R. P. Pal, 'Striyom ko pahile "hom rul" dijiye' [First Give Women 'Home Rule'], *Stri Darpan* (February 1917): 73–76. See 73.

33 Hukmadevi, 'Stri-jati kab tak juti ban kar santusht rahegi?' [For how long will the community of Women remain satisfied with being the shoes?], *Grihalakshmi kartik* (1974 [October/November 1917]): 323–328. See 324–325.

34 Sarojini Naidu (1879–1949) was born in Hyderabad to a Brahmin family. She received her education in England and married in 1898. She was involved in the major political campaigns on widow remarriage, women's education and women's franchise (in the later 1910s). From 1914 onwards Naidu became a supporter of Mahatma Gandhi and his *satyagraha* (truth-force) and non-cooperation movements. As the first woman ever she was elected President of the Indian National Congress in 1925. Apart from Naidu's political career she wrote poetry in English and is remembered as the 'nightingale of India'. See Radha Kumar, *The History of Doing. An Illustrated Account of Movements for Women's Rights and Feminism in India, 1800–1900.* (New Delhi: Kali for Women, 1993): 56–57.

35 Sarojini Naidu, "Shrimati Sarojini Devi Naidu ka vyakhyan" [Mrs. Sarojini Devi Naidu's Speech], *Stri Darpan* (February 1917): 61–62. See 61.

36 Tanika Sarkar, 'The Hindu Wife and the Hindu Nation: Domesticity and Nationalism in Nineteenth Century Bengal', *Studies in History* 8, (1992): 215–235.

37 Naidu, 'Shrimati Sarojini Devi Naidu ka vyakhyan' [Mrs. Sarojini Devi Naidu's Speech], 62.

38 *Ibid.*

39 *Ibid.*

40 Contributors to women's periodicals drew on different discourses when producing their writings for female audiences. In a forthcoming paper titled 'At the Margins of Empire: Feminist Configurations of Burmese Society in the Hindi Public (1917–1920)', I discuss how an Indian woman writer gathered sources from colonial administrative, Orientalist, and Indian nationalist discourses on Burma. This was not, however, to support civilizing discourses that centered on the 'savage woman'; on the contrary, the writer highlighted the 'advanced' status of women in Burma as a sign of civilization that warranted political emancipation. Nonetheless, she drew many of her arguments from an image of Burma as it had been produced by nineteenth and early twentieth century travelers, Orientalists and colonial officials.

41 Rameshwari Nehru, 'Stri ka kartavya' [Women's Duty], *Stri Darpan* (July 1917): 4–5. See 4.

42 Hukmadevi, 'Stri-jati kab tak juti ban kar santusht rahegi?' [For how long will the community of Women remain satisfied with being the shoes?], 326.

43 Chakravarti, 'Whatever Happened to the Vedic *Dasi*? Orientalism, Nationalism and a Script for the Past', 33.

44 *Ibid.*

45 Hukmadevi, 'Stri-jati kab tak juti ban kar santusht rahegi?' [For how long will the community of Women remain satisfied with being the shoes?], 323.

46 *Ibid.*, 323–324.

47 Dalmia writes on Guha's thesis of 'dominance without hegemony': 'Since, as Guha has convincingly shown, colonial rule never achieved hegemony, the indigenous Indian idiom always retained more than a measure of autonomy. The task, then, consists in working out how the two idioms overlapped, crossed or subverted each other, in order to flow and coalesce into the third idiom, which was the modern Indian. This third idiom could neither be a replica of the western, nor of the ancient Indian concept. The constituent elements formed a new compound "a new and original entity".' See Vasudha Dalmia, *The Nationalization of Hindu Traditions. Bharatendu Harischandra and Nineteenth-century Banaras*. (Delhi: Oxford University Press, 1997): 15.

48 Chakravarti, 'Whatever Happened to the Vedic *Dasi*? Orientalism, Nationalism and a Script for the Past', 28.

49 Ramchandra, 'Nari-jivan: pracin kal mem striyom ka sthan' [The Life of Women: Women's Place in The Olden Days], 98–103.

50 'Positive Power' and 'Negative Power' are used in the English language and script.

Chapter Seven

FROM 'SOCIAL REFORM' TO 'SOCIAL SERVICE': INDIAN CIVIC ACTIVISM AND THE CIVILIZING MISSION IN COLONIAL BOMBAY c. 1900–1920[1]

Prashant Kidambi

Introduction

The turn of the twentieth century marked a critical watershed in the history of Indian public discourse about the 'social question'. For the best part of the nineteenth century, the Indian intelligentsia had concentrated its energies on 'social reform', a term that denoted a desired transformation amongst high-status castes and communities of cultural practices that were perceived as being both irrational and the root cause of India's decline as a civilization.[2] The attention of social reformers had focused on 'traditional' indigenous customs such as prohibitions on female education, child marriage, polygyny, female infanticide, *sati*, *purdah* and the pitiable state of widows and *devadasis*, all of which were characterized as 'perverted, twisted, distorted practices born of ignorance and fear and followed without recourse to common sense'.[3] Social reformers were particularly concerned with the oppressed condition of women and viewed their emancipation 'as the first step towards progress'.[4] However, from the late 1890s onwards, members of the largely upper-caste Indian intelligentsia widened the debates on the 'social question' to include the condition of the lower orders of society. Thus, alongside the rhetoric and practice of 'social reform' there gradually emerged a new discourse of 'social service'.

Those who took to 'social service' sought to 'civilize' the urban poor by eradicating 'vices' such as drunkenness, gambling and prostitution, and inculcating in them 'enlightened' values regarding sanitation and hygiene. At the same time, proponents of the new ethic of 'social service' also believed that the welfare of 'the masses' was essential for the progress of society as a whole. 'All the work has only one aspect, so far as society is concerned', they declared, 'the weak, the needy, the helpless are assisted, and the vitality of the community is increased'.[5]

It is not intended to suggest, of course, that the boundaries between 'social reform' and 'social service' were clearly demarcated and sustained in practice.[6] The distinction is nonetheless a useful one in that it highlights, at a conceptual level, the differences in the objectives and orientations of these two modes of 'social improvement' in colonial India. In other words, whereas the thrust of nineteenth-century discourse of 'social reform' had been directed at countering what were perceived to be outmoded *internal* practices within a number of endogamous castes and communities (Hindu, Muslim and Parsi alike), the discourse and practice of 'social service' emanated from members of the high-status Anglophone intelligentsia and sought primarily to 'civilize' and discipline the poor. And while discourses of caste and community retained their salience, ideologies of 'nation' and 'class' emerged as key determinants of these endeavours.

Colonial Bombay in the early twentieth century was a principal locus of the new civic activism. Indeed, many aspects of the city's public life were conducive to this development. As a premier imperial city in the Indian Ocean region, it was a key junction for the global flows of ideas and ideologies. As one of the largest and most important administrative, commercial and industrial cities in colonial India, it was also home to a vocal and reform-minded intelligentsia. The rich associational traditions that had developed within the city during the late nineteenth century, the emergence of a vigorous urban public sphere, and the presence of philanthropic-minded men of wealth, were equally integral to the rise of new forms of social activism directed at the poor.

This essay focuses on a variety of civilizing initiatives undertaken by sections of Bombay's intelligentsia vis-à-vis the city's economically deprived and socially underprivileged classes. The discourses of 'social service' and 'nation-building' that underpinned these activities were informed by a variety of ideological impulses and produced an equally diverse range of initiatives. This essay focuses on three noteworthy aspects of these discourses and practices. First, it shows how a growing consensus among Bombay's reformist Hindu publicists and politicians about the need to reclaim the so-called 'depressed classes' triggered an 'internal civilizing mission' that sought to instil 'enlightened' values in the latter and thereby 'improve' and 'uplift' them. Second, it highlights the salience for urban middle-class formation of Indian disciplinary projects aimed at civilizing the poor. Finally, it also suggests that some institutional features of the 'social service' movement in Bombay might be viewed as the Indian version of a 'global civilizing mission' that saw elites and the middle classes in a number of cities across the world engaging in novel forms of civic activism in response to the perceived threat posed to the social order by rapid industrial urbanization.

Reclaiming the 'Depressed Classes'

During the late nineteenth century, many 'liberal' Hindus had begun to view the caste system as a pernicious and irrational mode of social organization that was an impediment to the progress of the 'Hindu nation'. Drawing on European eugenic, ethnological and evolutionary theories, as well as reformulated Brahmanical notions of ideal spiritual and moral conduct, reform-oriented intellectuals sought to argue that the institution of caste had depleted the 'natural vitality' of the 'Hindu race' and weakened its capacity for rational individual thought and action.[7] Adapting European 'organic' social theories to the Indian context they asserted that the well-being of the Hindu community as a holistic entity was determined by the health of its individual, interdependent parts.[8] Moreover, they also pointed out that by nurturing social divisions caste-based prejudices were inimical to the goals of 'higher national efficiency'.[9] As part of their critique of caste, reformist Hindu publicists, especially those who were actively involved in the National Social Conference (founded in 1887 by Mahadev Ranade, one of the most prominent liberal social reformers in late nineteenth-century western India), increasingly began to focus on the 'problem' of 'untouchability' and the need to 'uplift' the so-called 'depressed classes' through 'progressive' policies of social improvement. Their attacks acquired a new urgency from the late 1890s onwards in an intellectual and political context marked by growing anxieties about the fate of the 'Hindu race'. The social 'uplift' of the depressed classes, as Susan Bayly has noted, 'first began to be widely advocated in the reformist press at a time when the Census was reporting an alarming decline in population growth among Hindus relative to Muslims, Sikhs and Christians'. During the first decade of the twentieth century, the National Social Conference responded to such reports by passing resolutions that exhorted its members to 'reclaim' those sections of the 'depressed classes' who had chosen to convert to Christianity, Islam and Sikhism. Nor was the fear of racial decline restricted to 'liberal' Hindu reformers: across the ideological spectrum Hindu publicists and politicians voiced fears that rival communities were growing 'stronger and more vigorous in evolutionary terms'.[10] In an ideological context dominated by eugenic theories, as well as a widely entrenched social Darwinism that held that communities, races and nations were engaged in ceaseless competition, ideologues of all hues 'were oriented to strengthening and improving the Hindu community materially, physically and intellectually so that it could reverse a perceived sense of decline'.[11]

Central to the task of 'national regeneration', was the task of reclaiming the 'depressed classes'. One of the first Hindu social organizations to take an aggressive stance in this matter was the Arya Samaj. Founded in April 1875 by a wandering preacher, Dayanand Saraswati (1824–83), the adherents of the Samaj 'were enjoined to arrest the supposed decline of the Hindu nation by taking part in campaigns of shuddhi or reconversion so as to reclaim untouchable "converts" who had been "lost" to the Hindu nation through the missionary endeavours of these rival faiths'.[12] But in Bombay, it was the Prarthana Samaj (Society of Liberal Religionists; founded in March 1867 by some of Bombay's leading English-educated intellectuals) that took the lead in undertaking the 'uplift' of the 'depressed classes'. While they had engaged in some initiatives in the 1870s and 1880s to educate the city's 'labouring and artisan classes',[13] the members of the Prarthana Samaj had made no real effort to reach out to Bombay's 'untouchable' communities. This was to change during the early twentieth century. In October 1906, Vithal Ramji Shinde (1873–1944), a member of the Samaj, established the Depressed Classes Mission in the city.

Shinde, who belonged to a 'respectable' Maratha (caste title of dominant peasants in Maharashtra) family, had completed his college education at Poona, where he had encountered 'reformist' ideas drawn from a variety of intellectual sources: the writings of John Stuart Mill and Herbert Spencer, Unitarian theological doctrines and the lectures of Max Mueller on comparative religion.[14] During the late 1890s, he began to attend the meetings of Prarthana Samaj and was increasingly attracted by its tenets and activities. In 1898 he ceased to be a mere visitor and was formally inducted into the society. Three years later, Shinde sailed to England on a scholarship to attend a two-year course in the comparative study of religion at Manchester College, Oxford.[15] During his time at Oxford, he not only had the opportunity to consider religious ideas in the abstract, but also received training 'in the dissemination of religious thought and organization of prayer sessions for proselytizing activities'. On his return to India in October 1903, Shinde was appointed a 'missionary' of the Prarthana Samaj. In this capacity he carried out both organizational and proselytizing activities for the society.

It was as a 'missionary' for the Society that Shinde first became involved with the 'uplift' of the 'depressed classes'. As a 'proud' Hindu, he was deeply affected by the lack of empathy and concern amongst upper-caste groups for the plight of the 'untouchables'. As a 'missionary' of the liberal faith of the Prarthana Samaj, he believed it was his duty to 'protect' and 'uplift' the 'depressed classes'. At the same time, he also sought 'to get Hindus to see the moral, religious as well as political necessity of recognizing the untouchables to be a part of the Hindu body politic'.[16]

Shinde saw the Depressed Classes Mission as a 'messianic' organization that would work in a spirit of selfless service. His social work 'moved far beyond the prayers, sermons and modest mobilizations' that had hitherto been undertaken by the Prarthana Samaj.[17] Under his direction, and backed by eminent 'public men' such as Sir Narayanrao Chandavarkar, Dwarkadas Govardhan Sukhadia and Krishanji Pandurang Bhalekar, the Mission aimed to reach out to the 'untouchable' communities and work towards their social betterment. Indeed, in many ways Vithal Ramji Shinde's initiatives in these years anticipated by more than two decades Mahatma Gandhi's campaigns for the 'uplift' of the Harijans.

The Depressed Classes Mission sought to provide formal and informal education to children of the 'untouchable communities', as well as to extend aid to the indigent families amongst them. Accordingly, vernacular schools for the children of the 'depressed classes' were set up in working-class districts of the city, a Sunday school was commenced at Kamathipura and a philanthropic society was formed to serve destitute women belonging to the lowest castes. The Mission based its headquarters in a working-class tenement near the Globe Mill at Parel in order to enable the 'missionaries' to live in close proximity to the communities that they were seeking to serve. Members of the Mission 'undertook home visits to establish community contacts and to understand the problems of individual families'.[18]

The activities of the Mission continued to expand during the 1910s. By the end of the first decade of its existence, it ran eight schools (one of which imparted technical training), two devotional societies, a debating society, a students' hostel and a reading room. The Mission's headquarters in Parel continued to be 'the centre of all these institutions'. Interestingly, some of the Mission's schools also had a sprinkling of upper-caste pupils and an attempt was made to break down the social barriers by making all pupils share the same classroom. The emphasis within the school curriculum and pedagogic practice was on the 'formation of habits of self-control and self-help'. 'Self-government' amongst the pupils was encouraged 'through the agency of monitors, prefects, and sanitary inspectors appointed by a majority of votes in a biennial general election'. Students also formed mutual help societies which sought to foster 'fellow-feeling' and 'exemplary conduct'. Moreover, 'strict attention' was paid in these schools 'to cleanliness and tidiness' amongst the students. Boys and girls, it was said, were 'helped in their efforts to form cleanly habits by a supply of combs, brushes, towels, soap, and mirrors in the school premises'.[19]

Gopal Krishna Gokhale's Servants of India Society, founded in Poona in June 1905, also took a keen interest in the problems of the 'depressed classes'. Gokhale (1866–1915), widely acknowledged as one of the great Indian 'liberal' reformers, was deeply concerned about the plight of the 'depressed classes' and 'was one of the many nationalists who portrayed the success of Muslim, Sikh and Christian proselytizers in attracting low-caste and "untouchable" converts as a sign of Hindu weakness and racial decline'. The Servants of India Society sought to achieve national regeneration and spiritual awakening through 'constructive social work'.[20] Indeed, 'the 1905 constitution of the Society specifically mentioned an intention to help educate and elevate the 'backward' or 'depressed classes'. To this end, the Bombay branch of the Society set up night schools for the city's factory workers and also arranged lectures and magic lantern shows on a variety of wholesome topics.[21]

The principal figure in the Society's activities in Bombay was Gopal Krishna Devadhar (1871–1935). Born into a Chitpavan Brahmin family of modest means, Devadhar completed his education at Poona and worked for a while as a Marathi teacher for two Christian missionaries before joining Gokhale's Servants of India Society. His work as an activist for the Society took him to the United Provinces, where he helped Arya Samaj volunteers in conducting relief work in the wake of the severe famine that struck the region in 1907–08. Devadhar subsequently moved to Bombay in 1911 in connection with his work for the *Dnyan Prakash* newspaper. In Bombay, he soon became closely involved in conducting social work both amongst the 'depressed classes' and the working-class population more generally. In particular, he played an important part in the spread of the co-operative movement amongst various 'untouchable' communities of the city. For instance, he was instrumental in starting 'a number of co-operative societies for the redemption of the debts of the Harijan and other backward sections of the working classes in Bombay'. Devadhar also took a keen interest in the issue of 'mass education' and initiated measures to widen access to learning amongst women and the working classes. In 1918, he also helped to set up a new primary school for the 'backward' Shimpi community and was said to have been largely responsible for 'putting this institution on a sound financial basis'.[22]

Another prominent volunteer of the Servants of India Society in Bombay was Amritlal Thakkar (known popularly in later years as *Thakkar Bapa*), who hailed from a well-established middle-class Goghari Lohana family based in the Gujarati city of Bhavnagar. The Lohanas were a mercantile community that had taken with great enthusiasm to western education. After graduating as a civil engineer, Thakkar travelled to Africa to work on the construction of the Uganda Railway. On his return to India, he joined the Bombay Municipal Corporation in 1904 as inspector of the light railway that carried the refuse of the city out to the suburbs. It was in this context that Thakkar came into close contact with the Dheds, Chamars and Bhangis who were employed as sweepers and menial workers by the Bombay municipality and were universally regarded by the upper-castes as 'untouchables' on account of their 'polluted' occupation. Inspired by the activities of Vithal Ramji Shinde (with whom he had briefly come into contact) and the Depressed Classes Mission, Thakkar set out to ameliorate the wretched conditions of the municipal conservancy workers by setting up a school for them. He resigned from his job in the Bombay municipality in January 1914 and was admitted into the Servants of India Society shortly thereafter. He subsequently worked with Devadhar among the 'untouchable' communities employed in the Bombay municipality.[23]

There are two noteworthy points about the reforming mission of these 'liberal' Hindu activists vis-à-vis the 'depressed classes'. First, it is clear from their writings and pronouncements that the ethic of 'selfless service' adopted by these social workers was greatly inspired by the activities of Christian missionaries. For instance, Shinde's conception of 'messianic' social work was clearly influenced by contemporary Christian missionary activism.[24] Likewise, Devadhar was influenced by the 'persistent methods of work and the humanitarian sprit' of Christian missionaries and 'was never weary of saying that public workers in India must develop the missionary spirit if they wanted to achieve maximum success in their undertakings'. Thus, Christian doctrinal influences and activities 'helped transform the Hindu ideal of *sewa*, or service, into an energizing public doctrine'.[25]

Second, notwithstanding their invocation of theories of 'individual rights and capabilities', liberal Hindus who campaigned for the 'uplift' of the 'depressed classes' tended to work with idealized dichotomies of purity and impurity as well as 'propriety and impropriety'. Thus, an ostensibly 'impersonal rhetoric of nationality and public obligation' was suffused with Brahmanical notions of caste hierarchy, spiritual purity and moral piety. As a consequence, in attempting to 'reclaim' the 'depressed classes', Hindu 'nation-builders' sought to purge these communities of all those practices they regarded as 'unclean' and antithetical to the tenets of a 'universalizing puritanical Hinduism'. At the same time, however, they also sought to invest their civilizing mission with modern 'scientific' legitimacy by invoking the ideas of contemporary eugenicists, ethnologists and racial theorists, who were keen to draw 'clear distinctions between healthy and unhealthy manifestations of appetite and psychic energy'.[26]

'Civilizing' the Plebeian Public Sphere

Some initiatives to 'civilize' the poor were an integral part of the strategies of empowerment that served to define an emergent Indian middle class. Recent scholarship has shown how the making of the middle class in colonial India was a 'cultural project' fashioned through decisive interventions in the public sphere from the late nineteenth century onward.[27] A range of intermediate and high-ranking Hindu scribal and trading communities[28] as well as *ashraf* Muslim service gentry and commercial classes came to constitute themselves as new 'arbiters' of appropriate social conduct. Their interventions consisted of attempts to redefine notions of 'respectability' by braiding together Brahmanical and high Islamic notions of spiritual purity and moral piety with Victorian discourses of improvement and self-discipline.[29]

English-educated Indians had internalized both the colonial ethic of 'improvement' as well as modern 'governing conventions' regarding the disciplined conduct of the self within the public sphere.[30] From this vantage point, they viewed the public norms and practices of the poor with a mixture of distaste, contempt and anxiety. The urban poor were frequently characterized in the Indian press as 'illiterate', 'ignorant', 'backward' and given to wanton outbursts of passion and fury that transgressed the norms of 'civilized' public sociability.[31] Indeed, notwithstanding important differences, educated middle-class Indians shared with colonial ruling authorities a belief in the need 'to make the bazaar, the street, the *mela* – the arenas for collective action in pre-British India – benign, regulated places, clean and healthy, incapable of producing either disease or disorder'.[32] At the same time, as the new, self-proclaimed leaders of Indian society, their incipient quest for 'social sovereignty' rendered it equally imperative for members of the middle class 'to obtain the obedience of the poor' to the norms of bourgeois 'respectability'. As noted above, this bourgeois ideal consisted of an amalgam of redefined elite Hindu and Islamic 'pious norms' and Victorian moral strictures about appropriate public and domestic conduct. Hence, 'the mission of social and moral reform was a central element in the relation of the Indian elites to those whom they identified as the poor and the lower classes'.[33]

Zealous social activists in colonial Bombay thus took it upon themselves to 'civilize' the urban poor by disciplining their public conduct. Indeed, they targeted all those plebeian collective practices that were seen to contravene the norms of 'respectable' public behaviour. For instance, middle-class moralists repeatedly targeted alcohol consumption amongst Bombay's working classes and called for liquor shops to be closed on occasions such as festivals. Frequent allusions were also made in the Indian press to the connection between liquor drinking and the propensity of the lower orders to indulge in 'degenerate' and 'licentious' social behaviour. Temperance campaigns were launched to counter the spread of the 'drink habit' and encourage 'purity' and 'thrift' among the city's labouring poor.

Members of Bombay's intelligentsia also sought the suppression of popular modes of observing Muharram, which were regarded as being incompatible with the norms of 'public decency'. In particular, the Muharram *tolis* (the gangs that wandered about the neighbourhoods), which drew heavily on traditions of folk entertainment, became the target of sustained criticism. The most prominent of these traditions was that of the *tamasha*, a theatrical form whose combination of risqué humour and bawdy sexual innuendoes was extremely popular amongst the city's labouring poor. For the 'respectable' classes, however, Muharram increasingly came to epitomize the 'degeneracy' and lack of civility characteristic of Bombay's plebeian street culture.

Likewise, middle-class Hindu publicists and politicians found repugnant the popular mode of celebrating Holi (the Hindu festival of colours that heralds the onset of spring) and the 'unseemly excesses' that characterized it.[34] Concerns about these 'excesses' prompted the founding of a *Hollika Sammelan* in 1911 by some of the city's prominent reform-minded, 'liberal' Hindus: men like Sir Narayanrao Chandavarkar, Gopal Krishna Devadhar, N. M. Joshi, and others.[35] The aims of the committee that convened this 'social purity' movement were 'to create a strong public opinion against the excesses of Shimga'; 'to keep off young boys and persons belonging to the labouring and depressed classes from unhealthy influences and practices'; and 'to impress on the minds of the unthinking masses the fact that these unhealthy practices had absolutely nothing to do with religion'. In order to attain these objectives, the *Sammelan* sought 'to divert the attention of these people from the usual filthy practices to healthy amusements and to organize for this purpose counter-attractions'.[36] To this end, it organized sports events, *kirtans* and *bhajans* and other forms of 'social' entertainment to educate workers in the place of their more raucous activities during the festival.[37]

Alongside the disciplinary imperative there was a powerful pedagogic dimension to the 'civilizing mission' of the Indian intelligentsia.[38] As putative leaders of Indian society and convinced of their own superior rationality, members of this class increasingly saw it as their duty to 'educate' the poor and inculcate in them 'modern' norms of civic life. The plague epidemic had sharpened perceptions amongst the city's western-educated Indian middle class that the poor needed to be 'enlightened' about modern principles of sanitation and personal hygiene. Western epidemiological theories that attributed plague to filth and poverty were enormously influential in informing the attitudes of western-educated Indians towards the city's poor. Moreover, a number of middle-class observers also held that the 'unhygienic' habits and squalid living conditions of the poor were a menace to 'public health'.[39] Such beliefs increasingly prompted Indian educated elites to participate in campaigns to spread 'sanitary awareness' amongst the city's labouring classes.

An important institutional initiative in this context was the establishment of the Bombay Sanitary Association. Founded in 1903, the stated aims of the

Association were 'to create an educated public opinion with regard to sanitary matters in general', 'to diffuse knowledge of sanitation and hygiene' and 'to promote sanitary science'. At its outset, the Association declared its intention 'to employ male and female visitors of every caste and creed to visit the houses of the poor, to give popular illustrated lectures, to issue verbal and written instructions'[40] on a range of subjects such as the value of water, fresh air, sunlight, the 'evils of overcrowding', the care of children, pregnant women, the importance of personal cleanliness and hygiene, the health hazards of keeping animals in the house, the 'objectionable habit of using any spot for natural purposes', and the danger posed by accumulation of filth.[41]

Even though the Bombay Sanitary Association was the brainchild of Dr Turner, the city's British health officer, it was professional Indian middle-class men and women who came to dominate its activities. The tone of the new association was set at its inaugural meeting, which was attended, apart from the colonial elite, by a large number of prominent Indian members of the professional classes. The working committee of the new association was also predominantly composed of professional Indians, mostly lawyers and doctors, who were actively involved in civic politics.[42] Once the Association was established, western-educated Indian professionals played a crucial role in propelling its expansion. The sub-committees of the Sanitary Association largely comprised professional Indian men, who toured the different sections of the city 'with a view to bringing to the notice of the people the value of personal and domestic hygiene'.[43] The Association also engaged the services of two paid 'health visitors' who 'regularly visited the house of the poor morning and evening and explained to the people how to improve the condition of their rooms by ventilation, whitewashing, disposal of refuse and advise them on the prevention of disease – small pox, plague, phthisis, consumption and diseases of infants and the value of vaccination'. In turn, the health visitors submitted weekly reports to an honorary secretary (a role discharged by the health officer).[44]

The Bombay Sanitary Association arranged for lectures to be delivered by Indian doctors in the vernacular on topics such as 'vaccination, personal hygiene, treatment of infants, precautionary measures against plague and other infectious diseases'.[45] In March 1905, one Dr K. N. Gokhale delivered a lecture in Marathi 'to an audience consisting chiefly of mill and coolie women' at the Victoria Bandar in Colaba. On this occasion, there were said to have been 'about 500 to 600 women from the locality and the neighbouring mills'. During the course of his lecture the doctor impressed upon his audience the necessity of cultivating clean habits in order to ward off disease. After similar speeches by other speakers, the meeting concluded with a local school mistress exhorting the audience that 'the prosperity of the city depends on the healthy condition of the poorer classes and it is for this reason that the Municipality gives so much attention to the care of the poor and as such it is the duty of the poor to take advantage of the facilities offered to them'.[46]

Social Work and the Urban Poor

Some aspects of the 'civilizing mission' in Bombay's public life in these years might profitably be viewed as the Indian incarnation of a global phenomenon. In the period spanning the 1880s to the 1920s there developed a new public concern in a number of countries, both metropolitan and colonial, about the social costs and consequences of industrial urbanization. The rapid influx of a vast indigent proletarian population, the impact of rising numbers on the civic infrastructure and the 'discovery' of poverty all served to provoke intense debates amongst governing elites and the middle classes in cities across the world about the pressing challenges that confronted the urban social order.

One notable consequence of these developments was the emergence of a new civic activism directed at the urban poor in many industrializing societies. In England, for instance, the late nineteenth and early twentieth centuries witnessed the efflorescence of a 'popular and voluntaristic social-scientific culture', which was reflected in the activities of 'numerous local Charity Organization Societies'; socialist organizations such as the Fabian Society and the Independent Labour Party; the metropolitan and provincial 'ethical societies'; the 'university extension and settlement movements'; and 'a range of new civic associations devoted to the advance of social research and the modernization of social policy'.[47]

Significantly, the philosophy of social work that informed their activities challenged the predominant view that 'the poor were morally culpable in their condition and that philanthropy could stem destitution'. Social activists increasingly recognized during the last two decades of the nineteenth century that 'the poor needed advocates willing to call on new and wider resources'. The shift in attitudes was best exemplified by Canon Samuel Barnett, a member of the Charity Organisation Society, who argued in 1883 'that the condition of the poor was clearly beyond the best charitable efforts at alleviation'. The following year, Barnett founded Toynbee Hall in Whitechapel and thereby inaugurated the 'settlement house' movement. The idea of the 'settlement house' was 'to bring closer the classes through their residential contact, and thereby to inculcate the spirit of self-improvement in the working poor and social awareness in the rich'.[48]

Similar social initiatives also characterized civic life in the United States of America during what came to be known as the 'Progressive Era'. The 'settlement house' movement, for instance, spread to a number of cities in the United States and by 1911 there were over four hundred in that country.[19] Indeed, notwithstanding important differences of emphasis, 'reformers on both sides of the Atlantic shared many common anxieties about the concentration of social problems in large cities'.[50] Underpinning the Progressive movement in the United States was the notion that the modern city, far from constituting 'the most extreme form of the social disintegration of the traditional world', could be made to yield a 'more hopeful' future through active citizenship and public intervention.[51]

Recent research suggests that civic initiatives in cities as far-flung as Toronto and Tokyo were driven by similar ideas and impulses in this period. Toronto, for instance, had grown rapidly from the late nineteenth century onwards and experienced social problems similar to other cities in the industrializing societies of the West. Concerned about the growing civic problems and the widening 'rift between rich and poor', Canadian middle-class social activists embraced Canon Barnett's ideas and by 1914 there were six settlement houses in the city. The organizers of these settlement houses were impelled by a variety of desires and needs: the urge to create 'islands of enlightenment' in working-class districts; to use these 'as sites from which to launch social investigations and to test innovative schemes aimed at promoting the welfare of the poor on a very pragmatic level'; to break down class barriers in order 'to recreate a sense of community' within cities; and last but not least, to counter the 'very real threat' posed by immigrant cultures to the hegemony of 'middle-class Anglo-Celtic culture'.[52] Likewise, in Tokyo during the late Meiji era, rapid economic and social changes were a 'major stimulus to attempts to understand new phenomena such as urbanization and the emergence of an industrial working class'. Publicists and activists belonging to an emergent middle class defined as 'social problems' specific issues ranging from working-class living conditions to prostitution and took the initiative in finding solutions to them.[53]

The middle-class 'discovery of poverty' was also a feature of late imperial Russian cities such as St Petersburg and Moscow. As Adele Lindenmeyr has shown, fundamental socio-economic transformations during the late nineteenth and early twentieth centuries evoked increasing concern amongst educated Russians living in urban centres and prompted them to engage in new forms of voluntary action that sought to aid, discipline and reform the poor.[54] In particular, a number of private charitable organizations were established in 'response to the rapid growth of many towns, and to the devastating impact such growth had on existing urban housing, health, and public safety'. The founding of 'voluntary associations of various kinds was one of the means chosen to transform a threatening migrant mass into a sober, educated, industrious and urbanized population'.[55]

The global responses to the social consequences of industrial urbanization also registered their effects in colonial Bombay. Confronted and concerned by the far-reaching economic and social changes of their times – the rapid pace of industrial urbanization, the emergence of a vast proletarian population, and the growing class differentiation within the city – members of Bombay's educated classes adapted to their own ends the ideas and institutional forms deployed by their counterparts in other global contexts. This is not surprising given that the city's intelligentsia were highly aware of many of the intellectual debates and voluntary civic initiatives pertaining to the poor that animated the public sphere in the metropolitan West. During the early twentieth century 'dramatic increases in telegraphic and postal facilities served to accelerate the flow of information into the subcontinent'.[56] A number of educated and propertied Indians travelled aboard and came into contact with ideas circulating in the imperial public sphere. Indian publicists and activists were thus 'plugged into transnational processes and flows regarding organized philanthropy, social service and citizenship'.[57]

One of the first organizations in colonial Bombay that devoted itself to 'professional' social work was the Seva Sadan Society, which was founded in July 1908 by the Parsi social reformer Behramji Malabari. A report in the *Indian Spectator*, which described the aims and activities of the Society, stressed the need for 'wholesome students of the poor and the distressed, students of their compensations, students of the law of rewards and punishments, students of the Science of Prevention and of the Art of Consolation and Cure'. The report also contended that prior to the Society's establishment, 'there was no indigenous, non-proslytising, non-sectarian organisation for lovingly serving all the three races, independently of caste and creed'. The Society, whose trustees included men like Sir Narayanrao Chandavarkar, Sir Bhalchandra Bhatawadekar, Sir Vithaldas Thackersey and Gokuldas Parekh, primarily devoted its energies to improving the lot of destitute women. Its activities were divided 'into four broad departments – healing the sick, protecting the helpless, instructing the ignorant, and teaching some industry which enables poor women to earn their livelihood'.[58] According to the Sadan's charter of aims, one of its principal objectives was 'to utilize the waste human material'. For this purpose, it initially established 'a Home for the Homeless', and an 'Industrial Home'.[59] Over time, the Sadan expanded its infrastructure and established an Industrial Department for poor women that imparted skills such as sewing, cookery and embroidery. At the same time, it provided training to women social workers who were to 'exercise their vocation among the poor'. This included amongst other things 'the visiting of hospitals and the distribution of fruits, flowers, clothes, and sweets to indigent patients, the visiting of the quarters of the poor and the administering of relief to women, and the visiting of jails and prisons for affording relief to women prisoners'.[60]

But by far the most prominent of such initiatives was the Social Service League, which was established in March 1911 by some of the most prominent professional middle-class men in Bombay's public life.[61] The League was explicitly 'founded on a non-sectarian and broad basis, and its membership was thrown open to all persons without distinction of race or creed'.[62] Organizers of the League declared that their principal 'motive power' was 'a sense of the common brotherhood of man and the innate feelings of the universal love for mankind, pity for the sufferings of the miserable, and justice for all'. They also differentiated its work ethic from social service which was driven by a solely 'religious motive'. The League's work, they explained, 'may be commonly regarded as secular'. Indeed, if at all there was a religious basis to its work, it was the broad and liberal 'religion of humanity'. Furthermore, the method by which it aspired to achieve its aims was to make human beings 'capable of self-help in the improvement of their social condition by providing them with opportunities and placing them in favourable surroundings'.[63]

The League was especially concerned about the problems of the city, which were conceived in explicitly 'organic' terms. In the words of one activist, 'a city does not grow merely by more roads and houses, even better roads and higher-rent houses; but with the growth of the health, comfort, and progressive well-being of its citizens, in all matters and in all aspects in which men live together as social beings'. 'The well-being of the whole', he added, 'depends on the well-being and growth of the constituent parts'. Looking around them, local activists perceived a number of pressing problems in Bombay's teeming working-class neighbourhoods that prevented such a state of well-being from being attained: overcrowding, dirt, disease, drunkenness and other social vices such as 'gambling, incest, illegitimacy, or prostitution' with their attendant 'lowering of the general moral tone of the people'. In order to render the city 'a really healthy organism', they argued, it was necessary not only to eradicate these evils, but also to nurture 'various *positive* forms of social life and social work' that would help 'to raise the comfort and well-being of the people'. Furthermore, as 'the care-taker of the society in which he lives', it was the duty of the individual citizen to take an active part in social work. Thus,

We want, in a word, an army of charitable social workers, men and women who will give personal labour; who will develop the sympathetic spirit as servants of the people; men and women keenly alive to the duties and responsibilities of citizenship; men and women who will go to rescue and reform, to prevent and uplift. The initiative must come from the comfortable, the leisured, and the educated classes. It is they who must see with a new angle of vision, see those not seen before, nor cared [...]. It is they who must see first the distant vision of a healthy, happy, truly beautiful city.[64]

The League set itself a number of objectives in its founding charter. First of all, it aimed to collect and study 'social facts' and to discuss 'social theories and social problems with a view to forming public opinion on questions of social service'. Second, it was dedicated to the 'pursuit of social service generally and specially with a view to ameliorate the physical, moral, mental and economic condition of the people'. A third objective was the 'training of social workers'. The League's constitution also proclaimed its intention to undertake measures for the 'organization of charities and social work'.[65] In the years that followed, the League laid great emphasis on the practical side of its work. It campaigned for mass education, sanitary awareness and social purity; tried to raise public awareness about the importance and value of social service; and conducted relief work amongst the urban poor during times of distress.

However, the most significant feature of the League's activities was its adherence to a new ethic of 'social work' that was subsequently to prove very influential in Bombay's public life. Inspired by the model of Toynbee Hall and the 'settlement houses' that were established in north-eastern American cities during the Progressive Era, the leaders of the League aspired to initiate similar experiments in Bombay. For instance, its fourth annual report noted that, 'In England, America and other countries educated persons, inspired with the idea of improving the social condition of the poor classes, live in their localities and start various educational and social activities for raising their standard of living'.[66] Whilst admitting at the outset that the prevailing conditions in India made it 'difficult, if not impossible' for the League to establish such settlements, not least because of 'the great paucity of trained social workers', its organizers nonetheless made 'an humble beginning' by establishing social work centres in Tardeo, Chikhalwadi and Parel, 'three localities inhabited by a large number of labouring classes'. Here, the League commenced its activities by focusing on 'sanitation work' in order that 'after continuous work for two or three years a visible change for the better may be effected in the life of the people'.[67]

These measures paved the way for a major innovation in January 1917 when the League established a 'permanent settlement' at Parel. 'The basic idea of the settlement', the League's organizers explained, 'is that social workers should go and live with the poor, see their life at close quarters, try to help them in their close quarters, try to help them in their difficulties and raise their standard of life'.[68] The League accordingly rented a ground floor apartment on Parel Road and appointed two resident graduate workers to take charge of the new settlement's activities. This involved, in the first instance, setting up a library and free reading room; arranging lectures, first-aid classes, recreational activities such as drawing and music classes; and founding a cooperative credit society. The League's workers also engaged in street preaching and it was reported that on Sunday evenings, 'the singing band of the Branch attracts the passers-by into its compound, where lectures are given by various speakers on all sorts of practical and useful subjects'.[69] Significantly, the public lectures that the League organized were often delivered by Hindu religious figures and a number of them revolved around themes drawn from the great Indian epics.

In February 1918, the League opened a second permanent settlement at Ghelabhai Street in Madanpura, 'in the midst of a large population of Mahomedan weavers from Northern India', most of whom were said to be 'illiterate'. The settlement was placed under the charge of a Muslim resident graduate worker and, as in Parel, a range of activities were initiated including an Urdu Library, a free reading room, night schools, lantern lectures, fresh air excursions, cooperative societies for the weavers of the locality, fund-raising drives among local Muslim businessmen to fund scholarships for poor students of the community and general sanitation work. The last aspect of the work was seen to be especially important in a locality that was deemed to contain 'some of the most insanitary slums inhabited by the labouring classes'.[70] Indeed, the League noted that as a result of its activities, 'the three portions of Ghelabhai Street were [...] levelled, metalled and lighted' and that it had sent a large number of representations 'to the different departments of the Municipality, the Rent Controller and the Improvement Trust, regarding insufficient water supply, dilapidated condition of premises, improper situation of some latrines and urinals, erection of new urinals, insanitation in chawls, darkness in streets, illegal enhancement of rents, etc.'.[71]

The League's work also acquired deeper institutional roots in the city. In March 1918, it opened a 'Workmen's Institute' for the Currimbhoy Ebrahim group of mills. Funded by the industrial magnate Sir Fazulbhoy Currimbhoy, this institution undertook to provide the workers of this industrial conglomerate a range of 'welfare' services.[72] Shortly after this institution was set up, the League was invited to organize and supervise a similar venture for the Tatas. The Tata Sons Workmen's Institute commenced work in November 1918 and engaged in 'welfare' activities for the company's workers.[73]

Reflecting on its achievements, the League was able to claim that 'the natural social work conducted by it, and the active propaganda for the promotion of social service that it had carried out are responsible in no small degree for the favourable atmosphere that has been created in this city for the service in the cause of humanity'. Indeed, its annual report for 1918 declared confidently that, 'The spirit of social service is abroad; the air is full of it'. Young educated men, it noted, were coming forward in greater numbers than ever before 'to volunteer their services whenever necessity arises', many of whom were 'content even with the meagre remuneration if they are allowed an opportunity of serving the great cause'. Furthermore, the League's organizers argued, their recent activities had demonstrated the value of a new mode of social work, in which volunteers resided amongst the poor and impressed upon the latter, 'the grandeur of pure life, economy, self-respect, honesty and fellow-feeling'.[74]

But the League's activities were not free of their internal constraints and contradictions. Its financial resources were not only precarious but also highly dependent on charitable donations from the city's moneyed elites.[75] Such financial constraints undoubtedly played a part in prompting the League to undertake welfare work on behalf of corporate firms that were able to fund such activity. But this, in turn, rendered its motives suspect in the eyes of many workers. It is not surprising that the Social Service League was rapidly marginalized once the communists established their political supremacy over Bombay's working-class districts in the 1920s.

Significantly, while many of the League's activists had genuine sympathy for the plight of the working classes, they nonetheless partook of the dominant elite discourse, which represented the latter as ignorant, irrational and intemperate. Indeed, the difficulties that they encountered in conducting social work amongst the working classes served at times to confirm their inherent prejudices about the poor. Even though the activists of the League agreed that the task of social work was to make workers independent and self-reliant, their own outlook was paternalist and pedagogical. As a consequence, the rhetoric of 'service' was imbued with conservative impulses. In particular, their assumptions about the innate volatility of the poor prompted the leaders of the League to advocate social work on the grounds that it served to inculcate peaceful forms of self-expression in the working classes. Thus, in the wake of two massive general strikes in 1919 and 1920, N. M. Joshi declared that processes of socialization through education and the provision of other social amenities had a practical value in that,

> The danger of allowing a large mass of discontented working class population to brood over their wrongs secretly in an industrial city such as Bombay is really very great. They form a mass of combustible material waiting to catch fire at the slightest ignition, and threaten to be a source of constant danger to the peace of the city.[76]

Equally, the fervour of the League's activists was seldom reciprocated by the intended objects of their solicitude. Thus, the 'difficulty of securing regular attendance' at its night schools was said to have 'baffled […] the managers of these classes'. In some instances, night schools in working-class neighbourhoods had to be terminated or 'transferred from their original places to more suitable locations'. An article contributed to the *Social Service Quarterly* in July 1916 highlighted the travails of the earnest social activist. The writer recounted an incident that had occurred when he and his fellow volunteers sought to renew their acquaintance with a group of mill workers amongst whom they had previously conducted social work:

> Armed with the question papers of Mr. Devadhar, which when opened out, looked like Railway time-table sheets and were at first sight as intricate as a Bombay transfer-tram-ticket to a villager, we ventured on our first systematic inquiry. We failed. The young lady of the house wanted to know whether we were the census enumerators; if so, her 'Karbhari' (husband) was out, and any way it was no business of ours to find how many children she had. We went a few doors further. We reminded an old gentleman, leisurely combing his long hair, that we were old friends. Had not we shown him a lot of fine temples and other views only a week before? The old gentleman said he did not remember. It was one of his off-days and he was drunk. We tried to engage him in talk. He was very agreeable, and we were duly informed how rascally his neighbours were, what a hard lot it was to be in a Bombay mill, and how he had vowed he would beat his daughter soundly next time she slacked in work at the mills. We ventured upon some more personal inquiries regarding his debts, his income – to fill another column in Mr. Devadhar's table – and were politely shown the door.

On another such occasion, the writer recalled,

> I was [...] 'managing' the lantern for a friend, a great temperance worker, when he was showing some mill-hands a set of views illustrating the evils of drunkenness. And incidentally, this is what he happened to say: 'You men should in this country', shouted my friend, 'you men should follow the example of the Brahmins whom you all respect. *They* never drink'. A ripple of laughter greeted this remark, which only the innate politeness of an Indian crowd prevented from accumulating into guffaws of derisive laughter.

Reflecting on his experiences, the writer admitted rather ruefully that 'we do not know how to approach these strata of Indian society'. In particular, 'the young man from College is no way equipped for the work he wants to do'. 'He is deficient in the knowledge of his own vernacular', he concluded, 'and cannot make a five-minute speech before a group of working-men without larding his vernacular sentences with English words'. Hence, relatively little progress was possible 'in the collection of social facts unless the higher middle classes in this Presidency care to come into closer touch with the working-classes'. [77]

Conclusion

By way of a conclusion, it would be appropriate to reflect on the wider political significance of the civic activism of Bombay's intelligentsia in these years. Undoubtedly, the initiatives of Indian middle-class activists in the first two decades of the twentieth century were integral to the project of 'nation-building'. Thus, in Bombay, as in colonial North India, the new traditions of service-oriented social and philanthropic work inducted 'new social groups into public life', brought a number of institutions under Indian control and infused civil society with ideas of 'active citizenship' and 'selfless' devotion to the cause of the downtrodden. [78] Moreover, their engagement in social and philanthropic activities enhanced the self-worth and confidence of members of a class that had to contend with the humiliating condescension of the British colonial elite.

Undeniably, too, their civic activism strengthened the claims to public leadership of the educated middle class during the first two decades of the twentieth century. By the end of the First World War, educated men were able to tout their credentials as the 'real' leaders of the citizenry far more confidently than during the late nineteenth century. Their ascendancy within the urban public sphere was confirmed by the increasingly strident manner in which organs of the intelligentsia such as the *Bombay Chronicle* and organizations like the Social Service League spearheaded campaigns for democratic reforms in the realm of municipal governance. [79] In turn, the views of the intelligentsia were accorded more weight by colonial officialdom than they had been during the era of 'new imperialism'.

On the other hand, notwithstanding the zeal of social activists, the 'civilizing mission' of the Indian middle class did not result in 'bourgeois' cultural hegemony over Bombay's working classes. For instance, the moral crusades of middle-class moralists to stamp out liquor drinking appear to have ended in failure. The limited impact of the anti-liquor crusaders can be discerned in the frustration of one contemporary observer who declared that despite the efforts of the various temperance societies, 'the people had since returned to their old habits and there was not now a very small proportion of them who did not drink and who had been able to save money'. [80] Similarly, the activities of the *Hollika Sammelan* also received a lukewarm response from the lower classes. Referring to the activities of the *Sammelan*, one contemporary reported in 1912 that while its efforts were 'no doubt making themselves felt amongst the middle classes, who are ready to appreciate such reform', the working classes and the lower castes 'still enjoy the orgies which accompany this saturnalia with all the zest of their forefathers'.[81]

Perhaps the most significant long-term political consequence of their civic activism lay in the 'moral capital' that it gradually generated for middle-class publicists and social activists seeking to make contact with the poor. Certainly, the conduct of social work came over time to epitomize exemplary commitment, in the face of extreme personal hardship, on the part of individuals drawn from educated middle-class backgrounds who took to such activity. This aspect of the ethic of social service was to have a more enduring impact. Indeed, the 'moral capital' of the Indian nationalist movement during the inter-war period stemmed in large part from notions of 'disinterested selflessness', or ceaseless striving for the betterment of the conditions of the 'weaker sections', of voluntary work, personal asceticism and self sacrifice on the part of heroic individuals drawn from 'respectable' social backgrounds.[82] Mahatma Gandhi is generally viewed as the originator of this mode of social activism, and the Gandhian phase of Indian nationalism as the period when it first emerged in Indian politics. However, the ethic of social service can be traced back to an earlier era of civic activism that developed amongst the urban, educated middle-class men in their quest for public leadership.[83]

Notes

1 This chapter is a significantly revised version of chapter 7 ('Social Service', Civic Activism and the Urban Poor) from my book *The Making of an Indian Metropolis: Colonial Governance and Public Culture in Bombay, 1890–1920* (Aldershot & Burlington, Vermont: Ashgate Publishing Ltd., 2007), 203–34. I am grateful to Ashgate Publishing for permission to use it here, and would like to thank the University of Leicester for a semester's leave that allowed me to rework the essay for publication in its present form. I would also like to thank Carey Watt for his helpful comments and suggestions.

2 E. E. McDonald, 'English Education and Social Reform in Late Nineteenth Century Bombay: A Case Study in the Transmission of a Cultural Ideal', *Journal of Asian Studies* (hereafter *JAS*) 25, no. 3 (1966): 453–70. On the importance of social reform among Parsi and Muslim communities such as the Khojas, see also Amrita Shodhan, *A Question of Community: Religious Groups and Colonial Law* (Calcutta, 2001), 122–5; and Christine Dobbin, *Urban Leadership in Western India: Politics and Communities in Bombay City, 1840–85* (Oxford, 1972).

3 Geraldine Forbes, *Women in Modern India* (Cambridge, 1996), 17.

4 *Ibid.*, 15.

5 Manu Subedar, 'Social Service in India', *The Indian Review* (1912): 902.

6 For instance, organizations like the Arya Samaj, the Theosophical Society and the Ramakrishna Mission were engaged in both 'reform' and 'service' activities. Equally, prominent 'social reformers' frequently took the lead in organizing 'social service'

activities. See Carey A. Watt, *Serving the Nation: Cultures of Service, Association and Citizenship in Colonial India* (Delhi, 2005), 4.

7 Susan Bayly, *Caste, Society and Politics in India from the Eighteenth Century to the Modern Age* (Cambridge, 1999), 144–86.

8 Carey A. Watt, 'Education for National Efficiency: Constructive Nationalism in North India, 1909–16', *Modern Asian Studies* (hereafter *MAS*) 31, no. 2 (1997): 340–341; on the influence of 'organic' social theory in late Victorian Britain see Jose Harris, *Public Spirit, Private Lives: Britain 1870–1914* (Harmondsworth, 1994), 223–6.

9 Bayly, *Caste, Society and Politics in India*, 157.

10 *Ibid.*, 182–3.

11 Watt, 'Education for National Efficiency': 340.

12 Bayly, *Caste, Society and Politics in India*, 183.

13 Dobbin, *Urban Leadership*, 253.

14 M. S. Gore, *Vithal Ramji Shinde: An Assessment of his Contribution* (Bombay, 1990), 1–49; G. M. Pawar, *Vithal Ramji Shinde* (Delhi, 2000), 3–11.

15 Gore, *Vithal Ramji Shinde*, 142–6.

16 M. S. Gore, *Jotirao Phule and Vithalrao Shinde* (Bombay, 1986), 25.

17 G. P. Deshpande, 'The World and Ideas: The Case of Colonial and Ex-colonial Maharashtra', in V. R. Mehta and Thomas Pantham (eds), *Political Ideas in India: Thematic Explorations* (New Delhi, 2006), 113.

18 Gore, *Vithal Ramji Shinde*, 149.

19 *The Social Service Quarterly* (hereafter SSQ) II, no. 1 (July 1916): 35–41.

20 Bayly, *Caste, Society and Politics in India*, 182.

21 Watt, 'Education for National Efficiency': 355–62.

22 The details in this paragraph are culled from H. N. Kunzru (ed.), *Gopal Krishna Devadhar* (Poona, 1939). I am grateful to Carey Watt for bringing this source to my notice.

23 T. N. Jagadisan and Shyamlal (eds), *Thakkar Bapa: Eightieth Birthday Commemoration Volume* (Madras, 1949).

24 In this context see also Deshpande, 'The World and Ideas', 113.

25 Bayly, *Origins of Nationality*, 285.

26 Bayly, *Caste, Society and Politics in India*, 183–5.

27 Sanjay Joshi, *Fractured Modernity: Making of a Middle Class in Colonial North India* (Delhi, 2001).

28 For a summary, see Rosalind O' Hanlon, *A Comparison between Women and Men: Tarabai Shinde and the critique of gender relations in colonial India* (Oxford, 1994), 1–62.

29 Joshi, *Fractured Modernity*, 1–58. See also Gail Minault, *Secluded Scholars: Women's Education and Muslim School Reform in Colonial India* (Delhi, 1998).

30 Sudipta Kaviraj, 'Filth and Public Sphere: Concepts and Practices about Space in Calcutta', *Public Culture* 10, no. 1 (1997): 84; 92–3.

31 In this context, see also Nandini Gooptu, *The Politics of the Urban Poor in Early Twentieth-Century India* (Cambridge, 2001).

32 Dipesh Chakrabarty, *Habitations of Modernity: Essays in the Wake of Subaltern Studies* (Chicago, 2002), 77.

33 Gooptu, *Politics of the Urban Poor*, 14.

34 While the celebration of the festival amongst the upper classes was said to be 'a tame affair', for the mill workers of the city Holi was believed to be 'one continuous round of hilarity by day and night'. During the festival it was the practice among the working classes to organize *tamashas* in which young boys dressed up in female attire and moved

about the town collecting subscriptions for a final entertainment. Educated observers complained that like the Muharram *tolis*, these gangs sought to blackmail 'the Marwadis, or money-lenders, and threaten well-dressed people with a rub-down with their greasy or sooty bodies'. V. A. Talcherkar, 'The Shimga or Holi Festival and the Bombay Mill-Hands', *ITJ* XIV, no. 162 (1904): 176–8.

35 Kunzru (ed.), *Gopal Krishna Devadhar*, 103.

36 *Ibid.*, 104.

37 V. B. Karnik, *N. M. Joshi: Servant of India* (Bombay, 1972), 27–8.

38 In this context, see also Veena Naregal, 'Figuring the Political as Pedagogy: Colonial Intellectuals, Mediation and Modernity in Western India', *Studies in History*, New Series 17, no. 1 (2001): 18.

39 On middle-class representations of the poor in this context, see also David Arnold, 'Touching the Body: Perspectives on the Indian Plague, 1896–1900', in Ranajit Guha (ed.), *Subaltern Studies*, vol. V (Delhi, 1987).

40 *Bombay Gazette and Overland Summary* (hereafter *BGOS*), 29 August 1903.

41 *BGOS*, 16 January 1904.

42 *BGOS*, 29 August 1903.

43 *BGOS*, 4 February 1905.

44 *BGOS*, 10 February 1906. In 1905–06, the 'health visitors' were said to have made 4519 visits to different houses and 'advised the people in sanitation and hygiene'. *Ibid.*

45 *Ibid.*

46 *BGOS*, 4 March 1905.

47 Jose Harris, 'Political Thought and the Welfare State 1870–1940: An Intellectual Framework for British Social Policy', *Past and Present* 135, no. 1 (1992): 121.

48 Michael J. Moore, 'Social Work and Social Welfare: The Organization of Philanthropic Resources in Britain, 1900–1914', *The Journal of British Studies* 16, no. 2 (Spring 1977): 85–8.

49 Allen F. Davis, *Spearheads for Reform: The Social Settlements and the Progressive Movement 1890–1914* (New York, 1967).

50 David Ward, 'The Progressive and the Urban Question: British and American Responses to the Inner City Slums 1880–1920', *Transactions of the Institute of British Geographers*, New Series 9, no. 3 (1984): 299.

51 David Ward, 'Presidential Address: Social Reform, Social Surveys, and the Discovery of the Modern City', *Annals of the Association of American Georgraphers* 80, no. 4 (1990): 491.

52 Cathy L. James, '"Not Merely for the Sake of an Evening's Entertainment": The Educational Uses of Theater in Toronto's Settlement Houses, 1910–1930', *History of Education Quarterly* 38, no. 3 (1998): 287–311.

53 David R. Ambaras, 'Social Knowledge, Cultural Capital, and the New Middle Class in Japan, 1895–1912', *Journal of Japanese Studies* 24, no. 1 (1998): 1–33.

54 Adele Lindenmeyr, 'Charity and the Problem of Unemployment: Industrial Homes in Late Imperial Russia', *Russian Review* 45, no. 1 (1986): 1–22.

55 Adele Lindenmeyr, *Poverty Is Not A Vice: Charity, Society, and the State in Imperial Russia* (Princeton, 1996). See also Daniel Brower, *The Russian City Between Tradition and Modernity, 1850–1900* (Berkeley, 1990).

56 Watt, *Serving the Nation*, 32.

57 *Ibid.*, 203.

58 *Indian Spectator*, 24 August 1912.

59 *Indian Spectator*, 31 August 1912.

60 *SSQ* III, no. 4 (1918): 218.

61 Karnik, *Joshi*, 36–49.

62 G. L. Chandavarkar, *A Wrestling Soul: Story of the life of Sir Narayan Chandavarkar* (Bombay, 1955), p.163. The League had five classes of members based on the extent of monetary contribution. These ranged from life members who had made donations of over five hundred rupees to those in the lowest class who generally paid anything between one rupee and four rupees per annum.

63 'The Social Service League, Bombay: A Brief Record of Four Years' Work', *SSQ* I, no. 1 (1915): 21–25.

64 N. M. Muzumdar, 'The Social Problems of a City', *SSQ* II, no. 1 (1916): 27–35.

65 The Social Service League's charter of aims was usually published at the end of all its reports and publications.

66 *Fourth Annual Report of the Social Service League* (Bombay, 1915), p.13.

67 *Third Annual Report of the Social Service League* (Bombay, 1914), pp.14–15.

68 *Sixth Annual Report of the Social Service League* (Bombay, 1917), p.1.

69 *Ibid.*, 29–30.

70 *Seventh Annual Report of the Social Service League* (Bombay, 1918), 1–4.

71 *Twelfth Annual Report of the Social Service League* (Bombay, 1924), 25–26.

72 *SSQ* 3, no. 4 (1918): 226.

73 *Twelfth Annual Report of the Social Service League* (Bombay, 1924), 30–35.

74 *Seventh Annual Report of the Social Service League* (Bombay, 1918), 1–4.

75 For instance, the League's annual financial statement for 1923 showed that the principal donors to the General Fund were either philanthropic bodies like the N. M. Wadia Charities, the Ratan Tata Estate, and the Abdullabhoy Lalji Trust, or wealthy individuals such as Sir Dorab Tata, Cowasji Jehangir and Sitaram Poddar. Furthermore, the donations to the League's General Fund outstripped the money collected as annual subscriptions from its members. *Twelfth Annual Report of the Social Service League* (Bombay, 1924), 49–53.

76 N. M. Joshi, 'Wanted: A Workers' Educational Association for Bombay', *SSQ* 6, no. 1 (1920): 1–2.

77 L. G. Khare, 'Some Difficulties of the Social Worker', *SSQ* 2, no. 1 (1916): 23–27.

78 Watt, *Serving the Nation*, 202.

79 Sandip Hazareesingh, 'The Quest for Urban Citizenship: Civic Rights, Public Opinion and Colonial Resistance in Early Twentieth-Century Bombay', *MAS* 34, no. 4 (2000): 803–12.

80 *BPP SAI* XXVII, no. 22 (1914), para. 1071.

81 *BPP SAI* XXV, no. 11 (1912), para. 472.

82 For a discussion of the significance of a 'saintly idiom' in Indian politics, see W. H. Morris-Jones, 'India's Political Idioms', in T. R. Metcalf (ed.), *Modern India: An Interpretive Anthology* (London, 1971), 273–291.

83 On this point, see also Watt, *Serving the Nation*, 204–205.

Part Four

TRANSCENDING 1947: COLONIAL AND POSTCOLONIAL CONTINUITIES

Chapter Eight

FEMALE INFANTICIDE AND THE CIVILIZING MISSION IN POSTCOLONIAL INDIA: A CASE STUDY FROM TAMIL NADU c. 1980–2006[1]

Shahid Perwez

Introduction

This paper engages with the social and political responses to female infanticide in contemporary Tamil South India, as an instance of the continuation of the rhetoric and practice of the British colonial 'civilizing mission' in postcolonial India.[2] The term 'civilizing mission' refers to 'the grand project that justified colonialism as a means of redeeming the backward, aberrant, violent, oppressed, undeveloped people of the non-European world by incorporating them into the universal civilization of Europe'.[3] For the sake of this paper, I use a particular expression of the term to refer to an agenda or a discourse of civilizational otherness, which British colonizers deployed largely for the self-legitimation of their rule in the name of 'improvement', 'betterment', and even the 'social and moral progress' of the colonized.[4] While some historical analysis has been made with regard to understanding the 'civilizing mission' as a programme, concept and ideology in British India, its continuities in postcolonial India are rarely the subject of academic analyses.[5]

If at the heart of this mission were an ideology and a material programme of knowing, naming and ordering[6] public spaces and political relations, do the contemporary governments of independent India differ much on this count or have they abandoned such an approach? If the 'civilizing mission' campaign granted the colonial subjects what Srirupa Prasad has equated with Jacques Donzelot's notion of 'supervised freedom',[7] has the policing of families and communities been abandoned in postcolonial India in favour of a liberalized notion of freedom for individuals and families? In other words, has the tension between individual and collective choices or rights been resolved? While the 'self-legitimation' processes or the pragmatics of rule of the British Raj have indeed been replaced with a more democratic and legitimate mandate of the postcolonial state, the very philosophy and legacy of the colonial 'civilizing mission' continues to shape the conduct of postcolonial governments in South Asia. The shift in global discourse from 'improvement' to 'development' since the 1930s, in which most governments today have increasingly oriented their programmatic activities around welfare and development has, in fact, helped to continue the procedural and bureaucratic hegemony akin to a colonial 'civilizing mission'. This paper analyses the colonial civilizing mission approach implicit in postcolonial development initiatives by ethnographically studying the paternalist agenda and programming of the contemporary government in Tamil Nadu, as captured in its efforts to prevent female infanticide.[8]

Why Female Infanticide in Postcolonial Tamil Nadu?

A study of the postcolonial government's responses to female infanticide in contemporary Tamil Nadu is apposite for a number of reasons. First of all, while there have been ample colonial-ethnographic narratives on female infanticide in north-western India, there has hardly been any parallel enterprise undertaken in the southern parts of colonial India.[9] Most colonial and postcolonial discussions of female infanticide, as well as recent accounts of sex selective abortion, have assumed that they are a typically North Indian phenomenon, most strongly associated with rigid patriarchal kinship structure including dowry, unfavourable marriage patterns, lack of individual freedom, poor education, and strict rules of female seclusion.[10] Since the mid 1980s, however, there have been reports of widespread female infanticide in Tamil Nadu, reported both locally and in the national press.[11] The increasing number of reports of the prevalence of female infanticide in Tamil Nadu has attracted the attention of social scientists and demographers alike.

Secondly, in response to the media accounts of female infanticide in parts of the state, the Tamil Nadu government announced a series of highly publicized measures in 1992 to tackle the issue. Two such schemes that will be explored in this paper are the Cradle Baby Scheme (CBS) and the Girl Child Protection Scheme (GCPS), designed to 'save' and 'rescue' the girl children in the state. These programmes formally indicate that the Tamil Nadu government acknowledges the existence of female infanticide in Tamil Nadu, and that the practice needs to be eradicated. It was the first Indian state to do so.

Thirdly, these schemes and other government actions quickly met with scepticism and were criticized by activists, media, and Non-Governmental

Organization (NGO) groups. Responding to these criticisms, the government in Tamil Nadu embarked on a large-scale social mobilization against female infanticide involving not only NGOs, media and activists, but also academics and international donor agencies. One concrete manifestation of this collaboration was a large-scale social mobilization against female infanticide that took place in the Dharmapuri district in 1997.[12] The move was largely initiated by the team of a development economist (working as a Professor in the Indian Institute of Technology) and a government official (Commissioner of Health) under Tamil Nadu Area Health Care Project, financially assisted by the Danish International Development Agency (DANIDA).

Fourth, female infanticide in Tamil Nadu has been made a public health issue, as the direct responsibility of documenting female infanticide now lies with the Department of Public Health and Preventive Medicine. The Department has listed 21 possible causes of infant death, of which one – a non-medical cause – is termed as 'death due to social causes'. All suspected and/or confirmed cases of female infanticide are registered in this category, rendering the phrase 'death due to social causes' a euphemism for female infanticide in Tamil Nadu. The implication of this association suggests that governmental programmes on female infanticide have increasingly been merged with the programmes on countering population growth, sterilization programmes and providing maternal and child healthcare. The Directorate of Family Welfare claims on its website:

> Family Welfare Programme is intended to provide maternal and child health care and thereby to bring down the growth rate of population. It is also intended to avoid higher order birth (i.e. birth of more than two children in a family) and prevention of female foeticide and female infanticide. Most of the female foeticide and female infanticide are meted out to the foetus/new-borns who are third or fourth order conceptions/births. Family welfare programme aims at avoiding such higher order conceptions/births to prevent female foeticide and female infanticide.[13]

In line with this pronouncement, various committees have been formed at the district, block and village levels, bringing NGOs and health and nutrition workers together to watch, monitor and counsel 'high risk' pregnant women for undergoing sterilization using both persuasion and coercion.[14] The NGOs, many of whom are funded by international donor agencies, work in tandem with district and village-level government health officials to maintain close surveillance on these women and their families by creating monthly reports of all such mothers who are either pregnant or have delivered recently. As part of the close surveillance of the 'high risk' families, the NGO fieldworkers are required to work along with the Village Health Nurse (VHN) and the

Child Nutrition Worker (CNW). While the former government functionary is appointed under the DANIDA assisted programme, the latter is appointed under the Integrated Child Development Services programme. All of them are required to routinely detect and register all pregnancies, watch and monitor that progress, register the births and follow up on the births (particularly those of a female infant) until the mother is sterilized.

Such interventions often classify and portray women as objects of attention requiring governance, development and improvement. This is akin to the nineteenth-century colonial government's strategy to prevent female infanticide through close surveillance of the family focussing on the detection of pregnancies and the supervision of their progress, the registration of births and the monitoring of the welfare of the female infants.[15] The enlargement of governmental and non-governmental regulations, control and documentation on female infanticide in contemporary Tamil Nadu, therefore, provides an interesting example of modern ways of ordering public spaces and political relations that had once been symptomatic of the British colonial 'civilizing mission' in India. Furthermore, by adopting exclusive policy documents and measures to curb female infanticide in an individualizing and exceptional manner, and by subsequently linking the practice with the discourses around demographic social engineering (i.e. a massive family planning campaign), the state in Tamil Nadu has employed new political technologies – which Foucault has called 'bio-political', and which Donzelot has captured in the expression 'policing of families'.[16]

Description of the Government Policies and Programmes

In contemporary Tamil Nadu, the above-mentioned programmes, CBS and GCPS, have constantly figured in all public discussions about how to reduce – if not eradicate – female infanticide. These two schemes form fertile ground for analysing representations and language concerning the subject in Tamil Nadu. Casual reviews, evaluations and assessments of these two schemes have informed most of the academic and journalistic writings on female infanticide in Tamil Nadu since they were announced in 1992, though a thorough enquiry into these measures has not been attempted. Viewed from the perspective of women considering female infanticide, the schemes appear to be fraught with tensions and conflict both from the point of view of their 'concepts' and 'implementation'. Yet these schemes have survived and their proponents have pronounced them a huge success in curbing female infanticide. Though it is beyond the task of this paper to analyse the success of these schemes demographically, I wish to raise some analytical questions about their methodologies and ideologies.

It is worth noting here that the immediate and earliest response of the government to the publicized reports of female infanticide was one of denial and the making of false accusations and charges against the NGOs and the media. This was followed by a claim that the practice was confined to a particular place in the state (where it was first reported). Not surprisingly, then, these organizations were repeatedly harassed, ostensibly to discourage them from continuing to publicize the issue. In contrast, the response of government in Tamil Nadu changed from denial to acceptance when All-India Anna Dravida Munnetra Kazhgam (AIADMK) came to power in 1991, and when Jayalalitha became the Chief Minister. She launched these two schemes in 1992, becoming the earliest proponent of 'saving' babies in the state. Other than introducing these two schemes, earlier that year, there were also arrests by district police, particularly in Salem, of some families who were accused of committing female infanticide.[17]

Since the start of CBS and GCPS in 1992, there have been stories of interventions, conflicts, criticisms, denials, acceptances and the waxing and waning of the state's interest in the issue of female infanticide. Notwithstanding the fact that these schemes, in particular the CBS, have been severely criticized by NGOs and academics for both their conceptualization and implementation, they have continued to be at the centre of all interventions and discourses surrounding the status of 'girl children' and women's well-being in Tamil Nadu. Both these schemes have been amended and changed a couple of times since their inception and their popularity has periodically risen and fallen according to political shifts in the state. However, the irresistible notion of 'children of the state'[18] has maintained the vigour and vitality of these schemes. This was evident in the continued survival of the schemes even when the Jayalalitha-led AIADMK government, which 'gave birth to' and nurtured them, was not in power (1996–2001). Although the incumbent Dravida Munnetra Kazhgham (DMK) government, which replaced AIADMK between 1996 and 2001, rarely showed any commitment to continue the earlier regime's measures, this lack of political will on the part of DMK functionaries was contradicted by the proliferation of research and writings (mostly by NGOs, academics and activists) during the same period, and the agencies that had funded these research and the resultant interventions. Additionally, a similar move by the Indian central government in August 1997, in the form of introducing a series of 'financial incentives' to poor families having two surviving girl children, has provided further impetus and justification for such measures.

Having sketched the context, let us now consider these two schemes in more detail. The material for describing these programmes was gained from difficult interactions with district government officials, policy documents, various reports as well as some material from newspapers in Salem. I was often denied access to the data on the CBS and the GCPS as the junior officials of the concerned departments were explicitly instructed not to reveal this information to 'outsiders' (such as non-government officials and unknown people including independent researchers). However, a young and academically-motivated administrative officer of significant repute and power in the district eventually introduced me to a select few other government officials who were responsible for the Salem district's female infanticide programme.[19]

Cradle Baby Scheme

The CBS was devised as an immediate rescue mission in areas where female infanticide was believed to be rife. Cradles were to be placed outside primary health centres, hospitals and orphanages to receive the newborn female infants that may otherwise have been killed, and families were openly asked to abandon unwanted female infants in the cradle rather than kill them. The scheme was originally introduced in the three districts of Salem, Dindigul and Madurai. Since 2001, following the return of AIADMK to power, additional centres have been opened at Theni and Dharmapuri districts with an increased budget outlay by 2005–06 of Rs 680,000 for the scheme in each of the named districts. The scheme has gradually been extended to all districts of Tamil Nadu with the setting up of 188 cradle centres. Accounts of the number of children saved so far vary: between May 1996 and April 2001 (when the AIADMK government was no longer in power), only 13 babies were admitted under the CBS in Salem. Since May 2001, following the return of the AIADMK government to power, the scheme was revived and from that point until the completion of my fieldwork in September 2005, more than 600 babies came under the care of the Salem centre alone.

In the earlier days of the introduction of CBS, cradles were literally placed outside primary health centres, hospitals, orphanages and government offices for collecting babies. Usually people would leave their unwanted babies in the wee, dark hours of the night to avoid detection. By the time they were found in the morning many had already died. Succumbing to widespread criticism of the manner in which babies were collected, the district administration later changed the modalities. Now the baby's adoption from the villages is facilitated either with the help of a VHN, a CNW, or an NGO fieldworker. In a few cases, parents actually give their babies directly to the District Collector at the Salem administrative office. In Salem, this became a practice in December 2001 when the newly appointed District Collector began collecting babies himself every week on a designated Grievance Day, a day originally meant for hearing people's problems and complaints.[20] Such a move soon rendered Salem district as the busiest collection centre under this scheme.

Detailed statistics with regard to babies being registered under the CBS tell an interesting tale regarding the working of the scheme. Firstly, according to the register of District Social Welfare Office (DSWO), Salem has received a total of 710 babies between October 1992 and August 2005. Of these, 27 babies have been 'returned to biological parents', and 39 babies died due to 'health sickness'. Secondly, although the CBS was designed explicitly to counter the practice of *female* infanticide, there were at least 39 *male* babies accepted under the scheme in Salem. Were these male babies potential victims of *male* infanticide? A few government officials confirmed my doubt, although this was not a line of thinking that was officially entertained by them. Thirdly, the reasons for surrendering the baby under the CBS were quoted as 'poverty', 'physically deformed', 'unwed mother', 'father's death', 'mother's death', 'family disintegration', 'abandonment', 'rape', 'orphaned child' and 'more than two daughters'. Such a wide spectrum of reasons quoted by the biological parents while surrendering their baby under the care of the state seem to form the basis for the state's social theory of female infanticide. That is, government officials in Tamil Nadu essentially view female infanticide as a result of 'poverty'. The government uses 'female infant mortality rate' and 'gender discrimination' as an indicator and it sees 'family planning' as the most important goal, thereby orienting all its policies and programmes accordingly.

There have been mixed and often contradictory reactions to this scheme. On the one hand, many activists and NGOs have been keen to point out that while the state claims to be the custodian of any abandoned children, it legitimizes and encourages female infanticide by absolving parents of responsibility towards their daughters. Others have argued that the scheme actually encourages son preference as families can continue to dump the girl child in the cradles.[21] On the other hand, NGOs operating in the region have been hugely successful in implementing the CBS. For peaceful co-existence with the government departments, all NGOs working on female infanticide prevention are required, in principle, to demonstrate their proficiency in curbing the practice by publishing the statistics annually regarding babies that they had facilitated under the CBS. The NGO fieldworkers therefore spend considerable time and effort in the field in conjunction with the VHN and the CNW, finding families with 'high risk' mothers and then persuading the mothers to surrender the newborn to CBS if it happens to be a female child. More often than not these mothers are also coerced by both the VHN and the NGO fieldworkers into undergoing sterilization after the CBS facilitation, as can be seen in the account of a mother seeking to use the CBS included below.

Additionally, the role of the media has been paramount in declaring success and in consolidating these schemes socially. A significant shift in voicing the success of this scheme became particularly visible after the return of AIADMK government in May 2001. In particular, *The Hindu* – the largest Chennai-based English-language daily – has kept this particular scheme before the public by making it the subject of headlines from time to time. Here are a few examples: 'Cradle baby scheme revived', (19 June, 2001, *The Hindu*: Chennai); 'Cradle baby scheme not popular in Usilampatti, but female infanticide is on the decline' (30 November, 2001, *The Hindu*: Madurai); '302nd cradle baby in Salem Centre' (1 October, 2002, *The Hindu*: Salem); 'Cradle baby scheme has saved 653 children' (5 January, 2003, *The Hindu*: Salem); 'Need for cradle baby scheme must go' (28 October, 2003, *The Hindu*: Thanjavur); 'From cradle babies to Danish girls'[22] (27 December, 2003, *The Hindu*: Salem), and so on. Indeed, despite criticisms of this scheme, media seem to have promoted CBS to such extent that the scheme has come to be synonymous with female infanticide in Tamil Nadu.

Girl Child Protection Scheme

In contrast, the GCPS is a long-term financial incentive to keep girl children with their families by allocating public funds for each girl participating in the scheme. The scheme was earlier called the '*Puratchi Thalaivi* [revolutionary leader] Dr Jayalalitha Scheme for the Girl Child' and was later renamed the GCPS.[23] It was originally introduced as part of the Fifteen-Point Programme for Child Welfare designed by the AIADMK government between 1991 and 1996. A further three points were added to it by Jayalalitha in 2001 when she returned to power, renaming it as the Eighteen-Point Programme for the Welfare of Women and Children. Under the initial scheme, for every girl child under four belonging to a rural family that satisfied a number of criteria including that of the mother undergoing sterilization, Rs 2000 would be deposited in a special public fund maintained by the government. At age 20, the girl would receive Rs 10 000 either to pursue higher education or to get married. A sum of Rs 40 million was earmarked for the scheme at that time.[24]

Under the present scheme, families with a lone girl child or two girl children could benefit from an initial deposit with the Tamil Nadu Power Finance Corporation of Rs 22,200 and Rs 15,200 respectively, made by the government in the name of the child. The deposited money is to be given to the registered girl children only after 20 years, along with an annual payment of Rs 1,800 (interest accruing from the deposits) from the sixth year of the deposit to meet up the educational expenses of the child. The budget of the scheme was raised to about Rs 227 million in 2001, which was further increased to Rs 500 million in 2005–06.[25] The most significant addition to the revised scheme was an increase in the set of filtering criteria for the applicant families. I have divided them here into 'pre' and 'post' application criteria for the sake of clarity in the argument that follows.

Pre-Application Criteria

1. Either of the parents must be sterilized within a year of the child's birth.
2. Sterilization certificate must be issued by a public health official within a year of the child's birth.
3. Application to this scheme must be made within a year of the child's birth (this was extended to three years by Jayalalitha just before the Tamil Nadu Assembly Polls in 2006).
4. Parents must be resident in the state for the last ten years preceding the application.
5. The parents' age must not exceed thirty-five years.
6. For families with one daughter, the family income should be below Rs 50,000 per annum and for families with two daughters, it should be below Rs 12,000 per annum.
7. The gap between the two children should not be more than three years.

Post-Application Criteria

8. The maturity value shall be payable only if the girl children study up to Tenth Standard and appear for the Public Examination. If the children do not appear for the Tenth Standard Public Examination before the completion of twenty years of deposit, such children are not eligible to receive the maturity value and it shall be forfeited to the Government Account.
9. Every five years, families must come for renewal of the scheme at a specified date. If they fail to turn up on the specified date, such families will be disqualified from the scheme.
10. If either of the children dies, the money shall be forfeited to the Government Account.

On the one hand, the difficulties in meeting these criteria by most families led to an endorsement of the family's perception of girl children as a burden inasmuch as 'the schemes implicitly endorsed the communities' perception of girl children as a burden that the state would help them to bear'.[26] I will provide some context to the bureaucratic apathy in highlighting issues around the unsuccessful applications and in reinforcing the notion of daughters as liability, through Chellamma's narrative in the forthcoming ethnographic section (all names in the paper have been changed to pseudonyms). On the other hand, the inclusion and enlargement of these stringent and needless criteria into a pre- and post-application reflects the state's limited intervention towards target families for the scheme with a modest budget outlay. Some of the immediate responses to the revised scheme suggested: 'the amount allocated for the scheme would cover hardly one per cent of the 770,492 girl children in the 0–4 age groups from poor households [given the fact] that every year 196,684 girl children are born in poor households at a birth rate of 19 per 1,000 and by considering that 35 per cent of the population lives below the poverty line'.[27] It was therefore suggested that at least Rs 169 billion – instead of Rs 500 million – would be needed in order to cover all female children in the 0–4 age group.[28]

Consequently, there were more unsuccessful GCPS applications made in Salem than successful ones. According to DSWO, out of 3,540 GCPS applications made in Salem district, only 1,450 applications were cleared by the government as of August 2005; there were over 2,000 applications still pending for approval by the DSWO. Looking at such a dismal outcome of GCPS applications successfully made in Salem district by families with only girl children, one cannot help gauge the populist agenda inherent in GCPS which was mainly introduced, according to the Tamil Nadu government, 'to promote family planning, to eradicate female infanticide, and to discourage preference for male child'.[29]

The nature of such short-lived and highly-publicized measures is also reflected in the fact that when the AIADMK government was no longer in power between 1996 and 2001, the alternative DMK government put the cause on the backburner and made practically no effort to continue with the scheme.[30] This was also indicated in the case of CBS, by the fact that there was a sharp decrease in the number of babies received and transferred to adoption agencies (i.e. only nine babies) during the same period. The apparent lack of political will on the part of the DMK government that returned to power in 2006 to continue with the policies and programmes of its rival political party reflects the uncertainties that prevailed in people's minds during the AIADMK regime. The question 'What if Jayalalitha is ousted from power?' persistently echoed during my fieldwork. Considering the fact that the earliest beneficiaries of GCPS could receive the concluding benefits only in the year 2012, after completing twenty years of schooling (only for few of those first lot of applications successfully made back in 1992), the family's nightmares have come true in the wake of AIADMK's removal from office in 2006.

There are some other erroneous perceptions concerning this scheme. First, GCPS is based on the assumption that all those who kill or do not want daughters are poor, when empirical evidence suggests that the mass of those who are involved in selective elimination of female foetuses are relatively privileged. This poses a significant dilemma for state's responsiveness to female infanticide in that it seeks to differentiate the issues of killing babies pre-natally from that of aborting the female foetuses post-natally. Second, a strong focus on undergoing family planning without sons as the condition for availing GCPS again – quite akin to CBS – places the government outside and as an unwitting participant in maintaining the culture of son preference, with which it claims to engage. As argued below, the prevailing son preference means that parents may not be willing to undergo sterilization until they have a son. As far as I can tell, all those women who have applied for this scheme opted to do so for the reasons other than the logic of financial imperatives that the government so powerfully promotes.

Furthermore, at the local level, popular perceptions suggest that such a meagre financial incentive does not compensate for the major expenses incurred in bringing up a daughter – notably dowry expenses. On the other hand, some commentators also fear that the money, if ever received, could be used for meeting dowry expenses in a daughter's marriage.[31] Likewise, the government's push for the education of the girl children (through GCPS) without creating adequate infrastructure for schooling points to populist intentions rather than a desire to solve the problem.[32] Given this scenario, it is somewhat disappointing to see that GCPS has now been duplicated and introduced with more or less the same principles and criteria to the capital city (Delhi) of India since mid-2006, with a meagre budget outlay of Rs 100 million.[33] Similarly, the Indian Ministry of Women and Child Development has also proposed a 'conditional cash transfer scheme' for girl children with a budgetary provision of Rs 135 million within the proposed Integrated Child Protection Scheme of Rs 855 million being earmarked from the Union Budget of 2007–2008.[34]

Voices from the Field

While there have been mixed responses to CBS and GCPS in government, NGO and media commentaries, let us now look at the voices from the field. The following ethnographic data is not exhaustive, but it represents an important selection from my field-notes (collected through various interviews and frequent interaction with mothers, VHNs and the NGO fieldworkers in various places in Salem).

Scene I: Somewhere Between Mettur and Macheri, September 2004

In the initial days of fieldwork, I often used to spend time with the local NGO fieldworkers, discussing and participating in their events and meetings. In one of the monthly review meetings on female infanticide by the fieldworkers, I was told about one of the first instances whereby a mother was to 'surrender' her newborn female baby to the CBS. This was the fourth consecutive female child born to Munnusamy, aged 40, and Ayupunna, aged 35. Both of them worked as agricultural labourers and belonged to the Vanniyar caste. According to the NGO fieldworkers, the mother had threatened to kill her newborn baby in broad daylight when the concerned VHN refused to facilitate her baby under the CBS. The VHN refused because the mother persistently resisted sterilization. I asked the NGO fieldworkers if sterilization was a pre-condition to obtaining the CBS and they said no. In order to elicit a counter-response from the NGO fieldworkers, I supported the mother's standpoint on sterilization, to which an NGO official said: 'we cannot let it happen because if she is not sterilized now, she would continue procreating until a son is born to her. And this would give enough excuse for other neighbouring mothers to challenge our authority in the area'. I became interested in learning more about the mother who, in the words of local NGO director, had resisted taking the 'ownership of collective responsibility for female infanticide programme', which, in the context of everyday NGO practice, means a physical escape of the high risk mothers from the gaze of NGO surveillance. With the help of NGO fieldworkers, I therefore visited the family and talked to the mother at length. The following excerpt is presented here to give some understanding of the operational complexities of the CBS.

Interviewer: Why do you want to give your newborn under CBS?

Ayupunna: Who will bring up one more daughter for us? Who will pay for wedding expenses including *Nakka* [gold customarily required in wedding] and *Varu-dakshina* [dowry]? We are already so poor with three daughters and there is no son here. People have started looking down at us. No one helps today. You tell me how I could afford four daughters on our meagre income. Will government give us any money? They won't…

Interviewer: Why did you not undergo 'operation' [euphemism for sterilization] after the birth of two daughters like most people are doing now?

Ayupunna: How can I? I want a son. My *Jathagakarar* [astrologer] had already told me that a son is forthcoming in my *Jathagam* [horoscope]. But these people [the VHN and the NGO fieldworkers] are now telling me to undergo operation. Why must I do operation? I strongly need a son for my family.

Interviewer: What if a daughter is born again. Would you still believe in *Jathagam*?

Ayupunna: *Aamaa* [Yes]! We took this [the newborn] to the *Jathagakarar* and he said that the baby will bring ill-fate for all of us. That is why I do not want to keep this baby.

Interviewer: So, would you then keep this daughter of yours if you were to suddenly get a lot of money to bring her up [I immediately asked recalling what she had just said about dowry and heavy expenses in bringing up a daughter]?

Ayupunna: [After thinking for a while] *Illai* [No] … because her *Jathagam* made it known that she will only bring ill-fate with her.

[Field notes: Kanakavalli, 27 September, 2004]

Ayupunna's story reinforces the role of astrologers in the everyday lives of the people and their belief in *Jathagam* while deciding the fate of the newborn. Of late, the local NGO had identified astrologers as the major player in female infanticide and thus eventually began a series of activities around creating awareness and educating them (the *Jathagakaras*) for female infanticide prevention. However, such discourses are clearly absent in government quarters. The case of Ayupunna demonstrates the state's lack of knowledge about the cultural contexts in which practical decisions about reproduction are made, and hence its difficulties in dealing with such issues. The prevailing son preference indicates that most (though not all) parents may not be willing to undergo sterilization until they have a son.

Scene II: Attipatti, February 2005

During my stay in this village, an NGO fieldworker and close friend asked me to advise him regarding a difficult situation that had arisen following the birth of a third girl child in a poor agricultural Lambadi family. It was an eighth-birth. At least three children had reportedly died and the family now had two daughters and two sons as surviving children. Meanwhile, the couple decided to 'surrender' (an English term frequently used by both the NGO fieldworkers and the villagers) their new born daughter under CBS. The reason they gave to the local VHN (a government health official) was that they were living in abject poverty and so they could not bring up any additional children. The VHN denied facilitation for two reasons, as she quoted to me: one, the couple was not ready for sterilization; and two, there was a verbal order from the higher government health officials that transfer of babies must be discouraged as the district cradle centre was unable to cope with too many babies. She said: 'I cannot afford to facilitate another child for adoption under Cradle [Baby Scheme] as nowadays this is taken to mean our poor performance in the village. Such facilitations would also mean my poor performance in the family planning operations. Those sitting high do not understand how difficult it is for us to convince a family for sterilization when everybody here wants a son' (Interview with the VHN,

5 February, 2005). The statement made by the local VHN revealed to me some of the politics of adoption besides revealing some other facets of the handling of the CBS.

Indeed, on my visit to the Salem District Cradle Centre later, I found out that with two Auxiliary Nurse Midwives and two helpers, the centre could accommodate a maximum of ten children at a time. These children have to be kept at the centre for a minimum of two months (lest the biological parents wish to reclaim the child) before they can be transferred to government-licensed agencies. This means that if the centre is full of children (which it always is, particularly since 2001, as emphasized by the nurses at the centre), there is no question of further adoption until one or more of these children are transferred to adoption agencies for adoption by childless couples. It was only after visiting the cradle centre that I was able to understand why the CBS facilitation was regularly turned down by the VHN and other government officials during my fieldwork, as opposed to its promotion in early 2001. Furthermore, the explanation making rounds with the local health functionaries was that the district cradle centre had already received over 650 babies which is why the department could not afford any further collection of newborns.

Such a pronouncement had created trouble for both my NGO fieldworker friend and the VHN, as the family was adamant on giving away its baby. The family was continuously issuing threats to kill the baby. With the CBS option closed, both of them wanted to find a private adoption agency who would accept the baby. In this respect, my friend was unusually careful and seeking my help in understanding the complications regarding the legality of adoption deals. I failed to immediately understand why adoption was so problematic. In return, he told me of the fate of two young female teachers who came to this village some five years earlier and started a primary school for children. Soon they also got involved with 'social work' in the village. In an attempt to save babies from being killed, they began sending children (unwanted by the families) to private adoption agencies as the CBS measure had not yet reached the village. All they would do was contact one of the private adoption agencies they knew of and someone would come and take the baby away without doing any paperwork.

This ran for sometime without any trouble until one of the families – who earlier had abandoned their child – asked these two female teachers to return the child to them, as they realized that it was not the right thing to do. These women had no idea how to get back the child and no idea where the child had been placed and the adoption agency denied ever having accepted any children from them. Soon the issue was out in public. Amidst the controversies that became much deeper, and with media involvement, these two women had to face the wrath of the bureaucracy for a long time – until they were cleared of all charges against them. It was later found out that the adoption agency was involved in child-trafficking and had sold the child overseas. Eventually, the license of the agency was cancelled but these women's position and respect could not be restored so they left the village. Since then, the idea of adoption evokes fear, as it did to my friend and the VHN.

Scene III: Outside the District Social Welfare Office, Salem, August 2005

My female research assistant and I encountered Chellammal, aged 32, a mother and a GCPS applicant, outside the District Social Welfare Office and invited her for a cup of tea to hear her grievances. We had overheard her in a conversation with one of the welfare officers previously. She was roughly treated and threatened by the official with regard to her application for the GCPS. When we requested that she narrate her grievances to us, she was overwhelmed with emotion, broke into tears and spoke uninterruptedly.

Chellammal, who belongs to the Scheduled Caste, delivered her first daughter in 1993 and her second in 1995. Within a day of her second daughter's delivery at the government hospital in Salem she had undergone sterilization. Three months later, she submitted her GCPS application to the District Social Welfare Office. She was asked by the officer-in-charge to come back a week later as the officer-in-charge was retiring from her government service that week. A week later, when Chellammal approached the newly-recruited officer, she was asked to submit a fresh application, after which she was told to go home and wait for a government acknowledgement letter regarding the status of her application to GCPS. For two long years she waited for that letter. When she did not receive it, she again approached the office in 1997. She was again asked to fill out a fresh application. Since then, she had been visiting the social welfare office and had spent quite significant money in the hope that one day her application would be confirmed and her daughter's future would be secured. Here is an excerpt from a long talk that we had that day:

> **Interviewer**: Did you not wish for a son? Did you undergo sterilization particularly for GCPS application or was there some other consideration?
>
> **Chellammal**: Of course I desired for a son. But how could I have one when my *Swamy* [god] does not want me to have one. I had to undergo operation because both my previous deliveries were caesarean. Doctors have seriously warned me about the complication of a third pregnancy. If I had conceived for the third time, I would have died. That is why I immediately underwent operation after my second child's delivery.

Interviewer: Who advised you to go for GCPS then?

Chellammal: Many people in my locality had already applied [for GCPS]. If government gives money to us, why not take it, they say. But I have suffered so much from the government people. They are rude and heartless people. They never gave me an explanation nor did they give me a 'card' [referring to a money deposit book that GCPS beneficiaries get once their application is approved].

Interviewer: Did you particularly undergo sterilization after two daughters because you wanted to claim government money?

Chellammal: No money can equal the worth of a son. This [Rs] 20,000 is far too less [sic] for a son. I would choose a son rather than [Rs] 20,000 if I was asked. But I am an unfortunate woman. What can I do? Now I am cursing myself why *Swamy* gave me two daughters. How will I get them married?

Interviewer: Are there some people in your village who had successfully received the GCPS card?

Chellammal: Many people had applied for this money in my *jati* [caste/community], but no one had got a card so far. But I know many *panakkarar* [rich and influential people] who had got their cards. Because the *Panchayat* President belongs to their *jati*, so they got it. We have no one to help.

Interviewer: What about the NGO [...] working in your area? Have you not contacted them in this regard?

Chellammal: Why would they help us? They only come to us when there is a *Sangha* [Self-help Group] related work or when they need us.

[Reconstruction from field notes dated 22 August, 2005]

Indeed, Chellammal's explanation for opting GCPS runs parallel to that of many other families in the village, in that the reasons for (re)producing a daughter are different from what the government invokes through GCPS in its policy document. Neither son preference nor female infanticide is contained through GCPS. All those families who had applied to GCPS happened to have chosen sterilization for reasons varying from social pressure, shame, cultural, medical or other neutral reasons over the financial incentives promoted by the GCPS. Diagnosing female infanticide in terms of poverty and using financial logic to tie it to saving babies by the government only reinforces the social perception that daughters are an economic burden and thus need to be avoided. Added to this purposive lack of realization is the fact that very few families would, if at all, 'choose' to undergo sterilization before producing a son. Even some people in the government department have openly expressed to me that given the dominant son preference in their area, it would be unwise to believe that families would undergo sterilization in order to avail themselves of this scheme, without first producing a son. The following discussion provides some more support for my argument.

Scene IV: In the District Social Welfare Office, Salem, August 2005

Later, the same day, I became involved in a lengthy talk with the DSWO, who was in charge of managing both these schemes for the Salem district. The officer was a young woman in her early thirties, who had been the additional in-charge of social welfare (of one of the neighbouring districts), besides managing Salem district. With an unusually pleasant personality, she spoke at length. Let us look at these two schemes from a government official's perspective.

Interviewer: My first clarification, is family planning a pre-condition for [acceptance into the] Cradle Baby Scheme?

DSWO: No. It is not compulsory. But we encourage our staff to motivate couples for family planning. This is so because most of the cases that come to us are from 'high risk' families and families with higher order births.

Interviewer: Tell me more about CBS? How has it been helpful in curbing female infanticide?

DSWO: The scheme is quite instrumental in saving babies from female infanticide. We have 710 cases registered so far. In this year alone, we have received 92 babies. It is quite helpful to poor parents, those who do not want more daughters.

Interviewer: But there are some male babies in CBS as well? Were they potential victims of male infanticide?

DSWO: Male infanticide is also coming up in this district but it mostly relates to higher order births or unlawful sex and unwed mothers. There has been some campaign in the district for young girls to avoid sex before marriage.

Interviewer: What about the GCPS?

DSWO: Yes, the GCPS is meant to promote family planning, stop higher order pregnancies and birth, and eradicate female infanticide. It has been in operation since 1992 and has now been revised with an increased budget outlay.

Interviewer: Any idea, in terms of what kind of families, with what background is coming for this scheme?

DSWO: Well, ideally it is meant for poor families and to discourage preference for sons in the community. The scheme is quite popular in rural areas. Caste-wise, it is mostly Gounders and Vanniyars whose applications are visible.

Interviewer: Are these castes not already rich and politically powerful?

DSWO: Yes, you are right! These two caste groups are quite powerful and dominant in Salem area. But only poor [below poverty line] among them are applying to this scheme. That is why we look for their income certificate [during application].

Interviewer: Has anybody got the money so far?

DSWO: Not yet, the first beneficiary in the state would receive the money in 2012 only because the money would be credited to the girl's account at the age of 20 or thereafter, and only after she has completed her Tenth Standard [education] from a public school.

Interviewer: What is its future […] given the fact that some people in the village are apprehensive about whether the money would be credited to their account after 20 years?

DSWO: Honestly speaking, there is a big question mark to the GCPS; what if Ms Jayalalitha [the then Chief Minister] steps down from power in the next election? DMK government has no interest in such matters. I really doubt if the money would ever be released to beneficiaries. One of the major obstacles is the periodical renewal. Every five years, either of the parents has to come here and renew their account book at a certain date. If they failed to turn up on a specified date, such families would disqualify from the scheme. Many have already failed to do so.

Interviewer: Appreciating your honest remark on GCPS, can I ask if the government really thinks that people would opt for this scheme by undergoing sterilization rather than having a son first? If it is so, is not then the idea of discouraging son preference wrongly placed through this scheme?

DSWO: Well, what you are saying is absolutely right. Nobody who desires a son in the family would opt for this scheme and not a son. That is the single most cultural barrier that we are facing in our family planning campaigns. But we cannot compromise on our campaign [for family planning] solely due to this. The campaign has to go ahead.

[Reconstruction from field notes dated 22 August, 2005]

A similar concern has been earlier expressed by the district administration in the media with regard to a social mobilization campaign and other such strategies to combat female infanticide. For example, a decline in the Infant

Mortality Rate in Salem district 'from 108 per 1,000 in 2000 to 55 per 1,000 at present [2002]' has been attributed to 'measures such as activation of monitoring committees in 385 village *Panchayats*' (in order to bring pregnant women under surveillance and counsel high-risk couples for undergoing sterilization) and staging a number of 'field level social mobilization campaigns' (218 alone by 2002) to eliminate 'gender bias and (promote) adherence to small family norms'.[35]

It would therefore be wrong to suggest that government officials operate in a cultural vacuum. Some of them do have some understanding of the cultural reasons behind families' logic for son preference, although the same is rarely entertained (officially) by them. Furthermore, addressing the issue by promoting the small family norm on the part of the government functionaries does not seem to connect with the already established link between the implementation of the one-child-per-family policy and the resultant abandonment and infanticide of female children along with widespread abortion of female foetuses in China.[36] Nor do they pay attention to the negative relationship of population control measures and the declining life chances for female children and an over-all female disadvantage in India. Indeed, the implementation of a small family norm by current programmes will always be at the expense of catastrophic consequences for the girl-child population.[37]

During my fieldwork, extensive interaction with the mothers and the families led me to view the widespread practice of female infanticide as strongly linked with the era of intensification of family planning and small family norm that is arguably the result of a broader Indian discourse on 'overpopulation' in the context of poverty and development.[38] Yet the government's strategy on female infanticide prevention has been by pursued with an aggressive sterilization campaign that is only fraught with a conflict of interest between the state and the families. Indeed, the state's zeal for curbing female infanticide conflicts with the parental desire to preserve offspring selectively. Here, the tension of individual rights versus state prerogatives resonates along with the duty of the family and that of state in providing for the well-being of the children.[39] Taking a position whereby collective interest as defined by the state overrides that of individuals, the state in Tamil Nadu has claimed a more absolute intervention not only in providing resources to parents for maintaining female children (the GCPS) and bringing them under state custody (the CBS), but also in monitoring 'high risk' mothers, families, communities and villages. The logic behind this is, of course, the democratic proclamation that the state has a mandated duty to intervene in the matters such as female infanticide when families and communities fail to ensure their members' well being. Such a conflict of interests seems to take on the idea that both the state and society in India are caught in the transition between shifting conceptions of the rights of children.[40]

What instead emerges from this shifting conception of life and death of female neonates in Tamil Nadu is a claim by the state that female infanticide has now been controlled as it is evident from a sharp decrease in the Infant Mortality Rate. This was a staple explanation given to me or anybody else visiting government officials, particularly by the Deputy Director of Health Services of Salem, who is the head of Public Health for the female infanticide programme in the district. These claims remain unsupported by the infant mortality or infanticide figures because the government will not make them public. During my interactions with government officials, I was constantly led to believe that since female infanticide has been declining, 'sex selective abortion' must be increasing. With such a proclamation, it is clear that the discourse on female infanticide has now been extended to bring medical practitioners (gynaecologists in particular) under its gaze.

Some evidence of this claim was made visible publicly towards the latter part of my fieldwork when the Tamil Nadu government had asked, through the district administration, the members of women's self-help groups to increase surveillance and watch the 'scan centres' in their localities and report back on any misuse of scanning or sex-determining technologies. The job was entrusted to the Tamil Nadu unit of Indian Council of Child Welfare in Salem and Dharmapuri districts with a sum of Rs 2.5 million being sanctioned for the project.[41] Another instance of surveillance over scan centres came to my notice much later when one of the NGO directors, after having participated in a meeting summoned by the district administration, informed me that the district administration was planning to ensure that all scan centres in the district must submit their monthly register of all pregnant mothers who visited their clinics.

However, in reality, both the government and the NGO sector admitted having little or no control over the sophisticated and undetectable methods of sex selection that people employ while considering sex selective abortion. In this scenario, it is interesting to note that the supposedly backward people are now effectively appropriating modern technologies of sex determination for sex selective abortion and conveniently use them for their own subversive ends. What we have then is a sad outcome whereby female infanticide has not been eradicated but has simply escaped successful monitoring and surveillance amidst changes in the *modus operandi* of recording deaths. Recording now ranges from falsification of the sex of the dead infant, concealment of such deaths under medical cause with a strong support from the villagers and village-administrators, to changing of residence of pregnant mothers at the time of delivery. Moreover, the increase in sex selective abortion itself has been viewed by the government and NGO officials alike as a consequence of stringent and punitive actions against female infanticide that has been built up alongside vigorous propaganda and programmes on population control. The assertion that as fertility decreases female disadvantages in infancy is seen to increase has already been well established in the discourses on population control and female children's declining life chances (as now expressed through declining sex ratio).[42] Therefore, the pressures and constraints generated by biomedical modes of family planning (mainly government-led sterilization) campaign in Tamil Nadu continue to create, induce and maintain the cultural milieu of son preference under which female infanticide and sex selective abortion is made intelligible for those families wanting to control the number of children born to them.

Concluding Remarks

There have been arguments and counter-arguments made about whether postcolonial Indian governments differ much from the British colonial state in addressing social issues like female infanticide. Some scholars argue that the modern Indian state derives its stand on tackling female infanticide in Tamil Nadu from the colonial government's 'civilizing mission' discourses.[43] Others argue that the postcolonial state claims a more absolute mandate for intervening in social or women's issues than the British colonial administration, by claiming a democratic consensus that need not be reiterated.[44] It is also true that contemporary Indian governments are in a different situation from those of the colonial era because colonial officials deployed a discourse of civilizational otherness to justify colonial rule. Yet the language and structuring of the postcolonial state's programmatic activities appears to be guided by colonial practices and does not seem to differ significantly when it comes to questions of power and governance.

A close surveillance of the family that was required as part of the colonial strategy to prevent female infanticide in nineteenth-century northwest India mainly comprised the detection of pregnancies and supervision of their progress, including the registration of births and marriages.[45] In contemporary Tamil Nadu, a public-health-based approach, adopted more recently in conjunction with NGOs, has led to the formation of various committees at the district, the block and the village level bringing the NGO and health and nutrition workers together to watch, monitor and counsel all 'high risk' pregnant women. These mothers are likewise watched, supervized and coerced into submitting their female infants under state care should they be suspected of killing the newborn. What, then, is the difference in the two modes of governance – colonial and postcolonial? The only difference appears to be a kind of democratic legitimacy that the government in Tamil Nadu has ostensibly acquired to 'civilize' its own citizens, which was not the case with the British Raj having very limited basis for Indian political representation. Furthermore, the Tamil Nadu government's structured understanding of female infanticide as a 'backward' and 'criminal' practice and as practiced by the 'other' (by associating it, at least initially, with only few castes or tribes and with poverty, isolation, certain regions and cultural practices like dowry) is somewhat akin to a staple explanation in colonial-sociological analyses over female infanticide, in which terms like 'cruel' and 'barbaric' were frequently used to describe local cultural practices.[46]

Such an implicit continuity of rhetoric and practices to 'civilize' those groups and communities which were left out of the mainstream on the part of the contemporary Tamil Nadu government has served as a 'litmus test' to intervene in women's reproductive and sexual practices. Such intervention is linked to development and social change in areas like literacy, labour, untouchability and health, much as the colonial government made such links in its civilizing mission in nineteenth-century British India.[47] To retrieve the liberal democratic state for a project of welfare and development in the former colony runs the risk of using the postcolonial state for an explicit 'civilizing mission'.

In the final analysis, the origin and growth of the intervention of state and non-state actors regarding female infanticide control in contemporary Tamil Nadu corresponds to a historic rise of 'the social' – a practice of the government that Donzelot has masterfully analysed in his engagement with the state and the family in nineteenth-century France.[48] In a similar manner, because families failed to ensure the well-being and survival of female neonates in Tamil Nadu, the state, by appealing to its mandate, initiated policies and programmes to 'rescue' and 'save' the babies under the *tutelage*. This signalled a rise of 'the social' – a realm that was to lie between the state and civil society but instead became the target of intervention and regulation, and hence, the basis for welfare and development. It is this conceptual significance (i.e. bio-technical forms of power), that the state in Tamil Nadu has enacted with programmes like CBS and GCPS. These serve at best to 'police' and discipline the families rather than liberate them. The Tamil Nadu state has thus claimed the right to intervene in the lives of its female rural citizens in order to educate, survey and discipline them. This is very reminiscent of some of the worst aspects of the British colonial civilizing mission, in which the promise of development and freedom were replaced by an emphasis on discipline, paternalism and authoritarianism.

List of Abbreviations

AIADMK   All-India Anna Dravida Munnetra Kazhagam (All-India Anna
          Dravidian Progressive Federation)
CBS   Cradle Baby Scheme
CNW   Child Nutrition Worker
DANIDA   Danish International Development Agency
DSWO   District Social Welfare Officer
DMK   Dravida Munnetra Kazhagam (Dravidian Progressive
          Foundation)
GCPS   Girl Child Protection Scheme
NGO   Non-governmental organization
VHN   Village Health Nurse

Notes

1 The fieldwork data used in this paper has been previously presented at South
   Asian seminars at the London School of Economics and at Edinburgh University
   in October and November 2005. Also, a rather shorter version of this paper was
   presented, and won the essay competition, at the Sixth Berlin Roundtable Conference
   on Transnationality on 'Population Politics and Human Rights', co-organized by the
   Irmgard Coninx Foundation, the Social Science Research Center, and Humboldt
   University, Berlin, 14–20 February 2007. For its inclusion in this volume, I am thankful
   to Michael Mann for allowing it to be included among nine chapters written mostly
   by historians of colonial issues, and special thanks to Carey Watt for improving it with
   constructive comments.

2 For an exploration of the civilizing mission in the nineteenth-century colonial response
   to female infanticide in northwest India involving the surveillance and disciplining of
   the Rajput household, see Malavika Kasturi, *Embattled Identities: Rajput Lineages and the
   Colonial State in Nineteenth-Century North India* (Oxford: Oxford University Press, 2002).

3 Antony Anghie, *Imperialism, Sovereignty, and the Making of International Law* (Cambridge:
   Cambridge University Press, 2005), 3.

4 Michael Mann, '"Torchbearers Upon the Path of Progress": Britain's Ideology of a
   "Moral and Material Progress" in India: An Introductory Essay', in Harald Fischer-
   Tiné and Michael Mann (eds), *Colonialism as Civilizing Mission: Cultural Ideology in British
   India* (London, Anthem Press, 2004), 1–26.

5 See Harald Fischer-Tiné and Michael Mann (eds), *Colonialism as Civilizing Mission:
   Cultural Ideology in British India* (London: Anthem Press, 2004). For a historical exception
   on the rhetoric of its continuing operation in the context of international law, see
   Anghie, *Imperialism, Sovereignty, and the Making of International Law*.

6 See Melitta Waligora, 'What is Your Caste? The Classification of Indian Society as
   Part of the British Civilizing Mission', in Harald Fischer-Tiné and Michael Mann (eds),
   Colonialism as Civilizing Mission: Cultural Ideology in British India (London, Anthem Press,
   2004), 141–164.

7 For a notion of freedom that had to be forever policed in the context of nineteenth-
   century France, see Jacques Donzelot, *The Policing of Families* (London: Hutchinson,

1980). Also see Srirupa Prasad, 'A Review of Harald Fischer-Tiné and Michael Mann (eds) "Colonialism as Civilizing Mission: Cultural Ideology in British India"', *Journal of Colonialism and Colonial History* (online) 6, no. 1 (2005). Accessed: October 26, 2010, http://muse.jhu.edu/journals/journal_of_colonialism_and_colonial_history/v006/6.1prasad.html.

8 The material for this paper has been drawn from my PhD project on female infanticide and sex selective abortion in South India for which the ethnographic fieldwork was conducted in Salem district of Tamil Nadu between July 2004 and September 2005. The same also constitutes the basis of a chapter of my PhD thesis.

9 However, at least one source suggests that the killing of babies had existed among some communities of South India during colonial rule. In *Ethnographic Notes in Southern India*, Edgar Thurston writes that 'a horrible custom exists among the females of the Colliers', but he leaves us wondering whether it is infanticide of males, females or both even though he clearly mentions the prevalence of female infanticide among the Khonds and Todas. See Edgar Thurston, *Ethnographic Notes in Southern India* (Delhi: Cosmo Publications, 1975 [First published in 1906 by Superintendent, Govt Press, Madras]), 503.

10 For some of the contemporary scholarship on the subject, see Ester Boserup, *Women's Role in Economic Development* (New York: St. Martin's Press, 1970), Malavika Kasturi, *Embattled Identities*, Barbara D. Miller, *The Endangered Sex: Neglect of Female Children in Rural North India* (New Delhi: Oxford University Press, 1981), Veena Talwar Oldenburg, *Dowry Murder: The Imperial Origins of a Cultural Crime* (Oxford: Oxford University Press, 2002), James Tod, *Annals and Antiquities of Rajasthan, or the Central and Western Rajpoot States of India*. Reprinted in 2 volumes, (Delhi: M. N. Publishers, 1978 [First published in 1829 by Munshiram Publishers, Delhi]), and, L. S. Vishwanath, *Female Infanticide and Social Structure: A Socio-Historical Study in Western and Northern India* (New Delhi: Hindustan Publishing House, 2000).

11 For the first and foremost reporting on female infanticide in postcolonial Tamil Nadu, see 1985 vernacular Tamil article in *Junior Vikatan* by A. Soundarapandian, 'Varadatchanaikkup-payandu pen kuzhandaigalai kolgirargal', *Junior Vikatan*, 4 December ([in Tamil] 1985). For the 1986 *India Today* article in English, see S. H. Venkatramani, 'Born to Die: Female Infanticide', *India Today*, 31 (1986), 26–33.

12 Venkatesh Athreya and Sheela Rani Chunkath, 'Tackling Female Infanticide: Social Mobilisation in Dharmapuri, 1997–99', *Economic and Political Weekly* 35, no. 49 (2000), 4345–48.

13 Health and Family Welfare Department, Government of Tamil Nadu. Accessed: April 30, 2007. http://www.tnhealth.org/dfw.htm.

14 The term 'high risk', which is used to demarcate a sub-population from among the population of pregnant mothers, denotes two entities in everyday usages of the government and NGO programme. One, a pregnant mother who has previously given birth to one or more female children, and two, a geographical area where these mothers reside – it could be a village, a *Panchayat*, a Block, or a *Taluk*. That is why, it is not uncommon to hear discourses around both the 'high risk mothers' and the 'high risk areas'. The criteria for defining a woman and an area are inter-dependent, yet vary across Tamil Nadu.

15 Rajeswari Sunder Rajan, *The Scandal of the State: Women, Law and Citizenship in Postcolonial India* (Durham, NC: Duke University Press, 2003), 188.

16 For a notion of 'biopolitics', see Michel Foucault, *The History of Sexuality, Vol. 1: An Introduction* (London: Allen Lane, 1980 [translated by Robert Hurley]). Also see

Michel Foucault, 'Governmentality', in Graham Burchell, Colin Gordon, and Peter Miller (ed.), *The Foucault Effect: Studies in Governmentality, With Two Lectures by and an Interview with Michel Foucault* (Chicago: University of Chicago Press, 1991), 87–104. Jacques Donzelot, *The Policing of Families* (London: Hutchinson, 1980).

17 Sabu M. George, 'Female Infanticide in Tamil Nadu, India: From recognition back to denial.' *Reproductive Health Matters*, 5, no. 10 (1997), 127.

18 'Children of the state' is a term borrowed from Sunder Rajan, *Scandal of the State*, 177–211.

19 For a discussion on the methodological issues involved in such a study, see Shahid Perwez, 'Towards an Understanding of the Field within the Field: Researching Female Infanticide by Researching NGOs in Tamil Nadu', in Devi Sridhar (ed.), *Anthropologists inside Organisations: South Asian Case Studies* (New Delhi: Sage Publications, 2008), 96–116.

20 Asha Krishnakumar, 'Life and Death in Salem', *Frontline* (online), 19, no. 4 (2002). Accessed October 26, 2010, http://www.hinduonnet.com/fline/fl1904/19041300.htm.

21 Sharada Srinivasan and Arjun S. Bedi, 'Ensuring Daughter Survival in Tamil Nadu, India', Working Paper No. 477, *Institute of Social Studies*, (The Hague, August 2009).

22 One of the most propagated and highlighted stories around the success of CBS relates to the visit of two adolescent Danish girls to Salem district in an attempt to trace their biological parents who, back in 1992, abandoned them under CBS. By flashing the visual image of the girl's momentary integration (which lasted for an hour) with their biological parents, the media went on claiming the positive role of CBS in preventing female infanticide – even though one of the daughters was reportedly abandoned for the fact that she was born with polio.

23 Succumbing to the populist measures, the incumbent DMK government once again renamed it as '*Sivagami Ammaiya Ninaivu* Girl Child Protection Scheme' in 2006.

24 Asha Krishnakumar, 'A Programme without a Plan', *Frontline* (online), 19, no.3 (2002). Accessed October 26, 2010, http://www.hinduonnet.com/fline/fl1903/19030410.htm.

25 Government of Tamil Nadu, Chapter 2: Women and Child Welfare, *Social Welfare and Nutritious Meal Programme*, Policy Note, 2005–2006, Demand No. 43 (Chennai, 2006).

26 Sunder Rajan, *Scandal of the State*, 200.

27 Krishnakumar, 'A Programme without a Plan'.

28 *Ibid.*

29 Government of Tamil Nadu. Accessed August 21, 2005, http://www.tn.gov.in/policynotes/archives/policy2002–03/swnmp2002–03–2b.htm.

30 Krishnakumar, 'A Programme without a Plan'.

31 George, 'Female Infanticide in Tamil Nadu', 128.

32 Krishnakumar, 'A Programme without a Plan'.

33 Social Welfare Department Accessed July 31, 2007, http://www.socialwelfare.delhigovt.nic.in/cmsw/ns2006_gcp.htm.

34 Empowerpoor.com. Accessed July 31, 2007, http://www.empowerpoor.com/relatednews.asp?report=501.

35 *The Hindu*, October 01, 2002.

36 Susan Greenhalgh and Jiali Li, 'Engendering Reproductive Policy and Practice in Peasant China: For a Feminist Demography of Reproduction', *Signs*, 20, no. 3 (1995), 601–641.

37 Sabu George (2001) cited in Sunder Rajan, *Scandal of the State*, 184.

38 Sarah Hodges, 'Governmentality, Population and Reproductive Family in Modern India', *Economic and Political Weekly* 39, no. 11 (2004), 1157–63.

39 Sunder Rajan, *Scandal of the State*, 203.
40 *Ibid.*, 188.
41 *The Hindu*, August 20, 2004.
42 Sunder Rajan, *Scandal of the State*, 184.
43 Oldenburg, *Dowry Murder*, 41–72.
44 Sunder Rajan, *Scandal of the State*, 199.
45 *Ibid.*, 188.
46 Oldenburg, *Dowry Murder*, 41–72.
47 Sunder Rajan, *Scandal of the State*, 167.
48 Donzelot, *Policing of Families*.

References

Anghie, Antony, *Imperialism, Sovereignty, and the Making of International Law* (Cambridge: Cambridge University Press, 2005).

Athreya, Venkatesh and Chunkath, Sheela Rani, 'Tackling Female Infanticide: Social Mobilisation in Dharmapuri, 1997–99', *Economic and Political Weekly* 35, no. 3 (2000), 4345–48.

Boserup, Ester, *Women's Role in Economic Development* (New York: St. Martin's Press, 1970).

Donzelot, Jacques, *The Policing of Families* (London: Hutchinson, 1980).

Fischer-Tiné, Harald and Michael Mann, (ed.), *Colonialism as Civilizing Mission: Cultural Ideology in British India* (London: Anthem Press, 2004).

Foucault, Michel, *The History of Sexuality, Vol 1: An Introduction* (London: Allen Lane, 1980 [translated by Robert Hurley]).

———— 'Governmentality', in Graham Burchell, Colin Gordon, and Peter Miller (eds), *The Foucault Effect: Studies in Governmentality, With Two Lectures by and an Interview with Michel Foucault* (Chicago: University of Chicago Press, 1991), pp. 87–104.

George, Sabu M. 'Female Infanticide in Tamil Nadu, India: From Recognition Back to Denial?', *Reproductive Health Matters* 10, no. 10 (1997), 124–132.

Greenhalgh, Susan and Li, Jiali, 'Engendering Reproductive Policy and Practice in Peasant China: For a Feminist Demography of Reproduction', *Signs* 20, no. 3 (1995), 601–641.

Hodges, Sarah, 'Governmentality, Population and Reproductive Family in Modern India', *Economic and Political Weekly* 39, no. 11 (2004), 1157–63.

Kasturi, Malavika, *Embattled Identities: Rajput Lineages and the Colonial State in Nineteenth-Century North India* (Oxford: Oxford University Press, 2002).

Krishnakumar, Asha, 'A Programme without a Plan', *Frontline* (online) 19, no. 3 (2002). Accessed October 26, 2010: http://www.hinduonnet.com/fline/fl1903/19030410.htm.

———— 'Life and Death in Salem', *Frontline* (online) 19, no. 4 (2002). Accessed October 26, 2010: http://www.hinduonnet.com/fline/fl1904/19041300.htm.]

Mann, Michael, '"Torchbearers Upon the Path of Progress": Britain's Ideology of a "Moral and Material Progress" in India: An Introductory Essay', in Harald Fischer-Tiné and Michael Mann (eds), *Colonialism as Civilizing Mission: Cultural Ideology in British India* (London: Anthem Press, 2004), pp. 1–26.

Miller, Barbara D., *The Endangered Sex: Neglect of Female Children in Rural North India* (New Delhi: Oxford University Press, 1981).

Oldenburg, Veena Talwar, *Dowry Murder. The Imperial Origins of a Cultural Crime* (Oxford: Oxford University Press, 2002).

Perwez, Shahid, 'Towards an Understanding of the Field within the Field: Researching Female Infanticide by Researching NGOs in Tamil Nadu', in Devi Sridhar (ed.), *Anthropologists inside Organisations: South Asian Case Studies* (New Delhi: Sage Publications, 2008), pp. 96–116.

Prasad, Srirupa, 'A Review of Harald Fisher-Tiné and Michael Mann (eds) "Colonialism as Civilizing Mission: Cultural Ideology in British India"', *Journal of Colonialism and Colonial History* (online) 6, no. 1 (2005), accessed October 26, 2010: http://muse.jhu.edu/journals/journal_of_colonialism_and_colonial_history/v006/6.1prasad.html.

Soundarapandian, A., 'Varadatchanaikkup-payandu pen kuzhandaigalai kolgirargal', *Junior Vikatan*, 4 December ([in Tamil] 1985).

Srinivasan, Sharada and Bedi, Arjun S., 'Ensuring Daughter Survival in Tamil Nadu, India', *Institute of Social Studies*, Working Paper No. 477, (The Hague, August 2009).

Sunder Rajan, Rajeswari, *The Scandal of the State: Women, Law and Citizenship in Postcolonial India* (Durham, NC: Duke University Press, 2003), pp. 177–211.

Thurston, Edgar, *Ethnographic Notes in Southern India* (Delhi: Cosmo Publications, 1975 [reprint of the 1906 edition printed by the Superintendent, Govt Press, Madras]).

Tod, James, *Annals and Antiquities of Rajasthan, or the Central and Western Rajpoot States of India* (Delhi: M. N. Publishers, 1978 [reprinted in 2 volumes from the 1829 edition printed by Munshiram Publishers, Delhi]).

Venkatramani, S. H., 'Born to Die: Female Infanticide', *India Today* 31 (1986), 26–33.

Vishwanath, L. S., *Female Infanticide and Social Structure: A Socio-Historical Study in Western and Northern India* (New Delhi: Hindustan Publishing House, 2000).

Waligora, Melitta, 'What is Your Caste? The Classification of Indian Society as Part of the British Civilizing Mission', in Harald Fischer-Tiné and Michael Mann (eds), *Colonialism as Civilizing Mission: Cultural Ideology in British India* (London: Anthem Press), pp. 141–164.

Government Sources

Government of Tamil Nadu. Accessed August 21, 2005, http://www.tn.gov.in/policynotes/archives/policy2002–03/swnmp2002–03–2b.htm.

Government of Tamil Nadu. Chapter 2. Women and Child Welfare. *Social Welfare and Nutritious Meal Programme*, Policy Note, 2005–2006, Demand No. 43, (Chennai, 2006).

Health & Family Welfare Department. Government of Tamil Nadu. Accessed: April 30, 2007. http://www.tnhealth.org/dfw.htm.

Social Welfare Department. Accessed July 31, 2007, http://www.socialwelfare.delhigovt.nic.in/cmsw/ns2006gcp.htm.

Chapter Nine

PHILANTHROPY AND CIVILIZING MISSIONS IN INDIA c. 1820–1960: STATES, NGOs AND DEVELOPMENT[1]

Carey A. Watt

This paper analyses the meaning of three different engagements with charitable and philanthropic activity in India between c. 1820 and 1960: it looks at the East India Company's movement into philanthropic activities in the decades after 1820; then it explores the significance of philanthropy, social service and social work carried out by Indian organizations in a period of growing nationalism between roughly 1890 and 1947; and thirdly, the paper considers the approach taken toward philanthropy and social work by the newly independent Indian state in the 1950s.

The essay shows some surprising continuities over this 140-year period, as well as some important differences. In each of the three cases listed above, philanthropic and charitable initiatives were linked to issues of moral authority and political legitimacy. In most societies, and certainly in India, 'giving' resources or services as charity or relief, without expectations of personal reward, can enhance the giver's social or political status. Charitable and philanthropic actions can even support claims or aspirations to political leadership and authority. Indeed, historically there have often been expectations that kings and other wealthy or prominent individuals 'give' to their communities.[2] Rulers, in a sense, were responsible for the redistribution of wealth. It is not surprising, then, that in two periods when new states were being built, the Company state in the second quarter of the nineteenth century and the independent nation-state of India under Jawaharlal Nehru's leadership in the late 1940s and 1950s, embryonic governments took deliberate steps to involve themselves in charity, philanthropy or social work.

Service and philanthropic efforts undertaken by Indian social service organizations such as the Servants of India Society and social service leagues (or *seva samitis*) in the first decades of the twentieth century were also connected to questions of political leadership and legitimacy. However, these were non-state and nongovernmental bodies, and their memberships often espoused different ideas regarding the role of the state regarding charity. Prominent individuals at the centre of organized social service initiatives, such as G. K. Gokhale, Madan Mohan Malaviya, Lajpat Rai and Annie Besant, had direct links to the Indian National Congress. While such philanthropic and charitable activities have often been portrayed as apolitical social and cultural endeavours, in the case of charity there is commonly a fair degree of overlap between socio-cultural and political matters. At least indirectly, social service efforts showed how prominent and politically-active Indians were reaching out to wide sections of Indian society, across putative caste, class, religious and geographic boundaries. This was important at a time when the Congress leadership was derided by senior British officials as a microscopic and sybaritic urban elite with little concern for poorer Indians, and hence with no serious claims to moral or political authority, let alone self-government. Mohandas Gandhi's 'constructive work' of the 1920s, 1930s and 1940s was in many ways a continuation of these earlier philanthropic efforts, using some of the same personnel. Gandhian philanthropy also helped to enhance Congress' image and claims to moral authority, especially during the frequent intervals when there were no active political campaigns. Therefore, visible involvement in charity and philanthropy could have direct political benefits for emergent states as well as for political movements such as the Indian National Congress.

Claims to moral authority and political legitimacy usually depend on constructing or asserting notions of difference, 'otherness' and superiority, and this was particularly true of colonial regimes established overseas by European powers in the nineteenth and twentieth centuries. Such assertions of superiority are often understood as a form of cultural imperialism, in which claims of moral authority and legitimacy were made on the basis of supposedly greater cultural and civilizational progress.[3] In the context of European colonialism, claims to represent a higher stage of civilization were commonly linked to notions of enlightenment and the concomitant attributes of rationality, order, utility, modernity and progress, especially as they related to questions of science, technology, economic development and political governance. More intangible claims to moral superiority were made, too, whether about the nature of occidental Christianity or collective social and cultural attributes of moral fibre or 'character' as manifested through traits of self-control, discipline and 'industry'.

The articulation of claims to cultural superiority and difference lends itself to the justification of political power – and especially colonial rule – in terms of the 'civilizing mission': the necessity and duty to 'civilize' or 'uplift' the subject population to a higher level of civilization by instilling the values and building the institutions of the 'superior' governing group. Many different imperial powers have used civilizing missions to implicitly or explicitly justify colonial rule,[1] but one of the most prominent modern examples remains that of the creation of the British colonial state in India during the period from the late 1820s to the 1850s, under the rule of the East India Company.

Company officials from the early decades of the nineteenth century, such as James Mill and T. B. Macaulay, are well known for their claims of British civilizational superiority and, simultaneously, their fulminations about Indian and Asian difference in the negative sense of 'barbarity' and 'backwardness'.[5] By the time of Macaulay's stint as law member in the governor-general's council of Lord Bentinck from 1834 to 1838, during the so-called 'age of reform', these kinds of statements were used commonly as a justification for British rule, a rule or government which was deemed necessary in order to 'anglicize' Indian society. 'Anglicization' was of course the equivalent of becoming 'civilized' to superior British or European standards.

Since there was no coherent or homogenous ideology of British rule in colonial India, as Thomas Metcalf and D. A. Low have argued persuasively,[6] it is not surprising that there was no consistent, explicit ideology or policy of 'civilizing' India. Elements of a 'civilizing mission' informed many different types of official and non-official British pronouncements and activities, and they are often noticeable only as implicit or underlying assumptions rather than deliberate or conscious statements. Notions of cultural or civilizational superiority are frequently linked to the proclamations of Macaulay and the elder Mill, and related efforts to 'civilize' Indians through the 'positive' contributions of English-language education, the introduction of British notions of private property, and the legal codes, institutions or practices of good government that helped bring about a so-called *Pax Britannica* in India. Though Mill's *History* was first published in 1817 it had a considerable legacy and influence on colonial attitudes. It was the standard reference work on India in the nineteenth century and was used in the training of the Raj's mandarins and bureaucrats.[7]

This essay is not directly concerned with Mill or Macaulay, and it tries instead to build on recent scholarship that has been complicating our understanding of the 'civilizing mission' in modern India.[8] Regarding the nineteenth century, my objective in section one (below) is to explore how charity and philanthropy were connected to efforts to enhance the Company's legitimacy as the British consolidated their hold on India and began to construct their state as India's paramount power from the 1820s onward. The question of the 'civilizing mission' becomes relevant when the ideas, values and assumptions that underpinned the Company's charitable activities are examined. I am particularly interested in the British emphasis on 'superior' utilitarian charity and 'useful institutions', and the recurrent stress on encouraging discipline, work and productivity through charity.[9] Hence the focus is not so much on the supposed positive aspects of the civilizing mission, such as Enlightenment ideals of liberty and rationality, as on the darker aspects related to the growth of state power. The Company state had a strong military emphasis and it worked to 'civilize' Indians through pacification, coercion and discipline – to make Indians sedentary and productive subjects.[10]

While it may not be so surprising to uncover aspects of a 'civilizing mission' in Company charity in an era when the colonial state was only just getting established, the essay then moves forward chronologically to the late colonial period in section two, in the decades after 1890, to show how the leaders of Indian charity and social service efforts also betrayed attitudes of cultural and civilizational superiority toward existing Indian practices, ideas and social groups. This was perhaps partly a result of the internalization of British critiques of Indian charity (and culture), and the partial 'colonization of the Indian mind' under British rule in the nineteenth and twentieth centuries – and this itself was a result of cultural imperialism and the 'civilizing mission'.[11] But Indians also criticized many British practices and creatively adapted others to local circumstances while they simultaneously valourized India's 'living traditions' of service, relief and gift-giving. Nevertheless, in the early twentieth century there were emphases on institutionalization, efficiency and obedience that were at once different from and reminiscent of the Company's obsessions in the 1830s and 1840s. The Indian focus on cultivating patriotic *Indian citizens* to carry out acts of service and charity, in the new context of Indian nationalism, revealed a familiar concern with austerity and discipline even while it drew on Indian practices of asceticism. As we shall see below, this was as true of Gandhi's constructive work after 1920 as it was of the Swami Vivekananda's Ramkrishna Mission, Madan Mohan Malaviya's Seva Samiti or G. K. Gokhale's Servants of India Society.

The third and final section of the essay looks at postcolonial India. The new, independent and self-consciously 'modern' Indian state of the late 1940s and 1950s, under the leadership of Jawaharlal Nehru, took a significant interest in charity, philanthropy and social work. This makes sense since Nehru had been prominently involved in Indian public life since the 1910s, and he had close relationships with many key figures active in charity and social work during the late colonial era, including Malaviya, Gokhale and Gandhi. Yet the attitude of the new and independent India, led by a victorious 'freedom fighter' who had the backing of Gandhi in the 1930s and 1940s, is striking for its seeming similarities to the old attitudes of the East India Company. Some of the language had changed, and both the state and society were much bigger, but there remained much in common. As with the Company in the

1830s, the 'Nehruvian state' was frequently critical of Indian philanthropic efforts and it tended to support new state-affiliated efforts and new institutions related to Five-Year Plans and the Community Development scheme, such as the Bharat Sevak Samaj (BSS), created in 1952.[12] The Indian state assumed an active and intrusive role in India's civil society by putting itself at the centre, and this caused tensions with existing Indian voluntary organizations – which we could in fact call nongovernmental organizations or NGOs. Charity and social work were to be centralized and brought under the control of 'superior' experts in rational or scientific planning and development, and much stress was placed on using charitable activities to promote 'national discipline' and make Indians more efficient and productive.[13] Hence, India and Indians could be 'improved' or 'developed', morally and materially, through state-directed charity. The 'civilizing mission' of the nineteenth-century colonial state was ironically echoed in a liberated and independent India.

Now, with the main lines of the essay outlined and some preliminary observations about 'Nehru's India' pointing us back in the direction of the 1820s and 1830s, we can turn to a more detailed analysis of the Company's charity.

I. 1820–57: Philanthropy and the East India Company

After 1818 and the final defeat of the Marathas, the East India Company was the pre-eminent power in the subcontinent and it began the process of consolidating its authority and building its state. Its philanthropic efforts were an important part of this process, as Sanjay Sharma has shown, and they encouraged the expansion of the colonial state in the 1830s and 1840s.[14] Moreover, the British were keen to portray themselves as the only effective source of charity and benevolence in India, and representations of the Company's benevolence were used to bolster the legitimacy of British rule. Company charity was assumed to prove the cultural superiority of the British, representing improvement, progress, humanity and modernity under colonial rule – while highlighting the *difference* between the British and their new Indian subjects.[15] In keeping with the 'civilizing mission' and the need to justify colonial rule, Indian efforts were correspondingly excoriated in order to de-legitimize them.

Of course, Company philanthropy was not always as liberal, humane and progressive as it claimed to be, and it often supported the more brutal aspects of the civilizing mission. 'Civilizing' a population involved coercing it and disciplining it so that people would behave or operate in different ways, with more obedience and greater productivity. Since the beginnings of 'civilization' with the transition to agriculture and increasingly sedentary modes of living more than 5,000 years ago, this has been a consistent theme, and it became more prominent in the era of modern statebuilding after 1800. Hence, Company philanthropy was fundamentally oriented toward creating a disciplined and domesticated population that would be more industrious and productive.[16] While these objectives fit with the general tendencies of 'civilization' to 'fix' people in place, and to discipline and monitor them in order to extract more labour and productivity, they were especially applicable to the financial and economic needs of an emergent colonial state based on military fiscalism and anxieties surrounding matters of security.[17]

Indian charity – especially Hindu charity – was denounced as superstitious and irrational as well as ostentatious, ritualistic and wasteful.[18] Charity or 'giving' that went to brahmins, religious mendicants and itinerant or nomadic groups was singled out for its apparent impracticality and lack of efficiency.[19] Part of the problem was that most Company officials were unable to appreciate the complexity of Indian charity, whether in the sense of the overlapping social, cultural political and economic functions of kingly giving, or the subtlety and flexibility of the distribution of aid according to considerations of caste, status and other factors.[20] Colonial attitudes to philanthropy tended to be overly focused on functionality and utility, and on the importance of uniformity – another marker of civilized 'modernity' in the nineteenth century.[21]

Company philanthropy was interested in 'works of public utility'. 'Public' is a key term because philanthropic relief, for the British, was meant to serve collective public interests, and this included the interests of the state. This was charity as 'works of public utility' and it was set in opposition to supposedly inefficient 'private' charity,[22] and Indian charity was increasingly categorized as private. Private acts of charity were deemed useless or gratuitous because they were thought likely to promote slothfulness and indigence. The Company did not wish to see charity used to support or reward unproductive occupations and people because they did not contribute practically to the social and economic improvement of the state.

The East India Company held that useful and utilitarian charity had to be conducted through modern, rational and public institutions. The push to institutionalize philanthropy was part of a larger process of building public institutions such as schools, libraries and hospitals, with committees, managers and other modern attributes. The preference for institutionalized charity meant that existing forms of Indian giving deemed 'private' and wasteful by the British were gradually displaced and marginalized, and this trend was made worse by the harmful effect that the economic downturn of the 1830s and 1840s had on Indian elites.[23]

The term 'institution' represented specific values to colonial officials that were indicative of the superiority of modern European culture. Institutionalization meant greater rationality and productivity and it was linked to bureaucratization, standardization and normalization, which were key elements of modern states in the nineteenth century. Institutions also had more permanence and fixedness. In this sense, the process of building institutions was part of the 'civilizing' process. Modern philanthropic institutions on the British model were supposed to 'enable' more growth in the 'moral and material progress' of India, a key indicator for the 'civilizing mission' and justification for British rule.[24]

Institutions, however, can also be used by states to coerce, discipline and intimidate. After the north Indian famine of 1837 the Company became much more active in philanthropic relief. Newspaper stories from 1837 mentioned how the Company's relief efforts illustrated 'liberal management' and 'progress in science'.[25] Reports produced later, in the 1860s and 1890s, portrayed British efforts in 1837–38 as humane and benevolent, and they also gave them an illusion of coherence.[26] In the 1830s and 1840s, however, the Company state was primarily concerned with two things: security and economic productivity. As we have noted above, the emergent colonial state was also dominated by military men and it had a very martial tone. Thus humanitarian relief was not always the paramount objective, as British officials used philanthropy to reduce Indian mobility and settle Indians into useful work, while also making them more disciplined, industrious and productive. Charity and its 'coercive institutions' helped to create a more constraining 'disciplinary society' that served state interests.[27] In addition, it was in these decades that new, scientific approaches to prisons, punishment and discipline were elaborated.[28]

Company officials often distrusted Indians seeking charity, and they feared that state charity would be misused and indiscriminate relief would encourage greater indolence. There were also concerns that overly generous relief would attract itinerant labourers, religious mendicants or 'outsiders' from the princely states to seek British aid. Worries about itinerant groups added to existing anxieties in the late 1830s regarding 'the distressed state of the country' following the 1837 famine.[29] This was also the era of campaigns against *thuggee* and *dacoitee* (banditry and robbery carried out by gangs or brotherhoods), so concerns about itinerancy had a particular edge – though nomadic peoples have commonly been seen as threatening or dangerous by settled states.[30]

Liberal and humane Company charity was not focused on providing gratuitous relief or assistance, as one might expect given British denunciations of supposedly wasteful Indian charity. The Company had a more rational and scientific objective of finding the 'deserving poor' and employing them in 'works of public utility', thereby serving the interests of the Company state much more than the needs of Indian society.

The philanthropy of the colonial state in the 1830s and 1840s put Indians to work, giving them wages to build 'useful' permanent structures and institutions such as courts, police stations, jails, hospitals, wells, walls, inns and roads. Roads were given tremendous attention in these utilitarian charity programmes, and this made for a robust period of road building.[31] Roads served both security and economic purposes: they could link markets and facilitate the flow of goods while also allowing for more effective policing and surveillance. Clearly, the construction of courts, police depots and jails through Company philanthropic projects also contributed to the disciplinary capabilities of the colonial state.

Section I (East India Company) Conclusion

The East India Company's penchant for modern forms of 'rational' philanthropy based in institutions ostensibly met the moral and material objectives of British colonial rule and the 'civilizing mission' in the nineteenth century. In terms of moral improvement, charity oriented toward 'works of public utility' encouraged qualities of industry and discipline in the Indian population. Materially speaking, on the other hand, charity that made Indians more sedentary and productive contributed to the tranquillity of India and, ultimately, to the country's economic improvement. This would also contribute to the material betterment or profit of the British colonial state.

Company philanthropy was portrayed in a manner that enhanced British moral authority and legitimacy, even though such a positive gloss did not always match the reality on the ground in the 1830s and 1840s. The language of science, rationality, progress and modernity used to describe philanthropic 'works of public utility' was consistent with general discourses about civilizational superiority and justifications for colonial rule. British charity would help reform, improve and civilize India, and bring *Pax Britannica* as well as a *Civilis Britannica* to the subcontinent.[32] Moreover, the Company state proclaimed that it was the only source of efficient charity and relief, rhetorically marginalizing Indian efforts while also diminishing Indian claims to moral authority.

As we have seen, however, the practical emphasis on discipline, domestication and industry in Company philanthropy highlighted the martial aspects of colonial rule and the more brutal side of the 'civilizing mission'. Constraint and discipline trumped enablement and liberty. This supports David Washbrook's interesting argument about 'the two faces of colonialism' in India after 1818.[33] Superficially, the Company was reforming and modernizing India by disseminating the values of British culture and civilization, especially through education. In reality, however, these reformist and civilizing impulses were quite weak, and, fundamentally, until the late 1840s British colonial rule was more oriented toward achieving military objectives. The latter included pacifying the population and bringing it under greater state surveillance, while also generating income to support further military campaigns. Furthermore, the dominance of military concerns and attempts to define and fix India actually led to a more 'traditional' and less 'enlightened' India, and produced a more despotic form of government. These were the 'unintended' consequences of a civilizing mission carried out by a despotic and 'very military state'.[34]

Despite the partial success of Company efforts to de-legitimize Indian charity and promote modern forms of institutionalized philanthropy that benefited the state, older modes of 'traditional' Indian *dana* ('giving' or 'charity') persisted. Indian elites in the second half of the nineteenth century were able to negotiate the institutional forms of charity in the new colonial public sphere while still practising and patronizing Indian forms of giving.[35] Paradoxically, in the era of Crown rule, after the Rebellion and the demise of the Company in 1858, the colonial state also helped continue Indian styles of kingly *dana*. This was most conspicuous at the Raj's great durbar (court ceremony) audiences of 1877, 1902–03 and 1911–12.[36]

The ability of Indians to operate in two different worlds of charity served them well when ideas and practices of charity took on more nationalistic overtones after c. 1890. Macaulay's aspirations to create a class of 'brown Englishmen' who would accept the innate superiority of British culture and act as emissaries for these values did not turn out as he had expected, though many Indians did internalize some of the claims of British civilizational superiority and acknowledge that India had fallen behind in 'the march of progress'. But this was only a partial internalization of British values, and, at least in terms of philanthropy and voluntary service, Indians created new hybrid forms and took British influences in directions that subverted British claims to moral authority and legitimacy in India. Nonetheless, they continued the colonial civilizing mission, though now it was a case of an Indian self-civilizing mission directed at Indian youth and the lower castes and classes, often referred to as the 'Depressed Classes'.

II. Nationalism, Charity and Constructive Social Work, c. 1890–1947

The second case study looks at concerns regarding efficiency and discipline in Indian social service, philanthropy and social work institutions between roughly 1890 and 1940. These bodies – which we might call early 'civil society' or proto nongovernmental organizations (NGOs) – often had links to Indian nationalism and they were critical of colonial action (and inaction) in various social and cultural fields. They enhanced nationalist legitimacy because Indians publicly and visibly reached out to the broader Indian population, including marginalized groups such as the so-called 'Depressed Classes' in both rural and urban areas. They also contributed to the elaboration of an Indian associational culture and civil society that was animated by notions of active and patriotic citizenship. The vanguard of social service often had connections to the Indian National Congress, so the Congress garnered greater legitimacy and moral authority while the legitimacy of colonial rule was undermined in equal or greater measure.

Despite their nationalistic overtones, Indian social service and philanthropic organizations were also critical of India and Indians. They were extremely dismissive of many older forms of Indian charity. While informed by Indian 'living traditions' such as *dana* ('charity'), *seva* ('service') and *karmayoga* ('altruism'),[37] such organizations claimed to be on the side of modernity and efficiency. They favoured organized and institutionalized philanthropy for national development over what they considered to be wasteful forms of personal charity, and the elite leadership of these organizations consciously or unconsciously enforced their own caste, class, ethnic and gender values as normative 'civilized' and 'national' values.

As we have noted above, the list of Indian voluntary bodies in this period includes the Ramkrishna Mission, founded in the mid 1890s by Swami Vivekananda, the Servants of India Society, founded in 1905 by G. K. Gokhale, the Seva Samiti of Allahabad, founded in the 1910s by Madan Mohan Malaviya, and various Social Service Leagues established after 1900 – many of which were associated with the Servants of India Society. The Arya Samaj (founded in 1875) and Theosophical Society (founded in 1875 in the United States and moved to India in 1877), initially had more of a cultural and religious focus, but philanthropic concerns were present from the outset and became more pronounced from the 1890s onward. Voluntary and philanthropic organizations provided services in a number of areas, including education, health care, emergency relief assistance, policing and first-aid at fairs, and general efforts to uplift or improve poor, 'backward' and marginalized groups of Indian society.

The work of Gandhi's Constructive Programme can also be classified as voluntary or nongovernmental activity, particularly after Gandhi's 'retirement' from Congress politics in 1934 and his focus on 'untouchable' or Harijan uplift,[38] and it was carried on into the 1950s and 1960s by prominent Gandhians such as Vinoba Bhave. Moreover, though it is not often recognized or acknowledged, Gandhian constructive work was indebted to earlier social service organizations including the Servants of India and the Arya Samaj. After all, Gokhale – founder of the Servants of India Society – served as a mentor to Gandhi, and Gandhi spent some time working with the organization after his return to India in 1915, though he ultimately decided not to join the Society. Gandhi continued to cooperate with members of the Servants of India Society, such as G. K. Devadhar, into the 1930s.[39]

Indian social service or constructive work constituted an 'internal' or self-civilizing mission – Indians 'civilizing' fellow Indians – in various ways. The leaders of voluntary and philanthropic organizations tended to accept that Indians 'lagged behind' in the march of progress and needed to catch up to the world's more advanced civilizations.[40] Since the early nineteenth century and the rise of European colonialism, such advanced civilizations were supposedly represented by France, Great Britain and other European states. These scales or hierarchies of modernity, progress and civilization, which made Europe the universal and superior paradigm while relegating Asian and African societies to inferior positions near the bottom, were internalized by most urban, educated Indians in the nineteenth and early-twentieth centuries.

Thus, Indian politicians and activists generally worked within European social, economic and political paradigms – that claimed to be universal – in order to catch up to their colonial overlords and become sufficiently 'civilized' so as to 'deserve' national freedom and independence. Politically, Indians began to create parties such as the Indian National Congress (1885) that could operate according to the Westminster liberal democratic model while Indian capitalists began to improve and develop India economically and lay the groundwork for the transition to bourgeois modernity. Socially and culturally, Indians began to reform supposedly 'superstitious', 'backward' and 'barbaric' beliefs and practices, especially those that were denounced by British officials and non-officials, including missionary societies. It is not surprising, then, that in *A Century of Social Reform in India*, first published in 1955, Swaminath Natarajan argued that modern Indian social reform began in the 1830s with Rammohun Roy's Brahmo Samaj in Bengal.[41] Natarajan asserted that Indian social reform was initially stimulated by British education and missionary initiatives near Calcutta, then the seat of British colonial power, during the so-called 'age of reform' c. 1828–35. Of course, this was also the peak of the 'Anglicization' movement and the era of Macaulay. Therefore, we could extrapolate to say that if the first modern Indian nongovernmental organizations were inspired by the Raj's civilizing mission in the 1830s, then later voluntary associations in the twentieth century were also legatees of a colonial civilizing mission, even if their activities were informed by Indian notions of *seva* or *karmayoga*. Though groups such as the Arya Samaj and Theosophical society occasionally insisted on the superiority of the 'pure' beliefs, texts and institutions of ancient India, they also wanted to be modern, rational and scientific.

Moreover, Indian social service and social work in the early decades of the twentieth century was commonly animated by concerns about Indian – and especially Hindu – racial decline. Indians involved in voluntary associations believed that they had to improve and uplift the weaker and less productive parts of society to prevent further slippage in 'the scale of nations and races'.

Though debates once again borrowed from Indian concepts, such as the image of an organically-ordered society with castes and varna interlinked and interdependent as in the body of the primeval man Purusha, the European 'science' of race and eugenics was ubiquitous. The writings and ideas of Herbert Spencer were widely cited, and Spencerian notions of social efficiency underpinned an Indian movement for 'national efficiency' that echoed the concerns of the national efficiency campaign in Britain.[12]

The desire to increase Indian 'efficiency' was meant to make the people of the subcontinent more modern and better able to compete in the global struggle of nations and races, according to Spencer's theories of social Darwinism. The language of 'efficiency' may have replaced the emphasis on utilitarianism and philanthropy as 'works of public utility' in the East India Company's reform era, but older notions regarding the need to uplift and improve Indian society according to a 'universal' European civilizational referent remained relevant. In addition, members of new Indian social service and philanthropic institutions, along with journals such as the *Social Service Quarterly*, criticized 'traditional' Hindu charity as wasteful, indiscriminate and inefficient. Indian charity needed to be 'disciplined' and directed into proper channels – ideally through the management of Indian voluntary societies.[13] Ironically, much of this criticism was reminiscent of the Company's attacks on Indian charity in the 1830s and 1840s. It even used some of the same language, such as the term 'indiscriminate'.

Social service and philanthropic activities also evinced aspects of a civilizing mission in the sense that they represented the imposition of supposedly more modern and progressive urban values on Indians of lesser social status, particularly the 'Depressed Classes' and residents of rural areas. This is largely because the key members of social service organizations in the late colonial period were commonly educated urban elites of 'respectable' status.[14] Moreover, cities have been equated with civilization since the emergence of the first settled agricultural societies more than five thousand years ago, and both nationalism and colonialism were primarily identified with the Indian city from the 1880s until independence was achieved in 1947.[15]

Aside from being urban, the leaders of voluntary societies also tended to hail from middle-class and upper-caste or *ashraf* (Muslim 'respectable' or gentlemanly) background. Predictably, their caste and class values gradually came to define expectations of proper public comportment and emergent notions of Indian citizenship in the early decades of the twentieth century. Such qualities or values could be transmitted to youth, peasants and the Depressed Classes through educational initiatives, and education was a fundamental component of British and Indian civilizing missions. Poorer and more 'backward' Indians needed to be uplifted, improved and made more efficient through education. Education could take the form of direct and explicit teaching in schools or implicit and informal education through example and suggestion. Indian social service and voluntary bodies established a considerable number of educational institutions, including schools and educational conferences and leagues.[46] But a growing number of social servants carrying out nationalist *seva* (service) in urban and rural areas practically embodied the desired qualities of active and patriotic citizenship and thereby acted as positive examples to be emulated by 'lesser' Indians.

Notions of Indian citizenship, as opposed to the status of being a British colonial subject, attained greater importance in the early twentieth century as it became more apparent that Queen Victoria's promises of equality in the post-Rebellion proclamation of November 1858 were simply rhetorical. As Indian public life became more energized with the help of a growing network of voluntary associations and growing nationalism there was a corresponding interest in promoting Indian citizenship. Citizenship, it should be remembered, is that crucial and fundamental relationship between a state and its people. Charles Tilly presents citizenship as a set of transactions and negotiations regarding rights, entitlements and privileges as well as duties and obligations.[47] Individuals, groups of citizens or would-be citizens usually try to enhance their rights and entitlements and make governments honour their promises and pronouncements. States, on the other hand, generally try to limit citizens' rights and emphasize duties – whether in the interests of maintaining state or elite power, or for the supposed necessity of national progress and improvement. Ultimately, a state needs to have the consent of its citizens in order to establish its hegemony and rule effectively. This is especially true of democratic states but it is applicable in other situations, too, and it is relevant in the case of the Raj because the British claimed to be training Indians for self-government on the Westminster democratic model. Technically, Indians could not be 'citizens' of India while still under the yoke of colonial rule (as subjects of the British sovereign), but it was to be expected that ideals of citizenship would be discussed in the context of growing nationalism, concern about the treatment of indentured Indians overseas and a more vibrant Indian public life. What is surprising, perhaps, is that emergent definitions of the ideal Indian citizen were rather conservative and tended to stress expectations of obedience, discipline and self-sacrifice – both in the late colonial period and in postcolonial India during the late 1940s and 1950s.

One of the upper-caste values equated with modernity, progress, civilization and good citizenship was cleanliness. Notions of purity and pollution have been extremely powerful in India's majority Hindu society, with twice-born upper-caste groups sometimes referred to as 'clean castes' and members of the lower or Depressed Classes deemed 'unclean'. Cleanliness became identified with superior status and 'civilization', and was a part of Indian 'self-civilizing' missions as Prashant Kidambi has demonstrated in his essay on colonial Bombay c. 1900–1920.[48] In fact, educating colonial subjects about cleanliness, sanitation and good personal and public hygiene was a central tenet of European colonial civilizing missions.[49] An advertisement for Pears' Soap in 1899 asserted that 'teaching the virtues of cleanliness' was 'the first step towards lightening The White Man's Burden'. The reference to Kipling's newly-published 'White Man's Burden' poem is significant and the text went on to say that 'Pears' Soap is a potent factor in brightening the dark corners of the earth as civilization advances'.[50] In this sense, Indian social service organizations were not so different from British colonial authorities as they commonly included lessons about cleanliness and sanitation when working to uplift the 'dirty' and 'unhygienic' urban poor, the Depressed Classes or 'backward' villagers.

Other 'respectable' high-caste Brahminical qualities that seeped into emerging definitions of Indian citizenship circulated by social service organizations included generalized notions of *dharma*, piety and civility. While *dharma* could simply connote 'religion', in the context of new models of citizenship and public comportment the term's associations with 'proper conduct' and 'duty' are more noteworthy. This was consonant with the conservative tone of citizenship articulated by Indian elites at the forefront of philanthropic and voluntary initiatives. There was a consistent emphasis on duty, obedience and discipline: terms which reflected Victorian values at the heart of the colonial civilizing mission.[51]

These conservative and restrictive themes also help to explain Indian enthusiasm for the Boy Scout movement. Though Indians were not initially allowed to join the official Scout organization the first independent Indian Scout troops were started by Indian voluntary societies as early as 1910, particularly the Theosophical Society and Seva Samitis, just two years after the publication of founder Baden-Powell's *Scouting for Boys: A Handbook for Instruction in Good Citizenship*.[52] 'Good citizenship' to Baden-Powell meant training boys and young men of 'character' who would be obedient, disciplined and observant of their duty to the nation and empire. Scouts were also enjoined to be 'clean in mind and body'. Indian nongovernmental organizations were attracted to the idea of healthy young Indians actively and energetically working to improve society through acts of kindness and service, but they were also attracted to the Scout movement's stress on obedience to authority. In all of this there was a strong theme of paternalism, and the idea of training real or imagined 'children' for national or civilizational progress has been at the heart of civilizing missions since the early nineteenth century.

Ranajit Guha has argued that various disciplinary strategies were used by leaders of the Indian National Congress to mobilize Indians for nationalist campaigns during the Swadeshi and Gandhian eras.[53] During the 1905–08 Swadeshi movement, for example, Congress liberals such as Surendranath Banerjea used caste sanctions based on Brahminical ideals of purity and pollution to 'discipline and mobilize' Indians for participation in the political campaign. Those who failed to mobilize or join were subject to social boycotts in the form of the denial of services from priests, barbers, washermen, doctors and lawyers. As Guha puts it, oppressive and coercive 'traditional' caste disciplines were adapted to a modern nationalist context and became a 'new national dharma'. Guha also points out that Gandhi saw discipline as a 'mediating function' essential for mobilizing boisterous 'subaltern' groups, and for regulating and redirecting their 'enthusiasm' toward elite Congress ends. Gandhi's disciplinary efforts focused on crowd control and 'soul control'. That is, he demanded proper, disciplined (we might say 'civilized') behaviour at Congress events and he promoted *swaraj* not just as 'self-rule' in the political sense, but as personal self-discipline and self-control too.   .

While Guha's analysis of Congress efforts to 'discipline and mobilize' Indian subalterns is useful and interesting, it is also problematic because it limits its consideration of discipline to narrow political contexts related to Swadeshi and Non-cooperation. As we have seen, however, discipline was also extremely important in charitable societies and voluntary organizations. For example, the Holika Sammelan and Social Service League tried to tame and civilize the 'excessive' revelry and 'unhealthy' or 'filthy' practices associated with the annual Holi festival in Bombay during the 1910s.[54] Furthermore, colonial philanthropic institutions in the Company era promoted industry and usefulness, while the Salvation Army was a global nongovernmental organization very keen on promoting an authoritarian military-style civilization in India during the late nineteenth century.[55] For social service organizations such as the Servants of India Society or Ramkrishna Mission, emphasizing discipline helped mobilize youth to serve society while simultaneously imparting lessons about industrious or efficient behaviour to the general population.

Guha also fails to recognize that his title of 'discipline and mobilize' has a distinctly military connotation. In the first section of this essay we noted that the Company state of the 1830s and 1840s was 'a very military state' that was concerned with pacification, domestication and security. It was no surprise, then, that Company philanthropic initiatives were oriented toward promoting a productive form of discipline in 'works of public utility' that contributed to the state's military-fiscal interests. However, as the rise of the Salvation Army in the 1880s and the growing emphasis on a martial style of discipline in social service associations and the Indian public sphere in the early twentieth century shows, military values were being infused or transmuted into the institutions of civil society. The global appeal of the Boy Scout movement, including its appeal in India, provides further evidence of this tendency. That military technologies morphed into civilian or governmental applications will be familiar to careful readers of Foucault's *Discipline and Punish*, but it is worth restating this point here to stress how Indian NGOs and philanthropic societies could also be 'coercive institutions' that employed notions of discipline reminiscent of the military.[56] Such notions of discipline were intended to help mobilize Indians for the patriotic service of society, but they were also meant to educate Indians about proper 'civilized' behaviour and public comportment. The stress on selfless service and the insistence on disciplined or civilized behaviour were both oriented toward the improvement and uplift of Indian society within contemporary civilizational rankings of peoples and races.

Indian 'traditions' related to asceticism were also invoked to encourage greater discipline and austerity among the Indian population, and to encourage Indians to participate selflessly in work for national improvement. Like *dharma* and caste sanctions regarding questions of purity, older Hindu concepts and practices were adapted to a modern twentieth-century context. In the early twentieth century, selfless social service for the national good was often directly equated with being a *sannyasi* – one who has renounced his family, the life of the body and the material world to be free from earthly burdens and focus on spiritual matters. The 'traditional' emphasis on spiritual growth and devotion to one's religion was reworked by social activists from the 1890s onward to portray a *sannyasi* as someone who has forsaken family and wealth to serve his society and nation. Swami Vivekananda was a key figure in this process, since he took a vow of asceticism in the late 1880s to focus on practical service and uplift of the poor. Then, in 1894, he declared to his *gurubhais* ('brother gurus', fellow devotees of Sri Ramakrishna) that: 'We are Sannyasins, who have given up everything [...] To do the highest good to the world, everyone down to the lowest – this is our vow'.[57] His modern ascetic inclinations were later expanded and institutionalized in the Ramkrishna Mission and its Seva Ashrams from 1897 onward.

The ideal of the *sannyasi* as social servant was also prominent in Seva Samitis, Social Service Leagues, the Servants of India Society and the Arya Samaj.[58] At the Arya Samaj's high-profile Gurukul school in Kangri, northern India, students and parents were told that becoming a *sannyasi* represented the highest form of social service.[59] The Gurukul's *Vedic Magazine* even playfully invited John Bull, a personification of England, to open his eyes and appreciate the work of the Arya Samaj and 'earn the blessings of a Sannyasin'.[60] Members of the Servants of India Society, meanwhile, were expected to lead a pure personal life, take a vow of poverty and act as 'national missionaries'.[61] They were thus like national monks or ascetics.

Emphases on *sannyasi* asceticism were also very apparent in Gandhi's social and political campaigns in both South Africa and India, and they were infused with elements of martial discipline. Gandhi's social work initiatives became part of his 'Constructive Programme', which was inaugurated during the Non-Cooperation movement of 1920–2 though it had antecedents dating back to Gandhi's stay in South Africa (1893–1914). The Constructive Programme consisted of many different activities and objectives, including the promotion of communal harmony (especially between Hindus and Muslims), the eradication of untouchability, and the use of the *charkha* (spinning wheel) to make *khadi* (home-spun cloth – usually cotton) to aid in the attainment of economic self-sufficiency for India. Stress was placed upon the dignity of manual labour and *sarvodaya* or 'the welfare of all', but themes of 'uplift' through education and selfless *seva* or social service ran prominently through all of these activities.[62] Thus, while it would be incorrect to say that the Constructive Programme was solely about social service, voluntarism and philanthropy, it is clear that social service and 'uplift' through NGO or voluntary sector activities were core features of the programme.

The Constructive Programme was also fundamental to Gandhi's attempt to create or 'construct' an 'alternative modernity' and civilization.[63] In fact, Gandhi believed that the nationalist politics of the Congress could not free India from colonial rule on their own and he viewed the Constructive Programme as essential to achieving a broader and more fundamental *swaraj* or self-rule.[64] Since the publication of *Hind Swaraj* in 1909 Gandhi had been an incisive and unrelenting critic of 'Western civilization' and its claims to be the universal agent of superiority, progress and modernity, which in turn buttressed British claims to moral authority and the colonial civilizing mission in India.[65] Moreover, Gandhi criticized India's urban nationalist elites for uncritically accepting and internalizing the values and claims of Western civilization. In effect, their minds had been colonized by British culture and this is partly why Gandhi was so focused on India's peasants, who had not yet been contaminated or conquered by Western values in the early twentieth century.

Gandhi's civilizational ideal borrowed heavily from his understanding of ancient Indian traditions and institutions. Ironically, this was influenced by British colonial officials such as Henry Maine, who wrote about village communities in the 1870s, and Western Arcadians or pastoralists such as John Ruskin, Henry David Thoreau and Leo Tolstoy.[66] Gandhi's alternative civilization was to be based on *ahimsa* or non-violence, and it would combine material concerns with goals of moral and spiritual improvement. Moreover, it was to be a civilization based on rural India's villages and peasants. It would be a small-scale and de-centered society in which agriculture and the dignity of manual labour would be considered paramount. Clearly, Gandhi's civilization envisaged a very different kind of state and society, far removed from the kind of strong state envisaged in 'Western civilization' during the nineteenth and twentieth centuries – and desired by most Indian nationalists. As David Arnold and Partha Chatterjee have pointed out, Gandhi's civilizational model was increasingly discounted as bizarre, unscientific and 'out of touch' in the 1930s and 1940s as Congress became more powerful and independence grew nearer.[67] It was in the 1930s during the Depression, too, that the concept of the 'welfare state' gained many adherents, including Gandhi's protégé, Jawaharlal Nehru. Of course, this was also the era in which notions of social and economic 'development' guided by a strong, centralized state became extremely influential worldwide. It makes sense, then, that Gandhi 'retired' from the Congress and nationalist politics in 1934, since his views on state, society and civilization were being ignored and marginalized and he was disappointed in the Congress' lack of interest in his constructive work.[68]

Gandhi's Constructive Programme sought to create a society in which NGOs and the voluntary sector or civil society would play a major part. The programme led to the establishment of many institutions and organizations related to social service and the uplift or improvement of India's villages and the poor and marginalized in both rural and urban locales. The various organizations and institutions of the Constructive Programme added to India's growing voluntary or NGO sector (see the appendix for a list of some of the key organizations). In this sense, the Constructive Programme was a continuation of the work of earlier social service organizations such as the Ramkrishna Mission, various Seva Samitis and the Servants of India Society. These latter bodies contributed to the elaboration of an associational culture and the growth of a voluntary sector during the period between 1890 and 1920. Furthermore, in 1910 Gokhale articulated a vision of an Indian society abounding in small institutions that would 'develop the public life of the country'. This was a harbinger of Gandhi's ideal of a decentred and small-scale civilization in which NGOs would figure prominently,[69] and should not be surprising because Gandhian interest in service and uplift was influenced considerably by Indian social service initiatives in the early twentieth century.

The social work or NGO activity of the Constructive Programme had two general strands that we might identify as part of an internal civilizing mission. The first relates to efforts to educate and to uplift 'dirty' and 'backward' peasants and untouchables, and the second is about Gandhi's general stress on discipline, austerity and self-control. General or basic education and instruction regarding sanitation were key parts of Gandhi's constructive work, just as they were in earlier social service activities intended to uplift and improve the Depressed Classes. Cleanliness was clearly an important part of

Gandhi's alternative modernity and civilization. Thus, while the civilization that Gandhi was trying to create through the Constructive Programme claimed to be ethically and morally superior to the West's civilization, it put similar emphasis on the need to cleanse and uplift supposedly backward Indians. In this sense we might say that Gandhian NGOs at the centre of his constructive work were part of a parallel civilizing mission running alongside civilizing missions pursued by British governmental and nongovernmental agencies, as well as Indian nationalist modernizers.

David Arnold has noted that the 1917 Champaran campaign represented a key moment in Gandhi's attitude toward constructive work in India's villages. The condition of Champaran's villagers was a 'grim revelation' to Gandhi because they suffered from 'pathetic ignorance' and lived in filthy and unsanitary conditions: 'it was necessary to educate them, do sanitary work in the villages and "penetrate every department of their lives" – in short, to use the language to which Gandhi had become habituated in South Africa, to *civilise* them. Champaran marked, in effect, the birth of what came to be known as the Constructive Programme, designed to achieve "village uplift" and social reform'.[70] It also underlined the importance of the 'disinterested service of the people' to Gandhi, and he kept fifteen village workers in Champaran after the successful conclusion of his campaign.[71] The fact that urban and educated 'social workers' were needed to uplift villagers from their social misery and backwardness displayed another aspect of Gandhi's civilizing mission. The peasant masses needed to be awoken from inaction and dormancy too. As Jawaharlal Nehru recounted in *The Discovery of India*, 'He [Gandhi] sent us to the villages, and the countryside hummed with the activity of innumerable messengers of the new gospel of action. The peasant was shaken up and he began to emerge from his quiescent shell'. He then added that Gandhi wanted 'to waken these masses out of their stupor and static condition and make them dynamic'.[72] Moreover, as Ben Zachariah has argued, Gandhian programmes for village uplift in the 1930s and 1940s, such as the All-India Village Industries Association run by J. C. Kumarappa, were not so different from the British or Congress efforts that Gandhi criticized.[73] All viewed Indian villages as economically backward and in need of moral and material 'uplift' or 'development' through discipline and hard work.

Gandhi's Harijan campaign and the activities of the Harijan Sevak Sangh can also be considered part of a paternalistic civilizing mission. Many untouchables saw Gandhi's use of the term 'Harijan' for untouchables as condescending in the 1930s and later decades. Harijan literally means 'children of god' and the implication was that 'clean' and educated or 'mature' upper caste Hindus were justified in 'civilizing' backward and childlike untouchables. Once again, upper-caste values were reified as normative values for Indian citizenship. In 1936 the untouchable leader B. R. Ambedkar denounced Gandhi as a Bania who had become a Brahmin, and in 1943 he referred to Gandhi as a Hindu fanatic.[74] Regarding the Harijan Sevak Sangh, Ambedkar remarked that it did not include untouchables in its management and said that it made petty gifts to petty untouchables and aimed to 'tame' them to make the caste system safe for Hindus.[75] Ambedkar also noted that Gandhi and the Congress wanted to win the political support of untouchables by making promises they could not or would not keep.[76] To cite David Arnold once again, by the early 1930s Gandhi had established himself as the leading defender and reformer of Hindu society with 'an increasingly defensive and proprietorial attitude towards the Hindu community and its leaders' "civilizing mission"'.[77] He believed that educated and 'civilized' Hindus had a responsibility to uplift untouchables and elevate them to a position of moral respectability in India. Verrier Elwin, a lapsed Christian missionary turned social activist, also criticized Gandhian constructive workers for pushing *adivasis* (tribal peoples) to adopt their own upper-caste cultural values, including their strict and repressive views on alcohol and sexuality. David Hardiman has described the Gandhian approach to *adivasis* as 'education into citizenship'.[78]

As noted above, the second aspect of Gandhi's civilizing mission relates to his general stress on discipline, austerity and self-control. Ranajit Guha has highlighted how Gandhi's political campaigns tried to discipline peasants and enforce 'proper' behaviour, obedience and self-control at Congress events, but Constructive Programme activities carried out by Gandhian NGOs also emphasized the need to educate peasants and untouchables about the importance of discipline and hard work. Self-reliance through manual labour would be demanded of all citizens of India, and true freedom and independence could not be won and maintained without work-discipline.[79] This was similar in many respects to what the East India Company tried to do through its philanthropic initiatives in the 1830s.

Gandhi's definition of civilization also seemed to put a conservative stress on duties over rights. In *Hind Swaraj* he equated his civilization with 'duty' and 'good conduct' as in the sense of *dharma*.[80] This was reminiscent of conservative definitions of citizenship outlined by social service leaders such as Gokhale and Malaviya. The emphasis on duty and discipline was continued by J. C. Kumarappa, an authorized spokesman for Gandhi in the 1930s and 1940s. Kumarappa was head of the AIVIA and his seminal work *Why the Village Movement?* asserted that duties were more important than rights in a 'true culture' while also underlining the significance of hard work, self-discipline and Brahminical ideals.[81]

Furthermore, from 1906 onward Gandhi was a *brahmachari* ('celibate') and after his return to India in 1915 he was increasingly seen as a Hindu ascetic – a *sadhu* or *sannyasi*. In fact, Nehru stated that Gandhi represented India's ancient traditions of renunciation and asceticism.[82] Here, too, there were continuities with earlier social service, reform and voluntary organizations such as the Arya Samaj. There was a martial aspect to Gandhi's asceticism as well. His conception of asceticism drew on older ideals and practices of militant warrior ascetics such as the *nagas* and *tyagis*, who were important as mercenaries and traders in the seventeenth and eighteenth centuries.[83] Instead of militant ascetics who served as soldiers in ascetic *akharas* (brotherhoods), however, Gandhi's ascetics practised militant non-violence as *satyagrahi* (practitioners of Gandhi's 'truth-force') citizens and social workers who would construct a new and pure Indian civilization.

Symbolically, Gandhi's identification as an itinerant ascetic wearing few clothes and walking with a *lathi* (long wooden staff) helped increase his appeal to India's peasants and they constituted an allusive defiance of the British efforts to render Indians sedentary since the 1820s, but it also represented his commitment to an austere and simple life. Austerity, simplicity and non-acquisitiveness were important elements of Gandhi's 'alternative modernity' and the activists and institutions of his Constructive Programme propagated them as national or civilizational ideals – at least by example and persuasion if not by coercion or imposition. Nehru wrote in his autobiography that Verrier Elwin referred to Gandhi as 'a medieval Catholic saint'.[84] Krishna Kriplani stated less charitably that Gandhi wanted 'to erase the distinction between a monk and a head of family while effectively trying to make ordinary men behave like monks'.[85] In effect, then, the Constructive Programme helped to disseminate conservative and restrictive upper-caste and particularly Brahminical values as national norms in order to civilize 'lesser' Indians.

The emphasis on discipline and austerity was probably strongest in Gandhi's ashrams. Residents of the ashrams at Sabarmati and Sevagram were frequently referred to as 'inmates' and in Sabarmati they were obliged to follow a rigorous daily regimen that lasted from 4:00 am until 9:00 pm, including several hours of manual labour. Moreover, inmates were required to make a considerable number of vows, such as truthfulness, non-violence, fearlessness, tolerance, non-stealing, non-possession (poverty), *swadeshi* (self-reliance and economic self-sufficiency), physical labour, *brahmacharya* ('celibacy') and control of the palate. The emphasis was on a very simple and frugal existence with only enough basic and 'pure' food, clothing and possessions to sustain one's body and serve the country. As *brahmacharis* members of the ashram were required to abstain from sexual activity, even with their spouses. The ashrams were therefore characterized by themes of austerity and renunciation, and it is fitting that the Sabarmati constitution of 1915 stated that 'Ashram inmates will be in the stage of *sannyasis*'.[86] Some of Gandhi's Western disciples and associates noted the plain, disciplined and austere atmosphere of his ashrams. For example, Briton Catherine Mary Heilemann developed a desire to join Gandhi's Constructive Programme in the 1920s and eventually became an inmate of the women's or Mahila Ashram at Sevagram as Sarala Behn in 1936. Like other 'inmates', however, she commented that there was too much discipline and self-denial at Sevagram and not enough joy. Though she remained a committed Gandhian constructive worker until her death in India in 1982, she left Sevagram to found her own ashram – Lakshmi Ashram in the Himalayan foothills of northern India.[87] Since Gandhi's ashrams were microcosms of the Indian society that Gandhi was trying to create through his Constructive Programme, they also give us an indication of the discipline and austerity that he expected of Indian citizens in general. His alternative modernity and civilization was similar in many respects to the illiberal disciplinary civilization promoted by earlier British and Indian civilizing missions.

Section II (1890–1947) Conclusion

As with the putative charity of the East India Company, charity undertaken by social service organizations had political implications regarding legitimacy, moral authority and power. There were nationalistic overtones but, as we have seen, there were aspects of a 'civilizing mission' too – even in the 'alternative modernity' that Gandhi sought to establish through his Constructive Programme.

The fact that we can discern elements of a 'civilizing mission' in Indian voluntary and 'civil society' initiatives should be a reminder to us that 'civil society' is not always or only a positive force for freedom and empowerment, as persuasively argued by Susanne Hoeber Rudolph a decade ago in *Economic and Political Weekly*.[88] Several other chapters in this book have also drawn attention to the role that nongovernmental organizations have played in colonial or 'internal' Indian civilizing missions.[89]

Moreover, India's growing associational culture and voluntary sector in the first half of the twentieth century was rife with 'modern' notions and practices of uniformity, obedience, sacrifice and, above all, discipline. In order to become a 'citizen' and be included in the emergent Indian nation one had to subscribe to or at least tacitly acknowledge the superiority of such ideals based on upper-caste Hindu values. These themes remained prevalent as Indian social, economic and political leaders shifted their attention to 'national planning' and 'development' in the 1930s and 1940s, and the language of 'social service' and 'constructive work' was gradually overtaken by an emphasis on 'social work' and 'social welfare'.

III. 1947–1960: Philanthropy, Development and the Indian State

The third case study examines philanthropy and development under the 'Nehruvian' Indian state in the 1950s by looking at the Bharat Sevak Samaj (BSS), a supposedly non-official and non-political voluntary organization started by the Government of India in 1952. Nehru was sometimes outspokenly critical of existing Indian philanthropic and social welfare efforts, and he saw the modern state, supported by scientific planning, technology and expertise, as the principal agent for delivering welfare and social justice on a national scale. The voluntary associations and networks of India's existing civil society were not considered adequate for the task.

The new Indian state attempted to subsume social service and philanthropic efforts under scientifically planned and state-directed economic development and, beyond that, various social welfare projects linked to the first Five-Year Plans and the Community Development programme.[90] This led to tensions and conflict with existing social service and philanthropic organizations, because some organizations resisted government efforts that directly or indirectly conspired to marginalize them.

There are interesting and surprising parallels with the state-building efforts of the East India Company in the 1830s and 1840s. In both cases new states in precarious situations were seeking legitimacy and moral authority by presenting themselves as the only true and 'modern' source of benevolence and giving. Moreover, both also emphasized the importance of 'discipline' and 'industry' for the sake of social or national stability, improvement and progress. Discipline, utilitarianism and efficiency were consistently considered important attributes of progressive and civilized societies, whether in the mid-nineteenth century or the mid-twentieth. In addition, independent Nehruvian India also continued many themes that were apparent in Indian social service and voluntary organizations of the late colonial era that were associated with Vivekananda, Gokhale, Malaviya and Gandhi. Perhaps the most notable and interesting of these thematic continuities are evident in the stress put on the necessity of austerity, discipline and self-sacrifice for uplift, improvement and the national good. National ascetics were still needed in postcolonial India.

The Bharat Sevak Samaj was envisaged as an organization that would help mobilize Indians to support the first Five-Year Plan, released in draft form in July 1951 and implemented in December 1952. The plan was considered essential for India's economic development, which in turn was to facilitate the country's social development. The BSS idea was first mooted by Gulzarilal Nanda in 1950, though it apparently was brought to Nehru's attention sometime in 1951 under the name of the Bharat Seva Sangh.[91]

When Nanda started to promote the BSS he was Deputy Chairman of the Planning Commission and in 1952 he was the Minister of Planning, Irrigation and Power. Nehru expressed support for Nanda's proposal in early 1952, just after India's first national elections (which Nehru's Congress Party won) and a lengthy tour throughout the country. He was optimistic about finding a way to motivate Indians, particularly the youth, to undertake 'work entailing hardship' to help the country. Nehru believed that Indian citizens were looking for an opportunity to do something constructive and he saw a possible solution in Nanda's BSS proposal.[92]

In April 1952 the Planning Commission published an eponymous *Bharat Sevak Samaj* pamphlet and this was followed by Nehru's announcement to Chief Ministers in July that the BSS had been 'fathered by the Planning Commission'.[93] This comment reflected the role played by Nanda and the relationship between the BSS and the planning process, which was at the heart of Nehru's government. In August 1952 the BSS unveiled a draft constitution, which named Nehru as the Samaj's President.[94] In the months that followed Nehru inaugurated various BSS branches throughout India, though the organization received a further boost when the Community Development scheme was launched on 2 October 1952 (a calculated reference to Gandhi's *jayanti* or birthday celebration), just ahead of the formal start of the first Five-Year Plan in December.[95] The Bharat Sevak Samaj was a powerful and influential organization in the 1950s and 1960s. It still exists today, but only as a shadow of what it was 50 years ago. The organization's decline began in the late 1960s when allegations began to surface about financial irregularities and misuse of government property. A commission of enquiry was struck in 1969 and the publication of its report severely damaged the reputation of the BSS and ensured its continued decline in the 1970s.[96]

Gulzarilal Nanda's biographer, Promilla Kalhan, described the Bharat Sevak Samaj as 'a non-political, non-governmental organization for large-scale social work on a voluntary basis'.[97] In the summer and autumn of 1952 Nehru defined it as an organization 'meant for hard work to build up the nation', to encourage Indians to work selflessly without expectation of reward or office. The BSS would provide opportunities to serve the Motherland, but its real value would be in the 'work it puts in to remove the poverty of the people'.[98] During a speech in October 1952 he stated:

There is a new organization, the Bharat Sevak Samaj. This is a non-official outfit connected with the Planning Commission. It is a non-political organization, meant just to encourage voluntary work. Every person who joins it has to undertake to do some manual labour. It may be once a week. There are many kinds of work you can interest yourself in, like sanitation, or cleaning the village, the town, or the *mohalla* [neighbourhood], whatever it is. You can do work in the fields. The point is, we want the people of this country to do a great deal of voluntary service themselves.[99]

The Samaj was open to all adult men and women on either a part-time or full-time basis, and there were no restrictions regarding religious, caste or class affiliations. Members of political parties could join too, including members of the ruling Congress Party, as long as they joined as individuals and did not try to advance party interests. Nehru was adamant, however, that 'people of a communal bent of mind', including members of the RSS, Hindu Mahasabha, Ram Rajya Parishad and Jan Sangh, were not allowed to enlist in the BSS.[100]

In the block quote above Nehru listed cleaning, sanitation and agricultural work as possible areas in which BSS volunteers could be of service to the country. In other statements made by the Prime Minister – and in the BSS constitution – volunteers were encouraged to do manual labour in the form of building roads, tanks (water reservoirs), canals, embankments, dams and public buildings such as offices, schools, dispensaries or simple houses. For instance, the BSS was deeply involved in the Kosi River dam and embankment projects after 1954. Most of the Samaj's work was undertaken in rural areas, including efforts to increase agricultural productivity and 'grow more food', but sanitation and 'slum improvement' initiatives were pursued in urban areas as well.[101] Uplift and development efforts were also carried out among *adivasi* or tribal groups.

Overall, Nehru and Nanda wanted the BSS to spread an 'ethos of work, of building up India, aiming at raising the people of India, and raising ourselves', which included emphasizing the dignity of manual labour.[102] The BSS also ran training programmes including labour and social service work camps for students, as well as conducting 'social education' efforts to spread knowledge about India's economy and the Five-Year Plans. In addition, the BSS had a number of general goals to improve Indian public life: creating social awareness about India's problems and the need for unity, tolerance and mutual help, and creating awareness regarding the obligations of India's citizens; improving standards of honesty; fighting corruption and anti-social behaviour; reducing inefficiency and promoting economy; and encouraging 'the general adoption of the practice of austerity'.[103]

In April 1953 Nehru explicitly linked the BSS to India's first Five-Year Plan, which was implemented in December of the previous year. He explained that the Plan would depend on 'the enthusiastic cooperation of the people of our great country', and he then defined the function of the Samaj as: 'To facilitate and organise this public cooperation on a voluntary basis and on the widest scale possible is the main function of the Bharat Sevak Samaj'.[104]

Nehru's insistence that the Bharat Sevak Samaj was a 'non-official' and 'non-political' 'voluntary organization' makes it seem that the BSS was a nongovernmental organization or NGO.[105] The paradox is that it was an NGO or quasi-NGO that was conceived, planned and started by India's national government to encourage 'public cooperation' and support for government initiatives, including the all-important field of economic planning and development. It also received a great deal of financial support from the Government of India, and the Commission of Enquiry appointed in 1969 was evidently frustrated and unsure as to whether the Samaj should be categorized as a voluntary organization or as an arm of government.[106]

Moreover, as we have seen in section two of this chapter, there already was a vibrant voluntary sector in India by the time independence was achieved in 1947. Nehru and Nanda's push for the BSS was therefore a case of direct government interference and intervention in India's voluntary sector. On several occasions Nehru indicated that he was aware of the potential tensions that the BSS might create with existing Indian NGOs. 'One hesitates to start a new organization when there are so many. Obviously, any such organization would tend to overlap and conflict with the work of others'. He insisted, however, that the BSS was 'not going to act as a rival to any other organizations'.[107] The Samaj's constitution emphasized the necessity of cooperation with existing NGOs, but claimed that the BSS could become 'the focal centre for such collaboration'.[108]

An attempt to justify the establishment of the BSS was made with the argument that existing Indian voluntary and philanthropic organizations lacked the required levels of commitment and organization to do effective social service or uplift work,[109] and that they were not sufficiently 'national' in scope.[110] In fact, Nehru had strongly criticized 'social welfare' work as early as 1940. In an article which appeared in *The Hindustan Times* he expressed appreciation for 'the earnest men and women who devote themselves to the service of their fellow creatures', but he regretted that they did so in a 'somewhat narrow way': 'They do good work [...] Yet, it seems to me, that all this good work is largely wasted, because it deals with the surface of the problem only [...]. Any scientific consideration of the problem of social welfare must, therefore, inevitably go down to these [political and economic] roots and seek out the causes'.[111] Such criticism was repeated during the course of an address to the Indian Conference of Social Work in 1952 when he extolled Gandhi's work but said that other older organizations hardly affected the masses of India and did not speak their language.

Nehru's solution was 'National Planning' to pursue disciplined national progress.[112] This would use a scientific approach led by experts and technocrats of the Planning Commission, which had 'fathered' the BSS.[113]

Philanthropy and social service were viewed through the lenses of economic development, professional expertise, planning, science and technology. As B. R. Nanda put it, 'In Nehru's armoury the chief weapon for the assault on poverty was economic planning'.[114]

As in the case of the East India Company displacing Indian charitable institutions in the 1830s because their work was supposedly indiscriminate and superstitious, Nehru's new Indian state justified the marginalization of existing Indian NGOs in the 1950s on the basis of the state's claims to better organization as well as its rationality and use of scientific planning.

Voluntary and social service organizations were critical of the Government of India's decision to create and support the Bharat Sevak Samaj. Hridaynath Kunzru, who was a member of the Servants of India Society since 1909 and became its president in 1936, was fundamentally opposed to the BSS. In 1954 he explained that he was angered that the BSS tried to lure Shri Ram Bajpai, a key member of the Servants of India and an Indian Scout and Guide activist, to manage a training centre for camp organizers. Kunzru was also disturbed by the fact that the BSS was too close to the Congress Party and thus the Indian government. He believed government money would be better spent in encouraging the work of existing social service associations such as the Servants of India, Ramkrishna Mission and the Seva Samiti.[115] Nine years later, in 1963, Kunzru again criticized the BSS for not making better use of experienced educational and voluntary organizations in its labour and social service camps.[116] Similar misgivings about government interference in the voluntary sector were expressed by other associations such as Servants of the People Society (New Delhi) and the Social Service League (Bombay) in 'golden jubilee souvenir volumes' that appeared in the 1960s and early 1970s.[117]

Gandhian social and 'constructive workers' voiced their opposition to the BSS too. Activists such as J. C. Kumarappa and Vinoba Bhave were already concerned about the growth of centralized state authority under India's Congress government, and government sponsorship and funding of a supposed NGO added to their anxieties. The Gandhian journal *Harijan*, an important voice for Gandhi's Constructive Programme since its start in 1933, published a few articles critical of the Samaj. In June 1953, for example, Maganbhai P. Desai disputed Nehru's assertion that the BSS was a non-political and non-official organization. Desai bluntly called it a Congress body used to promote the Five-Year Plan. He also took issue with the claim that a vacuum existed in India relating to voluntary work on a well-organized national scale that could only be filled by the Bharat Sevak Samaj: 'There is another way also. Or rather we have had it already, which we called the Constructive Programme forged out by the people under Gandhi's auspices'.[118]

Despite such criticism and resistance, a state-directed and top-down approach to planning and development remained dominant in the 1950s. This was echoed in the state's top-down approach to civilizing Indians by taming and disciplining them in order to uplift them. In this respect, the Nehruvian government was closer to the East India Company than it was to the self-civilizing mission of Indian NGOs in the first half of the twentieth century. As Judith Brown has noted, Nehru was paternalistic and was occasionally referred to as 'the last Englishman to rule India' or 'the last Viceroy'. Moreover, he was sometimes 'sharply imperious towards and critical of Indians in ways that echoed the discourse of earlier British rulers', including complaints about Indians' laziness, lack of public commitment and narrowness of outlook.[119]

Nevertheless, the Nehruvian state civilizing mission of the 1950s, as embodied in the BSS, was often remarkably similar to the civilizing agendas of Indian voluntary organizations associated with Vivekananda, Gokhale and Gandhi. On the one hand, there was a general assumption that well-educated, upper-caste and urban Indians needed to educate and uplift rural Indians, including *adivasis*, and the urban poor. When responding to questions about the Samaj in the Lok Sabha in July 1952, for example, Nehru said the following: 'It is an idea to get large numbers of voluntary people to work in villages and elsewhere – city people to go to the villages and generally work with the others, etc.'.[120] The implication was that civilized citizens of the city would bring superior technical knowledge regarding sanitation, irrigation and agricultural production to 'different' and 'backward' villagers. Improvements, especially regarding sanitation, would also be applied to 'backward' urban slum dwellers. The BSS constitution also pointed to 'insanitary surroundings, low standards of essential amenities [and] lack of facilities for community life in most places' as an incentive for constructive activity in India's towns and villages.[121] Cleanliness and sanitation, those important markers of civilization and civilizing missions, remained key elements of Nehru's BSS civilizing mission in postcolonial India.

The Samaj's constitution also cited statistical evidence relating to per capita income, the kind of evidence that was so important to Nehru's planning experts such as P. C. Mahalanobis, to show that India 'stands almost at the bottom among the nations of the world' and was 'lagging behind'.[122] This type of language about 'lagging behind' and needing to catch up was similar to that used by Indian leaders of social service initiatives interested in social or national efficiency in the early twentieth century, though Nehru's planning experts put more emphasis on economic indicators as opposed to the stress on racial decline and eugenics at the turn of the twentieth century. Nonetheless, in both cases it was clear that Indians needed to be uplifted, 'raised up' and civilized according to universal civilizational standards based on the West's modernity. It is important, then, to remember that Nehru and Mahalanobis were deeply influenced by Western models of national development that put the economy, and particularly heavy industry, as the top priority. Mahalanobis admitted to 'an inferiority complex about economic matters' and set off on an educational tour of the United States, Europe and the Soviet Union in 1954.[123] Bhiku Parekh has argued that Nehru suffered from a gnawing sense of racial inferiority and susceptibility to foreign opinion in the late 1940s and early 1950s and believed that India had to 'catch up',[124] which helps to explain his invitations to American experts and the US-based Ford Foundation to help with Indian development in the early 1950s.[125] In fact, American expertise and the Indo-American Technical Cooperation Agreements, signed in 1952, played a considerable part in Nehru's Community Development Plan, which was linked in turn to the Bharat Sevak Samaj. Therefore, Nehru and his senior planning mandarins sought to modernize and civilize their fellow Indians largely according to Western standards and models, even if they were adapted to fit Indian conditions and Nehru's concept of 'a socialistic pattern of society'.[126]

The Nehruvian civilizing mission was deeply committed to the virtues of science and technology and set them in opposition to ignorance, superstition and backwardness. Thus, one of Nehru's goals was to foster a 'scientific temper' in all spheres of human activity in India.[127] Village-Level Workers in the Community Development scheme in the early 1950s were 'agents of change' charged with taking new ideas to the peasants, which included demonstrating scientific methods of planting seeds along with introducing chemical fertilizers and new crops.[128] In the mid 1950s Indian journalist and author Frank Moraes prepared a biography of Nehru that conveyed the Prime Minister's excitement about the enlightenment of the 'dark' or economically 'backward' areas of India. At a Community Projects Conference in May 1952 Nehru stated: 'There are far too many backward people in this country [...] you can safely say that 96 per cent of the people are economically very backward'. Once the Community Development programme got underway in October 1952 he could claim that: 'All over India there are now centres of human activity that are like lamps spreading their light more and more in surrounding darkness. This light must grow until it covers the land'. Moraes enthusiastically noted the importance of social service when he wrote the following: 'With improved health, better education and a growing sense of social service, rural India is slowly stirring to new life and reaching out to broader horizons'.[129] In the 1970s, E. N. Mangat Rai stated that community development 'produced a buzz of activity in the villages, which were constantly prodded and provoked to effort'.[130] Educated and knowledgeable agents of progress, aided by American expertise, were sent by the government from the cities to rural India to bring science, light and the 'buzz of activity' to an apparently backward and inert population. Of course, much of this was reminiscent of the earlier 'uplift' and 'civilizing' campaigns of Gokhale and Gandhi.

The Bharat Sevak Samaj's constitution asserted that problems of 'poverty and ignorance' had to be combated by 'social enlightenment and action'.[131] Nehru reinforced this principle in declaring that the Samaj's programme embraced 'community organisation especially in the Community Project areas, work camps for students, slum service, anti-malaria work and social education, as well as the spread of knowledge about the economic situation and the Five-Year Plan'.[132] He also stressed the importance of basic education for *adivasis*.[133] In sum, BSS volunteers were to help 'enlighten' India's urban poor, rural peasants and villagers, as well as tribal peoples, and this was a further indication of a civilizing mission in the Nehruvian era.

The paradox of the Samaj's civilizing mission is that Jawaharlal Nehru had experienced the arrogance and condescension inherent in the Raj's civilizing mission – and perhaps observed it in Indian social service organizations too - and actually cautioned directors and members of the BSS about patronizing the Indian people.[134] He warned about a 'superior approach' connected to service or *seva* and wanted volunteers to avoid any sense of 'barrier between the server and the served. I do not want that barrier. It is a kind of false pride, which one may develop while doing service. Therefore, I would like to have a rather comradely, cooperative approach where every person is served'.[135] B. N. Mullik, the Director of the Intelligence Bureau in the early 1950s, toured India's north-eastern tribal areas with the Prime Minister in 1952 and related a story about Nehru advising government officials not to 'assume any air of superiority' when dealing with *adivasis*. 'He mentioned the case of a Bharat Sevak Samaj worker who started giving Hindu names to the Nagas with the result that the Nagas had become hostile to him and this had come in the way of social work'.[136] Despite such occasional admonitions, Nehru's development initiatives and the work of the Samaj continued to manifest significant aspects of paternalism, superiority and a civilizing agenda directed at India's 'backward' peasants, urban poor and tribal peoples.

The other part of Nehru's civilizing mission carried out by the Bharat Sevak Samaj was providing tutelage to Indians about the virtues of discipline, industry and austerity, and this continued an important part of the earlier Indian and British civilizing missions in the nineteenth and twentieth centuries. As we have noted above, the BSS promoted ideals of hard work, the dignity of labour, selfless service and sacrifice for the national good and 'the general adoption of the practice of austerity'. Volunteers were instructed not to expect payment or reward for their service and were encouraged to be frugal and subsist on the barest of necessities, just like the Gandhians at Sevagram.[137] Moreover, the Samaj's constitution stressed the importance of service, sacrifice, obedience, discipline, efficiency and exactitude for part-time volunteers, while full-time *sevaks* were to observe the 'Service is Sacrifice' precept as well as the principles of obedience, work, exactitude, efficiency and discipline.[138] Discipline, obedience, hard work, efficiency and sacrifice were key qualities in the BSS, just as they were for Gandhi's constructive workers or earlier social servants of Gokhale's era. Indeed, Nehru was known to prize punctuality and discipline very highly, though in the mid 1950s some of his associates told visiting political scientist Michael Brecher that 'Gandhi was a much more ruthless disciplinarian'.[139] Moreover, as Ben Zachariah has pointed out, the Indian National Congress's development plans strongly emphasized discipline from the 1930s onward.[140] This would help modernize and civilize Indians morally and would assist the nation-building process by encouraging disciplined and responsible citizenship.

On 15 August 1947 Indians finally became real citizens of an independent India, followed by a universal adult franchise that was enshrined in the constitution of 1950 and successfully put into practice in the first general election in 1952. Moreover, despite India's enormous internal and external challenges in the aftermath of independence and partition, Nehru's government could now control and direct its own development. However, the promise of citizenship and development also raised Indians' expectations and put more pressure on national and state governments to deliver tangible social, economic and political benefits. Citizens were increasingly demanding rights and trying to claim entitlements, and many did so in a noisy and unruly manner.[141]

Dipesh Chakrabarty has recently studied Nehru's frequent complaints about a disruptive style of politics in the 1950s characterized by 'crowd action' and 'hooliganism', and how Nehru tried to counter this by instilling notions of unity and discipline in the Indian population.[142] In this respect Nehru often sounded like a 1950s Indian version of Robert Baden-Powell, the founder of the Boy Scouts. In his foundational 1908 text *Scouting for Boys*, Baden-Powell fulminated about 'bad citizenship' and 'hooliganism' in Edwardian Britain. The Scout movement intended to promote good citizenship, which depended on disciplined and obedient youth. The comparison is significant because Nehru was involved in Indian scouting initiatives from about 1920 onward and he eventually became the head of the Bharat (Indian) Scouts and Guides after 1947.[143]

Chakrabarty's article continues or extrapolates Ranajit Guha's 'Discipline and Mobilize', which analysed Congress efforts to discipline, control and mobilize Indians during the Swadeshi movement of the 1900s and the early Gandhian campaigns of the 1920s.[144] Like Guha, however, Chakrabarty also focuses narrowly on Congress politics and fails to consider how social and economic development initiatives carried out through NGOs or quasi-NGOs such as the Bharat Sevak Samaj were related to Nehru's efforts to train disciplined and obedient – and hence more 'civilized' – Indian citizens.[145]

The Samaj disseminated a conservative and restrictive model of Indian citizenship that emphasized duty, discipline, sacrifice and service above rights and entitlements – including the right to demonstrate and protest. As such, the BSS was an important part of Nehru's attempt to decrease Indians' expectations of rights and benefits while simultaneously raising the state's expectations of sacrifice, austerity and self-denial or asceticism for the national good. Therefore, the BSS was part of an attempt to tame or civilize Indians by changing their behaviour and expectations in order to maximize 'public cooperation' with the state's development programme for civilizational progress as defined in the Five-Year Plans.

Conclusion

It is interesting that philanthropic efforts seem to have been tied to questions of political legitimacy, moral authority and nation-building in vastly different contexts over more than 130 years, from the 1820s to the 1950s. Whether associated with colonial state-building efforts or aligned with Congress nationalism and opposed to the state (at least the colonial state), in each successive phase philanthropic and charitable initiatives claimed to be more scientific, more rational, more efficient and more modern than their predecessors. The rhetoric of science, utility, efficiency and development was used in relation to charity in order to buttress a state's or a movement's claims to leadership and authority. Discipline was a common theme, too, and discipline – if we can invoke Foucault's insights about modern 'disciplinary society' and its coercive or 'austere institutions' and regulations – is an important marker of modernity.[146] The analysis of Indian voluntary associations and NGOs provided in this paper shows how non-state 'civil society' institutions could employ disciplinary practices too.

Claims of representing progress and development indicated certain assumptions of superiority and perhaps a greater or more advanced 'civilization'. Charitable and philanthropic initiatives are ostensibly oriented to action in order to relieve or lessen hardship and misery, but they also represent and disseminate certain attitudes and values. Such values are usually assumed to be superior and more civilized than those espoused by the objects or recipients of philanthropy, and this is where we find evidence of the 'civilizing mission' in philanthropic efforts. We might expect this of charitable activities carried out by the British colonial state (and its non-official allies) in the subcontinent, but it is important to see that such civilizing or self-civilizing agendas were inherent in the work of Indian NGOs in the late colonial period – and in the voluntary and government sectors of independent India at the peak of the Nehruvian era in the 1950s.

Lastly, perhaps it is important not to be too cynical about 'uplift', 'improvement' and 'development' efforts undertaken by states and NGOs in India (and elsewhere) during the nineteenth and twentieth centuries. Despite common attitudes of implicit or explicit arrogance, paternalism, condescension and superiority in development efforts it is salutary to remember that many individuals, organizations and agencies – British and Indian – were motivated by an earnest desire to improve the moral and material conditions of the Indian people among whom they worked. As Frederick Cooper has recently noted, 'development' is often under attack today but it has survived many previous assaults from the left and the right because it has made a positive difference in the lives of impoverished and marginalized people – men, women and children who actually want 'development' and yet have sufficient agency to simultaneously demand greater rights.[117]

Appendix: Some Indian NGOs Connected to Gandhi's Constructive Programme c. 1915–1948

Satyagraha Ashram (1915, also known as Sabarmati Ashram): established in May 1915 on the outskirts of Ahmedabad near the Sabarmati river shortly after Gandhi's return to India. This was the third of Gandhi's four ashrams and his first in India.[118] Gandhi and his supporters used Sabarmati as a base for social and political campaigns focused on *satyagraha* ('truth-force' or firmness in the search of justice and truth) in the 1930s, and as centre for experiments oriented to constructing Gandhi's 'alternative modernity' through service of the Motherland.

Gujarati Vidyapith (1920): a college for national education that sponsored and supported rural schools in Gujarat (Gandhi's native region).

Sarva Seva Sangh (1923, Service for All Organization): the organization was founded by Jamnalal Bajaj, an industrialist and philanthropist who supported Gandhi, and it sought to have *lok sevaks* or 'servants of the people' undertake work for public welfare in Indian villages. David Hardiman describes it as a precursor to Vinoba Bhave's Sarvodaya Samaj and movement (Society for Uplift and Welfare of All), aiming at improving public welfare in all fields of life, founded after Gandhi's death in 1948.[119]

All-India Spinners' Association (1925): this was created as a branch of the Indian National Congress to promote use of the *charkha* (spinning wheel) and Indian *swadeshi* or economic self-sufficiency.

Khadi Seva Sangh (1928, 'Home-Spun Cloth Service Society'): to promote the spinning of *khadi* and economic self-sufficiency.

Go Seva Sangh (1928, 'Cow Service Society'): to protect India's cows but more fundamentally to promote better methods of animal husbandry and peasant agriculture.

Harijan Sevak Sangh (1933, 'Harijan Service Society'): for the eradication of untouchability and the uplift of India's untouchables.

All-India Village Industries Association (1934, AIVIA): to develop and promote village industries including spinning khadi and provide employment, dignity and self-sufficiency for those in India's six hundred thousand or so villages.

Gram Seva Mandal (1934, Village Service Society): founded by Gandhian Vinoba Bhave to promote the eradication of untouchablility and the spinning of *khadi* to help Indian villages and villagers.

Sevagram (1936, 'Service Village'): this was the last of Gandhi's four ashrams. It was located in a village named Segaon, near the city of Wardha and the geographic centre of India. It was in a harsh and difficult physical environment, but was a place where he and his supporters could experiment with efforts to uplift India's villages and untouchables.

Lok Seva Sangh (1948, 'People's Service Society'): On 11 January 1948, just weeks before his death and only months after India achieved independence, Gandhi called for the transformation of the Indian National Congress into the Lok Seva Sangh or 'People's Service Society'.

Notes

1 Research for this essay has been supported by a Junior Research Fellowship at Wolfson College (Cambridge), a SSHRC (Canada) postdoctoral fellowship, a Shastri Indo-Canadian Institute (SICI) fellowship in India, and the Research Office of St Thomas University. I am grateful to Michael Mann, Samira Farhoud, Dietmar Rothermund and David Arnold for comments and feedback, though I alone remain responsible for the content of the essay and any errors it might contain (unwittingly).

2 Sanjay Sharma, *Famine, Philanthropy and the Colonial State: North India in the Early Nineteenth Century* (New Delhi: Oxford University Press, 2001), 171–81; Nicholas B. Dirks, The *Hollow Crown: Ethnohistory of an Indian Kingdom*, second edition (Ann Arbor: The University of Michigan Press, 1993); and Bernard S. Cohn, 'Representing Authority

in Victorian India' in Eric Hobsbawm and Terence Ranger (eds), *The Invention of Tradition* (Cambridge: Cambridge University Press, 1983), 165–209.

3 The term civilization only came into widespread use in English during the nineteenth century in the age of British imperial expansion. Regarding cultural imperialism see Michael Mann, '"Torchbearers Upon the Path of Progress": Britain's Ideology of "Moral and Material Progress" in India. An Introductory Essay' in Harald Fischer-Tiné and Michael Mann (eds), *Colonialism as Civilizing Mission: Cultural Ideology in British India* (London & New York: Anthem Press, 2004), 1–26. See also Edward Said, *Culture and Imperialism* (New York: Vintage Books, 1994).

4 See Kenneth Pomeranz, 'Empire & "Civilizing Missions"', Past & Present', *Daedalus* 134, no.2 (Spring 2005): 34–45.

5 James Mill, *The History of British India* (New York: Chelsea House, 1968). Mill's text was first published in 1817. T. B. Macaulay, 'Minute of the 2nd February, 1835' in *Speeches by Lord Macaulay with his Minute on Education*, selected with an introduction and notes by G. M. Young (New York: AMS Press, 1979 [reprint ed., 1st pub. 1854]), 345–61.

6 Thomas R. Metcalf, *Ideologies of the Raj* (Cambridge: Cambridge University Press, 1996), and D. A. Low, *The Lion Rampant: essays in the study of British imperialism* (London: Frank Cass and Co., Ltd, 1973). See also Tim Allender, *Ruling Through Education: The Politics of Schooling in the Colonial Punjab* (New Delhi: New Dawn Press, Inc., 2006), 9–13, regarding the absence of any coherent British ideology in the Raj's educational endeavours in the Punjab in the 1850s and 1860s, and the relatively greater importance of immediate practical considerations.

7 Terence Ball, 'Mill, James (1773–1836)', *Oxford Dictionary of National Biography* (Oxford University Press, Sept. 2004), online edition, Oct 2007, accessed 9 February 2010; and Romila Thapar, *The Penguin History of Early India: From the Origins to A.D. 1300* (New Delhi: Penguin Books, 2002), 7. See Adam Knowles' chapter in Part One of this book, 'Conjecturing Rudeness: James Mill's Utilitarian Philosophy of History and the British Civilizing Mission', for more detail on Mill's life and his *History of British India*.

8 See Harald Fischer-Tiné and Michael Mann (eds), *Colonialism as Civilizing Mission: Cultural Ideology in British India* (London & New York: Anthem Press, 2004); Michael Adas, 'Contested Hegemony: The Great War and the Afro-Asian Assault of the Civilizing Mission Ideology', *Journal of World History* 15, no.1 (2004): 31–63, and Frederick Cooper, 'Writing the History of Development', *Journal of Modern European History* 8, no.1 (2010): 5–23. My thanks to Harald Fischer-Tiné for bringing the Cooper article to my attention.

9 See Sharma, *Famine, Philanthropy and the Colonial State.*

10 Michel Foucault's work on the disciplinary and surveillance practices of modern states is well known, but sociologists from Max Weber to Anthony Giddens have discussed these topics as well – including the tensions between 'liberty' and 'constraint' or 'enablements' and 'constraints' in modern societies. See Michel Foucault, *Discipline and Punish: The Birth of the Prison*, translated by Alan Sheridan (New York: Vintage Books, 1995); Christopher Dandeker, *Surveillance, Power and Modernity: Bureaucracy and Discipline from 1700 to the Present Day* (Cambridge: Polity Press, 1990); and Peter Wagner, *A Sociology of Modernity: Liberty and Discipline* (London & New York: Routledge, 1994).

11 'Decolonizing the mind' of the pernicious cultural legacies and residues of colonialism has been one of the principal objectives of postcolonial scholarship since the 1970s. On the issue of 'colonizing the mind' or how the cultural and discursive formations of colonialism 'colonized the minds' of colonial subjects (and others), see Edward

Said's *Orientalism* (New York: Vintage Books, 1978/1979), and, for a significant Indian postcolonial perspective, see Dipesh Chakrabarty's 'Postcoloniality and the artifice of history: Who speaks for "Indian" pasts?' in *Representations*, No. 37, Special Issue: Imperial Fantasies and Postcolonial Histories (Winter, 1992): 1–26. Gandhi alerted Indian nationalist elites to this problem in *Hind Swaraj* in 1909, and in this sense he was a precursor to late-twentieth-century postcolonial thinkers. See also Dipesh Chakrabarty, *Provincializing Europe: Postcolonial thought and historical difference* (Princeton, NJ : Princeton University Press, 2000), and Ania Loomba, *Colonialism / Postcolonialism* (Florence, KY: Routledge, 1998).

12 Bharat Sevak Samaj could be translated as Indian Volunteer Society, since the term 'sevak' denotes a person volunteering his or her 'seva' or service for society or the nation-state.

13 These themes and topics will be discussed further in section III, below.

14 Sharma, *Famine, Philanthropy and the Colonial State*. Sanjay Sharma's excellent study is referred to frequently in this section of the essay, and it constitutes the main source of information.

15 This neat and coherent portrayal of humanitarian British charity was more a product of famine reports and regional histories of the 1860s and 1890s. The reality of the 1830s was that there was much uncertainty and division about how to proceed. See Sharma, *Famine, Philanthropy and the Colonial State*, 135 (Crooke 1897) & 159 (1860s reports).

16 The importance of notions of 'industry' in this period has been discussed by Thomas Metcalf in *Ideologies of the Raj*, 31. In the late eighteenth and nineteenth centuries, the term connoted individual hard work, diligence and assiduity.

17 On military fiscalism see David Washbrook in 'Progress and Problems: South Asian Economic and Social History c. 1720–1860', *Modern Asian Studies* 22, no.1 (February 1988): 57–96. See also C. A. Bayly, *Indian Society and the Making of the British Empire*, New Cambridge History of India, II, 1 (Cambridge: Cambridge University Press, 1988), 79–89, on military despotism.

18 Sharma, *Famine, Philanthropy and the Colonial State*, 176–77.

19 Sharma, *Famine, Philanthropy and the Colonial State*, 171–92.

20 See Dirks, *Hollow Crown*, and Sharma, *Philanthropy and the Colonial State*.

21 The movement toward uniformity in the self-consciously modern nineteenth century is a key theme in C. A. Bayly's *The Birth of the Modern World, 1780–1914* (Malden, MA & Oxford: Blackwell Publishing, 2004).

22 Sharma, *Famine, Philanthropy and the Colonial State*, 149.

23 Sharma, *Famine, Philanthropy and the Colonial State*. Dirks' *Hollow Crown* also highlights the decline of kings and kingship under colonial rule in the nineteenth century. See Bayly, *Indian Society*, on the economic downturn.

24 As sociologists put it, institutions can enable autonomy and liberty, thereby contributing to greater progress and 'civilization'. See Wagner, *Sociology of Modernity: Liberty and Discipline*, xiii, 19–33. See 'The Carceral' in Foucault's *Discipline and Punish*, 293–308, regarding the importance of 'normality' as created and defended by judges, teachers and social workers, etc. 'Moral and Material Progress and Condition of India' reports were produced from the late 1850s onward. See Michael Mann's introductory essay, '"Torchbearers Upon the Path of Progress"' in Fischer-Tiné and Mann (eds), *Colonialism as Civilizing Mission*, regarding the importance of these 'moral and material progress' reports.

25 Sharma, *Famine, Philanthropy and the Colonial State*, 186–87.

26 See Sharma, *Famine, Philanthropy and the Colonial State*, 135 (W. Crooke's report in 1897) & 159 (1860s reports). The reality of the 1830s was that there was much uncertainty and division about how to proceed as the new state tried to establish itself.

27 See Foucault, *Discipline and Punish*; Dandeker, *Surveillance, Power and Modernity*; and Wagner, *Sociology of Modernity*.

28 Sharma, *Famine, Philanthropy and the Colonial State*, 154.

29 Sharma, *Famine, Philanthropy and the Colonial State*, 136–37.

30 See Kim A. Wagner, *Thuggee: Banditry and the British in Early Nineteenth-Century India* (Houndmills: Palgrave-MacMillan, 2007).

31 Sharma, *Famine, Philanthropy and the Colonial State*.

32 D. A. Washbrook, 'India, 1818–1860: The Two Faces of Colonialism', *The Oxford History of the British Empire*, vol. III, ed. Andrew Porter (Oxford: Oxford University Press, 1999), chapter 18, 395–421.

33 Washbrook, 'India, 1818–1860'.

34 Washbrook, 'India, 1818–1860', see the section 'A Very Military State', 404–08.

35 See Sharma, *Famine, Philanthropy and the Colonial State*, Douglas E. Haynes, 'From Tribute to Philanthropy: The Politics of Gift-giving in a Western City', *Journal of Asian Studies* 46, no. 2 (May 1987): 339–60; Douglas E. Haynes, *Rhetoric and Ritual in Colonial India. The Shaping of a Public Culture in Surat City, 1852–1928* (Berkeley: University of California Press, 1991); and Watt, *Serving the Nation*, chapter 3, 'From Dana to Associational Philanthropy', 65–96.

36 On the late nineteenth century durbars see Bernard S. Cohn, 'Representing Authority in Victorian India' in Hobsbawm and Ranger, (eds) *Invention of Tradition*. On the 1911 durbar see *The Historical Record of the Imperial Visit to India, 1911*. Compiled from official records of the Viceroy and Governor-General of India (London: John Murray [for the Government of India], 1914). To celebrate the 1911 durbar in Delhi gifts of food and other items were made all over north India.

37 *Dana* in this context would mean 'giving' or 'charity', *seva* would be 'service' and *karmayoga* would be disinterested or altruistic performance of one's duties, though by 1900 this also took on the sense of 'the altruistic service of humanity'.

38 Gandhi preferred to call India's untouchables Harijans or 'children of god'. Since about 1970 most untouchables have called themselves *Dalits* or 'the oppressed'.

39 For more information on early-twentieth-century Indian social service organizations and the links between Gandhi and these groups, see Carey A. Watt, *Serving the Nation: Cultures of Service, Association and Citizenship in Colonial India* (Delhi: Oxford University Press, 2005), chapter four 'From Seva to Social Service', 97–129 and pp. 179–81, 204–05 and *passim*. See also Prashant Kidambi's chapter (seven) in Part Three of this book, 'From "Social Reform" to "Social Service": Indian Civic Activism and the Civilizing Mission in Colonial Bombay, c. 1900–20'.

40 On the issue of 'lagging behind' see Carey A. Watt, 'Education for National Efficiency: Constructive Nationalism in North India, 1909–1916', *Modern Asian Studies* 31, no.2 (May 1997): 339–74, and Watt, *Serving the Nation*, the section entitled 'National Efficiency: Progress at the National Level', 44–47.

41 S. Natarajan, *A Century of Social Reform in India*, 2nd ed. (1962 [first published 1955]), 8.

42 On 'national efficiency' see Geoffrey R. Searle, *The Quest for National Efficiency: A Study in British Politics and Political Thought* (Berkeley and Los Angeles: University of California Press, 1971). In the South Asian context see Watt, 'Education for National Efficiency',

and Watt, *Serving the Nation*, 'National Efficiency: Progress at the National Level', 44–47.

43 Watt, *Serving the Nation*, pp. 67–70. *The Social Service Quarterly* was established in 1915.

44 See also Harald Fischer-Tiné, Prashant Kidambi and Shahid Perwez in Parts Two, Three and Four of this book, respectively, on the issue of middle-class and urban values in Indian 'self-civilizing' missions.

45 As Sunil Khilnani remarked, 'the British Raj lived in the city'. Sunil Khilnani, *The Idea of India* (New York: Farrar, Straus and Giroux, 1999), 116.

46 See Watt, *Serving the Nation*, the section of chapter five entitled 'Education Under Indian Control: The Institutional Foundation', 132–38.

47 Charles Tilly, 'The Emergence of Citizenship in France and Elsewhere', *International Review of Social History* 40, Supplement 3 (1995): 223–36.

48 See Prashant Kidambi, 'From "Social Reform" to "Social Service": Indian Civic Activism and the Civilizing Mission in Colonial Bombay, c. 1900–20', in Part Three of this book. See also Prashant Kidambi, *The Making of an Indian Metropolis : Colonial Governance and Public Culture in Bombay, 1890–1920* (Aldershot & Burlington, Vermont: Ashgate Publishing Ltd., 2007).

49 As Harald Fischer-Tiné's chapter on the Salvaton Army (Part Two) demonstrates, civilizing missions could also be directed at poor, working-class 'savages' and 'the great unwashed' in the 'home' or 'metropolitan' British population. Fischer-Tiné points out that Frederick Booth-Tucker, the head of the Salvation Army in India, believed that the Army's 'Soup, Soap and Salvation' formula was applicable worldwide.

50 The Pears' Soap advertisement is reproduced in Alice L. Conklin and Ian Christopher Fletcher (eds), *European Imperialism, 1830–1930:Climax and Contradiction* (Problems in European Civilization Series) (Boston & New York: Houghton Mifflin Company, 1999), 54. This is the page facing the editorial introduction to section two of the book, entitled 'The Imperial Mission', 55–95. Interestingly, the section begins with Kipling's 'The White Man's Burden', 58–59 and ends with Timothy Burke's essay 'Colonialism, Cleanliness, and Civilization in Colonial Rhodesia', 86–95 – in which issues of soap and cleanliness feature prominently.

51 On the compatibility of British Victorian values with Indian upper-caste and *ashraf* values see Harald Fischer-Tiné, 'National Education, Pulp Fiction and the Contradiction of Colonialism: Perceptions of an Educational Experiment in Early-Twentieth-Century India', in Harald Fischer-Tiné and Michael Mann (eds), *Colonialism as Civilizing Mission: Cultural Ideology in British India* (London & New York: Anthem Press, 2004), 236, and Prashant Kidambi's chapter in Part Three of the present volume. See also Susan Bayly, 'Hindu Modernisers and the "Public" Arena: Indigenous Critiques of Caste in Colonial India', in William Radice (ed.), *Swami Vivekanada and the Modernisation of Hinduism* (Delhi: Oxford University Press, 1998), 93–137, and Susan Bayly, *Caste, Society and Politics in India from the eighteenth century to the modern age* (Cambridge: Cambridge University Press, 1999). This topic is also explored in Watt, *Serving the Nation*, 15–16, 189–90.

52 See Watt, *Serving the Nation*, 50–52 and 116–20 and 151–58 on the Boy Scouts and Girl Guides in India. See also Carey A. Watt, 'The promise of "character" and the spectre of sedition: the boy scout movement and colonial consternation in India, 1908–1921', *South Asia*, New Series 22, no.2 (December 1999): 37–62, and Carey Watt, '"No showy muscles": the Boy Scouts and the global dimensions of physical culture and bodily health in Britain and colonial India', in Nelson R. Block and Tammy M. Proctor

(eds), *Scouting Frontiers: Youth in the Scout Movement's First Century* (Newcastle: Cambridge Scholars Publishing, 2009), 121–42.

53 Ranajit Guha, 'Discipline and Mobilize' in Partha Chatterjee and Gyanendra Pandey (eds), *Subaltern Studies VII: Writings on South Asian History and Society* (New Delhi: Oxford University Press, 2003), 69–120. *Swadeshi* literally means 'of our own country' and represented the practice of boycotting British-made goods in favour of supporting Indian industries and promoting Indian self-reliance.

54 See the discussion of Holi in Bombay in Kidambi's essay in Part Three of this volume.

55 See Harald Fischer-Tiné's chapter on the Salvation Army in Part Two of this volume.

56 Foucault, *Discipline and Punish*, 168–69. For a further discussion of this issue see Watt, '"No Showy Muscles"', 130–32.

57 Vivekananda is quoted in G. Beckerlegge, *Swami Vivekananada's Legacy of Service* (Delhi: Oxford University Press, 2006), 188.

58 See Watt, *Serving the Nation*, 104–07, and Beckerlegge, *Swami Vivekananada's Legacy of Service*, 150–69 and 187–88. See also Peter van der Veer, *Imperial Encounters: Religion and Modernity in India and Britain* (Princeton and Oxford: Princeton University Press, 2001), 46–50, 72–74, 99–100.

59 This was in 1914. 'They Teach but to Serve', by Professor Seva Ram and N. Pherwani, *Vedic Magazine and Gurukula Samachar*, VII, nos 9–10 (April & May 1914): 707–18.

60 Harald Fischer-Tiné, 'National Education, Pulp Fiction and the Contradiction of Colonialism', in Fischer-Tiné and Mann (eds), *Colonialism as Civilizing Mission*, 245. The Sannyasin referred to was probably Swami Dayananda, who founded the Arya Samaj in 1875 and was giving a fictional address to John Bull in the *Vedic Magazine*.

61 Watt, 'An Overview of the Servants of India Society, Seva Samiti (Allahabad), Theosophical Society, and Arya Samaj', *Serving the Nation*, Appendix II, 211–15.

62 When responding to questions about the Constructive Programme in the early 1940s Gandhi stated that it had as many as eighteen components but acknowledged that the Congress was only committed to supporting six of them. See 'The Implications of the Constructive Programme' (1940) and 'Constructive Programme: Its Meaning and Place' (1941) in *Mahatma Gandhi: The Essential Writings*, edited and introduced by Judith M. Brown, Oxford World's Classics (Oxford: Oxford University Press, 2008), 161–64 and 164–84.

63 The phrase 'alternative modernity' is borrowed from chapter four entitled 'An Alternative Modernity' in David Hardiman, *Gandhi in His Time and Ours: The Global Legacy of His Ideas* (New York: Columbia University Press, 2004), 66–93.

64 David Arnold, *Gandhi* (Harlow, UK: Longman / Pearson Education Ltd, 2001), 130.

65 See Mohandas K. Gandhi, *Hind Swaraj and Other Writings*, edited and introduced by Anthony J. Parel (Cambridge: Cambridge University Press, 1997).

66 See Mohandas K. Gandhi, *Autobiography – The Story of My Experiments with Truth*, translated from Gujerati by Mahadev Desai (New York: Dover Publications, Inc., 1983), 77, 120, 140, 265–75, and 'Gandhi's mission, and the influences on him' regarding Thoreau, Ruskin, and Tolstoy in *Mahatma Gandhi: The Essential Writings*, 28–34. See also Arnold, *Gandhi*, 68–70, Hardiman, *Gandhi*, 74–76.

67 Arnold, *Gandhi*, 184–85, 202–03, Partha Chatterjee, chapter four 'The Moment of Manoeuvre: Gandhi's Critique of Civil Society' and chapter five 'The Moment of Arrival: Nehru and the Passive Revolution', from *Nationalist Thought and the Colonial World. A Derivative Discourse?* (Tokyo and London: Zed Books Ltd., 1986), 85–130, 131–66.

68 Arnold, *Gandhi*, 184.

69 Watt, *Serving the Nation*, 171–77. The quote from Gokhale is on 171.

70 Arnold, *Gandhi*, 86. Emphasis added. Arnold also notes that the Congress was not an adequate vehicle for the scope of Gandhi anti-colonial objectives and his Constructive Programme represented 'the broader "civilising" objectives Gandhi had in mind'. See Arnold, *Gandhi*, 129. The 1917 Champaran *satyagraha* (Gandhi's 'truth-force' technique and movement characterized by morally-justified non-violent resistance) in Bihar was Gandhi's first political (and, as we have noted, social) campaign after his return to India in 1915. Gandhi's campaign aimed to improve the miserable conditions of Indian indigo workers exploited by European planters, and he won significant concessions within a few months.

71 See Mohandas K. Gandhi, *Autobiography – The Story of My Experiments with Truth*, translated from Gujerati by Mahadev Desai (New York: Dover Publications, Inc., 1983), Part V, chapters XII through XIX, 363–83, and Arnold, *Gandhi*, 86.

72 Jawaharlal Nehru, *The Discovery of India*, (Delhi: Oxford University Press, 1994 [first published 1946]), 361–62 and 363.

73 Ben Zachariah, 'In Search of the Indigenous', in Harald Fischer-Tiné and Michael Mann (eds), *Colonialism as Civilizing Mission: Cultural Ideology in British India* (London & New York: Anthem Press, 2004), 248–69.

74 On Gandhi as 'a Bania who became a Brahmin' see B. R. Ambedkar, 'A Reply to the Mahatma', appendix II of *Annihilation of Caste with a reply to Mahatma Gandhi; and Castes in India: their mechanism, genesis, and development* (Jullunder, Punjab: Bheem Patrika Publications, 1968 [originally published in 1936]), 116–27. On Gandhi as 'a fanatic Hindu' see B. R. Ambedkar, *Mr. Gandhi and the Emancipation of the Untouchables* (Jullunder, Punjab: Bheem Patrika Publications, 1943), 51–52, and 'Gandhi, a fanatic Hindu', in *Gandhi and Gandhism* (Jullunder, Punjab: Bheem Patrika Publications, c. 1970), 3–4. Gandhi was of the Modh Bania caste and therefore he was in the varna or caste group of Vaishya or the merchant castes, below the varnas of Brahmins (priests and learned and literate elites) and Kshatriya (rulers and warriors) but above the Shudras (labourers and artisans) and Untouchables (who performed ritually impure and polluting tasks). Thus, Gandhi was of a clean, twice-born caste group and, as David Arnold has noted, Banias held higher status in Gandhi's native Gujarat than in other parts of India. See Arnold, *Gandhi*, 21–22.

75 Ambedkar, *Mr. Gandhi and the Emancipation of the Untouchables*, 54.

76 See Ambedkar, 'Gandhi, The Doom of the Untouchables' in *Gandhi and Gandhism*, 59–61. Gandhi's launch of the Harijan campaign followed his 'epic fast' of September 1932 which was successful in derailing Ambedkar's attempt to win separate electorates for India's fifty million or so untouchables at the 1931 Round Table Conference in London and the subsequent Communal Award announced by British Prime Minister Ramsay MacDonald in August 1932. In a time of growing communal tension Gandhi and other Congress leaders were alarmed at the prospect of losing such a significant part of 'the Hindu community'.

77 Arnold, *Gandhi*, 177–78.

78 Hardiman, *Gandhi*, 147–51 and 153.

79 Hardiman, *Gandhi*, 78.

80 Hardiman, *Gandhi*, 68–69 and Arnold, *Gandhi*, 68. Hardiman points out that Gandhi used the Gujarati word *sudharo* as an equivalent for the English 'civilization' in the Gujarati version of *Hind Swaraj*, and that *sudharo* can be translated as 'good conduct' or

'good way of life', which to Gandhi meant living morally and curbing one's material desires and the fetishization of technology.

81 Zachariah, 'In Search of the Indigenous', 255–65. Kumarappa's *Why the Village Movement?* was first published in 1936 and had reached a fifth edition by 1949.

82 Nehru, *Discovery of India*, 340. A *sadhu* can also be a (Hindu) ascetic, like a *sannyasi*. A *brahmachari* is, more broadly, someone in the life-stage or ashram of *brahmacharya*. This is normally the period of studenthood from roughly the age of eight to twenty-five when upper-caste, 'twice-born' Hindu boys would start their education while observing a strict and celibate life, which included learning self-control and discipline. In practice, as Gandhi showed at the age of 37, one could take a vow of *brahmacharya* at any age.

83 On the interesting and complex history of ascetics in India see William R. Pinch, *Warrior Ascetics and Indian Empires* (Cambridge: Cambridge University Press, 2006), 231–255, Peter van der Veer, 'Taming the Ascetic: Devotionalism in a Hindu Monastic Order', *Man* (N.S.) 22, no.4 (Dec. 1987): 680–695, and C. A. Bayly, *Rulers, Townsmen, and Bazaars: North Indian Society in the Age of British Expansion, 1770–1870* (New York: Cambridge University Press, 1983). On Gandhi's creative assimilation of older Indian ascetic practices into his 'constructive' and political campaigns, see Daniel Adsett, 'Gandhi's New Ascetics: Non-violent Confrontational Renouncers in Twentieth-Century Indian Nationalism' (unpublished honours essay, St Thomas University, Fredericton, 2009).

84 Jawaharlal Nehru, *An Autobiography* (Delhi: Oxford University Press, 1989 [first published in 1936 by John Lane, The Bodley Head Ltd., London]), 403.

85 Quoted in Jacques Attali, *Gândhî, ou l'éveil des humiliés* (Fayard, Le Livre de Poche, 2007), 353–54.

86 'Draft Constitution of the Satyagraha Ashram' (before 20 May 1915) and 'New Constitution of the Satyagraha Ashram (1928)' in *Mahatma Gandhi: The Essential Writings*, 106–12 and 113–24. The quotation is from page 109.

87 See chapter five, 'Sarala Behn – Catherine Mary Heilemann (1901–1982)' in Sharon MacDonald, *Neither Memsahibs Nor Missionaries: Western Women Who Supported the Indian Independence Movement* (unpublished PhD dissertation, University of New Brunswick, 2010), 141–61.

88 Susanne Hoeber Rudolph, 'Civil Society and the Realm of Freedom', *Economic and Political Weekly*, 13 May 2000, 1762–69.

89 See Jana Tschurenev, 'Incorporation and Differentiation: Popular Education and the Imperial Civilizing Mission in Early-19th-Century India' and Harald Fischer-Tiné, 'Reclaiming Savages in "Darkest England" and "Darkest India": The Salvation Army as Transnational Agent of the Civilizing Mission' in Part Two, and Prashant Kidambi, 'From "Social Reform" to "Social Service": Indian Civic Activism and the Civilizing Mission in Colonial Bombay, c. 1900–20', in Part Three.

90 For an overview of economic development, planning and the Five-Year Plans see Dietmar Rothermund, *An Economic History of India: From Precolonial Times to 1986* (London, New York & Sydney: Croom Helm, 1988), 126–35 and 185–89.

91 Promilla Kalhan, *Gulzarilal Nanda: a life in the service of the people* (New Delhi: Indian Association of Social Science Institutions, Allied Publishers, 1997), 85, and Jawaharlal Nehru, 'To C. D. Deshmukh', New Delhi, 26 January 1952, *Selected Works of Jawaharlal Nehru* (henceforth *SWJN*), 2nd series, vol. 17, ed. S. Gopal (New Delhi: Jawaharlal Nehru Memorial Fund, 1995), 97–100.

92 Jawaharlal Nehru, 'To C. D. Deshmukh', New Delhi, 26 January 1952, *SWJN*, 2ⁿᵈ series, vol. 17, 97–100.

93 Jawaharlal Nehru, 'Letter to Chief Ministers', 5 July 1952, *SWJN*, 2ⁿᵈ series, vol. 18, ed. S. Gopal (New Delhi: Jawaharlal Nehru Memorial Fund, 1996), 631–42. The BSS was the twelfth of thirty-one issues addressed in the missive to Chief Ministers.

94 Nehru remained president of the BSS until his death in 1964, when Nanda replaced him. Kalhan, *Gulzarilal Nanda*, 89.

95 Gandhi was born on 2 October 1869. By starting the Community Development Programme on Gandhi's *jayanti* (birthday celebration) Nehru was surely trying to gain greater 'Gandhian' legitimacy for his government's initiative. Benjamin Zachariah also makes this point about Gandhi as 'a crucial legitimating icon' and Congress finding 'new uses for Gandhian ideas'. See Benjamin Zachariah, *Nehru* (London and New York: Routledge, 2004), 194.

96 *Commission of Enquiry Into the Affairs of the Bharat Sevak Samaj*, chaired by Justice J. L. Kapur, in Virendra Kumar (ed.), *Committees and Commissions in India, 1947–73*, vol. 9 (Delhi: Concept Publishing Company, 1975) 131–56, and Kalhan, *Gulzarilal Nanda*, 91–94.

97 Kalhan, *Gulzarilal Nanda*, 85.

98 Jawaharlal Nehru, 'An Augury for the Future', speech at the inauguration of the Madhya Bharat branch of the BSS in Indore, 15 September 1952, *SWJN*, 2ⁿᵈ series, vol. 19, ed. S. Gopal (New Delhi: Jawaharlal Nehru Memorial Fund, 1996), 91–92.

99 Jawaharlal Nehru, 'Unity in Diversity', speech at a public meeting, Shillong, 19 October 1952, *SWJN*, 2ⁿᵈ series, vol. 20, ed. S. Gopal (New Delhi: Jawaharlal Nehru Memorial Fund, 1997), 3–9. A *mohalla* is a neighbourhood or locality.

100 See Jawaharlal Nehru, 'Strength of the Bharat Sevak Samaj', a speech at a conference of BSS conveners, New Delhi, 7 May 1953, and 'To Gulzarilal Nanda', 23 May 1953, *SWJN*, 2ⁿᵈ series, vol. 22, eds Ravinder Kumar and H. Y. Sharada Prasad (New Delhi: Jawaharlal Nehru Memorial Fund, 1998), 127–28 and 129–30, respectively. The organizations Nehru mentioned were all Hindu fundamentalist and communalist parties that generally believed that India should be for Hindus only, and were active in anti-Muslim violence which destabilized India and undermined the country's secular and inclusive principles. Moreover, the Mahasabha and RSS (Rashtriya Swayamsevak Sangh) were linked to Gandhi's assassin, Nathuram Godse, and thus to the killing of Gandhi on 30 January 1948.

101 See Jawaharlal Nehru, 'The Functions of the Bharat Sevak Samaj', a note to M. O. Mathai, 1 October 1952, and 'A New Work Culture', speech at inauguration of BSS branches in Tamil Nadu, Mysore and Coorg, Madras, 10 October 1952, *SWJN*, 2ⁿᵈ series, vol. 19, 92–94 and 94–97, and 'Programme of Bharat Sevak Samaj', 24 April 1953, *SWJN*, 2ⁿᵈ series, vol. 22, 126–27. See also schedule II, 'Functions', of the Bharat Sevak Samaj constitution, http://www.bss.in/BSSCon3.htm (accessed 14 July 2010). A draft constitution of the BSS was published on 12 August 1952. The on-line version is not dated but the preamble appears to have been written in 1952 since it refers to 'our country which has just achieved independence'. Schedule III of the constitution appears to have been written – or at least updated – in 1962 as it refers to the BSS's 'life of about a decade'. Information taken or quoted from the BSS constitution has been corroborated by other sources such as the *Selected Works of Jawaharlal Nehru (SWJN)* and biographies of Nehru or G. L. Nanda.

102 Jawaharlal Nehru, 'A New Work Culture', Madras, 10 October 1952, *SWJN*, 2ⁿᵈ series, vol. 19, 94–97.

103 See Jawaharlal Nehru, 'Programme of Bharat Sevak Samaj', 24 April 1953, *SWJN*, 2nd series, vol. 22, 126–27, and Schedule II of the Bharat Sevak Samaj constitution, 2–3.

104 Jawaharlal Nehru, 'Programme of Bharat Sevak Samaj', 24 April 1953, *SWJN*, 2nd series, vol. 22, 126–27.

105 Nehru referred to the BSS as a 'voluntary organization' in Jawaharlal Nehru, 'India and the World', a speech at a meeting in Lucknow, 22 November 1952, *SWJN*, 2nd series, vol. 20, 19. The descriptors 'non-official' and 'non-political' were employed in the 19 October 1952 speech cited in the block quote above.

106 The BSS was given Rs. 3 crore (Rs. 30 million) for 30 different schemes between 1953 and 1967, plus the free use of many government buildings and properties. *Commission of Enquiry Into the Affairs of the Bharat Sevak Samaj*, in Kumar (ed.), *Committees and Commissions in India, 1947–73*, 131–33. Regarding the BSS as an arm of government see 142–44.

107 Jawaharlal Nehru, 'A New Work Culture', speech at inauguration of BSS branches in Tamil Nadu, Mysore and Coorg, Madras, 10 October 1952, *SWJN*, 2nd series, vol. 19, 94–97.

108 See the BSS constitution preamble: 'it has been from the outset stressed that the formation of the Samaj should not lead to any duplication of efforts or overlapping of activities. All agencies working in this field should collaborate and by mutual help greatly enhance the range and effectiveness of the entire programme of constructive voluntary activity in the country. Samaj can become a focal centre for such collaboration.' See http://www.bss.in/BSSCon1.htm (accessed 14 July 2010).

109 See Nehru's comments in 1956 regarding how local social work organizations in various cities and elsewhere 'were doing good work. But, taken as a whole, there was not only a complete lack of coordination but also no driving force.' Moreover, the new Central Social Welfare Board, established exactly one year after the BSS, on 12 August 1953, was charged with tackling social work issues 'for the first time . . . in an organized way' and reaching rural areas. This was an insult to existing NGOs. See Jawaharlal Nehru, 'To Abdul Kalam Azad', 8 June 1956 and 'To Abdul Kalam Azad', 9 June 1956, *SWJN*, 2nd series, vol. 33, eds H. Y. Sharada Prasad, A. K. Damodaran and Mushirul Hasan (New Delhi: Jawaharlal Nehru Memorial Fund, 2004), 205–08.

110 See the preamble BSS constitution, which referred to the need for useful work 'on a very large scale' and that 'no institution existed' for assuming the responsibilities of stimulating and mobilizing voluntary efforts on 'a nation-wide basis'. Nehru also referred to the BSS filling a vacuum in India: 'I have felt that there is a vacuum in India at the present time. There is a demand for this vacuum to be filled. I want to know how far the Bharat Sevak Samaj can fill that vacuum.' See Jawaharlal Nehru, 'Strength of the Bharat Sevak Samaj', New Delhi, 7 May 1953, *SWJN*, 2nd series, vol. 22, 127–28.

111 Jawaharlal Nehru, 'The Content of Social Welfare', *The Hindustan Times*, 20 October 1940, in *Jawaharlal Nehru: An Anthology*, ed. Sarvepalli Gopal (Delhi: Oxford University Press, 1980), 254–55.

112 See Nehru's address to the Indian Conference of Social Work, *Indian Journal of Social Work*, vol. XII, no. 4 (1951–52).

113 See Benjamin Zachariah on 'The Nehruvians and the Nehruvian Project', in Zachariah, *Nehru*, 187–93.

114 B. R. Nanda, *Jawaharlal Nehru: Rebel and Statesman* (Delhi: Oxford University Press, 1998), 193.

115 S. R. Venkataraman to Kunzru, 19 Jan. 1954, and Kunzru to Venkataraman, 21 Jan. 1954, Servants of India Society papers, S. R. Bajpai, file 44, 1954–55, Nehru Memorial Museum and Library, New Delhi.

116 Kunzru headed the Kunzru Committee, which was appointed in 1959 to study the BSS's physical education and youth welfare activities. Its report was completed in 1963. See the *Commission of Enquiry Into the Affairs of the Bharat Sevak Samaj*, in Kumar (ed.), *Committees and Commissions in India, 1947–73*, 137–38.

117 *Servants of the People Society, New Delhi: 50 Years in the Service of the People: Golden Jubilee Souvenir Volume* (New Delhi: 1972); Vaikunth L. Mehta, 'Social Service in a Welfare State' in *The Social Service League, Bombay: Souvenir, Golden Jubilee Celebration*, 20 March 1961, 93–100.

118 Maganbhai P. Desai, 'The Present Situation', *Harijan*, vol. XVII, June 6 1953, 108–09.

119 Judith M. Brown, *Nehru* (Harlow, UK: Longman / Pearson Education Ltd, 1999), 103, 137, 184–85. The quotation is from page 137.

120 Jawaharlal Nehru, 'Charges of Partisan Functioning of Government', from a speech in the Lok Sabha, 4 July 1952, New Dehi, parliamentary debates, *SWJN*, 2nd series, vol. 18, 283–95. The quote is from page 288.

121 BSS constitution, preamble.

122 BSS constitution, preamble.

123 Ramachandra Guha, *India After Gandhi: The History of the World's Largest Democracy* (New York: Harper Perennial, 2008), 215.

124 Bhiku Parekh, 'Jawaharlal Nehru and the Crisis of Modernisation', in *Modern Indian Culture and Society: Critical Concepts in Asian Studies*, vol. I, edited by Knut A. Jacobsen (New York: Routledge, 2009), 198–99.

125 The Ford Foundation (which arose out of the Ford Motor Company) was founded in 1936, but operated locally in Michigan till 1950, when it went national and international. New Delhi was the Ford Foundation's first overseas office, established in 1952. It remains the Ford Foundation's biggest overseas bureau today. Senior Foundation officials worked very closely with the Indian government in the 1950s and 1960s, and they designed and managed large-scale poverty reduction projects, especially in rural areas. Douglas Ensminger, the first Ford Foundation representative in India (1952–69) was reported to have had 'a close personal rapport' with Prime Minister Nehru. See 'Investing in Ideas, Innovations and Institutions: An Overview', by Mark Robinson, Chris Robinson and Gowher Rizvi, in *The Ford Foundation, 1952–2002: Celebrating 50 years of Partnership* (10 vols. plus the Overview).

126 See Guha, *India After Gandhi*, 215, for the quote about 'a socialistic pattern of society'.

127 Guha, *India After Gandhi*, 220–23.

128 This is based on the study made by anthropologist S. C. Dube in western Uttar Pradesh in 1954, as cited in Guha, *India After Gandhi*, 224.

129 The two Nehru quotations are from Moraes. See Frank Moraes, *Jawaharlal Nehru: A Biography* (New York: The Macmillan Company, 1956), 432–34.

130 E. N. Mangat Rai, *Patterns of Administrative Development in Independent India*, University of London, Institute of Commonwealth Studies Commonwealth Papers No. 19, general editor Prof. W. H. Morris-Jones (University of London: Published for the Institute of Commonwealth Studies The Athlone Press, 1976), 74.

131 BSS constitution, preamble.

132 Jawaharlal Nehru, 'Programme of Bharat Sevak Samaj', 24 April 1953, New Delhi, *SWJN*, 2ⁿᵈ series, vol. 22, 126–27.

133 Jawaharlal Nehru, 'To K.N. Katju', 10 November 1952, New Delhi, *SWJN*, 2ⁿᵈ series, vol. 20, 175–76.

134 Jawaharlal Nehru, 'Mobilization of Manpower', foreword written 25 April 1952 to a pamphlet, *Bharat Sevak Samaj*, published by the Planning Commission on 22 June 1952, *SWJN*, 2ⁿᵈ series, vol. 18, 29–30.

135 Jawaharlal Nehru, 'A New Work Culture', Madras, 10 October 1952, *SWJN*, 2ⁿᵈ series, vol. 19, 96.

136 B. N. Mullik, *My Years with Nehru, 1948–1964* (Bombay etc: Allied Publishers, 1972), 90–93. The quotation is from page 91.

137 Nehru made numerous references to Sevagram in the early 1950s and undertook an important trip to the Gandhian ashram in late October and early November 1952 to attend a Basic Education Conference. He fondly reminisced about his past work with Gandhi and was impressed by the 'extreme simplicity and artistry' of the conference as well as its low cost. See Jawaharlal Nehru, 'Letters to Chief Ministers', 20 November 1952, New Delhi, *SWJN*, 2ⁿᵈ series, vol. 20, 547–57.

138 See schedule III of the BSS constitution, which seems to have been revised in 1962 since it refers to the BSS's 'existence of a decade'.

139 Michael Brecher, *Nehru: A Political Biography* (London: Oxford University Press, 1959), 6. Brecher was visiting from McGill University (in Montréal) and spent several days travelling with Nehru in March 1956.

140 Benjamin Zachariah, *Developing India: An Intellectual and Social History c. 1930–50* (Delhi: Oxford University Press, 2005), 43–46, 242–53.

141 See Cooper, 'Writing the History of Development', 14–15, on this point. Cooper discusses how the rhetoric of development could encourage people to make claims on colonial and postcolonial states in the mid twentieth century. See Brown, *Nehru*, 141–42, regarding the growing policization of individuals and pressure groups leading to greater demands on the state, and Dipesh Chakrabarty, '"In the Name of Politics": Democracy and the Power of the Multitude in India', in Dipesh Chakrabarty, Rochona Majumdar and Andrew Sartori, eds., *From the Colonial to the Postcolonial: India and Pakistan in Transition* (Delhi: Oxford University Press, 2007), 31–54, on Nehru's concerns about noisy and inappropriate political behaviour in postcolonial India. Guha, *India After Gandhi*, 117, has written of 'the precocious existence of a "rights culture"' in India starting before independence and continuing into postcolonial India.

142 Chakrabarty, '"In the Name of Politics"'.

143 Regarding Nehru as head of the Bharat Scouts and Guides see Lakshmi Mazumdar (ed.), *A Dream Came True*, reprint (New Delhi: Bharat Scouts and Guides, 1997 [first published 1968]). Nehru worked with Gandhi to organize national volunteers in 1920 and Gandhi became the 'protector' of a National Boy Scouts Association in the early 1920s. On this point see Watt, *Serving the Nation*, 179, 186.

144 See the discussion of Ranajit Guha's 'Discipline and Mobilize' (2003) in section II, above.

145 It is interesting in this respect that Chakrabarty actually quotes a speech entitled 'Hard Work for Building a New India' that Nehru gave at the third All-India Bharat Sevak Samaj meeting in Nagpur on 12 March 1955 (though he mistakenly says it was held in Chandigarh), and yet does not discuss the BSS, planning or community development. See Chakrabarty, '"In the Name of Politics"', 34.

146 Foucault, *Discipline and Punish*, 231–56 and 293–308. We should note, however, that Foucault acknowledges that disciplinary methods and institutions existed before 'modernity' (see page 137), as does Ranajit Guha in 'Discipline and Mobilize'.
147 Cooper, 'Writing the History of Development'.
148 The first two ashrams were in South Africa: the Phoenix Settlement (established in 1904 near Durban) and Tolstoy Farm (established in 1910 near Johannesburg). The fourth was Sevagram (established in 1936 near Wardha in central India).
149 Hardiman, *Gandhi*, 202–03.

Afterword

IMPROVEMENT, PROGRESS AND DEVELOPMENT

Michael Mann

On the Legitimacy of the Civilizing Mission

More than 100,000 Indian soldiers, most of them hailing from the Panjab, fought in Great Britain's army on the battlefields of Belgium and northern France during the Great War of 1914–18, also known as World War I. Along the vast system of trenches criss-crossing Flanders and the Champagne region they were witness to how nations that understood and defined themselves as the most civilized ones of the world waged the most barbaric war that had hitherto been fought on the European continent if not worldwide. However, by far the largest numbers of Indian soldiers, namely more than 600,000, were sent to Mesopotamia to attack and ultimately invade the Ottoman Empire's eastern provinces, which later came to form Iraq.[1] Furthermore, since the 'Western powers' regarded the Ottoman Empire to be an 'Oriental' state, which was by definition (again according to Western understanding) a despotic regime and for that reason not a part of the world of civilized nations, military campaigns in the 'East' did not receive the same attention as did the west-European theatres of war, even though warfare in the former was as gruesome as in the latter.

Despite the disastrous warfare in Mesopotamia killing tens of thousands of Indian soldiers, it was the gruesome war in Europe which deeply influenced the Indian soldiers' perception of European powers, their 'culture of warfare' and, more generally, their civilizations. The barbarity of the trenches, in particular the gas-attacks, the relentless heavy artillery bombardments along with the huge amount of men and material that were destroyed – in short, industrial warfare – made Indian soldiers doubt the claims of superiority made by European nation states. Thus, it is not difficult to imagine why, in the eyes of many of the Indian soldiers returning to British India, imperial powers like France, Germany and Great Britain had not only lost their status as civilized people but, consequently, also their justification to civilize other people. The foundations of colonialism had been shaken by the eruption of savage warfare among these European states.[2]

As for the soldiers coming home, the political situation in British India was taking a turn from bad to worse. Instead of constitutional reforms being carried forward, which the returning soldiers as well as the political elite of India were expecting from the Government of India in New Delhi and the Imperial Government in London as reward for the Indian material and human contribution to the war, reforms were suspended. To aggravate the situation, the Rowlatt-Act, named after its author Mr. S. A. T. Rowlatt, stipulated strict rules and regulations for the Panjab. They were meant to act as preventive measures to suppress political unrest from the outset. For example, the act forbade assemblies of more than three persons. Yet this did not stop many Panjabis from gathering to debate the political situation. On 13 April 1919, approximately 3,500 people came together in Jallianwala Bagh, a former walled garden in Amritsar. To set an example, General Reginald Dyer ordered troops to march into the enclosed area and fire upon the peacefully assembled people. According to estimates, at least 400 persons were killed and some 1,200 wounded. Among the victims were men, women and children.[3] In the introduction to this volume, Carey Watt has already hinted at the Amritsar massacre's significance in pointing out the role of British violence and brutality undermining claims to a superior civilization.

Indian public opinion unequivocally regarded the 'Amritsar Massacre' as a brutal act of (British) barbarity. Within a few years, the British had lost credit as a civilized and civilizing nation, at least in the eyes of the Indian political class. The ensuing public debate questioned the ideological foundations of the civilizing mission and its essential assumptions of racial, cultural and moral superiority. Without a doubt, this ideology was at the core of all colonial legitimacy. To question this ideology meant questioning colonial rule as such. As far as radical public opinion was concerned, the legitimacy of colonial rule had ended following the events in Europe and Punjab, and in general, colonial legitimacy was in deep crisis. During the following decade the public sphere was preoccupied with two questions: firstly whether, if at all, the political class should cooperate with the colonial regime, at least temporarily; and secondly whether immediate independence should be demanded. In any case, the end of colonial rule was being envisaged. Even the British anticipated the end of their regime in South Asia, although in a distant rather than near future.[1]

An all-Indian public opinion had been emerging since the beginning of the twentieth century. Between 1905 and 1909, the Swadeshi-Movement in Bengal demanded and propagated the idea of 'home rule'. The agitation soon spilled over the borders of Bengal and, arguably for the first time, created the feeling of a national awakening. At the same time, the 'Fourteen Points' of American President Woodrow Wilson, promulgated on 8 January 1918, initiated an India-wide public debate. Wilson's proclamation regarding the right to self-determination for all people as nations prompted questions as to whether India already constituted a nation or whether that nation still had to be forged. This debate included the question regarding whether India was, at present, a civilized country or whether it still needed to be 'guided' and/or educated towards becoming a civilized people and nation.[5] In the heat of the debate, the Amritsar Massacre decided the latter question insofar as Great Britain could no longer be seen as a civilized nation justified in governing India. Conversly, the Rowlatt Satyagraha and Non-Cooperation Movement of Mohandas K. Gandhi in 1919 and 1920 as well as the Khilafat Movement demonstrated that the populace of British India was willing to act peacefully and collectively as a civilized nation, at least according to the contemporary understanding of the British and Indian political class and public opinion.[6]

However, the debate on self-determination and the end of the Non-Cooperation movement also demonstrates that the ideology of the civilizing mission had been internalized by most of India's nationalist politicians. The campaign was stopped by Gandhi after an infuriated crowd had set fire to a police station in Chauri Chaura burning several policemen – an act which Gandhi condemned as uncivilized. According to Gandhi, India had to act as a civilized nation. Yet, for several decades Indian reformers and politicians had claimed, firstly, that India had been a nation since time immemorial; secondly, that India was the homestead of the world's civilizations; and thirdly, that the values of that civilization simply had to be revitalized to build the nation.[7] To make this vision come true projects like the Arya Samaj's model Gurukul school in Kangri tried to educate young Indians in traditional values and modern sciences.[8] Modern sciences, i.e. 'Western' sciences, were regarded an appropriate means to uplift India's youth and to make it fit to rule the country. At the same time, however, Gandhi, among others, condemned Western sciences and technology as uncivilized because they promoted materialism and would therefore ruin all of India (not only the youth).[9] A similar point regarding concerns about the 'colonization of the mind' of urban, middle-class and Western-educated Indians has also been made in the introduction to this volume.

It was obvious, too, that among politicians, agitators, journalists and writers there existed no common idea, ideology or programme. Even if India and Indians did not need British assistance to improve and develop the country it was, nevertheless, commonly held opinion that the country and the people had to be 'developed' for self-government as an independent Indian nation. In this way the civilizing mission had been internalized, since it accepted the assertion that India's civilization remained 'backward', even at the beginning of the twentieth century. The debate reflected the British civilizing mission's notion that India was indeed unfit to rule itself and that the country (still) needed the benevolent and paternalistic guidance of the British. Denying this sort of colonial guidance or education, many Indian 'nationalists' were confronted with the dilemma that they still lacked a concept of civilization and, in particular, one which would be applicable to India. In short, this manifestation of mental asymmetry depicts only one, although one very important, aspect of the unequal colonial relationship between Great Britain and British India. Against this background it seems sensible to take a closer look at the origins and ideology of the civilizing mission.

On the Origins of the Civilizing Mission

First of all it makes sense to take a separate look at the each of the two words in the term 'civilizing mission'. The word 'mission' has its origins in the Medieval Latin word *missio* meaning instruction, task or duty. With a religious, particularly Christian background the connotation expands to the sending out of one or more persons who act in the name of god (or any other metaphysical being). Typically such persons, missionaries, communicate a spiritual idea or pursue a specific project inspired by divine instructions. The idea of a mission to disseminate a belief is strongly related to Christian religions, yet also to Islamic religions. In a non-religious secular context, however, the meaning of mission ranges from the sending out of persons on special charge to the psychological phenomenon of a 'sense of mission' (German: *Sendungsbewusstsein*) which becomes manifest in single persons, a group of persons or even in whole nations. A national sense of mission may have religious roots or backgrounds as it is the case, for example, in present-day USA.[10] Looking at the history of the beginning of the twenty-first century one may assume that there is a civilizing mission that is operating internationally. An indication of this may be seen in the infamous 'Coalition of the Willing' ready to attack Iraq in 2003, as Carey Watt has noted in section one of his introduction to this book, entitled 'Civilizing Missions Today?'.

The term 'civilization' refers to the overall cultural development of societies and has basically two connotations. First it describes a process of becoming a civilized society, and secondly it describes the condition, the state of being a civilized society. In contradistinction, uncivilized marks the lower or absent state of a group's or society's cultural development. According to Norbert Elias civilization is a multi-dimensional process of learning which constantly reacts to external pressure and permanently acts in accordance to internal norms by means of self-control.[11] Additionally, another distinction may illustrate the different associations of civilization. Civilization written with capital 'C' refers to *cives* originally denominating the ancient Roman citizen with his self-organizations. Therefore, 'Civilization' also denotes an urban culture, private and public law, arts and sciences and, more generally, politics that pursue and proliferate universalistic (of course Western) ideas of rule of law and human rights as they came to exist in Europe from the eighteenth century onwards. Civilization with a small 'c' and sometimes a plural 's' is a descriptive category referring to the anthropological, historical and social development of humans. Comparing 'Civilization' and 'civilizations', the first can be set up as an ethical category or scale to measure the latter.[12]

As one can imagine, such a concept of civilization developed during the European Enlightenment caused much critique. Already Montaigne and Rousseau, for example, argued that not civilization but nature is the first and last norm of egalitarian human life as incarnated in the 'noble savage'. Secondly, in the early nineteenth century western European philosophers denied the idea that an (alleged) universal rationality and universal natural law could justify the assimilation of deep cultural and civilizational differences. And thirdly, some present-day opinions state that there exists a basic and, therefore, undeniable incommensurability of cultures and civilizations as can be seen, for example, in different social norms and moral ideas, different beliefs and religions and ideas of values. Apart from these theoretical and philosophical concerns, the idea of the civilizing mission takes cultural differences for granted and creates, in the long run, asymmetries between the missionaries and those proselytized. A mission as a committed action of a 'master-culture' aims, on the one hand, at building civilization(s) and, on the other hand, at changing civilization(s),[13] implying, at best, a partial transformation of the existing civilization and, at worst, its utter destruction.

Seen from a more general perspective every form, and in particular the modern form, of the civilizing mission consists of two dimensions. The first is the horizontal one, in particular, the expansion related to the idea that the Christian mission should disseminate the divine message *per pedes apostolorum* among as many people and in as many countries and communities of the world as possible. Similar to the universal idea of an evangelical mission at the turn of the seventeenth century, the civilizing mission took, from its conceptual beginnings in the second half of the eighteenth century, an explicitly external and consequently global perspective. Second, the vertical dimension concentrates on a society's internal uplifting to better the material and moral condition of its people – in short: an inner mission.[11] It was in this context that 'improvement' and 'development' of any given society became the object of the civilizing mission, be it European or non-European. In the non-European, colonial context of the nineteenth century both dimensions were at work at the same time, yet it still has to be debated whether the prime object was the horizontal (external) dimension or whether – as the case studies of British India may suggest – the vertical (internal) dimension attracted the same if not more attention.[15]

Without a doubt, the idea and ideology of the civilizing mission are closely connected to a process which began around 1500 that Western historiography has described as 'European expansion'.[16] From its outset, European economic and political expansion went hand in hand with a civilizing (cultural) mission. As soon as local colonial power was established 'overseas' and territorial expansion was set in motion, economic, military and cultural penetration followed closely, taking place more or less simultaneously and thus mutually helping to stabilize nascent colonial regimes. In the case of the Spanish and Portuguese empires of the sixteenth and seventeenth centuries the civilizing mission was almost identical to the Christian (Catholic) mission which, in many instances, was implemented with violent force.[17] This was in stark contrast, for example, to the evangelical mission by the Danish-English-Halle Mission in Southern India during the first half of the eighteenth century and later throughout the nineteenth century after the East India Company's charter had opened British India for Christian missionaries in 1813. However, the Protestant mission failed almost entirely in British India.[18]

That failure indirectly indicates that an overall master-plan for a civilizing mission did not exist, not even in France during the late nineteenth and almost entire twentieth centuries where, in contrast to all other imperial powers, the *mission civilisatrice* was an integral part of the colonial ideology in word and deed. Apart from the missing master-plan, the civilizing mission was always (and only) the ideology of colonial, imperial and ultimately indigenous (colonized) elites comprising various (pressure) groups. Also, there was no particular British or French civilizing mission but institutions and organizations whose members propagated cultural values via, for example, judicial systems and moral regulations.[19] This may be the reason why the civilizing mission, including the Christian mission as a cultural ideology of modern colonialism, has received little attention from colonial and imperial historians.[20] However, as demonstrated recently, particularly in settlement colonies like Virginia (later USA), Boer (Dutch) South Africa and German South-West Africa (Namibia), a civilizing mission to uplift and develop the native population never even existed.[21] One may add Australia to this list too.

European settlement, it seems, often left no space for local people and, for the same reason, did not include the idea of assimilating, educating and developing indigenous people. In 'white settlement colonies' such as Canada and South Africa 'natives' were commonly segregated and separated in reservations or townships. Yet one has to remember that in Canada, for example, native children were forcibly removed from their families and sent to government or Christian 'residential schools' to 'civilize' them.[22] Also, still in the 1930s, the children of Icelandic settlers were separated from their parents and sent to Denmark for school education as the Danish settlement colony, without having any native population, was regarded as a backward place which required improvement through education. The development of so-called 'backward classes' and 'uncivilized people' through education was on the civilizing agenda of many nation states even in the second half of the twentieth century as the Indian example illustrates. Female education promoted by NATO forces and NGOs in Afghanistan since 2001 is part of the same process.

The non-existence of a master-plan meant that the civilizing mission was actually a highly elusive and flexible ideology and, at the same time, very adaptive to changing political, social and cultural environs. Due to these characteristics the civilizing mission served as an aggressive political instrument, since 'civilization missionaries' believed in the progress of humankind based on a teleological view of human history. As such, the civilizing missionaries became agents of progress and modernity. During the nineteenth century, however, the civilizing mission's ideology changed from an idealistic vision of universal cultural improvement and development as well as, ultimately, the assimilation of mankind, to espousing rude racial segregation based on genetic pre-disposition which in turn made assimilation and therefore mission impossible. However, this change did not mark the end of the civilizing mission, as the post-WWI mandate system of the League of Nations demonstrates.

Instead the civilizing mission became the 'white man's burden' and so, for the said genetic reasons, a permanent burden of the 'racially superior' white races. This was precisely what Rudyard Kipling meant when he welcomed the USA to the 'club of imperialists' in 1899, after the US had fought its expansionist war against Spain and annexed the Philippines. Ideologically (and practically) seen, the burden was twofold. On the one hand it included the extraction of natural resources from the colonies since, as it was firmly believed by the colonial administrators and ideologists, the indigenous population was not able to realize the potential value of natural wealth. On the other hand it meant governing the indigenous population because they were considered incapable of ruling over themselves. Permanent observation, instruction, guidance and policing were the only solutions for the overall threat emanating from such uncivilized countries and communities. Colonial politics were also aiming to prevent the uncivilized actions and activities from spilling over into the realm of the civilized nations.

The project of the civilizing mission, however, was relegated to the backburner of imperialism after the turn of the twentieth century, yet it was still valuable as an ideology that could be used or exploited at will. The civilizing mission was part of the Western world's strategies to establish and perpetuate hegemony over the 'East', the latter representing all non-Western societies and polities. After the end of European colonialism by c. 1980, important elements of the civilizing mission survived in diplomatic, academic and media vocabularies with terms like the 'Third World' and 'underdeveloped countries' implying that they still needed 'improvement' and 'uplifting'. Even today, the ideology of the civilizing mission is embedded in the political agenda of Western powers. Phrases like 'member of the world community' suggest that there are states which do not belong to that community, such as 'rogue states', which by definition cannot belong to the community of the civilized. There are also states which need some 'guidance' or 'discipline' to become 'proper' members of that community, including several if not most countries in Africa and, as Carey Watt has argued in his introduction, Iraq and Afghanistan. In any case the international community, sometimes reduced to a 'coalition of the willing', is obliged to help the people of oppressive (despotic) regimes to overcome the said political orders or to transform them into civilized (democratic) systems. 'Old Europe' was provincialized, representing old-fashioned civilization standards – at least according to the US administration's official reading.[23]

On the Outcomes of the Civilizing Mission

In the first section of his introduction to this volume, Carey Watt has shed some light on the more recent facets of the civilizing mission. Taking a long-term historical perspective, it becomes evident that since the end of the eighteenth century two salient aspects have been used to justify political-cum-military intervention by 'Western' states. One of these is the reproach of 'mismanagement' by a ruler or regime, ranging from 'Oriental despots' to 'rogue states' that sponsor 'terrorism'. To overcome or control the threat emanating from such regimes, the *ultima ratio* would be to depose and replace such a ruler and change the political regime. The second motif is the alleged aim to establish a better if not permanent peace order in a state or a region. The spectrum for such an order ranges from direct colonial rule and military occupation to financial aid by the World Bank and the International Monetary Fund. Both motifs, however, are interrelated and to some extent interchangeable. From this long-term perspective one may assume that the civilizing mission was, from the very beginning, not only a strategy to establish hegemony but that it was (and still is) based on faulty – if not bizarre and grotesque – premises. For example, conquest and the beginning of colonial relations including early attempts of civilizing missions actually turned civilized cultures like those of the North American 'Indians' or African tribal societies into savage and wild (colonial) societies which paradoxically required greater and more coercive efforts to civilize the now uncivilized, as in the case of Canada's 'residential schools' system described above.[24]

Similar processes and developments can be observed in present-day Somalia, Afghanistan and Iraq, to mention only the most prominent examples. Existing problems in some polities, societies and communities have often been aggravated by international intervention, with bombings, hijackings, kidnapping and piracy becoming the outstanding features of their uprooted political and societal entities. On the other hand, continuous 'assistance', 'guidance' and 'policing' seem to be the ever-appropriate strategy for controlling 'unstable' and therefore 'dangerous' regimes. American money and military aid sent to Pakistan to maintain control over atomic weapons and access to Afghanistan caused immense conflicts within Pakistan's political and social systems. Likewise, Afghan President Hamid Karzai's recent vote to cooperate with the Taliban and the inability of NATO's military forces to establish real peace or stability in the country indicates the rather troublesome situation into which Afghanistan has deteriorated since this 'international intervention' began in late 2001.[25]

Yet one also has to keep in mind that the civilizing mission was not only an instrument applied by imperialist powers to establish and maintain control over 'backward' and therefore 'uncivilized' people, but it likewise became a tool for the national governments of former colonies to maintain their newly established political regimes, whether democratic or dictatorial. In India, Nehruvian politics continued the internal civilizing mission well into the 1960s, with the state ever ambitious to turn (backward) peasants into (modern) citizens. Rural protest and dissent was officially characterized as anti-national to facilitate the postcolonial state's continued policing, controlling and manipulation of peasants. This has been particularly true since the so-called 'liberalization' of India's economy in 1991. India's economic growth demanded more natural resources than ever before and led to the displacement of local populations, particularly in the 'red belt' (ore area) of Chota Nagpur (being part of the present day federal states of Jharkhand, Chhattisgarh and Madhya Pradesh). This was justified by appealing to 'the national interest'. The same is true for the ongoing debate and, at the same time, the uprooting of millions of tribals and poor peasants, *eo ipso* 'backward people', caused by the Narmada dam project. One contemporary NGO-worker remarked that the spectacular *Avatar* film (2009)[26] effectively depicted the massive violence and brutality that is omnipresent in resource-rich areas of India. The displacement, resettlement and re-construction of allegedly backward people seems to be inherent in colonial and postcolonial politics. What is more, protest is commonly regarded by uncivilized people as an act of resistance which impedes development and, ultimately, the process of nation building.

To conclude, the civilizing mission is still on the political agenda of the Indian nation state as well as the larger 'international community'. The latter is mainly represented by the former colonial powers of Western Europe and the USA, though it has been joined by nation states from other regions of the world. Applicants include nations that were formerly colonies, and they must claim 'civilized status' and promise to maintain the existing global order. Furthermore, the military forces of NATO and the United Nations – euphemistically termed 'peacekeeping forces' or, more recently, 'counterinsurgency forces' – continue to propagate the ideology of colonial-era civilizing missions. As this book has demonstrated, the same holds true for the internal or self-civilizing missions of postcolonial nation states. While the tactics applied may have changed, the general strategies and targets have remained constant. Against this background it seems appropriate to re-think and re-evaluate the historical ideology of the 'civilizing mission' and to apply it as an epistemological category to national politics of former colonies (and presumably to many other nation states as well) as well as international politics and global strategies in the twenty-first century.

Notes

1 Briton C. Busch, *Britain, India, and the Arabs 1914–1921* (Berkeley etc.: University of California Press, 1971).

2 Budheswar Pati, *India and the First World War* (New Delhi: Atlantic Publication, 1996). Ravi Ahuja et al., *The World in World Wars. Experiences, perceptions and perspectives from the South* (Leiden: Brill 2010 forthcoming).

3 V. N. Datta and S. Settar (eds), *Jallianwalla Bagh Massacre* (New Delhi: Pragathi Publications, 2000).

4 Carl Bridge, *Holding India to the Empire (The British Conservative Party and the 1935 Constitution)* (London: Oriental University Press, 1988). Horst-Joachim Leue, *Britische Indienpolitik 1926–1932. Motive, Methoden und der Misserfolg imperialer Politik am Vorabend der Dekolonisation* (Wiesbaden: Steiner Verlag, 1981).

5 *Vide*, for example, *The Tribune* (Lahore), 29 the December 1918, *Punjab Native Newspaper Reports, 1896–1924. Selections from the Native Newspapers Published in the Punjab* Received up to 4th January 1919, vol. XXXII, No 1, 151, para 5a, p.4 [BL: IOR].

6 B. M. Sankhdhar (ed.) *World War I to Gandhi's Non-Cooperation Movement, 1914–20* (New Delhi: Deep and Deep Publisher,1999). During the Khilafat Movement which opposed Allied plans to abolish the Khalifat of the Sultan of Istanbul after WWI, Gandhi established an 'Indian national front' of Muslims and Hindus, though a very brittle one. *Vide* Gail Minault, *The Khilafat Movement. Religious Symbolism and Political Mobilization in India* (Delhi etc.: Oxford University Press, 1982, 2nd imprint 1999).

7 *Vide* the most prominent historiographical re-construction by Bal Gangadhar Tilak, *Orion or Researches into the Antiquity of the Vedas* (Bombay, 1893, 4th edn Poona: Tilak,

1955) and *idem*, *The Arctic Home in the Vedas* (Poona/Bombay: Ramchandra Govind, 1903).

8 Harald Fischer-Tiné, *Der Gurukul Kangri oder die Erziehung der Arya-Nation. Kolonialismus, Hindureform und 'nationale Bildung' in Britisch-Indien (1897–1922)* (Würzburg: Ergon-Verlag, 2003).

9 Mohandas K. Gandhi's *Hind Swaraj* was first published in the *Indian Opinion* in Gujarati, Gandhi's mothertongue, on December 11 and 18, 1909, thereafter as an English pamphlet by the 'International Printing Press, Phoenix, Natal', the printing press of Gandhi's ashram, in 1910.

10 Wolfgang M. Schröder, 'Mission impossible? Begriff, Methode und Begründung der "civilizing mission" aus philosophischer Sicht', in Boris Barth and Jürgen Osterhammel (eds), *Zivilisierungsmissionen. Imperiale Weltverbesserungen seit dem 18. Jahrhundert* (Konstanz: UVK Verlagsgesellschaft, 2005), 13–32, esp. 18–9. Christian missions and former colonial organizations like the Deutsche Kolonialverein may act as pressure groups.

11 Norbert Elias, *Über den Prozeß der Zivilisation. Soziogenetische und psychogenetische Untersuchungen.* 2 vols. Vol. 1: *Wandlungen des Verhaltens in den weltlichen Oberschichten des Abendlandes* (Frankfurt am Main: Suhrkamp Verlag, 1976, Vol. 2: *Wandlungen der Gesellschaft – Entwurf zu einer Theorie der Zivilisation*, Frankfurt am Main: Suhrkamp Verlag, 1976, paperback edition 1997), *vide* esp. vol. 2, 323–53.

12 Wolfgang M. Schröder, 'Mission impossible?', 22–4.

13 *Ibid.*, 29–30.

14 Jürgen Osterhammel, '"The Great Work of Uplifting Mankind". Zivilisierungsmission und Moderne', in Boris Barth and Jürgen Osterhammel (eds), *Zivilisierungsmissionen. Imperiale Weltverbesserungen seit dem 18. Jahrhundert* (Konstanz: UVK Verlagsgesellschaft, 2005), 363–425, see esp. 363.

15 This differs with Osterhammel's characterization. The example of British India may illustrate the fact that from a Calcutta/New Delhi perspective the vertical dimension was given more attention than the horizontal. From a London perspective, however, the horizontal dimension may have been more important.

16 It has to be kept in mind that some kind of integrating civilizing mission also existed in imperial China for centuries though it was by far not as elaborate and ambitious as was the case with European civilizing missions, Gang Wungwu, 'The Chinese urge to civilize: Reflections on change', *Journal of Asian History* 18 (1984):1–34.

17 Already contemporaries complained about the Spanish brutal conquista , cf. the latest account and interpretation by Daniel Castra, *Another Face of Empire. Bartholomé de las Casas, indigenous rights and ecclestical imperialism* (Durham etc.: Duke University Press 2007).

18 Michael Mann (ed.), *Europäische Aufklärung und protestantische Mission in Indien* (Heidelberg: Draupadi Verlag, 2006) and *idem* (ed.), *Aufgeklärter Geist und evangelische Missionen in Indien* (Heidelberg: Draupadi Verlag, 2008).

19 Osterhammel, 'The Great Work of Uplifting Mankind', 370.

20 Andrew Porter, 'Christentum, Kontext und Ideologie', in Boris Barth and Jürgen Osterhammel (eds), *Zivilisierungsmissionen. Imperiale Weltverbesserungen seit dem 18. Jahrhundert* (Konstanz: UVK Verlagsgesellschaft 2005), 125–47, esp. 126–8.

21 Boris Barth, 'Die Grenzen der Zivilisierungsmission. Rassenvorstellungen in den europäischen Siedlungskolonien Virginia, den Burenrepubliken und Deutsch-Südwestafrika', in *ibid.*, 201–28.

22 Over 150,000 aboriginal children (First Nations, Inuit and Métis) were placed in 'Indian Residential Schools' to be 'civilized' and converted to Christianity, and the Government of Canada made a formal apology on 11 June 2008 for its part in this civilizing mission. Julian Walker, *The Indian Residential Schools Truth and Reconciliation Commission* (Ottawa: Parliamentary Information and Research Service, 2009), 1–5. See also John Sheridan Milloy, *A National Crime: the Canadian government and the residential school system, 1879–1986* (Winnipeg: University of Manitoba Press, 1999).

23 Cf. Dipesh Chakrabarty, *Provincializing Europe. Postcolonial Thought and Historical Difference* (Princeton: Princeton University Press 2000. Reissue with a new preface by the author, 2008).

24 Osterhammel, 'The Great Work of Uplifting Mankind', 408.

25 For the US-American strategy as a technologically superior and therefore also civilizing power see Michael Adas, *Dominance by Design. Technological Imperatives and America's Civilizing Mission* (Cambridge MA etc.: Belknap Press 2006).

26 *Avatar*, written and directed by James Cameron (Twentieth Century Fox Film Corporation, 2009). Sanskrit-Hindi *avatār*: incarnation.

LIST OF CONTRIBUTORS

Harald Fischer-Tiné is Professor of history at the Swiss Federal Institute of Technology, Zurich. He has taught at the University of Heidelberg (where he received his PhD in 2000), Jacobs University in Bremen, and at Humboldt University, Berlin. He has published widely on modern South Asian history, imperial history and world history. His most recent book is entitled *Low and Licentious Europeans: Race, Class and 'White Subalternity' in Colonial India* (New Delhi: Orient Blackswan, 2009).

Prashant Kidambi is Senior Lecturer in colonial urban history at the School of Historical Studies, University of Leicester. He is the author of *The Making of an Indian Metropolis: Colonial Governance and Public Culture in Bombay, 1890–1920* (Aldershot: Ashgate, 2007). He has recently been awarded a Leverhulme Research Fellowship to work on a project that explores the social and cultural history of the first Indian cricket tour to Britain. He also continues to pursue his research interests in South Asian urban history in the colonial and postcolonial periods.

Adam Knowles completed an MA in South Asian history and continental philosophy at the University of Heidelberg, Germany. He is currently a graduate student in philosophy at the New School for Social Research in New York, where he is pursuing research on Martin Heidegger.

Andrea Major is Lecturer in wider world history at the University of Leeds. She completed her PhD at the University of Edinburgh in 2004 and published *Pious Flames: European Encounters with Sati 1500–1830* in 2006 (Oxford University Press). Her most recent research project was *Slavery and the Raj: Empire, Abolition and 'Unfree' Labour in India*, which was supported by the Leverhulme Trust.

Michael Mann is Professor of South Asian history and culture at Humboldt University, Berlin. He studied South Asian history, Hindi and German literature at Heidelberg University. Before moving to Humboldt University he taught at the South Asia Institute of Heidelberg University and the Historical Institute at FernUniversität in Hagen. His research is on the history of South Asia in the nineteenth and twentieth centuries, and he continues to publish widely on a variety of topics.

Shobna Nijhawan is Assistant Professor in Hindi at the Department of Languages, Literatures and Linguistics at York University in Toronto. She completed her PhD at the Department of South and Southeast Asian Studies at the University of California, Berkeley. She is currently working on Hindi ayurvedic and allopathic periodicals, and medicine and health issues in Hindi literature. She recently edited *Nationalism in the Vernacular: Hindi, Urdu and the Literature of Indian Freedom* (New Delhi: Permanent Black, 2010), and her monograph *Nationalism, Creativity, and the Hindi Public Sphere: Women's Periodicals in the Early Twentieth Century* will be published by Oxford University Press in 2011.

Shahid Perwez is Research Associate in the Department of Anthropology at the University of Durham. At Durham, he is working on the publication of a manuscript, along with Yulia Egorova, based on their fieldwork research on the Judaising movement of Dalits in coastal Andhra, South India. He completed his PhD in sociology and social anthropology at the University of Edinburgh in 2009. Based on his PhD thesis, he is also working on the publication of a book on female infanticide and sex selective abortion in Tamil Nadu.

Jana Tschurenev is Lecturer in the Institute of History at the Swiss Federal Institute of Technology, Zurich. She completed her PhD in comparative education at Humboldt University Berlin in 2009, in which she analyzed the emergence of modern elementary schooling in India and Britain in the early nineteenth century. Her current research interests include exploring women's organizations, feminism and moral reform activism from a global history perspective.

Carey A. Watt is Associate Professor of South Asian and world history at St Thomas University in Fredericton, Canada, and holds a PhD from the University of Cambridge. His research explores issues of citizenship, physical culture, Boy Scouts, philanthropy, NGOs and nationalism in South Asia and globally. He has published articles and book chapters regarding the history of colonial India, Scouting and postcolonial France, and his monograph *Serving the Nation: cultures of service, association and citizenship in colonial India* was published by Oxford University Press (New Delhi) in 2005.

INDEX

CPSIA information can be obtained at www.ICGtesting.com
224298LV00001B/4/P